SCIENCE IN THE BET MIDRASH:
Studies in Maimonides

SCIENCE IN THE BET MIDRASH:
Studies in Maimonides

Menachem Kellner

For Daniel and Alon

Library of Congress Cataloging-in-Publication Data

Kellner, Menachem Marc, 1946-
  Science in the Bet Midrash : studies in Maimonides / Menachem Kellner.
    p. cm. -- (EMUNOT: Jewish philosophy and Kabbalah)
  ISBN 978-1-934843-21-5
  1. Maimonides, Moses, 1135-1204. I. Title.
  BM546.K47 2009
  296.1'81--dc22
                        2009008077

Book design by Olga Grabovsky, Rivka Kellner

Published by Academic Studies Press in 2009

28 Montfern Avenue
Brighton, MA 02135, USA
press@academicstudiespress.com
www.academicstudiespress.com

TABLE OF CONTENTS

PART ONE
APPROACHES TO THE STUDY OF MAIMONIDES

PART TWO
RELIGIOUS FAITH AND DOGMA

PART THREE

SCIENCE AND TORAH

PART FOUR

UNIVERSALISM

BY WAY OF PERSONAL INTRODUCTION

n 1973 I received a Ph.D. in philosophy from Washington University in St. Louis, with a dissertation on "Civil Disobedience in Democracy: A Philosophical Justification." My dissertation advisor and afterwards my dear friend was the late Steven Schwarzschild (1924-1989). My choice of dissertation topic reflected the fact that I was a true child of the sixties, and that I had been convinced by my teachers that philosophers *did* philosophy and did not write about its history. As a product of various yeshivot in the USA and Israel, I also started college wanting to prove that an observant Jew could be as good a secular academic as the best of them (a wish reflected, perhaps, in the fact that for years mine was the only kipah on the campus of Washington University).

After I finished my degrees I discovered that, while there were no jobs for philosophers, there were plenty of openings for people who had some knowledge of Jewish studies. I also discovered that I enjoyed teaching Judaica and researching the history of Jewish philosophy more than I ever enjoyed "doing" philosophy – and so never looked back.

Just as my career choice was unplanned, so was much of the arc of that career. I was hired by the University of Virginia (and later by the College of William and Mary) to teach religious ethics (on the strength of my dissertation) and Judaic studies. Out of the combination of those two fields grew my first book, the anthology *Contemporary Jewish Ethics* (New York, 1978 and 1985). Sometime in the mid-1970's David Bleich – whom I had met thanks to the Academy for Jewish Philosophy which he had founded with Norbert Samuelson and David Silverman – called me at my home in Richmond, Virginia (I was teaching at the University of Virginia in Charlottesville, but we lived in Richmond since we needed "shuls and schools"). He asked me to translate a chapter of Isaac Abravanel's *Rosh Amanah* for a compilation of texts on Jewish dogma which he was compiling. This became his anthology, With Perfect Faith (New York, 1983).

One thing led to another and I ended up translating the whole Rosh Amanah (under the title, Principles of Faith) for the Littman Library of Jewish Civilization – with whom I have since enjoyed a wonderful relationship – and publishing (in 1993) a scholarly edition of the original Hebrew text with Bar-Ilan University Press. I had begun working on this during a trial year at the University of Haifa in 1978-79. While working on these books I came to realize that a proper introduction to Rosh Amanah demanded an account of Jewish dogmatics from their inception with Maimonides. This led to a dozen or so articles in English and Hebrew culminating in the publication in 1986 of Dogma in Medieval Jewish Thought: From Maimonides to Abravanel (Oxford University Press for the Littman Library of Jewish Civilization). A Hebrew translation followed (Jerusalem, 1991), the initiative of my late friend Meir Ayali; other friends and colleagues helped me translate different chapters. As these words are being written, a Chinese translation of the book is being prepared by a scholar at Shandung University. (I am looking forward to the movie and sequels.) My interest in dogma culminated in my third Littman book, Must a Jew Believe Anything? (2000; second expanded edition, 2006).

Others of my books had similarly accidental origins. In conjunction with my work on dogma, I had published an article in Hebrew on the status of Gentiles in the messianic era, suggesting that Maimonides' innovative attempt to ground Judaism on a firm dogmatic footing reflected a messianic definition of 'Who is a Jew?'. I argued that in Maimonides' view, the difference between Jew and Gentile would disappear by the time the messianic era reached fruition. I gave the article to a friend in my synagogue in Haifa, the late Asher Waggenberg, who was sure that Maimonides could not have taught what I imputed to him. I promised to write an article showing not only that Maimonides held those views, but that he of necessity held them because of his antecedent philosophical commitments. That planned article turned into Maimonides on Judaism and the Jewish People (SUNY Press, 1991). The book eventually appeared in Serbian translation, thanks to the initiative of Rabbi Asiel of Belgrade (until I actually saw the book, I was half-convinced that the whole thing was a complicated practical joke).

In another case of serendipity leading to a book, I once attended a lecture by a well-known scientist affiliated with Habad who insisted that since Maimonides' *Mishneh Torah* had been written with divine inspiration, Jews today were duty-bound to accept as accurate the pre-Copernican account of the solar system found in the first chapters of "Laws of the Foundations of the Torah." I said to myself: "that may be the Habad view of Maimonides, but was it Maimonides' view of Maimonides?" This, and friendship with Gad Freudenthal, led me to write a series of studies on Maimonides and science (several of which are included in this volume and others which are scheduled to be republished in the companion volume on Gersonides) and also Maimonides on *'The Decline of the Generations' and the Nature of Rabbinic Authority* (SUNY Press, 1996). I no longer remember what prompted *Maimonides on Human Perfection* (Atlanta, 1990), but I certainly remember the effort invested in it by Lenn Evan Goodman, the editor of the series in which it appeared.

Near the beginning of my career I shared an office at the University of Virginia with Norbert Samuelson; it is hardly surprising, then, that Gersonides became and remained an object of interest to me. I no longer recall what prompted me to critically edit (Ramat-Gan, 2001) and translate (New Haven, 1998) his commentary on Song of Songs, but it was a project to which I devoted several intense and satisfying years (and on which I received a great deal of help from my friend and neighbor Professor Nisan Ararat and my daughter Rivka). I cannot say the same thing about my translation of Maimonides' *Book of Love* for the Yale Judaica *Mishneh Torah* series (New Haven, 2004). Ivan Marcus invited me to take on the project and I asked my son Avinoam what he thought of the idea. He said, "It can't hurt, Aba, for a few years you will write articles on Rambam's approaches to prayer while you are working on the translation." Well, Avi was wrong: the book is extremely dry and technical with very little in the way of philosophical materials.

Steven Schwarzchild, z"l, planted seeds in me, some of which took a long time to bear fruit. He never succeeded in making me a devotee of Kant or Hermann Cohen (or of vegetarianism, pacifism, socialism, and non-Zionism), but through him I absorbed Cohen's reading of Maimonidean Judaism as what Cohen (and Schwarzschild) would have called regulative and what I have come to call institutional and nominalist. The fullest expression of that approach is found in my fourth Littman book, *Maimonides' Confrontation with Mysticism* (2006) – a misleading title for a book which is really not about mysticism at all. That book also gives voice to something else I learned about Maimonides from Steven Schwarzschild – the Great Eagle's uncompromising universalism (the subject of several of the essays in this volume). It was at the urging of Ken Seeskin, and with his support, that I edited a volume of Steven's Jewish writings, *The Pursuit of the Ideal* (SUNY Press, 1990). To my great sorrow, I received word of Steven's totally unanticipated passing while working on the index to the volume. I had come to know, and admire, Ken Seeskin thanks to the aforementioned Academy for Jewish Philosophy and all three of my SUNY Press books appeared in the Jewish philosophy series he edited; a series which has so enriched the field.

I met Steven Schwarzschild shortly after my father, Rabbi Abraham Kellner (1909-1965) passed away. These men are two of the most important influences on my life, personal and professional, the third being Jolene Shoulson Kellner, my wife, my confidant, and my teacher of all things important. Growing up in the home of an Orthodox rabbi who loved all things Jewish, and who sincerely tried to love all Jews and, indeed, all of God's creatures, I found that Schwarzschild's emphasis on Judaic universalism struck a familiar chord. Growing up in the home of an Orthodox rabbi who combined deep human warmth with a certain Litvak impatience with nonsense, I found that Maimonidean rationalism also struck a familiar chord.

Moving to Israel in 1980 (much to Jolene's surprise – she never believed I really meant it) and thus realizing my father's never fulfilled dream of aliyah, I found that Maimonides was not an object of antiquarian interest, but a participant in the debates over the nature and future of the Jewish state. I also found in many places an Orthodoxy not characterized by universalism, by rationalism, and by open-hearted tolerance. This lent my studies and writings an urgency they had lacked before our aliyah. The move to Israel also brought me into close touch with a circle of wonderful colleagues (*menschlichkeit* seems to be the hallmark of Israeli scholars of medieval Jewish philosophy – which marks them off radically, I regret to say, from too much of the rest of the Israeli professoriate), among whom I would like specifically to thank Meir Ayali (z"l), Ya'akov Blidstein, Naomi Cohen, Moshe Idel, Raphi Jospe, Zev Harvey,

Sara Klein-Braslavy, Danny Lasker, Ze'ev Levy, Avraham Melamed, Mordechai Pachter, and Colette Sirat.

Over the last several years my life has been enriched by a group of wonderful doctoral students, by my Sabbath study partners (Avram Montag and Joel Bigman), by three loyal friends who call themselves the Kellner Commandos (Eliezer Zitronenbaum, Yisrael Stockman, and Hayyim Schachal). But most of all, Jolene and I have been enriched by Avi's Rina and her two wonderful boys, Daniel and Alon. It is to them, grandchildren-in-love, that this book is dedicated.

Acknowledgements

The present volume (and the soon to be published companion volume of studies on Gersonides) is the fruit of an initiative of the indefatigable Dov Schwartz, whose many contributions to the study of medieval and modern Jewish thought have put all his colleagues in his debt. At a stressful time for my family Dovi reaffirmed my faith in academic collegiality and integrity and for that, even more than for this book, I thank him.

All of the articles in the volume have been revised for their publication here. I have updated references, tried to make gendered language more sensitive, and have sought to reduce overlap and repetition. Hebrew and Arabic terms are transliterated without diacritical marks.

Over the years, many relatives, friends, and colleagues have generously helped me in my work. I here happily record my gratitude to: Harvey Chisick, Shalomi Eldar, Seymour Feldman, Gad Freudenthal, David Gillis, Lenn Evan Goodman, Bernard Goldstein, Julian Hartt, Zev Harvey, Giora Hon, Avi Kadish, Hannah Kasher, Jolene Kellner, Yisroel Kellner, Howard Kreisel, Maurice Kriegel, Tzvi Langermann, Daniel J. Lasker, Tyra Lieberman, Gilbert Meilaender, Avraham Melamed, Yisroel Miller, Avram Montag, Chaim Rappoport, Norbert Samuelson, Michael Schwarz, Steven S. Schwarzschild, z"l, Kenneth Seeskin, Colette Sirat, Baird Tipson, and Isadore Twersky, z"l.

I acknowledge with gratitude permissions received from the original publishers of the chapters of this book (listed in the introductions to each section).

PART ONE

INTRODUCTION TO PART ONE
Approaches to the Study of Maimonides

The essays in this section all deal to one degree or another with the question of how to read Maimonides. As Maimonides himself explains in the Introduction to the *Guide of the Perplexed*, the Torah has an esoteric level which it would be inappropriate to teach publicly. Like the first Moses, therefore, were he to write anything about Torah, Maimonides would have to write esoterically, i.e., to address dramatically different audiences simultaneously. As I often tell my students, Maimonides has to write both for my haredi friends and for me simultaneously, and write in such a fashion that we all believe that ours is the correct interpretation. What, then, is the secret that Maimonides hides?

Leo Strauss thought that it was that Maimonides was fundamentally an orthodox Aristotelian, and thus only pretended to be what today would be called an orthodox Jew. It is this approach which leads Shlomo Pines (in his introduction to his translation of the *Guide*) to call Maimonides' halakhic enterprise only an "avocation." I do not believe that any close student of the *Mishneh Torah* –not to mention the Commentary on the Mishnah, the Book of Commandments, and the responsa– could be anything but amazed by this insouciant dismissal of that field to which Maimonides devoted most of his energy and most of his intellect throughout his life. Maimonides also devoted astonishing amounts of energy to the mundane affairs of the Egyptian Jewish community of his day. Is this the behavior of a man who believed that if immortality of any sort is possible, it depends upon the development of one's intellect? Every moment spent away from philosophical reflection is a moment wasted, never to be regained. Let it also be noted that after Maimonides finished writing the *Guide of the Perplexed* in about 1191, he wrote no more philosophic or scientific texts, whereas he never ceased occupying himself with his "avocation."

So, what is the secret that Maimonides hides? He himself tells us: the rabbis of the Talmud used the expression *ma'aseh bereshit* for what the Greeks called physics and used the expression *ma'aseh merkavah* for what the Greeks called metaphysics. So why is this important? The consequences of these equations are momentous. Maimonides imports what we today would call science into the heart of Torah ("Laws of the Foundations of the Torah," I.1). This is allied to his universalism (Jews are distinguished from non-Jews *only* by behavior and belief [knowledge]) and to his conception of the commandments of the Torah as tools (which could in principle have been different), whose importance lies in the end they serve, and not in themselves. That being the case, true reward and punishment are not connected to behavior, no matter how saintly or how vile.

Maimonides hid these secrets from his fellow Jews, not out of fear of reprisal (protected as he was by his good friend, al-Qadi al-Fadl, he had no reason to fear them), but out of *noblesse oblige*. Exposing simple Jews (and their philosophically no less simple rabbis) to these truths could only lead to perplexity (in the best of circumstances) or to falling away from observance (in the worst of circumstances), neither of which Maimonides had any interest in promoting.

One God wrote two books, as it were: Torah and Cosmos. The truly devout Jew realizes that he or she must study both books, or only have access to half of God's oeuvre. The chapters in this first section of the book, then, all deal with how Maimonides, I am convinced, would want to be read.

The chapters in this section originally appeared in the following places:

"Reading Rambam: Approaches to the Interpretation of Maimonides," *Jewish History* 5 (1991): 73-93. This was originally a review-essay focusing on Marvin Fox, *Interpreting Maimonides: Studies in Methodology, Metaphysics, and Moral Philosophy* (Chicago: University of Chicago Press, 1900). The portions of the essay dealing with Fox's important book have not been reproduced here.

"Strauss' Maimonides vs. Maimonides' Maimonides: Could Maimonides have been *both* Enlightened and Orthodox?" *Leela*, December, 2000: 29-36. A Hebrew translation appeared the following year in *Iyyun* 50 (2001): 397-406.

"The Literary Character of the Mishneh Torah: On the Art of Writing in Maimonides' Halakhic Works," E. Fleisher, G. Blidstein, C. Horowitz, and B. Septimus (eds.) *Me'ah She'arim: Studies in Medieval Jewish Spiritual Life in Memory of Isadore Twersky* (Jerusalem: Magnes Press, 2001): 29-45.

"Is Maimonides' Ideal Person Austerely Rationalist?" *American Catholic Philosophical Quarterly* 76 (2002): 125-143.

CHAPTER ONE:
Reading Rambam –
Approaches to the Interpretation of Maimonides

M*iddah ke-neged middah,* says the Talmud (Sanhedrin 90a), is how human being are rewarded and punished for their actions. "Measure for measure" is the way Shakespeare put it; either way, it is what has happened and is happening to Maimonides, and deservedly so. The Rabbis of the Mishnah and Talmud presented the heroes of the Bible us if they were rabbinic sages who spent most of their time in *yeshivot* and courts of Jewish law, devoting their spare time, as it were, to the wars and intrigue that so dominate their activities in the pages of the biblical story.[1] Maimonides served the Rabbis in their own coin, presenting them essentially as philosophers of an Aristotelian mold, who cloaked their metaphysical concerns in *aggadah* so as not to upset or harm the uninitiated. It is only fair, then, that Maimonides himself is presented as everything from a late convert to Kabbalah,[2] to an halakhist who in truth disdained philosophy,[3] to an Aristotelian philosopher, whose own innermost thoughts stood in conscious opposition to normative Jewish teachings.[4]

There is a further sense in which the situation is both fair and appropriate. Maimonides was one of the few major medieval halakhic decisors to claim that laws derived by the rabbinic sages from the Bible through the use of the "thirteen principles of biblical exegesis" were rabbinic in their authority (*d'rabbanan*), that they did not derive their authority directly from the text of

---

1 See Diamond, "Biblical Monarch."

2 See Scholem, "From Philosopher to Cabbalist."

3 See, for example, Kellner, "Kotler."

4 This appears to have been the position of Shlomo Pines and of Leo Strauss.

the Torah *(d'oraita)*.[5] What, then, was the point of the derivation from biblical texts? The biblical verses, Maimonides maintained, were used as an *asmakhta,* or prooftext, a kind of biblical hook on which to hang rabbinic law. Similarly, Maimonides is used as an *asmakhta,* a kind of medieval authority on which to base all manner of modern positions.[6]

Why have Maimonides' writings have aroused such debate through the generations? I here offer a new way of looking at one aspect of the Maimonidean controversies; I also suggest to historians who work in areas outside the pure history of ideas that attention to those ideas can be crucial to their work as historians. My point is that in following the details of the unfolding debates, in concentrating on the social roles of the protagonists, historians are in danger of losing sight of the fact that the debates were prompted by and usually focused on Maimonides' writings. Attention to these writings affords insights into aspects of the controversies that otherwise might be missed.

The debate over what Maimonides said, over just who in fact Maimonides was, and the use of Maimonides as an authority to justify all sorts of different religious and ideological positions, is not a modern phenomenon. On the contrary, it began almost immediately with the publication of Maimonides' writings. These writings stimulated a long-festering and remarkably acrimonious debate about the proper relationship between revelation and reason throughout much of the Jewish High Middle Ages.[7]

Maimonides stood at the center of this debate partly because of his great authority. He had proved his bona fides as a master halakhist and communal leader before publishing his philosophic work, *Guide of the Perplexed.* Maimonides wrote the first running commentary on the entire Mishnah; he wrote the

---

5   This is presented and defended by Maimonides in the second of the fourteen principles with which he prefaces his *Book of Commandments.* For a detailed analysis, see Kassirer and Glicksberg, *Me-Sinai.*

6   To give just one example. Maimonides is cited as an authority by those who favor territorial negotiations between Israel and the Arabs, as well as those who reject the idea out of hand. Similarly, both the "Rebbe of Lubavitch" (Menachem Mendel Schneersohn, 1902-1994) and the "Rebbe of Leibowitz" (Yeshayahu Leibowitz, 1903-1994) presented themselves as authentic Twentieth Century spokespersons of Maimonides. Further on this, see Lasker, "Maimonides' Influence."

7   For a recent study providing an entry into the huge bibliography on the debates, see Stern, "Philosophical Allegory."

first compendium of the 613 commandments of the Torah that had a clear-cut rationale; most important, he wrote the first comprehensive code of Jewish law and organized it on logical lines. His was a masterful personality, he had influence at court, and he headed a great Jewish community. Maimonides thus was known and highly respected throughout much of the Jewish world before the publication of the *Guide of the Perplexed.*

Why, then, did his writings stimulate such debate? Scholars have pointed to two main reasons. The first has to do with esotericism. Near the opening of the *Guide of the Perplexed* (I, Introduction, p. 18) Maimonides advertised his intent to write in ways that hid his true views from the unworthy:

> In speaking about very obscure matters it is necessary to conceal some parts and to disclose others. Sometimes in the case of certain dicta this necessity requires that the discussion proceed on the basis of a certain premise, whereas in another place necessity requires that the discussion proceed on the basis of another premise contradicting the first one. In such cases the vulgar must in no way be aware of the contradiction; the author accordingly uses some device to conceal it by all means.

Maimonides further advertises his intent in the introduction to the third part of the *Guide,* which opens with a discussion of *ma'aseh merkavah,* the most obscure of the "secrets of the Torah" (p. 416):

> I shall interpret to you that which was said by Ezekiel the prophet, peace be on him, in such a way that anyone who heard that interpretation would think that I do not say anything over and beyond what is indicated by the text... On the other hand, if that interpretation is examined with a perfect care by him for whom this Treatise is composed and has understood all its chapters – every chapter in its turn – the whole matter, which has become clear and manifest to me, will become clear to him so that nothing in it will remain hidden from him.

With these statements Maimonides precipitated a cottage industry in Jewish intellectual circles, and has kept his interpreters busy ever since for close to a millennium. He also invited debate over his meaning and turned himself into a hook on which a bewildering array of opinions has been hung. Heterodox ideas were attributed to Maimonides during his lifetime[8] and for generations after his death.

But Maimonides became a focus of debate for more important historical reasons. One of these is well known and has been subjected to concentrated scholarly and theological scrutiny: because of who he was and what he wrote, Maimonides forced Jews to attend to the question of the place of reason and revelation in their faith. The resulting debate has been interpreted by scholars as a conflict over the place of rationalism in Judaism and also as reflecting socio-economic battles within the Jewish community.[9]

There is, however, another, even more important, reason for the ongoing debate about Maimonides – one that has been overlooked by most scholars. Simply put, whether Maimonides intended it or whether it was clearly understood by those who argued over his writings, to the cumulative effect of his teachings was to undermine the authority of the rabbis as a class, in particular, the authority they exercised in matters that extended beyond the narrowly legal.[10]

I do not mean that Maimonides consciously or unconsciously attempted to "subvert the dominant rabbinic oligarchy, to undermine the influence of an insensitive, seemingly entrenched, religious establishment which lorded it over its charges." In this view, "the popularization of *halakha* through the *Mishneh Torah,* the conversion of Jewish law from an esoteric to an exoteric discipline, would threaten the exclusive authority of the rabbinic leadership class. Its judicial role would be usurped by increasingly learned members of other classes, and the hierarchical structure of the community, which had come under attack for various reasons, would collapse."[11]

---

8 On this, see Diesendruck, "Samuel and Moses ibn Tibbon" and Ravitzky, "Samuel ibn Tibbon."

9 For this latter approach, see Saperstein, "Conflict."

10 Haim Hillel Ben-Sasson ("*Ha-Rambam*") argues that in his debates with contemporary ge'onim Maimonides was self-consciously rebelling against institutionalized rabbinic authority. My point here is that Maimonides' life and writings add up to an argument against the notion of intellectual authority as such. In support of Ben-Sasson's thesis, by the way, note should be taken of a passage in Maimonides' letter concerning the opposition to his writings in the Baghdad Yeshiva. When religious figures reach positions of authority, he wrote, they often lose their fear of heaven. See Baneth's edition of *Iggerot ha-Rambam*, p. 63. The issues taken up here are dealt with more expansively in Kellner, *Decline* and also in Kellner, "Rabbis."

11 I quote from Twersky, who discusses this view but does not adopt it himself. See "Mishneh

Maimonides may or may not have had such a political goal in mind when he wrote the *Mishneh Torah* and his other books; he is silent on the subject, and therefore we have no way of knowing. I am suggesting something different here: one of the consequences of Maimonides' writings, taken as a whole, is the undermining of the *intellectual,* as opposed to the social and economic, authority of rabbinic scholars and halakhic decisors *as such.* Many aspects of Maimonides' literary activity encourage intellectual independence and argue against the notion that rabbinic erudition, whether modest or vast, bears authority in non-halakhic spheres.[12]

Maimonides' commentary on the Mishnah sought to open that text as never before, explaining its reasoning and conclusions so that it could be used a source of Jewish law.[13] One of the most popular sections of the commentary is the eight-part introduction to Tractate Avot. In his introductory remarks to this text Maimonides insists that one should accept the truth, whatever its source.[14] His argument is with individuals who reject an idea because its author

---

Torah," p. 268.

12 Maimonides' demand that Jews unquestioningly accept his "thirteen principles of faith" on pain of exclusion from the Jewish people and the world to come is no refutation of this thesis. The "thirteen principles" had particular political/halakhic goals in mind, and, moreover, were addressed to those individuals, rabbis and laity, for whom the sort of intellectual independence Maimonides prized would be dangerous. See Kellner, *Dogma*, pp. 34-49 and below, chapter 9, "Could Maimonides Get Into Rambam's Heaven?"

13 Heschel, *Maimonides*, pp. 36, 75, and 83.

14 Maimonides' text reads:

Know that the things about which we shall speak in these chapters and in what will come in the commentary are not matters invented on my own nor explanations I have originated. Indeed, they arc mailers gathered from the Sages in the Midrash and the Talmud and other compositions of theirs, as well as from the discourse of both the ancient and modern philosophers, and from the compositions of many men. Hear the truth from whoever says it. Sometimes I have taken a complete passage from the text of a famous book. Now there is nothing wrong with that, for I do not attribute to myself what someone who preceded me has said. We hereby acknowledge this and shall not indicate that 'so and so said' and 'so and so said,' since that would be useless prolixity. Moreover, identifying the name of such an individual might make the passage offensive to someone without experience and make him think it has an evil inner meaning of which he is not were. Consequently, I saw fit to omit the author's name, since my goal is to be useful to the reader.

I quote from the translation in Weiss and Butterworth, *Ethical Writings*, p. 60. Note Maimonides' explicit reference here to readers who might reject a truth brought in the name of an author objectionable to them.

is in some way unacceptable. This is implicitly a negative argument against authority: Maimonides is arguing against the notion of an "anti-authority," an individual whose views must be rejected because of who he or she is,[15] just as a religious authority is an individual whose views must be accepted because of who he or she is.[16]

The *Mishneh Torah,* as claimed by some of its supporters, potentially freed Jews from dependence on rabbis for all matters of standard halakhah.[17] But more than that, Maimonides tells us that part of his goal is to free Jews from the need to devote their lives to Talmud study. He planned

> that no other work should be needed for ascertaining any of the laws of Israel, but that this work might serve as a compendium of the entire Oral Law ... [such] that a person who first reads the Written Law and then this compilation, will know from it tile whole of the Oral Law, without needing to consult any other book between them.[18]

It is likely that Maimonides intended by this dramatic and revolutionary statement to free Jews who had already achieved a high level of Talmudic eru-

---

15 For an example of just this, see Lamm, *Torah Umadda,* pp. 52-53.

16 For other texts in which the same idea finds expression, see *Guide* III.8, where Maimonides states that the Sages, unlike Aristotle, erred in claiming that the movement of the spheres made sounds. He explains that there is nothing wrong with attributing error to the Sages in these matters:
"[The Sages themselves] in these astronomical matters preferred the opinion or the sages of the nations of the world to their own. For they explicitly say, 'The Sages of the world have vanquished' [Pesahim 94b]. And this is correct. For everyone who argues in speculative matters does this according to the conclusions to which he was led by his speculation. Hence the conclusion whose demonstration is correct is believed." The truth is what counts, not the identity of the person who said it. We find a similar idea in the *Mishneh Torah,* "Laws of the Sanctification of the New Moon," XVII.24: "In that all these matters are established with clear proofs that are beyond reproach, such that one cannot possibly doubt them, we do not concern ourselves with their authors, whether they were composed by prophets or by gentile authors. For with respect to everything the reason of which has been discovered, and the truth of which has been made known through proofs that are beyond reproach, we rely upon he who said it." Further on these texts, see Kellner, *Decline,* and my discussion of R. Aaron Kotler's attempt to attribute a diametrically opposed view to Maimonides, in "Kotler."

17 For a contemporary statement to this effect, see the letter of Sheshet ben Isaac Benveniste of Saragossa to R. Meir ha-Levi Abulafia, published in Marx, "Texts," p. 427. For more on Sheshet and his letter, see Septimus, *Hispano-Jewish,* pp. 46-48. On the democratizing effect of the *Mishneh Torah,* see Twersky, *Introduction,* pp. 334-36, and Septimus, pp. 40 and 73. See also Twersky's important comments in "The Mishneh Torah," pp. 268-269.

18 This passage appears in the introduction to the *Mishneh Torah,* just before the list of commandments, p. 4b.

---

dition to move on to the study of Torah in its truest and deepest sense, namely, metaphysics.[19] Be that as it may, the upshot of his position was in effect to remove from the heart of the Jewish curriculum the one arena in which rabbis are the undisputed masters: Talmud.[20]

In both the *Mishneh Torah* and the *Guide of the Perplexed* Maimonides subtly restricts the authority of the Sages of the Talmud. He sharply distinguishes their role as transmitters of the Sinaitic revelation from their role as individuals reporting on their own ideas and interpretations, or reporting on the best science of their day. Thus, regarding questions concerning the coming of the Messiah, Maimonides writes:

> Some of our Sages say that the coming of Elijah will precede the advent of the Messiah. But no one is in a position to know the details of this and similar things until they have come to pass. They are not explicitly stated by the Prophets. Nor have the Rabbis any tradition with regard to these matters. They are guided solely by what the scriptural texts seem to imply. Hence there is a divergence of opinion upon the subject.[21]

In describing the messianic world, then, the Sages are simply interpreting biblical verses as best they can. In effect, Maimonides is saying that their interpretations carry no more authority than our own.

In two places in the *Guide* Maimonides tells us that the Rabbis of the Talmud erred in matters of science. In II.8 (p. 267) and III.15 (p. 459) Maimonides explicitly attributes such error to the Sages, saying in the second passage:

---

19 I defend this interpretation in *Perfection,* pp. 13-39 and in "*Mishneh Torah*-Why?" See also Kasher, "Talmud Torah." Moshe Halbertal has defended a much more radical reading of Maimonides here. See "*Mishneh Torah.*"

20 Note should also be made of the fact that in "Laws of the Study of Torah," I.7 and III.10, Maimonides forbids scholars of Torah in the most uncompromising way from making their calling into a living. He flatly forbids Jews to charge a fee for leaching the Oral Torah, and further forbids them to live at the expense of others in order to study Torah. Maimonides was as good as his word; we have no record that he ever taught for a fee and he certainly supported himself. For discussions of Maimonides' attitude towards the subsidizing of rabbinic scholarship, see Septimus, "'Kings, Angels, or Beggars'" and Kanarfogel, "Compensation."

21 "Laws of Kings and their Wars," XII.2. This text is analyzed below in ch. 18, "Maimonides' *True Religion* – for Jews, or All Humanity?

Do not ask me to show that everything they [the Sages] have said concerning astronomical matters conforms to the way things really are. For at that time mathematics were imperfect. They did not speak about this as transmitters of the dicta of the prophets, but rather because in those times they were men of knowledge in those fields or because they had heard these dicta from the men of knowledge who lived in those times.

I am certain that Maimonides did not mean to be overtly revolutionary. But let us examine the upshot of his claim. We must follow the dicta of the Sages, Maimonides tells us, when they transmit Halakhah; not when they interpret the Bible or teach science. If the authority of the Sages of the Talmud is restricted in this way, how much more so the authority of contemporary rabbinic scholars!

Another passage in the *Guide* was understood by its medieval readers as explicitly undercutting the authority and standing of Talmudists. In his famous "parable of the palace" (*Guide* III.51) Maimonides seems to be disparaging experts in rabbinics vis-à-vis experts in the physical and metaphysical sciences.[22] In his commentary on the chapter Shem Tov cites what appears to have been a fairly typical reaction to the parable:

Many rabbinic scholars said that Maimonides did not write this chapter and if he did write it, it ought to be hidden away or, most appropriately, burned. For how could he say that those who know physics are on a higher level than those who engage in religion, and even more that they are with the ruler in the inner chamber, for on this basis the philosophers who are engaged with physics and metaphysics have achieved a higher level than those who are immersed in Torah![23]

---

22 I say "seems to disparage" because, as I understand the parable, Maimonides was not comparing rabbis to scientists, to the disadvantage of the rabbis, but, rather, was comparing rabbis *simpliciter* to rabbis who had gone on "to master the sciences." See my *Perfection*, pp. 14-30. But even as I read it, and especially since very few rabbis actually fulfilled this ideal, the parable turns out to be an attack on the authority of rabbis as such.

23 For other medievals who read the text as did Shem Tov, see *Perfection*, pp. 15-17. It should be noted that this attempt to cast doubt on the authenticity of offensive Maimonidean texts is not limited to the Middle Ages. R. Jacob ben Zvi Emden (1697-1776) entertained the possibility that the *Guide of the Perplexed* was not written by Maimonides, the author of the *Mishneh Torah*. See Schachter, "Rabbi Jacob Emden."

These various ways in which Maimonides' writings tend toward the limitation of rabbinic authority are best summarized in a well-known letter of his. Commenting on the dicta of certain Talmudic Sages who affirmed astrology, Maimonides wrote:

> Similarly, it is not proper to abandon matters of reason that have already been verified by proofs, shake loose of them, and depend on the words of a single one of the sages from whom possibly the matter was hidden. Or there may be an allusion in those words; or they may have been said with a view to the times and business before him... A man should never cast his reason behind him, for the eyes are set in front, not in back.[24]

One must never give up one's reason and rely upon the authority of another.[25] This call to intellectual independence is the leitmotif of Maimonides' work as a whole and finds expression in one way or another on almost every page he wrote.[26] But rabbinic scholars as a class must find this threatening, especially when their own rule is challenged.

The danger of Maimonideanism,[27] then, as it must have been perceived, if even only inchoately, by the rabbis of his day, is not only that Maimonides adopts a universalistic conception of Judaism[28] and imports a gentile philosophy into the very heart of the faith,[29] but that his approach to life and Torah

---

24 "Letter on Astrology," in Lerner and Mahdi, p. 235.

25 In this same letter Maimonides also argues against the popular notion of accepting as true things that are written in books, even ancient books, just because they are written there.

26 See also Twersky, "Epistemology." Twersky's examples deal with Maimonides' discomfort with *some* contemporary rabbis, but they also support the thesis advanced here. I do not want to exhaust the reader by citing examples of this approach of Maimonides *ad nauseum*, and limit myself to just one more: the discussion of the nature of the *aggadah* near the beginning of Maimonides' introduction to *Helek* can be read as undermining the authority of Maimonides' rabbinic contemporaries, the overwhelming majority of whom, on Maimonides' own testimony there, understood *aggadot* literally, not allegorically. For an English translation of the text, see Twersky, *Reader*, pp. 402-23. Historical background to the discussion is provided in Langermann, "Letter of R. Shmuel," and in Stroumsa, *Reshito*.

27 I borrow this expression from W. Z. Harvey. See his interesting essay, "Return."

28 See the chapters in this volume on Maimonides' universalism.

29 This criticism was, in effect, made by Isaac Abravanel. Commenting on the words with which Maimonides opens the *Mishneh Torah* – "The foundation of all foundations and pillar of all the sciences is to know that there exists a First Existent" ("Laws of the Foundations of the Torah," I.1) – Abravanel expostulates: "Of what concern is it of ours whether or not this

undermines rabbinic authority, especially of those rabbis who insist on the basis of their mastery of rabbinic literature that they have the right to determine Jewish theology and politics.[30]

Analyzing the social roles of the dominant figures in the various debates over the writings of Maimonides in the High Middle Ages supports my reading of rabbinic responses to Maimonides. With few exceptions those who took what can in broad terms be called anti-philosophical positions were authoritative rabbinic scholars or their followers; similarly, almost without exception, those who defended the Maimonides who called upon us never to forget that our eyes are set in the front of our heads were intellectuals with neither formal nor informal rabbinic authority.

This demands a bit more explanation. Aviezer Ravitzky has drawn our attention to the existence of a self-conscious school of Jewish philosophers founded by Samuel ibn Tibbon (died ca. 1232), the translator of Maimonides' *Guide*.[31] Members of this school saw themselves as engaged in a joint project – a project that distinguished them from their more traditionally oriented contemporaries. That project was the furthering of rationalist values and teachings. These individuals saw themselves as good and faithful Jews (indeed, as the best and most faithful of all Jews), and *as such* devoted their time to scientific and philosophical studies, leaving halakhic matters to the halakhists. Philosophical studies were so important to them that they often ignored their more traditional rabbinic studies, betraying without shame their ignorance of basic matters. Opposed to the intellectuals were traditionalist scholars, those whom I have here called "rabbis," who may not have opposed philosophy per se, but certainly insisted that Jews devote the lion's share of the time available to the study (and implementation) of halakhic texts.[32]

---

foundation is the pillar of gentile sciences?" *Principles*, p. 76. On Abravanel's attitude towards Maimonides, see Lawee, "Good," and Hoch and Kellner, "Voice."

30 On the contemporary repercussions of this attitude, and its connection to medieval debates, see Kellner, "Rabbis."

31 See Ravitzky, "Mishnato," and "Samuel ibn Tibbon."

32 This distinction was drawn by several medievals, including Profiat Duran (Efodi), Elijah Delmedigo, and the latter's student, Shaul ha-Kohen Asheknazi. For details, see Hoch and Kellner, "Voice." See also Kellner, *Dogma*, pp. 66-69.

The issue may be better understood if we cast it in the following terms. After his death, Maimonides' followers ranged themselves into two opposing camps. The "halakhic" Maimonideans – those for whom the Rambam of the *Mishneh Torah* was crucial, who viewed Maimonides as fitting without difficulty into the line of halakhic decisors beginning, in effect, with Moses and continuing to them and through them to their disciples and descendants – were opposed by the "philosophic'" Maimonideans. Such thirteenth-century and fourteenth-century figures as Samuel ibn Tibbon, Jacob Anatoli, Zerahiah ben Shealtiel Hen, Isaac Albalag, Moses of Salerno, and Shem Tov ibn Falaquera come to mind. These men were to a large extent part of a self-consciously defined group sharing a common intellectual agenda, including the writing of philosophy in Hebrew (unknown before the time of Samuel ibn Tibbon), the translation of scientific texts into Hebrew, and the philosophical interpretation of Scripture (often presented esoterically). These "philosophic" Maimonideans were further characterized by their appreciation of the high level of intellectual sophistication among the gentiles (and not among the Jews, as Samuel ibn Tibbon often complained),[34] by their relatively low level of halakhic erudition, and by their feeling that they were a tiny saving remnant swimming in a sea of ignoramuses.[33]

These individuals, who, in Their own eyes at least, were intellectuals *(maskilei ha-muskalot)* in the strictest sense of the term, were loath to accept the authority of rabbis as such. In this (correctly, I have tried to show), they were following in the footsteps of Maimonides.

The rabbis, the halakhic Maimonideans, like their intellectualist opponents, the philosophic Maimonideans, were also part of a defined group sharing a common intellectual agenda. The main authorities for this group were other rabbis – heads of courts, halakhic decisors, and authors of works of rabbinic scholarship. Those who opposed Maimonides, or, more accurately, those who opposed the social consequences of his philosophical teachings, were not nec-

---

33 Compare Samuel ibn Tibbon's lament in his *Commentary on Ecclesiastes* that "many of our generation" reject Maimonides while only "one in a city, two in a family" properly appreciate the master. The text is cited by Ravitzky in "Samuel ibn Tibbon," p. 89. See also ibn Tibbon's comments in the last chapter of *Ma'amar Yikavvu ha-Mayyim.*

essarily aware of the points I have adduced here, but they certainly seemed to realize that they were faced with a very serious threat.

That complex of historical phenomena known as the "Maimonidean controversy" was an event of major social and political significance, shaking the Jewish communities of Spain, Provence, and even France for well over one hundred years. I have tried to suggest here that historians who focus on the events themselves or see them primarily in terms of "class struggle" or as a reflection of a debate over particularism and universalism in Judaism, but who ignore Maimonides' writings themselves, will in the end at best see and present only a partial picture.[34]

Who was the Maimonides whose writings so upset the rabbis of his and later generations? He was not the radical Maimonides presented by readers who understand him as a self-conscious heretic, hiding his true views behind a cloak of insincere orthodoxy. Had Maimonides' rabbinic contemporaries and near contemporaries understood him thus, there would have been no controversy. He would have been anathematized altogether, or, at the very least, ignored. Maimonides was deeply convinced that one must master the Torah before going on to science and philosophy – but go on one must (if one has the abilities). This Maimonides insists on the freedom to explore ideas, affirming that it is the truth that counts, and that it is the truth that must be accepted, no matter what its source. This Maimonides uses philosophical texts to interpret Scripture and Midrash; and this Maimonides explicitly rejects the idea that a person's role or position, no matter how exalted, has any bearing on the truth or falsity of what that person says.

In the twentieth century Leo Strauss gave renewed impetus to the old questions, who really is Maimonides and what did he mean to say? In a series of gnomic studies, illuminated by flashes of brilliance, Strauss forcefully reminded the scholarly world of what it should never have forgotten: the *Guide of the Perplexed* is an esoteric work and may not be taken at face value.[35] Strauss

---

34 A noted historian of medieval Jewry once told me that he could not care less "whether or not the active intellect had a tail." My point here is that such questions should be of interest to the social historian, not just to the historian of ideas.

35 The most important of Strauss's writings in this connection are "The Literary Character" and "How to Begin." Recent critiques of Strauss include Seeskin, *Searching*, and Davidson, *Maimonides*.

apparently felt that what Maimonides wished to keep hidden he, Leo Strauss, had no right to make public, and so he kept his understanding of Maimonides' secret doctrine obscure.

Having been reminded that Maimonides had a secret doctrine, scholars have set to work seeking to determine what it is. An example of this is useful here. Throughout his writings, both halakhic and philosophic, Maimonides presents a doctrine, that, if not surprising in Aristotelian terms, is surprising in traditional Jewish terms: human perfection consists of nothing other than perfection of the intellect, which, in turn, consists of nothing other than a high degree of competence in metaphysics. Practical perfection (observance of the commandments, moral behavior) is *at most* a necessary propaedeutic for intellectual perfection.

At the very end of the *Guide of the Perplexed*, however, Maimonides seems to reject this intellectualist framework, closing the book with the following:

> It is clear that the perfection of man that may truly be gloried in is the one acquired by him who has achieved, in a measure corresponding to his capacity, apprehension of him, may He be exalted, and who knows His providence extending over His creatures as manifested in the act of bringing them into being and their governance as it is. The way of life of such an individual, after he has achieved this apprehension, will always have in view *loving-kindness, righteousness,* and *judgment,* through assimilation to His actions, may He be exalted, just as we have explained several times in this treatise.

What is to be made of this? Is Maimonides suddenly abandoning his intellectualist perception of human behavior and substituting a call for practical perfection in the world? If so, what form must this practical perfection take? Many scholars hold on to the intellectualist interpretation of human perfection, explaining this passage in various ways.[36]

Others affirm that the call for a practical *imitatio Dei* in the passage just quoted must be understood as normative for any interpretation of Maimo-

---

36 Modern scholars who so interpret Maimonides include Isaac Husik, Alexander Altmann, Harry, Zvi Blumberg, and the early David R. Blumenthal. In the Middle Ages this was the interpretation of Samuel ibn Tibbon and Shem Tov ibn Falaquera. For details, see Kellner, *Perfection*, pp. 67-68.

nides' views on human perfection. These scholars are divided into three groups. Hermann Cohen, Julius Guttmann, and Steven Schwarzschild are the most prominent representatives of the trend in Maimonidean interpretation that holds that the way in which humans satisfy the call to practical perfection is through moral behavior.

Shlomo Pines launched a frontal attack on the intellectualist reading of Maimonides, discerning in Maimonides' work an esoteric doctrine, according to which the sort of intellectual perfection ordinarily thought to be the supreme purpose of human life is actually impossible. He was thus led to affirm that the best life is the practical life. Together with his student Lawrence Berman, Pines developed a Straussian reading of Maimonides, according to which the best life is one of political leadership.

Isadore Twersky, David Hartman, Shalom Rosenberg, and I have proposed that according to Maimonides one imitates God by obeying His commandments after and in conjunction with achieving the highest level possible of intellectual perfection.[37]

We have before us, then, a four-way debate concerning Maimonides' true views on a single issue: human perfection. Multiplying by the many issues (creation, immortality, freedom of the will, providence, etc., etc.) about which there is debate concerning Maimonides' true views, one quickly sees how complex the thicket of Maimonidean hermeneutics is!

There are two widely accepted ways of viewing Maimonides. One may be called vertical; the other, horizontal. In the first view, Maimonides is situated in a chain of Jewish tradition stretching back to Moses, and is seen primarily as a halakhic decisor. It is primarily in this tradition that Maimonides' views are studied and understood. In the second view, Maimonides is located in the context of contemporary or near-contemporary Muslim philosophy, and it is in relation to thinkers like al-Farabi that his views are studied and understood.

The correct interpretation, in my opinion, is that Maimonides must be understood as standing at the nexus of both vectors, the vertical one stretching back to Moses and the horizontal one encompassing his philosophical contemporaries and near contemporaries. Maimonides was convinced that one could and must live simultaneously in both these worlds.

---

37 For details on all this, see *Perfection*, pp. 7-11.

CHAPTER TWO:
Strauss' Maimonides vs. Maimonides' Maimonides: Could Maimonides have been *both* Enlightened and Orthodox?

L eo Strauss' view of Maimonides is based upon an unresolvable quarrel which Strauss posits between Enlightenment and Orthodoxy, between unbelief and belief, between Athens and Jerusalem.[1] Strauss asserted that there occurred a medieval Enlightenment similar to that of the Eighteenth Century. As in the later Enlightenment, medieval intellectuals had to choose between Orthodoxy and Enlightenment. Strauss' Maimonides was an enlightened man and thus could not remain Orthodox.[2] Would Maimonides himself agree with this assessment, that he was forced to choose between Enlightenment and Orthodoxy and privately preferred the former while publicly affirming the latter? In this essay I shall argue that Maimonides was no Straussian reader of himself. This argument has been made before;[3] here I hope to present new reasons for rejecting Strauss' way of reading Rambam.

Strauss, it appears to me, was misled in his approach to Maimonides in two important ways. First, his understanding of the "Aristotelian enlightenment" in terms of the value-free nature of natural science and his depiction of it in narrowly intellectualist terms was much too 18th century in tone and substance.[4] Second, Strauss' insistence that "the leading idea of the medieval Enlightenment that has become lost to the modern Enlightenment and its heirs, and through

---

1 Leo Strauss, *Philosophy and Law*, pp. 27, 31, 38.

2 I realize that Strauss never made himself this clear but trust that most of his readers will agree with my assessment. One of his closest students, Werner Dannhauser, so interpreted him in a symposium at the University of Haifa in December, 1999.

3 For recent and convincing critiques of Strauss on Maimonides, with citations of other relevant studies, see Seeskin, *Searching*, pp. 177-188 and Davidson, *Maimonides*, pp. 393-410.

4 *Philosophy and Law*, pp. 105-107.

an understanding of which many modern certainties and doubts lose their force [is] the idea of Law"[5] crucially misrepresents the notion of law at issue.[6] Maimonides' intellectualism is less strict and austere than Strauss thought, and his notion of law is much different from that alleged by Strauss.

Strauss, as I understand him, presents Maimonides as seeing the ideal human in purely and austerely intellectualist terms, as nothing more than a rational animal.[7] Strauss' Maimonides seems to adopt a view (held afterwards explicitly by Gersonides[8]) according to which that which makes us human, and in consequence that which survives our deaths, is only what we know. On this view, the human subject counts for nothing, the objects of knowledge, for everything. This Maimonidean-Gersonidean position follows from the adoption of the idea that human beings are rational animals. From this it follows that all that is not rational in us we share with animals. Our animal-like characteristics are to be despised: subjugated where they can be and regretted where they can not be.

The Maimonidean view thus understood sees the mind, not as a collection of talents inhering in a substrate, but as a collection of concepts. Someone once said of a boring town in the US: "there's no there there". In the view of the Straussian Maimonides: "there's no I there." Characters from the television series, *Star Trek*, will help us understand Strauss' Maimonides. They are Mr. Spock, a half human and half "Vulcan," who strives to be guided by nothing but logic, and Dr McCoy, a passionate physician:

> Spock and McCoy represent two different philosophical traditions on the relation between reason (the mental faculty that produces and assesses beliefs) and

---

5 *Philosophy and Law*, p. 39.

6 It is this alleged centrality of the idea of law which leads Strauss to read Maimonides (and other ancient and medieval thinkers) as being much more concerned with issues of politics than was really the case.

7 For a critique of this view, see ch. 4 in this volume, "Is Maimonides' Ideal Person Austerely Rationalist?"

8 Gersonides, 1288-1344, held that what makes us human is our abstract knowledge. Warren Zev Harvey has shown that for Gersonides, any abstract knowledge "counts" while for Maimonides it must be knowledge of metaphysical matters. See his "Crescas' Critique of Philosophic Happiness." Gersonides' intellectualism led him to deprecate the importance of human beings vis-a-vis the separate intellects. This aroused much anger against him, anger which could have been directed against Maimonides as well. See my "Cultured Despisers."

passion (the mental faculty that produces desires and emotions). According to the ancient Greek philosophers Plato and Aristotle, the human condition is a struggle between reason and passion – a struggle that reason ought to win. According to the other tradition, most closely associated with the eighteenth-century Scottish philosopher David Hume, there is no conflict at all, and passion is preeminent.[9]

Mr. Spock tries to embody what is often presented as the Maimonidean ideal of a human being: a person in whom reason has wholly vanquished passion.[10]

The physicist Freeman Dyson once observed, concerning an autistic woman of his acquaintance:

> [she] has no concept of her own identity, she doesn't understand the difference between 'you' and 'I' – she uses pronouns almost indiscriminately. And so her universe is radically different from mine. Concrete social relations are for her very, very difficult to comprehend. On the other hand, with anything abstract, she has no trouble...Because these are people whose intelligence is intact, but something at the center is missing.[11]

There can be no doubt that Maimonides accepts Aristotle's definition of human beings as rational animals.[12] In terms of our genus, we are animals (as opposed to pieces of furniture or meteorological phenomena). Our specific difference, that which distinguishes us from all other members of the animal kingdom, is our rationality. Everything that is not a direct reflection of rational thought – hopes and fears, love and hates, desires, needs, passions – is a consequence of our animal nature.

---

9 Hanley, *Is Data Human?* pp. 6-7.

10 Strauss, I believe, was aware of the fact that philosophers lived human lives among human beings, out of (unfortunate) necessity; they sought to be guided by intellect alone, not by tradition, convention or sacred scripture. In what might be called their non-philosophic capacity, they sought to develop admirable human characters. In this sense, the analogy to Mr. Spock might need to be modified.

11 Quoted by Sacks, *Anthropologist*, p. 229.

12 This view was already attributed to Aristotle in the ancient world, but my friend Moshe Grimberg and I have not been able to find any place where he actually says so in as many words. There can be little doubt that Aristotle actually agrees with the definition (see, for example, Nicomachean Ethics, X, viii, 1179a24-30), he just never actually stated it explicitly. For Maimonides' adoption of this view, see *Confrontation*, p. 57n.

Maimonides' intellectualism finds many expressions in surprisingly dispa-rate contexts: the definition of human beings and their perfection; the defi-nition of subhumans; immortality; the relationship between commandments and moral perfection; the attainment of providence and prophecy; the differ-ence between animals and humans; and universalism and messianism.[13]

According to Strauss, on Maimonides' conception of the ideal Jewish hu-man being a Jew fulfills the commandments of the Torah not only because they are commanded by God, and not only because obedience to these com-mandments has beneficial consequences for the individual and her society, but because through this obedience one can achieve a very high level of moral perfection. Moral perfection is itself a step towards the true human perfection, which is the apprehension of truths, especially concerning God, to the great-est extent that one can apprehend them. The truly perfected individual has subjugated all feelings, all passions, and all desires to reason, has eliminated from her consciousness everything personal, lives her outward life on "auto-pilot," as it were, and devotes her inner (and truer) life to the contemplation of abstract truths. Every aspect of living not connected to that contemplation is ignored to the greatest extent possible. All that distinguishes one perfected individual from another is the level of abstract truth which each has compre-hended.[14] This view of Maimonides has been held, to one degree or another, not only Leo Strauss, but by thinkers as diverse as Samuel ibn Tibbon,[15] Ger-sonides, and Isaac Husik.[16]

Maimonides certainly seems to open himself to the charge that he sees the perfected human being as a coldly rational thinking machine, dispassionately weighing evidence and calculating results. But there are a number of reasons for revising this view. Let us look at a few of them briefly.

As I understand Maimonides, one who wishes perfectly to fulfill the com-mand of *imitatio Dei* must achieve the highest possible level of intellectual

---

13 For details, see see ch. 4 in this volume, "Is Maimonides' Ideal Person Austerely Rationalist?"

14 In this, perfected individuals are like the separate intellects. See "Laws of the Foundations of the Torah," II.5.

15 See Kellner, "Maimonides and Samuel ibn Tibbon."

16 See Husik, *History*, pp. 299-300.

perfection[17] and then descend Jacob's ladder (or return to the Platonic cave), in order to participate in the governance of one's society according to the principles of loving-kindness, righteousness, and judgment.[18] This, however, cannot be done by a person who is wholly divorced from the needs of one's society, uninterested in the well being of its citizens and ignorant of how to order their affairs in the best possible way. To put the matter bluntly, after a lifetime of devotion to Torah study (which includes halakhah, physics, and metaphysics), the person who wishes to imitate God must also become an expert on human nature and on plumbing.

This point needs expansion. Maimonides appeared to hold that knowledge was transformative. A person who spends a lifetime of effort perfecting herself morally and then intellectually, practicing rigid self-discipline while with great difficulty plumbing the depths of understanding of the basic structure of the cosmos, is not the same person who started the quest, only now with more knowledge. This is a person transformed, an individual whose reaction to the understanding gained with so much difficulty is to "recoil affrighted, and realize that he is a small creature, lowly and obscure, endowed with slight and slender intelligence, standing in the presence of Him Who is perfect in knowledge."[19] This is the person who realizes that the greatest perfection open to him or her is to imitate the ways of God, in practicing loving-kindness, judgment and righteousness in the world.[20] But there is more than simple realization here: unlike Plato's philosopher, who must be forced to return to the cave and become a king, Maimonides' individual transformed-by-knowledge wants and needs to imitate God. Such a person is driven by *love* of God (a point to which I shall revert below) to sacrifice her own selfish needs by putting herself at the service of vastly inferior people.

---

17 It may be appropriate to note here that the nature of the intellectual perfection prized by Maimonides may be somewhat different from discursive reason as usually understood. The highest levels of knowledge are apparently intuitive, and may even be experiential. See Blumenthal, *Philosophic Mysticism*, Faur, *Homo Mysticus* and Loewe, "*Credat Judaeus Appella?*"

18 For defense of this interpretation see Kellner, *Perfection*.

19 "Laws of the Foundations of the Torah," II.2, p. 35b; compare IV.12.

20 See *Guide* III. 54 and my exposition of the end of the *Guide* in *Perfection*.

To repeat: Maimonidean intellectual perfection is not simply a matter of adding knowledge, in the way in which we can add memory to our computers. Breadth of knowledge and depth of understanding transform the knower. This issue may be better understood in light of Maimonides' understanding of the point of moral striving. We practice moral behavior, not only so that we do the right thing, but also so that doing the right thing becomes part of our personality. In "Eight Chapters" and in "Laws of Moral Qualities" Maimonides develops a position which focuses at least as much on character as it does on deed: a major reason for giving charity is not only to alleviate poverty, but so that we ourselves become charitable people. Similarly, the perfected knower is in a real sense transformed into a different and better person by the knowledge gained.

Another matter on which Maimonides is often misunderstood is prophecy. The prophet is not simply a super-philosopher, a point importantly emphasized by Jose Faur in his *Homo Mysticus*. The philosopher becomes a prophet thanks to imagination. But prophets are not just morally perfected super-philosophers with active imaginations. They are alive to aesthetic experience as well.[21]

Three other points should be introduced here in order to round out our picture of the prophet. These are the compulsion felt by a prophet to prophesy, the fact that prophets differ in respect to two qualities necessary for prophets, courage and divination, and the ways in which all human beings (prophets emphatically included) differ one from the other. With respect to each of these, Maimonides makes it clear that prophets are much more than simply superior philosophers.[22]

Another relevant issue is love of God. Is love of God equivalent to knowledge of God or something more? Maimonides, I have shown elsewhere,[23] maintains that we achieve love of God *through* the apprehension of God's being as it is in truth to the greatest extent possible for us. That does not mean that loving God is nothing other than knowing about God.[24]

---

21 *Guide of the Perplexed* II.36 (p. 371). Further on this, see the recent and interesting discussion in Bland, *Artless Jew*, pp. 74-108.

22 See ch. 4 in this volume, "Is Maimonides' Ideal Person Austerely Rationalist?"

23 Ibid. and also ch. 19, "Spirituality and a Life of Holiness."

24 See my introduction to my translation of Maimonides' *Book of Love*.

Modern readers of Maimonides are led to misunderstand him, I think, because we think of reason in terms made natural to us by thinkers like Descartes, with his search for clear and distinct ideas, torn out of any human context, on the one hand and by thinkers like Hume, who posited a vast gulf between fact and value, on the other hand. We look at reason as cold and calculating, as a tool for deducing theorems and getting from means to ends. But for the medievals, passionate love literally "made the world go round." The heavenly spheres do not know God in some coldly dispassionate, "scientific" way only, but are brought by that knowledge to the love of God. That love in turn makes them strive to be like God. The outermost sphere "is moved by its love for God, and, being moved, communicates motion to the rest of the universe."[25]

Thus, for Maimonides and thinkers like him, reason is a source of motivation.[26] And thus he so naturally invokes the Song of Songs in the last chapter of the *Guide of the Perplexed* and makes love an outcome of knowledge. Learning carried out properly transforms the learner into a new kind of person.[27]

Despite all this, Strauss' picture of Maimonides is not entirely incorrect: Lessing may have preferred the eternal search for truth to being given all the truth on a silver platter, but I doubt that Maimonides' would have. But he certainly would have recognized that having that truth was not simply a matter of piling fact upon fact, deduction upon deduction; it was a matter of passionate love. The Maimonidean intellectual does not live in a value-free world. Prophets, the ultimate intellectuals, are not all alike, differing only in intellectual attainments. They differ crucially as well with respect to their abilities to govern, the strength of their imaginations, the compulsion they feel to prophesy, their courage, and their abilities as diviners. In each of these qualities, prophets differ *qua* prophets.

The point I am raising here is of some importance for our understanding of Maimonides. If human perfection is nothing other than intellectual perfection, then determining what we can in fact know becomes crucially important. Indeed, much of the best research and writing on Maimonides has focused on this issue. In this, Strauss' influence seems pronounced. If, as many Strauss-

---

25 Lewis, *Discarded Image*, p. 113.

26 On this see Seeskin, *Searching*, p. 121.

27 The last two paragraphs owe much to Kenneth Seeskin.

influenced interpreters of Maimonides believe, Maimonides was pessimistic about the possibility of actually achieving intellectual perfection, then in truth the only perfection open to human beings is practical perfection, whether in the realm of halakhah, morals, or politics.

But, as I hope to have made clear here, Maimonides' enlightened individual is transformed by the search for knowledge into someone new and better than she was before, uses imagination, courage, and divination in her search for prophecy, and seeks to love God in ways not limited to abstract intellectualizing. There is much room for us to seek to become ever more perfect even if true metaphysical knowledge remains beyond our grasp. There is nothing in this conception of enlightenment which makes it fundamentally incompatible with Orthodoxy. Nor is there anything in this conception of enlightenment which forces one to think that the only truly perfected person is the one who founds or improves polities.

This brings us to a consideration of Strauss' claims about the centrality of law. Strauss, I believe, ignores an important Maimonidean distinction between two kinds of law. This distinction is brought out by the fact that in scientific and dogmatic contexts Maimonides holds that one falls into error, while in halakhic contexts, one makes mistakes.[28] This reflects the fact that for Maimonides, halakhah is a system of formal rules, independent of "reality" in an important sense while science describes reality. The clearest example of this position with respect to halakhah is the following:

> It is plain and manifest that the laws about ritual impurity and purity are decrees laid down by Scripture and not matters about which human understanding is capable of forming a judgment; for behold, they are included among the divine statutes.[29] So, too, immersion as a means of freeing oneself from ritual

---

28 Giora Hon has analyzed the concepts of mistake and error. Hon associates "mistake with avoidable ignorance. A mistake can be avoided since checking procedures are known and available. By contrast, error is associated with unavoidable ignorance..." After analyzing the distinction, Hon suggests "that the distinction between mistake and error can constitute a clear demarcation line between propositions whose truth-values depend on rules and their applications, and those which involve in the assignment of their truth-values elements of reality other than rules, that is, elements whose claim to knowledge is incomplete, for example, sense data." See Hon, "Going Wrong," p. 6.

29 This statement is interesting in light of the claim made by Maimonides in the *Guide of the Perplexed* that the divine statutes (*hukkim*) can be understood. On the whole issue see Stern,

impurity is included among the divine statutes. *Now "ritual impurity" is not mud or filth which water can remove, but is a matter of scriptural decree and dependent upon intention of the heart.* Therefore the Sages have said, If a man immerses himself, but without special intention, it is as though he has not immersed himself at all. Nevertheless we may find some indication of all this: just as one who sets his heart on becoming ritually pure becomes so as soon as he has immersed himself, *although nothing new has befallen his body,* so, too, one who sets his heart on purifying himself from the impurity that besets men's souls – namely, evil thoughts and wicked moral qualities[30]– becomes pure as soon as he consents in his heart to shun those counsels and brings his soul into the waters of pure reason. Behold, Scripture says, *I will sprinkle pure water upon you, and you shall be pure: I will cleanse you from all your ritual impurity and from all your fetishes (Ezek. 36:25).* May God, in His great mercy, purify us from every sin, iniquity, and guilt. Amen.[31]

These being the case, it not surprising that the consequences of "honest mistakes" in halakhah are relatively modest. In this Maimonides should be contrasted with Nahmanides who held that even inadvertent sinning damages the soul of the sinner.[32]

Maimonidean science and dogma, on the other hand, relate to "elements of reality other than rules." Going astray in these contexts has extremely serious consequences: one loses one's immortality. Another way of putting this point, one which makes clearer its importance for understanding the kind of religious thinker Maimonides was, is as follows: for Maimonides, halakhah is, in a significant sense, arbitrary[33] (i.e., it could have been other than it is), while science is not.

Problems.

30 *De'ot ra'ot.* For many reasons I would prefer to follow Herbert Danby (in the Yale Judaica Series translation) and translate this as "false convictions" but I fear that would be incorrect. On the expression *de'ah* as "moral quality" in Maimonides, see *Guide of the Perplexed* III.35, p. 535.

31 "Laws of Immersion Pools," XI.12, p. 535, with emendations and emphases added. Further on this text, see *Confrontation,* pp. 136-139.

32 See Nahmanides to Lev. 4:2 and 18:29 and the discussion in *Confrontation,* pp. 44-52.

33 For my problems with this term, see *Confrontation,* p. 36n.

This point needs to be made clearer. The need for moral law, political law, and ritual law reflects the fact that post-Adamic human beings are not governed by intellect. In that sense, such laws are a necessary aspect of the human condition. But the specific details of the laws of the Torah reflect what might be called historical accident. Since Abraham chose God more than God chose Abraham (at least according to Maimonides), and because the Torah was given to the descendents of Abraham because they were his descendents,[34] it follows that the Torah could have been different. Had Abraham been a Navajo, for example, and not a Hebrew, the Torah would have been written in the Navajo language and the specific histories, laws, customs, and ceremonials would have reflected Navajo, not Hebrew realities. Furthermore, since, according to Maimonides, many specific ceremonials were instituted in order to make Jews as unlike idolaters as possible, had the Sabian idolaters of Moses' time practiced their idolatry differently, Judaism would be practiced differently. In this sense, the laws of Judaism are arbitrary: they could have been different.

This should help us to understand why Maimonides is, (following well-established precedent) long-suffering when it comes to mistakes in halakhic contexts, but very "short-suffering" when it comes to errors in what may be called, for the sake of convenience, the "scientific" context (which context includes dogma). This follows from his view that (at least part of) science deals with ultimate reality as opposed to halakhah which is a structure or construct in a real sense independent of that reality.

In a series of passages in the *Guide of the Perplexed* (I.5, I.32-33, and III.56) and in his Commentary on the Mishnah (Hagigah II.1) Maimonides makes clear that error in scientific contexts can be dangerous. In the *Guide of the Perplexed* (I.34, p. 73) Maimonides uses an interesting allegory to explain the danger:

> One of the parables generally known in our community is that likening knowledge to water. Now the Sages, peace be on them, explained several notions by means of this parable; one of them being that he who knows how to swim brings up pearls from the bottom of the sea, whereas he who does not know,

---

34 See *Confrontation* , pp. 77-83.

drowns. For this reason, no one should expose himself to the risks of swimming except he who has been trained in learning to swim.

Maimonides' view of the danger of scientific error is a reflection of his adoption of the theory of the acquired intellect, according to which the children of
human parents are born as human beings only in potentia, and that if they do
not actualize their intellects, and thus realize the specific difference of human
beings (*rational* animals), they remain as they were born, potential but not
actual human beings. One actualizes oneself as a human being through the
correct apprehension of metaphysical truths. Errors in metaphysics, therefore,
keep one from becoming fully human and further keep one from one of the
consequences of being human, achieving a share in the world to come.

The same issues underlie Maimonides' unforgiving attitude towards errors
in matters of dogma. Such errors cannot be forgiven, for the person making
them excludes herself from the world to come.[35]

To this point I have suggested that Maimonides distinguishes between
mistakes in halakhic contexts, which have relatively modest consequences,
and errors in scientific and dogmatic consequences, which have profound
consequences. I have further suggested that this reflects his perception of
halakhah as a system of rules imposed upon reality as opposed to reflecting
reality. Maimonides holds views of the nature of ritual purity and impurity, of
holiness, and of the consequences of sin, which contradict those of many of
his predecessors and successors in the Jewish tradition and which only make
sense in the context of a view of halakhah as a system of essentially arbitrary
rules fundamentally independent of reality.

In sum, Maimonides sees halakhah as constituting a social reality, not as
reflecting an ontological reality. To adopt a modern idiom, "halakhah" is the
name given to a set of rules which create a "game" called "Judaism." These
rules are "arbitrary," but not in the sense that they are not expressions of God's
wisdom and benevolence, but in the sense that they could have been different
(as is proved by Maimonides' explanation for why God commanded the Jews
to bring sacrifices). Violations of these rules can have serious consequences

---

35 I have expanded upon and supported this interpretation of Maimonides in a number of
studies, most recently in *Must*. See also below, ch. 9, "Could Maimonides Get Into Rambam's
Heaven?"

on a psychosocial level, leading up to and including the death penalty, but it has no and can have no direct consequences on an ontological level. Obedience to the commandments in and of itself does not gain one entry to the world to come.

In the final analysis, and this, I submit, Strauss failed to grasp, religious and political laws play much less an important role in Maimonides' understanding of the world and of our place in it than do laws of nature. The whole point of religious and political laws is to enable us to grasp the laws of nature and in that fashion become fully human. Since philosophers are much more than "autistic" thinking machines, they must also live in a psycho-social reality and thus need and are obligated by the institutional laws of halakhah no less than their intellectually less favored contemporaries.

Law is central for Maimonides the philosopher and for Maimonides the rabbi. But the laws which are thus central are not the "political" laws of the Torah, but the deeper laws hidden behind them, the laws which govern the natural world in which we live.

Maimonidean Orthodoxy makes no demands which an "enlightened" individual cannot meet. In his own mind, Maimonides was thoroughly enlightened and thoroughly orthodox and saw no need to choose between the two.

CHAPTER THREE:
The Literary Character of the *Mishneh Torah*: On the Art of Writing in Maimonides' Halakhic Works

Isadore Yizhak Twersky ushered in a new era in the academic study of Maimonides with his seminal article, "Some Non-Halakic Aspects of the *Mishneh Torah*." In my own 'footnotes' to this article, i.e., the studies I have written thanks to its inspiration, I have sought to elaborate different aspects of Maimonides' central teaching as expressed by Twersky, that the quest for wisdom (*hokhmah*) "is absolutely indispensable for religious perfection – is indeed the crowning achievement" (p. 96). In his elegant essay, Twersky showed how for Maimonides the process of intellectualization "is woven uninterruptedly and unabashedly from his earliest writings through the *Moreh Nevukhim* and on through all his responsa. It is especially discernible in the texture of the *Mishneh Torah*" (p. 96).

Here I will call further "attention to some motifs of Maimonidean rationalism... allusively incorporated into the *Mishneh Torah*" (p. 95). In particular, I wish to draw attention to certain stylistic features of Maimonides' writing in the *Mishneh Torah*.

There are many passages in the *Mishneh Torah*, a few examples of which I will examine here, in which Maimonides writes in what might be called a quasi-esoteric vein. He writes simultaneously for several audiences without drawing explicit attention to that fact.

Maimonides, it appears to me, had in mind three different kinds of readers when he wrote the *Mishneh Torah*. In the first instance, the work was addressed to rabbinic scholars, talmudists, who had no interest in philosophical issues, no grounding in philosophical texts, and who probably viewed such issues and texts as at best irrelevant to their spiritual lives. In the second instance, the work was addressed to rabbinic scholars, talmudists, who had gone beyond the pale of talmudic studies to the realms of logic, physics, and metaphysics without in any way giving up their prior allegiances. These were individuals like Maimonides himself as I understand him, individuals for whom rabbinic studies were not an end in themselves, but a preparation for the study of the wisdom (*hokhmah*) of the Torah properly understood. Thus, I do not see Maimonides' audience as divided between "Talmudists" and "philosophers" but between talmudists *simpliciter* and philosophical talmudists.[1] Maimonides probably had in mind a third group as well, talmudists on their way to becoming philosophical talmudists, for whom I suspect Maimonides hoped the *Mishneh Torah* to be crucially valuable."[2]

---

1 Maimonides presents this gradation in the famous "parable of the palace", *Guide of the Perplexed* III. 51. On this issue there, see my *Perfection*, pp. 13-33. As will be made clearer in the next note, there is little doubt that Maimonides prized philosophical talmudists over "plain" talmudists (and, among Jews, over "plain" philosophers).

2 The distinction I make here between talmudists *per se* and philosophical talmudists is hinted at in a number of places in Maimonides" writings. See, for example, in addition to the "parable of the palace" (see previous note), *Guide of the Perplexed* I, Introduction, just before the seven causes of contradictions (pp. 16-17):

> To sum up: I am the man who when the concern pressed him and his way was straightened and he could find no other device by which to teach a demonstrated truth other than by giving satisfaction to a single virtuous man while displeasing ten thousand ignoramuses – I am he who prefers to address that single man by himself, and I do not heed the blame of those many creatures. For I claim to liberate that virtuous one from that into which he has sunk, and I shall guide him in his perplexity until he becomes perfect and finds rest.

In that this passage was addressed to a rabbinical scholar who had grown perplexed by his exposure to the philosophical sciences, it appears that the "ten thousand ignoramuses" were talmudists ignorant of philosophy. At the very beginning of his Introduction (p. 5) Maimonides expressly distinguishes between those who have engaged in no study but "the legalistic study of the Law" and those who have gone further, for whom the *Guide of the Perplexed* was written (see also p. 10). The point comes out as well in *Guide* 1.32-33; III.31 (p. 523) and in one of Maimonides "popular" writings, *Essay on Resurrection*: "I have met some who think that they are among sages of Israel – by God, they indeed know the way of the Law ever since childhood, and they battle in legal discussions – but they are not certain if God is corporeal, with eyes, hands and feet, as the Bible says, or if He has not a body". Maimonides goes on to call these people "exceedingly deficient folk... who, although they consider themselves sages in Israel, are in fact the most ignorant..." He further states that he decided not to teach basic religious truths in the *Mishneh Torah* in the "idiom of inquiry since examination of these roots requires skills in many fields, of which, as I pointed out in the *Guide*, the learned in the Torah know nothing". I cite from the translation of Abraham Halkin in *Crisis and Leadership*, p. 212. See ibid p. 223.

Talmudists read Maimonides' words, and because of the context, vocabulary, and style think that they are reading a wholly traditional text, totally unobjectionable, and fully consistent with conventional religion as popularly understood. The more philosophically aware audience reads the same passage and finds in it statements consistent with some of the more daring Maimonidean theses expressed (later) in the *Guide of the Perplexed.*

It is my understanding that Maimonides wrote in this fashion in order to protect talmudists from exposure to ideas which might cause, rather than solve, perplexity. Maimonides had no interest in confusing such people. On the contrary, his desire to be helpful to them was such that he made clear attempts to teach them without upsetting their traditional beliefs. This approach finds expression in the following text:

> Know that the things about which we shall speak in these chapters and in what will come in the commentary are not matters invented on my own nor explanations I have originated. Indeed, they are matters gathered from the discourse of the Sages in the Midrash, the Talmud, and other compositions of theirs, as well as from the discourse of both the ancient and modern philosophers and from the compositions of many men. Hear the truth from whoever says it. Sometimes I have taken a complete passage from the text of a famous book. Now there is nothing wrong with that, for I do not attribute to myself what someone who preceded me said. We hereby acknowledge this and shall not indicate that 'so and so said' and 'so and so said', since that would be useless prolixity. Moreover, the name of such an individual might make the passage offensive to someone without experience and make him think it has an evil inner meaning of which he is not aware. Consequently, I saw fit to omit the author's name, since my goal is to be useful to the reader. We shall explain to him the hidden meanings in this tractate.[3]

It turns out that the ancient and modern philosophers to whom Maimonides is referring here are Aristotle and Alfarabi.[4] It was Maimonides' intent

---

3   I cite the text from the Introduction to "Eight Chapters" as it is translated in Weiss and Butterworth, *Ethical Writings*, p. 60

4   See Davidson, "*Shemonah Perakim.*"

to help his readers; if explicit references to the great thinkers of the past would be counter-productive, then he would do without such references. So, too, in the *Mishneh Torah*: if making some of his positions explicit would only drive away readers who would otherwise benefit from study of his work, Maimonides had no compunction about writing such that his ideas would be clearly understood only by those who could read them in their broader philosophical context.[5]

I do not mean to say here that Maimonides held positions which he thought his talmudist readers should reject. In his own eyes, his positions were those of the Torah, properly understood. Positions which deviated from his were illegitimate, not the other way around. Maimonides, however, was a realist, and understood the Jews of his day (and, I might add, many in our own day), the power of habit, and the unwillingness of people to give up ideas to which they had grown accustomed.[6] Rubbing the faces of such people, so to speak, in explicit expositions of his (correct, Jewishly orthodox, but withal unusual) ideas would in no way bring them to accept the truth. They had to be brought to it gradually and in his role as educator (a role which I think can be seen in every single thing he wrote) Maimonides sought to do that.

But there were others, a tiny minority,[7] who could understand the truth, appreciate it, and accept it. It would have been sinful not to give hem at least a glimpse of the truth, and Maimonides sought to do that also in all of his works, the *Mishneh Torah* most emphatically included.

Maimonides, it seems to me, sought to write as the Torah writes, "in the language of human beings." The Torah was written on several levels, the uppermost suitable for the talmudist uninterested in or incapable of understanding the true meaning of the Torah, which is presented to the philosophically sophisticated in deeper levels. If the Torah itself was written by God in this

---

5   It is also possible that Maimonides was trying to protect himself from unwelcome criticism, but he gives very little indication in his writings that he was afraid of such criticism and I doubt that this matter was a prominent part of his thinking.

6   On this, see *Guide* I. 31, pp. 66-67. See my discussion of this issue in *Decline*, pp. 43-49.

7   See Maimonides' comments in his introduction to Helek, the tenth chapter of Mishnah Sanhedrin, where he speaks of a group whose "members are so few in number that it is hardly appropriate to call them a group...". I cite the translation from Twersky, *Reader*, p. 408.

fashion, is it any surprise that Maimonides, motivated by that very Torah to walk in God's ways, wrote his "repetition" of the Torah in this fashion?

A good example with which to begin our discussion is the very first sentence of the *Mishneh Torah*, "Laws of the Foundations of the Torah," I.1:

> The foundation of all foundations, and the pillar of all the species of wisdom,[8] is to know that there exists a First Existent, that He gives existence to all that exists, and that all existent beings, from the heaven to the earth and what is between them, exist only due to the truth of His existence.

The traditionalist reader of this passage notes the following things:

- The first letters of the first four Hebrew words spell out the tetragrammaton, as is the case in many devotional works.

- Acceptance of God's existence is presented as the foundational belief of Judaism.

- God is characterized as creator of all things.

- Everything that is not God derives its existence from God, and without God cannot exist.

The more philosophically literate and sophisticated reader of this passage notes the following things:

- The 'foundation' of religion is made equivalent to the 'pillar' of the sciences; they both teach the same thing: God's existence.[9]

- The Jew is here called upon to *know* that God exists; such knowledge entails being able to prove that God exists, using the tools of logic and philosophy.[10]

---

8 I.e., the axiom of all the sciences.

9 Isaac Abravanel took note of this fact, and did not like it. See *Rosh Amanah*, chapter 5, 4th objection (p. 63); *Principles*, p. 76. Abravanel realized that by *hokhmot* here Maimonides meant what we call today "sciences" (although today we do not count metaphysics as a science). See further below, note 25.

10 For a discussion of the difference between "knowledge" and "belief" in this context, see pp. 353-358 in Manekin, "Hebrew Philosophy."

- God is characterized as the source of existence, not necessarily as the cause of all that exists. In other words, God can exist without the world, but the world cannot exist without God. With such a view God and the world can have existed in this relationship from all eternity. This formulation is as acceptable to Aristotle, who denies the creation of the world, as it is, for example, to R. Akiva, who presumably affirms it.

- God is here called "the first existent", as opposed to the more usual biblical, rabbinic, or traditional names one would expect to find in a halakhic work; the language calls to mind a parallel text by Alfarabi, a text which turns out upon examination to be a literary source for much of what Maimonides writes in "Laws of the Foundations of the Torah."[11]

- God's "truth" is here called the source of all existence. The attentive reader notes that this strengthens the last two points: God is presented as the metaphysical basis of all that exists. The well-educated reader further remembers Aristotle's claim (*Metaphysics*, ii, 993b20-30) that eternal things are true, and as such are the cause of being of other things.[12]

A text which on the face of it presents no problems for the conventional reader of the *Mishneh Torah* at the same time opens a window into the mind and soul of its author for the reader familiar with the language, ideas, and issues of medieval philosophy.

Maimonides himself instructs us to read "Laws of the Foundations of the Torah," ch. 1 in the way I have presented it here. In *Guide of the Perplexed* I.71 (pp. 181-182) he explains that,

the proofs for the oneness and existence of the deity and of His not being a body ought to be procured from the starting point afforded by the supposition

---

11 See Kraemer, "Opinions." For valuable further explication of the philosophical issues raised in these points, see W. Z. Harvey, "Maimonides" First Commandment."

12 See Fox, *Interpreting*, p. 243 for more on this. On "truth" as "essence" see Baneth, "Terminlogy," p. 258.

of the eternity of the world, for in this way the demonstration will be perfect, both if the world is eternal and if it is created in time. For this reason you will always find that whenever, in what I have written in the books of jurisprudence, I happened to mention the foundations and start upon establishing the existence of the deity, I establish it by discourses that adopt the way of the doctrine of the eternity of the world.

Maimonides hastens to assure the readers of the *Guide of the Perplexed* that the reason for this is not that he believes 'in the eternity of the world, but that [he] wish[es] to establish in our belief the existence of God, may He be exalted, through a demonstrative method as to which there is no disagreement in any respect'.

Whatever one may think about Maimonides' position on creation, there is no doubt that in "Laws of the Foundations of the Torah" he "mentioned the foundations" and sought to establish the existence of God. We are thus surely right in reading 'Foundations' I.1 as it is presented here, as teaching an Aristotelian conception of God as the metaphysical ground of being, as opposed to a conception of God as creator of the cosmos. Maimonides' stylistic strategy enables him to get the point across to the reader who can benefit by it, while keeping the less sophisticated reader in the dark. But this second reader is not misled: the existence of God is indeed the foundation of all foundations, the Jew is required to accept that teaching (the first commandment in the Decalogue according to Maimonides and the first of the 613 commandments), even if only as a matter of belief, not knowledge, and God is indeed the creator of the cosmos and not only the metaphysical ground of its being. Maimonides has succeeded in reaching out to two very different audiences here, instructing both, and harming neither.

Maimonides' comment in the *Guide of the Perplexed* tells us something very important: he expected at least some readers of the Mishneh Torah to realize that he was proving God's existence with arguments which assumed the eternity of the universe and had to explain to them in the *Guide of the Perplexed* why he did that. This is important evidence in favor of my contentions concerning the diverse nature of the audience addressed in the *Mishneh Torah*.

"There is another text in "Foundations of the Torah" where Maimonides' ability to address two different audiences simultaneously finds emphatic expression:

It is among the foundations of religion to know[13] that God causes human beings to prophesy, and that prophecy does not rest upon anyone but a sage great in wisdom, powerful with respect to his [moral] qualities – [i.e.] one whose passions do not overpower him with respect to anything in the world, but, rather, through his intellect he always subdues his passions – and who has a very broad[14] and well-established[15] intellect. A person filled with all these qualities, sound of body, upon entering *pardes* and continuously dwellings upon those great and remote matters,[16] and having an intellect prepared[17] to understand and conceive them, and who continues to sanctify himself, by separating himself from the ways of most people who walk in the darkness of the times, and who zealously trains himself and teaches his mind not to have any thoughts concerning vain things, the nonsense of the time and its snares, but his mind is always directed above, bound under the throne in order to understand those sacred and pure forms, and who examines the entire wisdom of God from the first form till the navel of the world,[18] learning from this God's greatness,[19] the holy spirit immediately rests upon him, and at the time the spirit rests upon him, his soul mingles with the degree of the angels known as *Ishim* and he be-

---

13 To know, not only to believe. See n. 10 above.

14 For a similar use of *rehavah*, see "Foundations", IV:11. A "broad" mind is one of the prerequisites for understanding metaphysics. I do not know what Maimonides means precisely by this term.

15 Or, "well-prepared". This phrase, *ve-hu de'ah rehavah nekhonah ad me'od*, gave me a lot of trouble. *Nakhon* either means "well-established", "prepared for", or "correct". Maimonides' contemporary, R. Abraham ben David of Posquieres, uses it in the latter sense often in his glosses to the *Mishneh Torah* ("Laws of the Sabbath",12:14 and 20:12, for example) and Maimonides himself uses it in that sense in a few passages in the *Mishneh Torah* (in "Laws of Slaves", 6:7 and "Laws of Testimony", 2:2). But in quite a number of passages he uses the expressions *de'ah nekhonah* or *mahshavah nekhonah* as a synonym for *de'ah meyushevet* ("settled intellect"). There is only one passage in which *de'ah nekhonah* means "correct intellect" ("Repentance," IX.1).

16 I.e., the matters which constitute *pardes*.

17 *Nekhonah*

18 I.e., from the outermost limit of the cosmos to its very center.

19 Compare "Foundations", II.1-2.

comes another man, and understands through his intellect that he is not as he was, but has risen above the degree of other wise humans, as it says of Saul: *You will prophesy and become another man* (1 Sam. 10:6).

The talmudist reader of this passage will be very comfortable with it, since so much of the language is taken from biblical and rabbinic texts.[20] On the face of it, there is nothing in this text to upset such a reader. Maimonides reminds us that prophecy is one of the principles of Judaism (as defined himself in his Commentary on the Mishnah[21]) and that prophecy is restricted to one who is very wise, powerful in the mishnaic sense controlling one's desires,[22] and one who has broad and correct understanding (*de'ah*).[23] When such a person, who

---

20 Among these, we may note especially the following: the expression *ve-ein ha-nevu'ah halah ela al hakham gadol be-nevuah, gibbor be-middotav* reflects Nedarim 38a. The word *be-mahshakei* is unusual, and the Jewishly erudite reader will remember that he or she has only seen variants of it in four biblical texts (Ps. 74:20, 88:7, 143:3, and Lam. 3:6). So too with the expression *mitkadshim*, with its biblical overtones. The expression *tahat ha-kisse* calls to mind the rabbinic expression, *tahat kisse ha-kavod*, which is found close to two dozen times in rabbinic literature (Shabbat 152b, etc.). In these passages, it is taught that the souls of the righteous are stored under the throne of glory. Maimonides, I submit, was sure that his talmudist readers would associate the phrase with the "righteous" as they understand the term (individuals who have scrupulously fulfilled the commandments out of love), while the philosophical reader, who has studied Maimonides' account of eschatology in *Helek* will know that the "real" righteous are those who have perfected themselves intellectually, through the study of metaphysics, after having achieved a high level of moral perfection (in the case of Jews, through the fulfillment of the commandments). Similarly with the expression *tabbur ha-arez* which shows up over a dozen times in rabbinic writings. There are, of course, more examples in this passage of Maimonides' use of biblical and rabbinic phraseology, but these are the most distinctive.

21 For Maimonides' discussion of dogma, see Kellner, *Dogma*, pp. 10-65.

22 In line with the dictum in *Avot* IV, 1, "Who is powerful? He who subdues his passions".

23 Maimonides apparently uses the term *de'ah* and *da'at* interchangeably in this passage (a matter which has led to confusion in the mss., but that need not concern us here). Maimonides himself defines the term *de'ah* in *Guide of the Perplexed* III. 51 (p. 621) as referring to intellectual apprehensions, not to imagination; for thought concerning imaginings is not called *knowledge [de'ah]* but *that which cometh into your mind* (Ezek. 20:32). Since, according to Maimonides' epistemology, our intellects are constituted by that which we know, the terms *de'ah* and *da'at* can also mean "intellect". In his commentary on *Avot* III.17 Maimonides explains the term *da'at* as referring to the product of our intellectual endeavors, the achievement of abstract knowledge (especially concerning God and forms which exist independently, i.e., the angels, i.e., the separate intellects). God and the angels are precisely the subject matter of metaphysics, Further on Maimonides' use of these terms, see Baneth (above, n. 12), pp. 260-262 and on the epistemological issues raised here, my "Gersonides on the Active Intellect" (to be republished in the companion volume to this one).

is also healthy and physically unimpaired, studies those disciplines known in the tradition as *pardes*, is devoted to those great matters, is wholly separated from unimportant nonsense and concentrates on nothing bur divine matters and the wisdom inherent in God's creation, then the divine spirit rests upon him or her. When that happens the individual's soul meets those angels called *ishim* and the prophet becomes someone new altogether.

So much for the philosophically uneducated talmudist reader. What does the reader who has carefully read the *Sefer ha-Madda* to this point and is furthermore familiar with Maimonides' own theory of prophecy (as later expressed in the *Guide of the Perplexed*), find in our passage? Something quite different. This reader finds the naturalistic account of the *Guide of the Perplexed*. There Maimonides maintains that prophecy is a perfection of the prophet, and that God's only role in the process is to make it possible. God does not choose or send prophets; rather, God establishes the circumstances in which prophecy can take place (and it is in that sense that the phrase, "that God causes human beings to prophesy," must be read in our passage). *Anyone* having certain qualities who works hard enough will achieve prophecy. Maimonides does allow for an exception: God can work a miracle and cause an otherwise qualified individual not to achieve prophecy. But not so here in the *Mishneh Torah*: when one has satisfied certain conditions, then "the holy spirit immediately rests upon him" – God does nothing (in the sense of direct, immediate intervention), the person seeking prophecy does everything. When that person has satisfied all relevant criteria, the divine spirit *immediately and automatically* rests upon him or her, with no specific action or decision by God.[24]

What are the conditions which the prospective prophet must satisfy? Let us examine them, one after the other.

---

24 It is true that in "Foundations", VII.5 Maimonides writes, "Those who seek to prophesy are called the *children of the prophets* (II Kings 2:3, etc.). But, even though they direct [or, possibly, prepare] their intellects, it is possible that the [divine] presence will rest upon them and it is possible that it will not." One can either see this as a refinement of the earlier statement in VII.1, moving from what Maimonides was later to call the "philosophic" view of prophecy to the view of the Torah (according to which God can miraculously withhold prophecy from someone who has satisfied all the conditions to become a prophet), or, one can understand it as I do, and read the passage as saying that not everyone who tries to achieve prophecy necessarily succeeds in satisfying all the required conditions.

- The candidate for prophecy must be exceedingly wise (literally: a great sage in wisdom).[25]

- The person must be powerful with respect to personal qualities. Maimonides explains that such a person uses intellect to control his or her physical desires.[26]

- The individual seeking prophecy must have an exceptionally "broad and very sound intellect."

---

25 Maimonides' use of the words "wise person" (hakham) and "wisdom" (hokhmah) demand attention. Maimonides uses the term hokhmot (plural of hokhmah) to mean the specific philosophic ("scientific") disciplines (as in the first sentence of the Mishneh Torah; see above, note 9); as such, it reflects the Arabic ilm. The general term, hokhmah, he defines in Guide of the Perplexed III. 54 as meaning the apprehension of true realities which lead towards an apprehension of God, the acquisition of arts, the acquisition of moral virtues, and to the aptitude for stratagems and ruses (p. 632). "It has accordingly become plain", he continues, "that the term wise [person] [hakham] can be applied to one possessing the rational virtues, to one possessing the moral virtues, to everyone skilled in a practical art, and to one possessing ruses in working evil and wickedness" (p. 633). One who knows the Torah in its true reality is wise in two respects: the rational virtues and the moral virtues. Maimonides furthermore notes that the knowledge of the Torah and "wisdom" had become (unfortunately) separated over the generations. There can be no doubt then that the "sage great in wisdom" spoken of here refers to a person possessing the rational and moral virtues. In the present context, the talmudist reader is no doubt meant to think of the term in connection with the phrase talmid hakham "rabbinic scholar" while the philosophically trained reader realizes that Maimonides is here writing about a person who has achieved mastery of physics and metaphysics. Further on Maimonides' use of the term, see Twersky, Introduction, index, s.v. hokhma, Baneth, p. 263, and Kasher, "Hakham."

26 The use of intellect to control one's desires (an idea which ultimately derives from Plato) is mentioned by Maimonides in a parallel text, the seventh of the "Eight Chapters" (Weiss and Butterworth, p. 81), a text worth quoting here in full:

Know that no prophet prophesies until after he acquires all the rational virtues and most of the moral virtues, i.e., the most important ones. This is their saying: "Prophecy only comes to rest upon a wise, powerful, and rich man" [after Shabbat 92a and Nedarim 38a]. "Wise" undoubtedly included all of the rational virtues. "Rich" refers to one of the moral virtues, I mean, contentment, for they call the content man "rich". This is what they say in defining the "rich man": who is rich? He who rejoices with his lot" [Avot IV, 1]. That is, he is content with what time brings him, and he is not pained at what it does not bring him. Similarly, "powerful man" refers to one of the moral virtues, I mean that he governs his powers as thought dictates – as we explained in the fifth chapter. This is their saying: "Who is a powerful man? He who conquers his impulse" [Avot IV.1].

In the fifth chapter, to which Maimonides makes reference here, we are taught that one ought to subordinate all the soul"s powers to a single goal, the perception of God, i.e., the study of metaphysics. On these texts see ch. 11 below, "The Virtue of Faith."

- The individual in question must be physically unimpaired. This brings to mind the second of the 'four perfections' which Maimonides enumerates in *Guide of the Perplexed* III.54 (wealth, health, morals, intellect). Furthermore, Maimonides teaches us in other passages in the *Sefer ha-Madda* that a healthy body is a prerequisite for studying wisdom.[27]

When a person, satisfies these four criteria, prophecy[28] will immediately, automatically, and naturally result if further steps are taken:

- The person must enter *pardes*. In "Laws of the Foundation of the Torah," I.4, and especially in IV.13, Maimonides makes clear that *pardes* means the study of physics and metaphysics.[29]

- One must continue studying the great and remote matters (which in "Foundations" IV.13 we learn means metaphysics).

---

27 "Laws of Moral Qualities", III.3 and IV.1, and "Laws of Repentance", IX.1. In the first of these passages Maimonides hints that the study of wisdom is equivalent to worshipping God. This is another example of the phenomenon studied in this chapter. The talmudist reader will understand the wisdom spoken of as rabbinic teaching while the philosophically attuned reader will realize that Maimonides is actually referring to the study of metaphysics. Further, on the importance of unimpaired health, see *Guide of the Perplexed* II. 36. Maimonides there teaches that a perfected imagination is a prerequisite for prophecy (p. 369) and that the imagination is a bodily faculty (p. 372).

28 A number of commentators (N. Rabinovitch, in *Yad Peshutah* and M.D. Rabinovitch in the Mossad ha-Rav Kook edition of *Sefer ha-Madda*) understand Maimonides here to be speaking of the "holy spirit" and not of prophecy. In *Guide of the Perplexed* II. 45 Maimonides maintains that speaking or writing by virtue of the holy spirit is a pre-prophetic state. I assume that these commentators do not want to admit that Maimonides is speaking of prophecy here because they are sensitive to the problematic of making prophecy a perfection of the prophet as opposed to a gift of God. Their position, however, is untenable for a number of reasons. First, Maimonides introduces the discussion in this paragraph as dealing with prophecy proper; why read him as if he changed the subject of the paragraph in midstream? Second, in his Introduction to his "Eight Chapters" (Weiss and Butterworth, p. 60) Maimonides uses the term "holy spirit" as synonymous with prophecy. Sara Klein-Braslavy draws attention to Maimonides' inconsistency on this matter in her *Shlomoh ha-Melekh*, p. 167. Klein-Braslavy notes there that Maimonides uses the terms "spirit" and "prophecy" interchangeably in *Guide of the Perplexed* I.40. Klein-Braslavy cites our text as another example of the interchangeable use of "holy spirit" and "prophecy."

29 On this matter see ch. 14, "Maimonides' Allegiances."

- One must be further willing to separate oneself from the common run of humanity and train oneself to think of nothing but 'the sacred and pure forms under the throne' (i.e., the separate intellects).

- One must examine God's wisdom as exemplified in the created cosmos, from the first form down to the navel of the world,[30] i.e., devote oneself to the study of physics (including astronomy) and metaphysics.

All this done, the holy spirit immediately rests upon one and one's soul (*nefesh*), i.e., one's intellect,[31] achieves contact with that level of angels called *ishim*, and one becomes an entirely new person, a level beyond normal savants, i.e., beyond the wise who have not achieved prophecy. The careful reader of *Sefer ha-Madda* knows that *ishim* is the name given to angels of the tenth (and lowest degree), those who speak with prophets.[32] The philosophically attuned reader, or the reader who comes back to this passage after careful study of the *Guide of the Perplexed*, knows that what traditionalists call "angels" the philosophers call "separate intellects"[33] and that the tenth (and "lowest") of these intellects is called the Active Intellect. It is through the Active Intellect that God addresses prophets: "know that the true reality and quiddity of prophecy consist in its being an overflow overflowing from God, may He be cherished and honored, through the intermediation of the Active Intellect" (*Guide* II.36, p. 269).[34]

The account of prophecy implied in this text is more radical than that propounded in the *Guide of the Perplexed*, since it does not mention the possibil-

---

30 See "Foundations", II.9.

31 The careful reader of the *Mishneh Torah* recalls from "Laws of the Foundations of the Torah", II.2, that it is the *nefesh* which thirsts to know God, from III.11 that it is through the *nefesh* that we know, and from IV.8-9 that the *nefesh* is our form. The reader of the *Mishneh Torah* who has already studied the *Guide of the Perplexed* will also know that *nefesh* is "a term denoting the rational soul, I mean the form of a man" (II.41, p. 91). We are also told there that "it is a term denoting the thing that remains of man after death." We know from many texts that what remains of a person after death is what he or she knows; on this latter, see Kellner, *Perfection*, pp. 1-5.

32 "Foundations", II.7.

33 II.6 (pp. 262-263) and II.12 (p. 280). For a fuller discussion of Maimonides on angels, see Kellner, *Confrontation*, ch. 8.

34 On prophecy, see ch. 4, "Is Maimonides' Ideal Person."

ity of God's miraculous intervention to withhold prophecy from an otherwise qualified individual. This is consistent with what we saw above: in the *Mishneh Torah* Maimonides adopts extremely naturalist positions, but conceals them from the non-philosophical talmudist reader. In so doing Maimonides succeeds in teaching truth at different levels to distinct audiences; he allows the less philosophically attuned audience to draw deductions from his writings which are both consistent with what they believe and not inconsistent with the truth known to Maimonides and carefully imparted to his philosophically more alert audience. God *is* the ultimate cause of prophecy. The traditionalist understands this to mean that God chooses prophets, 'speaks' to them, sends them on specific missions, etc. The philosophically astute talmudist realizes that prophecy is a natural phenomenon, caused by God in the way in which all natural phenomena are caused, indirectly, without specific acts of divine volition, operating through unchanging nature.

In the text before us, then, we find that Maimonides succeeds impressively in teaching truth to the philosophic talmudist while both not lying to the non-philosophical talmudist and keeping the truth taught to the former hidden from the latter.

While the phenomenon to which I am drawing attention here is most pronounced in "Laws of the Foundations of the Torah," it is not only found there, as the following text, "Laws of the Recitation of the Shema," I.2 (which deals with a straightforwardly halakhic issue), illustrates:

> What does one recite? The three paragraphs beginning with the words *Hear* (Dt. 6:4-9); *If, then, you obey* (Dt. 11: 13-21); and *The Lord said* (Num. 15:37-41). One recites the paragraph *Hear* first because it contains a commandment concerning Gods unity, love of God, and study, which is the basic principle upon which all depends. After it, *If, then, you obey*, since it commands obedience to all the other commandments. After that, the paragraph concerning the fringes, since it also contains a command to recall all the commandments. (Num. 15:38)

The second sentence of this passage reads as follows in Hebrew: *umakdimin likrot parashat shema mipnei she-yesh bah yihud ha-shem, ve-ahavato, u-talmudo, she-hu ha-iikar ha-gadol she-ha-kol talui bo.* The interpretation of one word here, *talmudo*, makes a tremendous difference to the meaning of the passage. What does the non-philosophical talmudist understand here? Such a person reads the sentence as follows: "One recites the paragraph *Hear* first because it contains a commandment concerning God's unity, love of God, and study of Torah, which is the great principle upon which all depends."[35] Our talmudist reads this sentence with great satisfaction: the study of *Torah* is made "the great principle upon which all depends" and it is in part because that study is found in the first paragraph of *Shema* (*you shall teach them diligently to your children* – Dt. 6:7) that the first paragraph is the first of the paragraphs of the *Shema*.

The philosophically more alert reader of the *Mishneh Torah* finds something else here, different from, but by no means inconsistent with, what the talmudist finds. Such a reader must understand the key term, *talmudo*, to mean the study of God, and not the study of God's Torah.[36] The study of God, as is taught in the first four chapters of the *Mishneh Torah*, involves the study of physics and metaphysics, not the study of Talmud as ordinarily understood. Maimonides, of course, has nothing against the study of Cod's Torah as the talmudist understands it, but the obligation to undertake that study is not the issue here, at least for the reader of this passage who has carefully read the *Mishneh Torah* to this point.[37]

Why do I say this? I take Maimonides to be teaching that we recite Dt. 6:4-9 first because of the first verse, *Hear, O Israel, the Lord, our God the Lord is one.* This verse indeed teaches "the great principle upon which all depends," namely God's existence and unity. In "Laws of the Foundations of the Torah," I.6, Mai-

---

35 Hyamson translates: "and studying his words"; Kaplan has: "and the studying of Torah"; M.D. Rabinovitch explains the passage as referring to the commandment of Torah study; N. Rabinovitch adopts the same position, referring back to *Berakhot* 2b. These modern translators and interpreters follow the understanding of this term implicitly held by the *Lehem Mishneh* and *Kesef Mishneh*. I have only found one modern who understands the passage properly and that is, not surprisingly, Rabbi Joseph Kafih in his edition of the *Mishneh Torah*. I treat this text futher in Kellner, "Philosophical Themes."

36 Of course, the philosophically more alert reader, who has also studied Twersky"s "Some Non-Halakic Aspects", will know that Talmud for Maimonides can mean the philosophical disciplines. On this, see also Kasher, "*Talmud Torah*" and Kellner, "*Mishneh Torah* – Why?"

37 If the amount of commentary on the first four chapters of the *Mishneh Torah*, or the times these chapters come up in the responsa literature are any indication, then very few traditionally minded talmudists have ever actually read these chapters carefully.

monides uses the same exact expression, "the great principle upon which all depends," with reference to God's unity.[38]

One should not be confused by the reference to the love of God in the Maimonidean text before us. It calls to mind the passages in the *Guide of the Perplexed* in which Maimonides teaches us that love of God is proportionate to knowledge of God.[39] Knowledge of God, of course, results from the study of physics and metaphysics (our knowledge of immaterial entities and our understanding of the limitations of what we can actually know about God). The student of Maimonides who has read and assimilated the *Guide of the Perplexed* knows that love of God finds its finest expression, not in the study of Talmud as ordinarily understood, but in the study of physics and metaphysics. This, too, is hinted at in the passage under discussion.

We have examined three passages in which Maimonides addresses at the same time conventionally minded rabbinic readers of the *Mishneh Torah* and philosophically aware students of the same text.[40] Part of his artistry as an au-

---

38 So also, in "Laws of Idolatry", I.3.

39 In "Laws of Repentance," X.6 Maimonides makes the point that love of God is proportionate to knowledge of God, and that one fulfills the commandment in the *Shema* to love God (Dt. 6:5) only by knowing God. This point finds expression as well in *Book of Commandments*, positive commandment 3 (another text in which Maimonides writes successfully for diverse audiences at the same time). See further, *Guide of the Perplexed* I.39, III.28 (p. 512), and especially III.51 (p. 621): "Now we have made it clear several times that love is proportionate to apprehension." Further on love of God in Maimonides, see the introduction to my translation of *Book of Love*, Lasker, "Love of God," and ch. 19, "Spirituality and a Life of Holiness," below.

40 There are, of course, many other instances of the phenomenon to which I have drawn attention here in Maimonides' writings. In almost every place where Maimonides discusses the nature of divine retribution in this world and the next, for example, he allows the rabbinic reader to think that fulfillment of the commandments is the key to reward and punishment while indicating to his philosophical readers that there is no punishment for sin after death and that survival after death is a function of intellectual perfection. For details see the appendix, "Maimonides on Reward and Punishment," to my *Must*. Another text in which Maimonides' artistry as an author simultaneously addressing diverse audiences is particularly evident is his commentary to Mishnah *Hagigah* 2:1, translated and briefly analyzed in Kellner, "Maimonides on Hagigah." Other relevant examples from the Mishneh Torah include "Laws of the Sabbath", II.3 (on which, see Newman, "Women, Saints, and Heretics"); "Laws of Theft and Loss," VI.11 (on which, see Lichtenstein, "Torah and General Culture," p. 222), "Laws of Prayer and the Priestly Blessing," XVI.7 (compared to *Sotah* 38b and *Numbers Rabbah* 11); and "Laws of Tefillin, Mezuzah and the Torah Scroll," VI:13, especially in light of the comments made in the commentary of Rabbi Eliyahu Touger in his translation of the text, p. 130. I discuss this text in "Philosophical Themes." We find the same phenomenon in the commentary on the Mishnah. See *Makkot* III.17, where Maimonides asserts "It is one of

thor, as well as a thinker, is to address each audience in a way in which it will not only not be harmed, but actually benefited. The audience of talmudists remains unaware of the philosophic message of the text it is reading, while those beginning the study of philosophy may be prompted to go further in their studies because of passages like those under discussion; the accomplished philosopher-talmudist will fully understand what the master is teaching and, if he or she is a faithful student of Maimonides, will approve the intention to teach the (philosophical) elite while not perplexing or upsetting the (rabbinic) masses.

the fundamentals of the belief in Torah that if a man fulfills one of the 613 commandments properly and in a fitting manner, and he does not associate with it a worldly aim at all, but rather does it for its own sake from love, as I explained to you, he merits the world to come..." Given the Maimonidean equivalence between love of God and knowledge of God, this text clearly means something different than what it says on the surface.

CHAPTER FOUR:
Is Maimonides' Ideal Person Austerely Rationalist?

Maimonides is regularly thought to have seen the ideal human in purely and austerely intellectualist terms, as nothing more than a rational animal. This picture of Maimonides is insufficiently nuanced and reflects a notion of intellectualism thinner and more pallid than that actually held by him. But this view is often attributed to him because Maimonides seems to adopt a view (held afterwards explicitly by Gersonides) according to which that which makes us human, and in consequence that which survives our deaths, is only what we know.[1] On this view, the human subject counts for nothing, the objects of knowledge, for everything. This Maimonidean-Gersonidean position follows from the adoption of the idea that human beings are rational animals. From this it follows that we share with animals all that is not rational in us.

THE STANDARD PICTURE OF MAIMONIDES' IDEAL HUMAN BEING. What I will call Maimonides' "hyper-intellectualist" (and hence elitist)[2] understanding of the nature of human nature is well known and need not be examined at length here.[3] There can be no doubt that he accepts Aristotle's definition of human

---

1 Gersonides, 1288-1344, held that what makes us human is our abstract knowledge. Zev Harvey has shown that for Gersonides, any abstract knowledge "counts" while for Maimonides it must be knowledge of metaphysical matters. See his "Crescas and his Critique of Philosophic Happiness." Gersonides' intellectualism led him to deprecate the importance of human beings vis-a-vis the separate intellects. This aroused much anger against him, anger which could have been directed against Maimonides as well. See my "Cultured Despisers" to be republished in the companion volume to this one.

2 Maimonides' intellectualist elitism is a prominent and well-known feature of his thought. See, for example, the end of his Introduction to the *Guide of the Perplexed*, p. 16. For another emphatic example, see II.36, p. 372. For discussion, see *Confrontation*, pp. 15-17.

3 For a medieval expression of this, see Kellner, "Maimonides and Samuel ibn Tibbon." For a

beings as rational animals.[4] In terms of our genus, we are animals (as opposed to pieces of furniture or meteorological phenomena). Our specific difference, that which distinguishes us from all other members of the animal kingdom, is our rationality. Everything that is not a direct reflection of rational thought –hopes and fears, love and hates, desires, needs, passions–is a consequence of our animal nature.

In order to understand Maimonides' position on these matters we must glance at his theory of the soul. Maimonides adopted a variant of a fairly standard medieval Aristotelian account of the nature of the human soul. According to this approach humans are born with a potential to learn, which they may or may not actualize; it is in this capacity and its actualization that our humanity lies. We are born with differing capacities to learn and to know; to the extent that we actualize that capacity by learning abstract truths we become actual intellects–we have actually *acquired* an intellect. If we fail to actualize our intellectual potential, that capacity with which we were born is wasted, and nothing survives the death of our bodies.[5]

Maimonides' intellectualism finds expression in a suprisingly large number of contexts. It is to these that I turn briefly here.

DEFINITION OF HUMAN BEINGS AND THEIR PERFECTION. Humans are said to have been created in the image of God only because of "the intellect that God made overflow unto man and that is the latter's ultimate perfection" (*Guide* I.2, p. 24). What does it mean to have such an intellect in as perfect a fashion as possible? It consists in one's "knowing everything concerning all beings that it is within the capacity of man to know in accordance with his ultimate perfection"

---

modern expression, see Husik, *History*, pp. 299-300. If I understand him correctly, Leo Strauss also seems to adopt the hyperintellectualist view of Maimonides described here. See his *Philosophy and Law*, p. 105 (where Strauss gives a Gersonidean explanation of the role of the imagination in prophecy); compare also Eve Adler's introduction to the book, p. 14 and ch. 2 above, "Strauss' Maimonides."

4   In his earliest work, *Logical Terms* (= *Treatise on Logic*), Maimonides wrote: "Rationality we call man's difference, because it divides and differentiates the human species from others; and this rationality, i.e., the faculty by which ideas are formed, constitutes the essence of man" (ch. 10; Efros trans., pp. 51-52). For some of the consequences of this acceptance of this definition of rational animals, see below, ch. 18, "Maimonides' *True Religion*."

5   A magisterial account of these matters may be found in Davidson, *Alfarabi*. Davidson discusses Maimonides on 197-207.

(III.27, p. 511). This perfection is purely intellectual; Maimonides continues: "It is clear that to this ultimate perfection there do not belong either actions or moral qualities…"

Thus, to be human, to actualize our potential for Godlikeness, is to know all that we can know. It is only this knowledge which makes us human: moral behavior and moral virtues are, Maimonides holds, necessary propadeutics to human (intellectual) perfection, but are not parts of it *per se*.[6]

SUBHUMANS.[7] Maimonides does not flinch from a necessary consequence of his view of humans as defined by their intellects: individuals born of human parents who have not achieved a minimum level of intellectual perfection are subhuman. "You know," Maimonides writes in *Guide of the Perplexed* I.7 (pp. 32-33), "that whoever is not endowed with this form [of the intellect]… is not a man, but an animal having the shape and configuration of man." Such human-appearing animals are actually more dangerous than simple beasts, since they can misuse their unrealized intellectual perfection for evil. So great is the danger of unrealized humans that "it is a light thing to kill them, and has even been enjoined because of its utility" (III.18, p. 475).[8] Such beings, Maimonides further tells us near the end of the *Guide* (III.51, p. 618), "do not have the rank of men, but have among the beings a rank lower than the rank of man but higher than the rank of apes."[9]

---

6   For further relevant texts, and for discussion of interpretations other than that offered here, see Kellner, *Perfection*, pp. 1-5 and the studies cited there. To these may be added Kreisel, *Political Thought*, pp. 88-92, 128-141, and 164-175.

7   For a valuable discussion of matters raised in this section, see S. Harvey, "New Islamic Source," pp. 55-59.

8   For examples of this "utility" see *Book of Commandments*, positive commandments 186 ("apostate city"), 187 ("seven nations") and 188 ("Amalek") and negative commandment 49 ("seven nations" again) and the corresponding passages in the *Mishneh Torah*. See also *Guide*, I.37 and I.54.

9   Compare further Maimonides' comment in his commentary to Mishnah Hagigah II.1, to the effect that it would have been better had unrealized humans not come into the world. For the text and discussion, see Kellner, "Maimonides on Hagigah II.1." This doctrine was strenuously criticized by Hasdai Crescas who was particularly offended by the fact that on this doctrine little children, who had never sinned, but who had also never had the chance to develop their intellects, would have no share in the world to come. See his *Or ha-Shem*, II.6.i.

There are a number of passages in his writings[10] where Maimonides makes comments about non-Jews which seem at variance with the overwhelmingly universalist tenor of his writing, in that they seem to be presented as less than fully human. These passages may best be understood in terms of Maimonides' hyper-intellectualist conception of what it means to be a human being, coupled with his pessimism about the likelihood of most non-Jews (or very many Jews, for that matter) actually achieving intellectual perfection.[11]

IMMORTALITY. A further consequence of Maimonides' purely intellectualist description of what it means to be human is his position that to the extent that humans achieve immortality this is due solely to their intellectual achieve-ments.[12] All that survives death (to the extent that anything does) is what we have learned. This is a position that Maimonides espouses in all this major writings. The point is made in his commentary on the Mishnah,[13] in the *Mishneh Torah*,[14] and in the *Guide of the Perplexed*.[15] Viewing existence in the world to come in these terms, it is no surprise that Maimonides made fulfillment of the commandments of the Torah in particular and moral behavior in general only prerequisites for achieving a share in the world to come, not guarantors

---

10 In particular, Commentary on Mishnah Bava Kamma IV.3, "Laws of Damage by Chattels," VIII.5, "Laws of Forbidden Intercourse," XII.8-10, and "Laws of Kings and their Wars," X.12. For disucssion of these passages, see ch. 17 below, "Was Maimonides Truly Universalist?"

11 For Maimonides, ethical perfection is, as I will show below in this chapter, difficult to achieve without the Torah, and is a necessary prerequisite for intellectual perfection. Without the discipline provided by the Torah, it is much harder for non-Jews than for Jews to achieve the level of ethical perfection necessary to advance to true (human) perfection. See also ch. 11 below, "The Virtue of Faith," note 6 and ch. 18, "Maimonides' True Religion."

12 There is considerable debate among Maimonides' contemporary interpreters over whether or not humans can actually achieve immortality ("a share in the world to come") or not. For details, see Kreisel, *Political Thought*, pp. 142-43 and 242-43. Alfred Ivry has succinctly summarized one view of eternal beatitude which arises from Maimonides' writings: "...the intellect which survives our death is not a discrete entity, but part of the universal truth which is ultimately one." Ivry, " Logical and Scientific Premises," p. 78. Maimonides' understanding of the happiness of the righteous after death was explicitly criticized by Crescas. See Harvey, "Crescas vs. Maimonides."

13 Sanhedrin, Introduction to *Perek Helek*, Kafih ed., vol. 4, p. 204.

14 "Laws of the Foundations of the Torah," IV,9, "Laws of Repentance," VIII.2-3, and "Laws of Phylacteries," VI.13.

15 I.30 (63), I.40 (90), I.41 (91), I.70 (174), I.72 (193, implicitly), I. 74 (220), III.8 (432-33), III.27 (511), III.51 (628), and III.54 (635).

of it. Halakhic and moral perfection are ultimately irrelevant to what happens in the hereafter.[16]

COMMANDMENTS AND MORAL PERFECTION. Maimonides' understanding of the role of practical behavior in the perfected life is particularly important, since the question of how to live one's daily life is crucially important to the Jewish tradition, and Maimonides' position seems so different from the way in which the tradition developed to his day and continued to develop after him. On the one hand, Maimonides was convinced that one cannot achieve any significant level of intellectual perfection without antecedently achieving and maintaining a very high level of moral perfection.[17] He was also firmly convinced that obedience to the commandments of the Torah was the very best tool available to bring one to moral perfection. From this it follows that (at least in the pre-messianic world) relatively few non-Jews will, in fact, actually perfect themselves as human beings.

The commandments of the Torah are thus given to perfect Jews morally. This point is emphasized at the very end of the *Guide of the Perplexed* where Maimonides teaches that:

> all the actions prescribed by the Torah – I refer to the various species of worship[18] and also the moral habits that are useful to all people in their mutual

---

16 Maimonides' view on this matter was well-understood by R. Solomon ben Abraham ibn Adret (c.1235 – c.1310), the leading halakhist of his generation, who complained about Maimonides' view (without explicitly identifying it as such), "Are the pious men of Israel without philosophy not worthy of an afterlife?" The text appears in Adret's *Responsa*, vol. 1., p. 387. I cite it as translated by Moshe Halbertal in *People of the Book*, p. 119.

17 *Guide of the Perplexed* I.34, pp. 76-77: "...the moral virtues are a preparation for the rational virtues, it being impossible to achieve true, rational acts–I mean perfect rationality – unless it be by a man thoroughly trained in his morals and endowed with the qualities of tranquillity and quiet." See further I.5 (28), I.62 (152), II.32 (361), II.36 (369, 371, 372), III.27 (510), III.54 (635). In the Commentary on the Mishnah, see Hagigah II.1, Sanhedrin I.3, the 5th of the Eight Chapters, and Avot III.11. In the *Mishneh Torah* see "Laws of the Foundations of the Torah," VII.1 and "Laws of Ritual Baths," XI.12.

18 This includes all matters relating to prayer, to the Temple cult (and in consequence, all matters of ritual purity and impurity), to the liturgical calendar, etc. These represent a very large percentage of the six hundred thirteen commandments of the Torah. One could easily make the case that Maimonides is referring here to all the ritual commandments of Judaism (*bein adam le-makom*).

dealings[19]–that all this is not to be compared with this ultimate end and does not equal it, *being but preparations for the sake of this end.*[20]

This passage offers two important lessons: the commandments of the Torah inculcate moral qualities which improve us in our relations with one another; and this moral improvement is not our ultimate end, but only a preparation for it.

It is hard to overstate how bizarre this claim is from a traditionally Jewish perspective: fulfillment of the commandments of the Torah, while obligatory, important, and beneficial, is not the way in which a Jew truly worships God.[21] Such obedience in and of itself does not even guarantee one a share in the world to come.[22]

PROVIDENCE AND PROPHECY. Maimonides' explanations of what one must do in order to enjoy a measure of divine providence and how one becomes a prophet are further expressions of his intellectualism. With respect to the former is he is very clear.[23] Remarkably, Maimonides measures divine providential care in accord with the degree of one's intellectual perfection.

With respect to prophecy, Maimonides is less purely intellectualist in his approach, although his doctrine is easy to present in purely intellectualist terms, as he does in *Guide* II.36. Many of his interpreters, taking his intellectualism as foundational, wonder about the need for the perfection of the imaginative faculty emphasized there (p. 369). But there can be no doubt that for Maimonides intellectual perfection is a crucial prerequisite for becoming a prophet.

---

19 I.e., all the commandments relating to inter-personal behavior (*bein adam le-havero*).

20 III.54, p. 636 (emphasis added). Compare also III.27, p. 511. Further on this, see Kellner, "Rabbis."

21 True divine worship, according to Maimonides, is silent (intellectual) meditation in the presence of God. See *Guide of the Perplexed* III.51. The Jewish liturgy is an accommodation to distressing historical realities. See "Laws of Prayer," I. It is useful here to compare Maimonides with Judah Halevi who, in effect, defines Jews, not as rational animals, but as praying animals. See his *Kuzari* III.5.

22 For justification of this reading of Maimonides, see Kellner, *Must*, pp. 149-163.

23 III.17, p. 473.

ANIMALS AND HUMANS. What do humans share in common with other animals? In the first instance, it is the fact that we and they are animals.[24] From this it follows that human beings can be literally beastly. But, to be beast-like is to destroy our humanity, or, more precisely, not to raise ourselves above our animal origins. Thus, for example, the Torah demands physical cleanliness so that we not be like beasts.[25] A true human being exercises self-restraint, eats only what is beneficial, and acts rationally, not instinctually.[26]

Our animal origins can be expressed in more positive ways as well. Maimonides holds that we share many characteristics with animals. For Maimonides, parental love is a quality shared by animals and human beings,[27] as is the ability to exercise our imaginations (I. 73, p. 209). But, everything which we share in common with animals is, in the final analysis, animal-like, and not truly human. All that is ours, truly ours, through which humans are humans, is our intellects. True human perfection, Maimonides holds,

> consists in the acquisition of the rational virtues–I refer to the conception of intelligibles, which teach true opinions concerning divine things. This is in true reality the ultimate end; this is what gives the individual true perfection, a perfection belonging to him alone;[28] and it gives him permanent perdurance; *through it man is man.*[29]

UNIVERSALISM AND MESSIANISM. Maimonides' intellectualism explains two further and related features of his thought. He is notorious for having adopted "universalist" positions.[30] Maimonides consistently distinguishes among

---

24 This is a point to which Maimonides makes offhand reference in a number of places. See, for example, II.36, p. 371 and II.40, p. 381.

25 This is how Maimonides explains Dt. 23:13-14 in *Guide of the Perplexed* III.41, p. 566.

26 See the fifth of Maimonides' "Eight Chapters." For an English translation, Weiss and Butterworth, *Ethical Writings*, p. 76.

27 See *Guide of the Perplexed* III.48, pp. 599 and 600.

28 As opposed to possessions, health, and morals, the other three perfections discussed in this passage.

29 III.54, p. 635 (emphasis added).

30 For further discussion, see Kellner, "Universalism." To put the issue briefly, Maimonides, unlike Halevi for example, did not posit any intrinsic difference between Jews and non-Jews. Jews as Jews have no innate advantage over non-Jews. Jews who follow the Torah, on the other

people, not on the basis of their religion, race, gender,[31] or place of origin, but only on the basis of their intellectual attainments. He is very insistent in distinguishing between those who are "in" and those who are "out." All humans are in, all non-humans are out; all humans have a share in the world to come, no non-human has a future life. To be human means to have achieved some minimal level of intellectual perfection. To achieve that, one must be rigidly self-disciplined.[32] Obedience to the Torah is not the only route to self-discipline, but it is surely the best. Non-Jews, in consequence, may achieve full human perfection, but, lacking the Torah, clearly have a harder time than Jews.[33]

This intellectually-based universalism leads Maimonides to envision an end to history in the messianic era in which all humans would worship God together, equally; at that point there would be no Jews and non-Jews, only servants of the Lord.[34] As he puts it at the very end of the *Mishneh Torah*, the one preoccupation of the whole world will be to know the Lord.[35] It is for that reason that there will be no famine, war, jealousy, or strife. It is for that reason also that blessings will be abundant and comforts within the reach of all.

THE STANDARD PICTURE REVISED. To this point I have sketched out what I have called the standard picture of Maimonides' conception of the ideal Jew:[36] one who fulfills the commandments of the Torah, not only because they are commanded by God, and not only because obedience to these commandments has beneficial consequences for the individual and her society, but because through this obedience one can achieve a very high level of moral perfection.

---

hand, have a tremendous advantage. More on this, see *Confrontation*, ch. 7.

31 In affirming the ontological (not halakhic or sociological) equality of men and women, Maimonides goes very much against the grain of his times. On this see Melamed, "Maimonides on Women" and Kellner, "Philosophical Misogyny."

32 For Maimonides, "self-discipline" is what morality is all about.

33 For an interesting expression of this, consider the explanation offered for circumcision in *Guide of the Perplexed* III.49 (p. 609). On this, see Josef Stern, *Problems and Parables*, pp. 96-97.

34 For a defense of this interpretation of Maimonides, see Kellner, *Judaism*, pp. 33-48 and below, ch. 18, "Maimonides' *True Religion*."

35 Which means the study of metaphysics.

36 Maimonides wrote for and about Jews; thus my language here. Even though he is led to a thoroughgoing universalism this seems to me to be more of a consequence of his intellectualism, rather than a goal he sought to arrive at.

Moral perfection is itself a step towards true human perfection, which is the apprehension of truths, especially concerning God, to the greatest extent that one can apprehend them. The perfected individual has subjugated all feelings, all passions, all desires, to reason, has eliminated from one's consciousness everything personal, and devotes one's inner life to the contemplation of abstract truths. Every aspect of living not connected to that contemplation is ignored to the greatest extent possible. All that distinguishes one perfected individual from another is the level of abstract truth which each has comprehended.[37]

In what follows I will suggest that this view is too one-sided and ignores important elements of Maimonides' view of the perfected human being.

HUMAN PERFECTION REVISITED. As I understand Maimonides, one who wishes perfectly to fulfill the command of *imitatio Dei* must achieve the highest possible level of intellectual perfection[38] and then *descend* Jacob's ladder (or return to the Platonic cave), in order to participate in the governance of one's society according to the principles of loving-kindness, righteousness, and judgment.[39] This, however, cannot be done by one who is wholly divorced from the needs of society, uninterested in the well being of its members and ignorant of how to order their affairs in the best possible way.

This point needs expansion. Maimonides appears to hold that knowledge is transformative. As already noted above in chapter two, a person who spends a lifetime of effort perfecting herself morally and then intellectually, practicing rigid self-discipline while with great difficulty plumbing the depths of understanding of the basic structure of the cosmos, is not the same person who started the quest, only now with more knowledge. This is a person transformed, an individual whose reaction to the understanding gained with so much difficulty is to "recoil affrighted, and realize that he is a small creature, lowly and obscure, endowed with slight and slender intelligence, standing in

---

37 In this, perfected individuals are like the separate intellects. See "Laws of the Foundations of the Torah," II.5.

38 It may be appropriate to note here that the nature of the intellectual perfection prized by Maimonides may be somewhat different from discursive reason as usually understood. The highest levels of knowledge are apparently intuitive, and maybe even experiential. See Blumenthal, *Philosophic Mysticism* and Faur, *Homo Mysticus*.

39 For defense of this interpretation see Kellner, *Perfection*.

the presence of Him Who is perfect in knowledge."[40] This is the person who realizes that the greatest perfection open to him or her is to imitate the ways of God, in practicing loving-kindness, judgement and righteousness in the world.[41] But there is more than simple realization here: unlike Plato's philosopher, who must be *forced* to return to the cave and become a king, Maimonides' individual who is transformed by knowledge *wants* and needs to imitate God. Such a person is driven by *love* of God.

Maimonidean intellectual perfection is not simply a matter of adding knowledge, in the way in which we can add memory capacity to our computers. Breadth of knowledge and depth of understanding transform the knower. This issue may be better understood in light of Maimonides' understanding of the point of moral striving. We practice moral behavior, not only so that we do the right thing, but so that doing the right thing becomes part of our personality. In "Eight Chapters" and in "Laws of Moral Qualities" Maimonides develops a position which focuses at least as much on character as it does on deed: a major reason for giving charity is not only to alleviate poverty, but so that we ourselves become charitable people. Similarly, the perfected knower is in a real sense transformed into a different and better person by the knowledge gained. I will return to this point in my conclusion.

PROPHECY.[42] Maimonides defines prophecy (*Guide*, II.36, 369) as follows:

Know that the true reality and quiddity of prophecy consists in its being an overflow overflowing from God, may He be cherished and honored, through the intermediation of the Active Intellect, toward the rational faculty in the first place and thereafter toward the imaginative faculty. This is the highest degree of man and the ultimate term of perfection that can exist for his species; and this state is the ultimate term of perfection for the imaginative faculty. This is something that cannot by any means exist in every man. And it is not something that can be attained solely through perfection in the speculative sciences and through improvement of moral habits, even if all of them have become as fine and good as can be. There is still needed in addition the

---

40 "Laws of the Foundations of the Torah," II.2 (p. 35b); compare IV.12.

41 See *Guide* III. 54 and my exposition of the end of the *Guide* in *Perfection*.

42 See Howard Kreisel's magisterial *Prophecy* for a comprehensive discussion of Maimonides' views in their broadest context.

highest possible degree of perfection of the imaginative faculty in respect of its original natural disposition.

Maimonides emphasizes here that in addition to moral and speculative perfection, a candidate for prophecy must have a highly perfected imagination. What is the imagination? It is, as Jose Faur reminds us, "a faculty that humans share with other members of the animal kingdom.[43] It constitutes a lower level of consciousness, distorting reality, and is incapable of providing valid criteria to know the real universe."[44] What precisely does the imagination do? Maimonides explains:

You know, too, the actions of the imaginative faculty that are in its nature, such as retaining things perceived by the senses, combining these things, and imitating them. And you know that its greatest and noblest action takes place only when the senses rest and do not perform their actions. It is then that a certain overflow overflows to this faculty according to its disposition, and it is the cause of the veridical dreams. This same overflow is the cause of prophecy. There is only a difference in degree, not in kind (II.36, p. 370).

The imagination acts directly on sense perceptions, manipulating them, combining them into new forms (which do not exist outside of the imagination). Unlike reason, which abstracts its information from sense perceptions, seeking to free itself to the greatest extent possible from them,[45] the imagination takes sense perceptions as its raw material, refashioning and reshaping them, but never freeing itself from them. Part of being a prophet, the highest category of human, is having a perfected imagination. Human perfection, therefore, is more than simply perfection in abstract knowledge.

Prophecy, according to Maimonides, can only be achieved after years of preparation (Moses became a prophet at the age of 80, and Joshua near the age

---

43 Maimonides writes: "Now the imaginative faculty is indubitably a bodily faculty" (II.36, p. 372).

44 Faur, *Homo Mysticus*, p. 70. It is crucial to remember that current use of the term imagination is not identical with the way in which Maimonides uses the term. See Wolfson, *Studies*, chapters 15-18. Recent studies include Faur, "Maimonides on Imagination," Harvey, "Theores of Imagination," and Ravven, "Spinoza and Maimonides."

45 In this I am reading Maimonides as if he were a Gersonidean. See my "Gersonides on the Active Intellect" to be republished in the companion volume to this one.

of 60[46]). The "sons of the prophets," those individuals who sought to become prophets, Maimonides informs us, "always engaged in preparation" (II.32, p. 362). One becomes a prophet only after a lifetime of perfecting oneself morally and intellectually.[47] Such a long period of time must have its impact upon the human personality.

The importance of the imagination in the process of prophecy must be emphasized. It helps us to understand what Maimonides means when he says: "Now with regard to everything that can be known by demonstration, the status of the prophet and that of everyone else who knows it are equal; there is no superiority of one over the other" (II.33, p. 364). In terms of what is known, the prophet has no advantage over the philosopher.[48] The prophet is not simply a super-philosopher, a point importantly emphasized by Faur in his *Homo Mysticus*. The philosopher becomes a prophet on account of the imagination. Faur explains: "By applying imagination to the realm of reason the prophet transcends the boundaries of pure rationality. In conjunction with reason the imaginative faculty becomes a creative force, enhancing the rational faculties of the individual, creating a new form of cognition, that of dynamic creativity."[49]

---

46 II.32, p. 362.

47 Furthermore, Maimonides continues, "it is our fundamental principle that there must be training and perfection, whereupon the possibility arises to which the power of the deity becomes attached" (p. 362). This teaching is a "fundamental principle," not some unimportant aspect of the doctrine of prophecy (since it requires that prophets first be what we would call philosophers).

48 I use "philosopher" where Pines translates "man of science." Since the sciences in question are Aristotelian physics and metaphysics, I think my translation here is less confusing. With respect to the issue at hand, it must be recalled that prophets are superior to philosophers in their grasp of speculative matters; that superiority, however, is connected to the perfection of their imaginative faculty:

Know that the true prophets indubitably grasp speculative matters; by means of his speculation alone, man is unable to grasp the causes from which what a prophet has come to know necessarily follows. This has a counterpart in their giving information regarding matters with respect to which man, using only common conjecture and divination, is unable to give information (II.38, p. 377).

Prophets, it seems, can jump to true speculative conclusions in a way that ordinary philosophers cannot. This is similar to their unusual abilities to foretell the future or describe events they have not seen.

49 P. 73. I remain to be convinced that Faur's emphasis on the creativity of the prophet reflects a Maimonidean as opposed to contemporary sensibility, but aside from that I find his

It is only by ignoring Maimonides' own statements about the role of the imagination in the prophetic consciousness that one can be led to depict Maimonides' perfected human being as a kind of coldly rational thinking machine.

But there is more. Prophets are not just morally-perfected super-philosophers with active imaginations. They are alive to aesthetic experience as well. In summing up his doctrine of prophecy, Maimonides writes (II.36, p. 371) that a person born with a superior constitution, who has taken advantage of it "to obtain knowledge and wisdom until he passes from potentiality to actuality and acquires a perfect and accomplished human intellect and pure and well-tempered human moral habits," and who abolishes the desire for bestial things (especially sex), and has no wish to dominate others or be held in esteem by them, is the ideal candidate for becoming a prophet. "Now there is no doubt," he continues,

> that whenever–in an individual of this description–his imaginative faculty, which is as perfect as possible, acts and receives from the intellect an overflow corresponding to his speculative perfection, this individual will apprehend divine and most extraordinary matters, will see only God and His angels, and will only be aware and achieve knowledge of matters that constitute true opinions and general directives for the well-being of men in their relations with one another.

It is in this context (after dismissing sex, and its parent sense, touch) that Maimonides comments: "As for the other sensual pleasures–those, for instance that derive from the sense of smell, from hearing, and from seeing–there may be found in them sometimes, though they are corporeal, pleasure for man as man, as Aristotle has explained." In every other context with which I am familiar, Maimonides restricts the phrase "man as man" to intellectual comprehension.[50] But here we are told that such sensual pleasure can belong to us as human beings. Kalman Bland has emphasized this point:[51] would-be prophets

---

exposition extremely helpful. For a comprehensive discussion of prophets and philosophers in Maimonides' thought, see Kreisel, "Sage and Prophet."

50 See, for example, III.54, p. 635.

51 See his *Artless Jew*, "Medieval Jewish Aesthetics," and "Beauty."

take advantage of refined aesthetic experiences in order to help them achieve prophecy.[52]

Three other points may be introduced here to round out our picture of the Maimonidean prophet. These are the compulsion felt by a prophet to prophesy, the fact that prophets differ in respect to two qualities necessary for prophecy, courage and divination, and the ways in which all human beings (including prophets) differ from each other.

With respect to the first, Maimonides (II.37, pp. 374-75) notes that philosophers and prophets may manifest divine emanation to the extent that it improves them alone, "or such that from that individual's perfection there is something left over that suffices to make others perfect." Philosophers who achieve this higher level of perfection are moved to teach and write books. With respect to prophets, "sometimes the prophetic revelation that comes to a prophet only renders him perfect and has no other effect. And sometimes the prophetic revelation that comes to him *compels* him to address a call to the people, teach them, and let his own perfection overflow toward them." An individual who prophesizes only because of an overpowering feeling that he or she must do so is much closer to Jeremiah (who wished to "conquer" his prophecy and cease speaking in God's name but found that God's word *was like a raging fire in my heart, shut up in my bones; I could not hold it in, I was helpless* [20:9]) than to a cold, dry, abstract thinking machine, as the standard picture of Maimonides would have it.

In II.38 Maimonides tells us that all human beings have courage in some degree and all humans have some ability to exercise what we might call "intuition," or the ability to jump quickly to correct conclusions about events which we have not witnessed (because we were not present, or because they have not yet taken place). Prophets differ widely in these abilities (p. 377), although all prophets must have them to an exceptional degree. So we find that prophets are individuals blessed with differing degrees of courage and intuition, neither of which are abilities connected to the theoretical intellect. One's degree as a

---

52 See "Laws of the Foundations of the Torah," VII.5 and the 5th of the Eight Chapters. It is true that Moses prophesied without benefit of the imagination, but Moses was not a "normal" prophet and cannot be taken as an ideal actually to be emulated. Note should also be made in this context of the role of joy in prophecy. On this see the important comments of Blidstein, "Joy in Maimonides," at pp. 158-160.

prophet, therefore, is not simply a matter of how much metaphysics one has learned, but is also, crucially, a matter of how brave one is, and how strong one's native intuitive abilities are.[53]

None of this should really surprise us. After all, "it has been explained with utmost clarity that man is political *by nature* and that it is *his nature* to live in society" (II.40, 381; emphasis added).[54] This being the case, we could hardly expect Maimonides to depict prophets, the most perfect of all humans, in ways which fundamentally ignore their own political character. Courage is not some secondary characteristic superadded to the essence of the prophet, but of her very essence. So too, it would seem, are political abilities, qualities of leadership, etc.

In this same chapter Maimonides notes that members of non-human species are alike; in all the ways that count, each horse is like every other horse. Humans, however, differ widely from each other. Given this, could Maimonides really have posited a view of the prophet which entirely ignores everything but his or her reasoning ability, a view that abstracts from the prophet each and every distinguishing characteristic, leaving as truly human (and as truly prophetic) only what the prophet has learned of metaphysical matters? Prophets, as the most perfect humans, are not understood by Maimonides as thinking machines, but as concrete individuals, whose individuality is part of their prophethood, not something to be overcome.

LOVE OF GOD. All Jews are commanded to love God: *You shall love the Lord your God with all your heart and with all your soul and with all your might* (Dt. 6:5). What is the nature of this love? Maimonides is often depicted as if he held love of God and knowledge of God to be identical.[55] This is not quite true.

---

53 Note that Maimonides stresses the individuality of prophets in II.29 (p. 377): "Know that every prophet has a kind of speech peculiar to him, which is, as it were, the language of that individual, which the prophetic revelation peculiar to him causes him to speak to those who understand him."

54 On the political character of human beings in Maimonides' thought, see Melamed, "Maimonides on the Political Character."

55 For recent studies of Maimonides on the love of God, see my Introduction to Maimonides' *Book of Love*, the studies cited there, and Lasker, "Love of God."

Let us look at the texts in which Maimonides speaks of knowledge and love of God. He raises the issue explicitly first in "Laws of the Foundations of the Torah," II.1 (p. 35b, emphasis added):

> And what is the way that will lead to the love of Him and the fear of Him? When a person contemplates his great and wondrous works and creatures and from them obtains a glimpse of His wisdom which is incomparable and infinite, he will *immediately* love Him, praise Him, glorify Him, and long with an exceeding longing to know His great name...

Maimonides tells us here that love of God is an immediate consequence of knowing God; he does not reduce one to the other.

But there are other texts in which he seems more or less to equate the two: "One only loves God with the knowledge with which one knows him. According to the knowledge will be the love: if the former be little or much, so will the latter be little or much..."[56] What Maimonides actually says here is that the more one knows God, the more one loves God. He does not say that love of God is nothing more than knowledge of God.

A passage in the *Guide of the Perplexed* (I.39, p. 89) seems to support both interpretations:

> As for the dictum of Scripture: *And thou shalt love the Lord with all thy heart* (Dt. 6:5) – in my opinion its interpretation is: with all the forces of your heart; I mean to say, with all the forces of the body, for the principle of all of them derives from the heart. Accordingly the intended meaning is...that you should make His apprehension the end of all your actions.

On the one hand, we are told here that in order to fulfill the Scriptural command to love the Lord, one must use all the forces of one's body. On the other hand, we are further told here that the goal of using all the forces of one's body to love the Lord is make knowledge of God the end of all our actions. Everything we do should serve the end of furthering our knowledge of God.[57] The

---

56 "Laws of Repentance," X.6, p. 92b.

57 There are some passages where Maimonides makes this explicit. "Laws of Character Traits," III.2 (p. 49b): "A man should direct all his thoughts and activities to the knowledge of God, alone." All one's activities, even cohabitation, should have thus ultimate end in view.

points made here are expressed again towards the end of the *Guide* (III.28, pp. 512-513):

> *...with all thy heart, and with all thy soul, and with all thy might* (Dt. 6:5). We have already explained[58]... that this love becomes valid only through the apprehension of the whole of being as it is and through the consideration of His wisdom as it is manifested in it.

In this passage, Maimonides seems to present love of God as a consequence of knowledge of God, and not as the same thing.

Near the end of the *Guide* (III.51, p. 621), Maimonides reiterates the relationship of dependence between love and knowledge: "Now we have made it clear several times that love is proportionate to apprehension." The more we know God, the more we love God.

What is the nature of this love we are commanded to have for God? Maimonides tells us in "Laws of Repentance," X.5 (p. 92b):

> What is the love of God that is befitting? It is to love God with a great and exceeding love, so strong that one's soul (*nafsho*) shall be knit up with the love of God such that it is continually enraptured by it, like love-sick individuals whose minds (*da'atam*) are at no time free from passion for a particular woman, and are enraptured by her at all times...even intenser should be the love of God in the hearts of those who love Him; they should be enraptured by this love at all times...

Maimonides reiterates the point again in X.6 (p. 93a), "It is known and certain that the love of God does not become closely knit in a man's heart till he is continuously and thoroughly possessed by it and gives up everything else in the world for it..." and makes much the same claim in some passages in the *Guide*, defining the passionate love of God (Ar: *ishq*) as "...an excess of love, so that no thought remains that is directed toward a thing other than the Beloved..."[59]

---

58 In "Laws of the Foundations of the Torah," II.1-2 and the fifth of the "Eight Chapters" among other places.

59 See Harvey, "Love."

Let us now look at the last passage in the *Guide* (III. 52, 630) in which the issue comes up explicitly:

> You know to what extent the Torah lays stress upon love: *With all thy heart, and with all thy soul, and with all thy might* (Dt. 6:5). For these two ends, namely love and fear, are achieved through two things: love, through the opinions taught by the Law, which include the apprehension of His Being as He, may He be exalted, is in truth; while fear is achieved by means of all actions prescribed by the Law, as we have explained.

Maimonides' position here is tolerably clear: we achieve love of God through the apprehension of God's being to the greatest extent possible for humans. This does not mean that loving and apprehending God are the same.[60]

CONCLUDING REMARKS. Maimonides certainly seems to open himself to the charge that he sees the perfected human being as a coldly rational thinking machine, dispassionately weighing evidence and calculating results. I have tried to show here that this is not a fair assessment.

For Maimonides, reason is a source of motivation. And thus he naturally invokes the *Song of Songs* in the last chapter of the *Guide of the Perplexed* and makes love an outcome of knowledge. Learning carried out properly transforms the learner into a new kind of person.

But, despite all this, the standard picture of Maimonides sketched out at the beginning of this paper is not entirely incorrect: Lessing may have preferred the eternal search for truth over being given all the truth on a silver platter, but I doubt that Maimonides would have. But he certainly would have recognized that having that truth was not simply a matter of piling fact upon fact, deduction upon deduction; it was a matter of passionate love.

---

60 Compare further, Benor, *Worship*, pp. 56-58. For a very useful discussion of love and knowledge in Maimonides see Kaplan, "Rav Kook."

PART TWO

INTRODUCTION TO PART TWO
Religious Faith and Dogma

Aristotle may have never actually said in so many words that human beings are best defined as rational animals, but there can be little doubt that were he asked he would have accepted the definition. Be that as it may, many ancient philosophers accepted the claim as authentic aristotelianism, and it is one which Maimonides certainly adopted. To be rational for the medievals is not only to exercise rational thought, but to *know* the truths arrived at rationally. Maimonides' adoption of this position had momentous implications for his thought, leading to many of his more unusual positions.

These include:

- universalism: maximizing one's natural intellectual abilities, neither birth nor behavior, is what makes one a fully-fledged human being.

- instrumental view of the commandments of the Torah: they were tools given to perfect humans morally and socially, a pre-requisite for achieving the truly human end of rational understanding, not as ends in themselves, or as theurgically effective instruments (and since they are tools, there is no reward, in the commonly accepted sense of the term, for their fulfillment, and no punishment, in the commonly accepted sense of the term, for their violation).

- elitism: most (potential) human beings, because of laziness or force of circumstances, remain unfulfilled in their humanity and ought to serve as instruments in the hands of those who have reached philosophical enlightenment (who in turn ought to seek to imitate God and guide and protect the intellectually less fortunate).

- esotericism: for their own good, the masses must be protected from exposure to the truths understood after much effort by the intellectually more perfected.

None of these positions had much impact on Judaism after Maimonides and many people today who revere his memory and devote themselves to the study of his *Mishneh Torah* would probably deny that he held them. But one consequence of his acceptance of Aristotle's definition of human beings had dramatic impact on subsequent Jewish self-understanding: the unprecedented idea that Judaism has dogmas in the strictest sense of the word. Since humans are defined as such by what they know, the Torah must teach truths. From here it is a short step to systematic theology (absent from rabbinic writings) and from systematic theology it is a short step to dogmatics (equally absent from rabbinic writings).

In a series of books and studies, some of them collected here, I sought to examine Maimonides' dramatic innovation in Judaism, and also sought to clarify some of the implications of that innovation.

The chapters in this section originally appeared in the following places:

"Heresy and the Nature of Faith in Medieval Jewish Philosophy," *Jewish Quarterly Review* 77 (1987): 299-318. Reprinted in: *The Jewish Philosophy Reader*, ed. Daniel H. Frank, Oliver Leaman, and Charles Manekin (London: Routledge, 2000).

"What is Heresy?" *Studies in Jewish Philosophy* 3 (1982): 55-70. Reprinted in N. Samuelson (ed.), *Studies in Jewish Philosophy: Collected Essays of the Academy for Jewish Philosophy*, 1980-85 (Lanham, MD: University Press of America, 1987): 191-214. A Hebrew version of this article appeared as: "Inadvertent Heresy in Medieval Jewish Thought: Maimonides and Abravanel vs. Duran and Crescas?" *Jerusalem Studies in Jewish Thought* 3 (1984): 393-403.

"Maimonides' 'Thirteen Principles' and the Structure of the Guide of the Perplexed," *Journal of the History of Philosophy* 20 (1982): 76-84.

"Maimonides, Crescas, and Abravanel on Exodus 20:2–A Medieval Jewish Exegetical Debate," *Jewish Quarterly Review* 69 (1979): 129-157.

"Could Maimonides Get Into Rambam's Heaven?" *Journal of Jewish Thought and Philosophy* 8 (1999): 231-242.

Review of Marc Shapiro, *The Limits of Orthodoxy: Maimonides' Thirteen Principles Reappraised* for *Edah Journal* 4.1 (Iyyar, 5704).

"The Virtue of Faith," Lenn E. Goodman (ed.), *Neoplatonism and Jewish Thought* (Albany: SUNY Press, 1992): 195-205.

The books in which I address issues of dogma in Judaism are:

Dogma in Medieval Jewish Thought. Oxford: Oxford University Press, 1986. (paperback reprint: 2004). Hebrew translation: *Torat ha-Ikkarim ba-Philosophiah ha-Yehudit Bimei ha-Benayim*. Jerusalem: WZO/Hillel ben Hayyim Library, 1991.

Must a Jew Believe Anything? London: Littman Library of Jewish Civilization, 1999. Second edition, revised and expanded: 2006.

Isaac Abravanel, *Rosh Amanah (Principles of Faith)*. Hebrew text edited, with introduction and notes, and companion texts from Duran, Crescas and Bibago. Ramat Gan: Bar Ilan University Press, 1993.

Principles of Faith by Isaac Abravanel (translation, introduction, notes). London: Littman Library of Jewish Civilization, 1981. (paperback reprint: 2004)

CHAPTER FIVE
Heresy and the Nature of Faith in Medieval Jewish Philosophy

Two very different conceptions of the nature of heresy and the question of who is a heretic are to be found in medieval Jewish texts.[1] I wish to suggest here that these different conceptions reflect (not surprisingly) different answers to the question "Who is a Jew?" and that these different answers reflect in turn different conceptions of the nature of religious faith. In other words, the controversy over the nature of heresy was a dispute not over what Jews were expected to believe (the content of faith) so much as over what it means to say that a person is a believer (the nature of faith). We may say that the question is less one of theology than of epistemology.

Maimonides, as is well known, laid down thirteen specific doctrines which every Jew qua Jew had to accept. Failure to accept even one of these doctrines caused a person to be excluded from the community of Israel, both in this world and in the next. This is what he says at the end of his statement of the principles:

> When all these foundations are perfectly understood and believed in by a person, he is within the community of Israel and one is obligated to love and pity him and to act towards him in all the ways in which the Creator has commanded that one should act towards his brother, with love and fraternity. Even were he to commit every possible transgression, because of lust and because of being overpowered by the evil inclination, he will be punished according

---

1 By "heresy" I refer to the idea usually expressed in Hebrew by terms such as *kefirah*, *minut*, and *epikorsut*. I cannot define the term further at this point since in this paper I hope to prove, inter alia, that the exact meaning of the term was a matter of dispute in the Middle Ages. The issue of heresy usually arose in the medieval period in the context of discussions of dogma. On that subject see my *Dogma*.

to his rebelliousness, but he has a portion [of the world to come]; he is one of the sinners of Israel. But if a man doubts any of these foundations, he leaves the community [of Israel], denies the fundamental, and is called a sectarian, *epikoros,* and one who 'cuts among the plantings'.[2] One is required to hate him and destroy him. About such a person it was said, *Do I not hate them, O Lord, who hate thee?* (Ps. 139: 21).[3]

This statement (especially when read in conjunction with parallel texts[4]) teaches a number of important lessons: first, that entry into the community of Israel depends upon the perfect understanding and acceptance of Maimonides' Thirteen Principles;[5] second, that a person who accepts these principles is thereby rendered worthy of all the benefits of being a Jew;[6] third, that sinning (i.e., violating specific precepts of the Torah) does not cost one either one's membership in the community of Israel or one's portion in the world to come; fourth, that an individual who doubts any one of the principles excludes himself or herself from the community of Israel and by implication from the world to come;[7] fifth, that such a person must be hated and destroyed.[8] It is clear from this that Maimonides construes as heresy the denial (or even questioning) of one or more specific teachings. Maimonides gives no reason to assume furthermore that a person who denies one of his Thirteen Principles without thereby intending heresy (out of ignorance, stupidity, poor education, or whatever) is any the less a heretic. Just as a rose is a rose is a rose, so also heresy is heresy is heresy, no matter what the intentions of the heretic.[9]

---

2   The reference is to Elishah ben Abuyah. See Hagigah 15a.

3   My translation here is based upon the text presented in the Kafih edition, vol. 4, p. 217.

4   See Maimonides' commentary on M. Sanhedrin X.2, XI.3 and his commentary on M. Hullin I.2. See further "Laws of Testimony," XI.10.

5   For an analysis of the full implications of this revolutionary claim, see chapter seven of my *Confrontation.*

6   Maimonides codifies the obligation to love a fellow Jew in "Laws of Moral Qualities" VI.3.

7   This is implied by the fact that the mishnah on which Maimonides is commenting here (see below) deals precisely with the question of who does and who does not merit a share in the world to come. Maimonides makes the point explicitly in "Laws of Repentance" III and in his commentary on Sanh. X.2 and XI.3.

8   See "Laws of Idolatry" X.1, "Laws of Testimony" IX.10, and "Laws of the Murderer" XIII.14.

9   See ch. 6 below, "What is Heresy?"

Maimonides' clear position on the issue of condemning as heretics all who deny certain Torah teachings was explicitly accepted by at least two other medieval thinkers: Abraham ben Shem Tob Bibago (died ca. 1489),[10] and Isaac Abravanel (1437-1508). In his *Derekh 'Emunah* (completed about 1480),[11] Bibago analyzes Maimonides' Thirteen Principles in detail and responds to a number of possible objections to them. The second of these objections involves the question of why one should be considered a heretic for denying a principle of the Torah if one's denial was not motivated by rebelliousness. Bibago attributes this objection to R. Abraham ben David of Posquieres (Rabad)[12] and responds to it in the following way:

> Rabad's statement is really amazing to me, since if it were correct everyone who denied a principle without meaning to do so would have an excuse and a portion in the world to come. [Even] the belief of the Christians would not be inconsistent with true felicity, since they understand Scripture literally and think that the intention of the verse is as they believe it. [On this basis] they would not be called heretics and sectarians. It would be possible to find a man who does not believe in any one of the principles or beliefs of the Torah because of his failure to understand the meaning of the Torah. [On this position] such a one could be called neither a sectarian nor a heretic. All this opposes reason and faith.[13]

Thus for Bibago reason and faith join hands in rejecting the idea that a person who innocently denies a principle of the Torah is no heretic.

In his lengthy disquisition on Maimonides' Thirteen Principles, entitled *Rosh Amanah*, Isaac Abravanel adopts Bibago's position and quotes him nearly word for word.[14] He makes the following addition to Bibago's statement:

---

10 On Bibago see Lazaroff, *Bibago*.

11 The book was printed completely only once (Constantinople, 1521). Selections from it were critically edited by Fraenkel-Goldschmidt.

12 On R. Abrahm ben David (12th cent.) see Twersky, *Rabad*.

13 *Derekh Emunah*, p. 10ld.

14 But without acknowledging his indebtedness to Bibago. On the question of Abravanel's free use of the writings of others see Abravanel, *Principles*, p. 219, and *Dogma*, chapter 7, n. 74 (p. 278).

These things are intolerable according to both the faith of Torah and correct reason. For a false doctrine about any one of the principles of faith turns the soul from its true felicity and will not bring [one] to life in the world to come, even if the opinion is held without intention to rebel. It is like poison which consumes the spirit of him who eats it, *and his spirit will be gathered to God* (Job 34:14), even if he ate it thinking that it was good and healthy food. Similarly, heresy and false belief in the matter of principles of religion will expel the soul of man and without a doubt make it impossible for him to inherit the world to come.[15]

Maimonides, Bibago, and Abravanel, then, disallow inadvertence as valid ground for a plea of exculpation in the question of heresy. By this I mean to say that they do not see the issue of intent as relevant to the definition of heresy, nor do they see inadvertence as an exculpating factor in judging heresy. This strict and no-nonsense approach to the question of heresy represents a theological *novum* in Judaism, ignoring as it does the entire category of *shegagah* (inadvertence) which plays such an important role in halakhah. While in the Middle Ages this view was not recognized for the theological novelty which it was, it did not go unchallenged. It was explicitly rejected by Maimonides' contemporary and critic, Rabad of Posquieres, and by R. Simeon ben Zemah Duran (1361-1444).[16] I have argued elsewhere[17] that there is very good reason to suspect that R. Hasdai Crescas (died ca. 1412) joined Rabad and Duran in rejecting the Maimonides-Bibago-Abravanel position, and that R. Joseph Albo (15th century) was ambivalent on the issue.[18]

The central focus of the opposition to Maimonides is a well-known statement of his. In "Laws of Repentance" III.7 Maimonides codifies as law that:

Five classes are termed sectarians [*minim*]: he who says that there is no God and that the world has no ruler; he who says that there is a ruling power but that it is vested in two or more persons; he who says that there is one Ruler, but that He has a body and has form; he who denies that He alone is the First

---

15 *Principles*, p. 113.

16 On Duran, see Kadish, "Duran."

17 In "What is Heresy?"

18 For information on all these figures, see Kellner, *Dogma*; on our issue specifically, pp. 151-155.

Cause and Rock of the universe; likewise he who renders worship to anyone beside Him, to serve as a mediator between the human being and the Lord of the universe. Whoever belongs to any of these five classes is termed a sectarian (p. 84b).

Sectarians, Maimonides goes on to tell us, "have no portion in the world to come, but are cut off and perish, and for their great wickedness and sinfulness are condemned for ever and ever." Rabad composed a series of critical glosses on the *Mishneh Torah*, the work in which "Laws of Repentance" is found. On the statement cited above, with specific reference to Maimonides' third class of sectarians (believers in God's corporeality), Rabad comments as follows:

Why has he called such a person a sectarian? There are many people greater than, and superior to him, who adhere to such a belief on the basis of what they have seen in verses of Scripture, and even more in the words of the aggadot which corrupt right opinion about religious matters.[19]

In typically forceful language[20] Rabad here defends the naive corporealist from Maimonides' charge of heresy. Rabad is not defending the view that God has a body;[21] he is, however, defending those Jews who, because they mistakenly understood certain scriptural verses and aggadot literally, believed that God has a body. In other words, Rabad allows for the category of inadvertence to play a role, not just with respect to commandments involving actions but also with respect to heresy; a person who inadvertently (*bi-shegagah*) commits what otherwise would be considered heresy is no heretic.[22]

---

19 I cite the text as translated by Twersky in his *Rabad*, p. 282.

20 There exists a less forceful version of this gloss. See Twersky, *Rabad*, pp. 282-286, and ch. 6 below, n. 8.

21 See Twersky's discussion of the subject, *ad loc*. On the question of medieval Jews who may have believed in a corporeal God, see *Dogma*, chapter 1, n. 159 (p. 233) and, more recently, Kanarfogel, "Anthropomorphism."

22 This conclusion is not, strictly speaking, warranted by the text. It is conceivable that Rabad (a) admits the existence of principles of Judaism; (b) does not consider belief in incorporeality to be such a one; and (c) excuses inadvertent heresy only with respect to beliefs which are not principles. Were this the case, we could say that Rabad excuses the naive corporealist, but only because belief in God's incorporeality is not a principle of faith. There is, however, absolutely no evidence that (a) is true. This is so for the following reasons: Rabad was not familiar with Maimonides' Commentary on the Mishnah, the text in which the Thirteen Principles appear (see Twersky, p. 107). Maimonides' claim that Judaism has dogmas or principles of faith was an absolute *novum* in Judaism (see my *Dogma*, pp. 1-9 and *Must*, chapts. 1-3). It

Rabad's gloss here is quoted (in the more polite version) by Duran in chapter 9 of his *Ohev Mishpat* (Venice, 1590, p. 146). Duran then expresses himself in the following items:

> You also ought to know that one who has properly accepted the roots of the Torah but was moved to deviate from them by the depths of his speculation, and who thereby came to believe concerning one of the branches of the faith the opposite of what has been accepted as what one ought to believe, and tried to explain the verses of Scripture according to his belief-even though he errs, he is no denier. For he was not brought to this deviation by heresy at all, and if he found a tradition from the Sages to the effect that he ought to turn from the position he had adopted, he would do so. He only holds that belief because he thinks it is the intention of the Torah. Therefore, even though he errs, he is not a denier and sectarian according to what is agreed upon by our people, since he had accepted the roots of the Torah as he should.

Duran here expands upon Rabad's statement, making clear the importance of intention to the definition of heresy. The inadvertent denier denies Torah teachings because he or she thinks that the Torah itself commands such denial. The heretic, on the other hand, is the person who, fully knowing that the Torah teaches a particular doctrine, goes ahead and denies it nonetheless.[23]

As indicated above, there are good grounds for linking R. Hasdai Crescas with Rabad and Duran as against Maimonides, Bibago, and Abravanel on the issue of inadvertence in heresy. Crescas' position, however, is complex and there is no clear-cut text which I can cite in support of my claim.[24] Such, however, is not the case with Crescas' well-known student, R. Joseph Albo. Although Albo appears to be ambivalent on the issue, in one place (*Ikkarim* I.2) he clearly allies himself with the Rabad-Duran-Crescas camp:

---

stretches belief to maintain that Rabad independently arrived at a position identical or even importantly similar to Maimonides' great *novum*. But let us assume that this is wrong. It is still highly unlikely that (b) would be true. After all, had Rabad indeed adopted the view that Judaism has dogmas, it is very unlikely that he would fail to include in his list of dogmas the claim of God's incorporeality, especially since he was familiar with Maimonides' argument ("Laws of the Foundations of the Torah" 1.7) that incorporeality is an absolutely necessary corollary of unity. On this see also Twersky, pp. 283-284.

23 The interpretation of Duran offered here is defended in detail in *Dogma*, ch. 3.

24 I refer the reader to my detailed argument in "What is Heresy?"

It is proper to say this in justification of those Jewish scholars who deal with this subject.[25] Every Israelite is obliged to believe that everything that is found in the Torah is absolutely true, and anyone who denies anything that is found in the Torah, knowing that it is the opinion of the Torah, is a heretic.... But a person who upholds the Torah of Moses and believes in its principles, but when he undertakes to investigate these matters with his reason and scrutinizes the texts, is misled by his speculation and interprets a given principle otherwise than it is taken to mean at first sight;[26] or denies the principle because he thinks that it does not represent a sound theory which the Torah obliges us to believe; or erroneously denies that a given belief is a fundamental principle, which however he believes as he believes the other dogmas of the Torah which are not fundamental principles;[27] or entertains a certain notion in relation to one of the miracles of the Torah because he thinks that he is not hereby denying any of the doctrines which it is obligatory upon us to believe by the authority of the Torah[28] – a person of this sort is not a heretic. He is, rather, classed with the sages and pious men of Israel, although he holds erroneous theories. His sin is due to error and requires atonement.[29]

In this passage Albo adopts Duran's principle that basically one is obliged to accept that all that the Torah teaches is true. Once one does accept it, but is led –either by philosophical speculation or by honest exegesis of Scripture– to adopt certain types of heterodox positions, one does not thereby become a heretic who forfeits one's share in the world to come. Albo discusses four types of heterodox positions to which one might be led by faulty speculation or faulty exegesis and which do not remove one from the community of Israel: (1) misinterpretation of a principle; (2) denial of the truth of a principle; (3) denying that a particular belief is a principle, while not denying that the belief is true and truly taught by the Torah; and (4) misinterpreting a miracle. Persons who err in any of these ways are not heretics, are not excluded from the community of Israel (indeed, they may be classed among "the sages and

---

25 I.e., the subject of the principles of the Torah.

26 E.g., Maimonides' treatment of resurrection: see Albo's *Ikkarim* 1.2 (Husik's translation, p. 54)

27 E.g., Maimonides' treatment of creation: see *Ikkarim* 1.2 (p. 51).

28 Possibly a reference to Gersonides; see *Ikkarim* 1.2 (p. 52).

29 *Ikkarim* 1.2 (pp. 49-50).

pious men of Israel"), and although they have sinned and must expiate their sin, they are not denied a share in the world to come.

Albo goes on to give various examples of "sages and pious men of Israel" who, misled either by philosophy or their failure to understand Scripture properly, adopted one or more of the heterodox positions listed above.[30] "We say, therefore," he concludes, "that a person whose speculative ability is not sufficient to enable him to reach the true meaning of scriptural texts, with the result that he believes in the literal meaning and entertains absurd ideas because he thinks they represent the view of the Torah, is not hereby excluded from the community of those who believe in the Torah, heaven forfend! Nor is it permitted to speak disrespectfully of him and accuse him of "perverting the teaching of the Torah" (Avot III.15) and class him among the heretics and sectarians.[31]

Thus we find Albo staunchly defending those Jews who are led to mistaken beliefs by honest mistakes in their understanding of Scripture. "That man alone," Albo tells us, who knows the truth and deliberately denies it, belongs to the class of the wicked whose repentance is rejected. But the man whose intention is not to rebel, nor to depart from the truth, nor to deny what is in the Torah, nor reject tradition, but whose sole intention is to interpret the verses according to his opinion, though he interprets them erroneously, is neither a sectarian nor a heretic.

Albo concludes this chapter with the following declaration (I.2, p. 54):

> It is clear now that every intelligent person is permitted to investigate the fundamental principles of religion and to interpret the verses [of the Torah] in accordance with the truth as it seems to him. And though he believes concerning certain things which earlier authorities regarded as principles, like the coming of the Messiah and creation, that they are not fundamental principles, but merely true doctrines, which the believer in the Torah is obliged to believe..., he is not a denier of the Torah or its principles.

---

30 Albo cites as examples the statement in Gen. Rabbah 3 that "temporal sequence existed before creation" and the discussion in *Pirke de-Rabbi Eliezer* 3 on the primordial matter out of which the world was created. On this text, see *Confrontation*, pp. 68-76. Albo also refers to an interpretation of the story of Balaam's ass which was adopted, as we know, but as Albo does not mention, by both Maimonides (*Guide* II.41) and Gersonides (in his commentary to Num. 22).

31 *Ikkarim* 1.2 (p. 52); Albo goes on to support his position by citing Rabad's gloss to "Repentance" III.7.

We have before us, therefore, two very clearly opposed views. The first, that of Maimonides, Bibago, and Abravanel, holds that every Jew is required to accept certain teachings[32] and that the rejection of any of these teachings for any reason constitutes heresy. On this account the category of inadvertence (*shegagah*) simply does not obtain with respect to questions of doctrine. The second view, that of Rabad, Duran, Crescas, and Albo, does allow for *shegagah* with respect to doctrinal matters. This view does not by any means deny that the Torah teaches certain doctrines; nor does it deny that some of these doctrines may be singled out and categorized as dogmas or principles of faith. This view, however, does distinguish between a person who purposefully denies Torah teachings knowing that they are Torah teachings, on the one hand, and a person who denies the very same Torah teaching without realizing that he or she is thereby contradicting the Torah, on the other hand. The first person is condemned as a heretic while the second may be excused as mistaken.

We can make the point clearer by examining some cases. Let us say that a person purposefully denies some teaching that is not a principle of faith because he or she purposefully rejects the Torah; all would agree that such a person is a heretic. Maimonides would count such a person as a heretic because his or her purposeful denial of Torah teaching involves a rejection of his eighth principle, Torah from heaven. Duran would count such denial as heresy because that is exactly how he defines it: knowing and purposeful rejection of any Torah teaching. What about the case of a person who denies a principle innocently (i.e., through what we have been calling inadvertence)? Maimonides would count such a person as a heretic, while Duran would not. This last case must be contrasted with the case of a person who inadvertently denies some teaching not included in the principles. In such a case, both Maimonides and Duran would admit that such an individual is no heretic.

In other words we may say that the two views of the nature of heresy delineated here reflect two different conceptions of what it means to be a Jew. The first conception defines a Jew as a person who holds certain specific doctrines. There may be some disagreement over what these beliefs are, but no disagree-

---

32 Maimonides and Abravanel do, of course, disagree on how many teachings a Jew must accept. For Maimonides it is thirteen; for Abravanel it is every doctrine taught by the Torah. See *Principles*, p. 28.

ment over the fact that to be a Jew means to accept certain specific teachings.[33] Once that is accepted, it follows as a matter of course that a person who rejects any of the specified teachings has failed to fulfill one of the cardinal requirements of being a Jew. It is no surprise that, in this conception, such a person is condemned as a heretic and excluded from both the community of Israel and the world to come

The opposed view is also willing to define a Jew in theological terms but refuses to specify the precise and exact teachings which must be accepted in order to count as a Jew. In this view, "there is only one principle of the Torah: to believe that everything included in the Torah is true."[34] It is acceptance of the Torah in general which defines a person in theological terms as a Jew. Once the Torah is accepted wholeheartedly, innocent deviations from the exact letter of its teachings can be accepted for what they are – mistakes. One can be mistaken about details of Torah teachings without thereby impugning its overall truth. This dispute reflects a yet more basic disagreement, a controversy over the question of what faith or religious belief actually is. It is almost a commonplace to distinguish between "two types of faith",[35] between belief that something is the case and belief in something or someone, between "theology" and "depth theology."[36] These two ideas are so often and so easily contrasted that one is tempted to forget how important and fundamental the distinction actually is and suspect that it cannot stand up to close scrutiny. Kenneth Seeskin subjected the distinction between intellectual acquiescence to the truth of a proposition ("belief that"), on the one hand, and trust, loyalty, and commitment ("belief in"), on the other hand, to acute analysis and confirmed the pre-philosophical intuition that we have here a distinction with an important difference.[37]

---

33 I do not mean to ignore the halakhic definition of a Jew as an individual born of a Jewish mother or properly converted to Judaism. In phrasing the issue here in theological terms I simply follow Maimonides' lead. Maimonides, in effect, added a theological dimension to the halakhic definition. Further on this, see Kellner, "A Suggestion" and *Confrontation*, chapter 7.

34 Duran, *Ohev Mishpat*, p. 9.

35 The title of Martin Buber's book on the subject.

36 Heschel, *Search*, p. 7.

37 See Seeskin, "Faith." The points made here are developed in much greater detail in Kellner, *Must*.

In general, when the Bible and the Talmud use the word *emunah* ("faith"), it relates not to propositions but to dispositions, not to assent but to consent,[38] not to intellectual acquiescence but to loyalty and faithfulness. Short of an exhaustive textual analysis, I cannot prove this contention. I shall, instead, cite a number of examples from rabbinic literature[39] which support my position. I have not chosen these examples at random. Rather, they are drawn from places where we would expect to find evidence of the propositional conception of faith had the idea been so understood by the rabbis.

The first text is central to all discussion of dogma in Judaism, since it is the only place in the entire corpus of rabbinic literature where we find what appears to be a systematic attempt to specify what teachings a Jew must hold in order to merit a portion in the world to come.[40] M. San. 10.1 reads as follows:

> All Israelites have a share in the world to come, as it states, *Thy people are all righteous, they shall inherit the land forever* (Is. 60:21). But the following have no share in the world to come: he who says that there is no resurrection, that the Torah is not from heaven, and the *epikoros*. R. Akiba says: Even he who reads the external books and he who whispers upon a wound, saying *I will put none of the diseases upon thee, which I have put upon the Egyptians: for I am the Lord that healeth thee* (Ex. 15:26). Abba Saul says: Even he who pronounces the Name according to its letters.

According to this mishnah there are six things that cost a Jew his or her share in the world to come: denying resurrection, denying the divine origin of the Torah, being an *epikoros*, reading certain types of forbidden literature, using Scripture magically in order to heal, and pronouncing God's name (the tetragrammaton) as it is spelled.

Let it be noted that of these six items the last three are clearly actions, not beliefs. Let it be further noted that the Gemara understands the third, *epikoros*,

---

38 The formulation is Seeskin's.

39 For biblical examples see Gen. 15:10, Dt. 32:2, Prov. 20:6, and Job 4:18. For important confirmation of the thesis advanced here N. J. Cohen, "Analysis," especially pp. 7-8 and the fuller discussion in Kellner, *Must*, chaps. 1-2.

40 This is certainly the way in which Maimonides understood the mishnah. I cite the text according to his version.

in purely actional terms.[41] The remaining two issues (resurrection and Torah from heaven) may very well relate to specific disputes which occupied the authorities whose views are expressed in the mishnah. But even if they do not, this mishnah is still a far cry from the systematic statement of necessary beliefs that it is often presented as being.[42] Had the rabbis of the Mishnah really believed that Jewish faith was measured by acceptance of carefully delineated specific teachings, this mishnah would have been a natural place for them to list these teachings. That they failed to do so is indirect evidence for the thesis that "faith" or "belief" was not so understood. Had the rabbis defined Jewish faith in terms of its propositional content, there is another place where we would expect to find some systematic discussion of those specific teachings which a person had to hold in order to be considered a faithful Jew: discussion of conversion. Given the fact that the rabbis were constrained by the halakhic definition of a Jew as a person born of a Jewish mother or properly converted to Judaism, they had very little control, so to speak, over the beliefs of a person born Jewish; but they surely could lay down explicitly what beliefs a person converting to Judaism had to adopt. But when we turn to the central Talmudic discussion of conversion (Yev. 47a-b) this is what we find:

> Our rabbis taught: If at the present time a man desires to become a proselyte, he is to be addressed as follows: "What reasons do you have for desiring to become a proselyte? Do you not know that Israel at the present time are persecuted and oppressed, despised, harassed, and overcome by afflictions?" If he replies, "I know, and yet I am unworthy," he is to be accepted forthwith and given instruction in some of the minor and some of the major commandments.... He is also to be told of the punishment for the transgression of the commandments.... And as he is informed of the punishment for the transgression of the commandments, so is he also informed of the reward granted for their fulfillment.

---

41 See B. Sanh. 9b-11a. This, of course, is no proof that this was the opinion of the author of this mishnah. But the Gemara gives no hint of any nonactional interpretation of the term. On the use of the term in rabbinic literature, see Labendz, "Epicurean".

42 Note that the holders of these deviant views are not labeled heretics by the rabbis. I argue in *Must* that the term 'heretic' with its overtly theological baggage (and its covertly Christian baggage) is an inappropriate translation for rabbinic terms such as *kofer, min, epikoros.*

The entire emphasis here is on the teaching of the commandments, as opposed to the acceptance of any catechism. We find then that in two crucial places –discussions of who will and will not merit a share in the world to come and who may or may not be converted to Judaism– that the rabbis give no indication of having adopted a propositional definition of the concept of *emunah*. For had they so interpreted it, they surely would have been careful, wherever they were able, to exclude from the community of Israel in this world and in the next individuals of defective faith, and would have specified how to measure the wholeness or defectiveness of that faith. I should like to adduce one more example (Mak. 23b-24a), one in which we find the Talmud actually defining the term *emunah*. The concept is defined, as we shall see, not in terms of specific teachings or propositions which can be accepted or rejected, but in terms of the performance of the commandments:

R. Simlai, as he was preaching, said: Six hundred and thirteen precepts were communicated to Moses, three hundred and sixty five negative ones, corresponding to the number of solar days [in the year], and two hundred and forty-eight positive ones, corresponding to the number of members of a man's body.... David came and reduced them to eleven [principles], as it is written, *A Psalm of David. Lord, who shall sojourn in Thy tabernacle? Who shall dwell in Thy holy mountain? [i] He that walketh uprightly, and [ii] worketh righteousness, and [iii] speaketh truth in his heart, that [iv] hath no slander upon his tongue, [v] nor doeth evil to his fellow, [vi] nor taketh up a reproach against his neighbor, [vii] in whose eyes a vile person is despised, but [viii] he honoreth them that fear the Lord, [ix] he sweareth to his own hurt and changeth not, [x] he putteth not out his money on interest, [xi] nor taketh a bribe against the innocent. He that doeth these things shall never be moved* (Ps. 15).

The Talmud continues, citing Isaiah who reduced the six hundred and thirteen commandments to six principles, Micah who reduced them to three, and Isaiah again who is said to have reduced them to two. The pericope ends as follows: "Amos came and reduced them to one [principle], as it is said *For thus saith the Lord unto the house of Israel: Seek ye Me and live* (Amos 5:4). To this R. Nahman ben Isaac demurred, saying: [Might it not be taken as meaning] Seek Me by observing the whole Torah and live?[43] But it is Habakkuk who came and based them all on one [principle], as it is said, *But the righteous shall live by his faith* (Hab. 2:4)."

We have here before us a text which begins with the six hundred thirteen commandments of the Torah and which, by a series of graduated steps, reduces them to one: that the righteous shall live by his faith *(be-emunato)*. *Emunah* is defined here not in terms of its propositional content but in terms of fulfilling the commandments of the Torah.

These three strategically chosen texts support the contention that *emunah* as generally used by the rabbis of the Talmud is best understood in terms of loyalty, faithfulness, and commitment, rather than in the intellectualist terms of acquiescence in (or rejection of) certain specified doctrines.

We may compare this conception of faith with the conception found in a number of medieval Jewish philosophic and halakhic works. Saadiah Gaon sought to convert the *amanat* of Judaism ("doctrines accepted as an act of religious faith") into *itiqadat* ("doctrines subject to an attitude of firm belief as the result of a process of speculation").[44] This latter term (ordinarily rendered into Hebrew as *emunot* and into English as "beliefs") Saadiah defines as follows:

> It behooves us to explain what is meant by *itiqad*. We say that it is a notion that arises in the soul in regard to the actual character of anything that is apprehended. When the cream of investigation emerges [and] is embraced and enfolded by the minds, and through them acquired and digested by the souls, then the person becomes convinced of the truth of the notions he has thus acquired. He then deposits it in his soul for a future occasion or future occasions.[45]

The subject of *itiqad*, then, are propositions which are either true or false. Judaism for Saadiah, it must be emphasized, is a matter of both *amanat* and *i'tiqadat*, specific discrete propositions.

Maimonides presents a similar definition of the term (*Guide* I.50, p. 111): "Know, thou who studied this, my treatise, that *itiqad* is not the notion that is

---

43 Perhaps an implied critique of St. Paul's understanding of the commandments?
44 See Altmann, "Translator's Introduction," pp. 19-20 and H. A. Wolfson, "Double Faith," pp. 585, 587-88, and 597.
45 Saadiah, *Beliefs*, Introduction, ch. 4, p. 14.

uttered but the notion that is represented in the soul when it has been averred of it that it is in fact just as it has been represented."[46] Furthermore, Maimonides uses this term, and its Hebrew cognate *da'at*, consistently in the context of religious beliefs.[47] For Saadiah and Maimonides, then, religious belief was more than a matter of trust, loyalty, and faith; it was also a matter of the affirmation or denial of certain propositions.

Further, and striking, evidence concerning Maimonides' view on this matter may be found in the *Mishneh Torah*. In "Laws of Forbidden Intercourse" XIV Maimonides codifies the procedure for conversion, basing himself upon the texts from Yevamot cited above. He writes:

> In what manner are righteous proselytes to be received? When a heathen comes forth for the purpose of becoming a proselyte, and upon investigation no ulterior motive is found, the court should say to him, "Why do you come forth to become a proselyte? Do you not know that Israel is at present sorely afflicted, oppressed, despised, confounded, and beset of suffering?" If he answers, "I know, and I am indeed unworthy," he should be accepted immediately. He should then be made acquainted with the principles of the faith, which are the oneness of God and the prohibition of idolatry. These matters should be discussed in great detail; he should then be told, though not at great length, about some of the less weighty and some of more weighty commandments. Thereupon he should be informed of the transgressions involved in the laws concerning gleanings, forgotten sheaves, the corner of the field, and the poor man's tithe. Then he should be told of the punishment for violation of the commandments. How so? The court should say to him, "Be it known unto you that before entering into this faith, if you ate forbidden fat, you did not incur

---

46 Further on this, see the notes *ad loc.* to Michael Schwarz's Hebrew translation of the *Guide*, the sources cited there, and now E. Kafih, "*Moreinu*," pp. 308-309.

47 Maimonides opens his commentary on M. Sanhedrin chapter 10 (*Perek Helek*) (which contains his Thirteen Principles) with the following words: "I have seen fit to speak here about many principles concerning very important doctrines [*al-itiqadat*]." See Kafih's edition, p. 195. He concludes his discussion with the following statement (cited above): "When all these foundations are perfectly understood and believed in by a person he is within the community of Israel" (Kafih, p. 217). See further Nuriel, "Faith" and Kellner, "Religious Faith." Nuriel shows how Maimonides uses *al-iman* (= *emunah*) in the sense of "trust" with no reference to cognitive content. The term appears rarely in the writings of Maimonides, since he understands the content of faith in terms of specific teachings. See also ch. 11 below, "The Virtue of Faith."

the penalty of extinction; if you desecrated the Sabbath, you did not incur the penalty of death by stoning. But now, having become a proselyte, should you eat forbidden fat, you will incur the penalty of extinction, and if you should profane the Sabbath, you will incur the penalty of death by stoning." This, however, should not be carried to excess nor to too great detail, lest it should make him weary and cause him to stray from the good way unto the evil way. A person should be attracted at first only with pleasing and gentle words, as it is said first, *I will draw them with cords of a man, and only then with bonds of love* (Hos. 11:4).

This statement, when compared with its Talmudic source, is seen to be really quite remarkable. Maimonides introduces references to the "principles" of religion, insists that we expatiate upon them in great detail, and prohibits lengthy discussion of the commandments. According to Maimonides, then, conversion seems to involve the acceptance of what might be called "the yoke of specific beliefs" more importantly than the acceptance of the "yoke of commandments." Where the rabbis of the Talmud shied away from references to the acceptance of specific beliefs, Maimonides makes it centrally important.

One more example: Abraham Bibago (died c. 1489) subjects the concept of *emunah* to minute analysis in his book *Derekh Emunah* and defines it in terms of the specific beliefs (*helqei emunah*) which form its content. "Do you not find some people," he complains, "who call themselves believers [*ma'aminim*] and members of the Mosaic covenant and who, if you ask them the number of their beliefs and what they are, put their hands upon their mouths?"[48] Bibago goes on to say that one who cannot number and "define his beliefs in his mind" ought not properly to be called a believer at all. We have here very clear evidence that Bibago understood *emunah* in terms of its propositional content.[49]

We have before us, then, evidence of two distinct understandings of the nature of religious faith: one, which I have labeled biblical and Talmudic, un-

---

48 I.e., cannot answer (compare Micah 7:16); *Derekh Emunah*, p. 94b (in Fraenkel-Goldschmidt's selections, p. 289).

49 For a further example see Albo, *Ikkarim* 1.19 (p. 165): "Belief in a thing means a firm conception of the thing in the mind, so that the latter cannot in any way imagine its opposite, even though it may not be able to prove it. Examples are, belief in the axioms..."

derstands faith primarily in terms of the attitude of the believer. A religion conceived of in these terms has no need of theological systemization. The second conception of faith defines it in terms of the specific propositions which the believer accepts or rejects. It is this conception of faith which gives rise to statements of dogma, and it is thus no surprise that we find none in biblical and rabbinic literature. A person defining *emunah* in this fashion would have good reason to be upset if the propositions held were incorrect. An attitude of trust in God, for example, is not compromised if some of one's specific conceptions concerning God are mistaken. But if one's faith in God is defined in terms of certain specific propositions about God, then that faith is certainly defective if one affirms incorrect propositions about Him.

We may now understand how these different attitudes towards the nature of belief underlay the different conceptions of heresy which we have discussed here. If we define "belief" in fundamentally attitudinal terms, we can allow for a person to be considered a good and faithful Jew even if he or she is mistaken with respect to certain teachings of the Torah. The one has literally nothing to do with the other. If, on the other hand, we define "belief" in terms of its specific content, then, while we would certainly demand of the faithful Jew an attitude of trust, loyalty, and commitment to God and to His Torah, we could not be satisfied with that, but would also be forced to judge the faithfulness of every Jew in terms of the specific doctrines which he or she affirms or denies.

All this is clear in retrospect. It was not so clear to the medieval figures whose texts we have been analyzing. This is indicated by the fact that strict consistency would demand that a thinker who defined "belief" in what I have called biblical-rabbinic terms ("belief in") should reject the notion of dogma or principles of faith altogether. This is emphatically not the case: Duran, Crescas, and Albo all put forward dogmatic systems of one form or another. They were willing to follow Maimonides' lead in laying down principles of faith for Judaism, even as they resisted adopting the conception of faith which underlay his system of dogmas.[50]

---

50 I return to issues addressed in this chapter in *Dogma*, *Must*, and "Religious Faith."

CHAPTER SIX
What is Heresy?

I n this chapter I propose to examine the question, what is heresy? I will discuss a medieval debate on the issue, attempt to make a small contribution to the better understanding of that debate, and utilize the lessons drawn from our discussion of the medieval debate in order to examine the issue in its contemporary perspective. Questions of heresy often turn on precise linguistic formulations and one of the central points I wish to make here turns on Hasdai Crescas' analysis of the proper usage of the term 'commandment'.

To make my intention clear from the outset, I will examine different understandings of what constitutes heresy in Judaism in an attempt to develop a definition of heresy which is consistent with the demands of the Jewish tradition yet sufficiently flexible to allow for a measure of tolerance on theological issues within Judaism. This is more than a purely theoretical issue since the laws concerning relationships with heretics are quite clear. In a text to which we shall have occasion to return, Maimonides informs us that we are commanded to hate and destroy the heretic. In the *Mishneh Torah* ("Laws of Idolatry, II.5) Maimonides codifies as halakhah that heretics (*minim*) "are in no way to be regarded as Jews," and that "it is forbidden to speak with them or to reply to them at all." We are further commanded (X.1) with respect to heretics "to destroy them and hurl them into the pit of destruction."

What, then, is a heretic?[1] Maimonides is, perhaps, the first Jewish thinker to address the issue. In his well-known commentary to M. Sanhedrin X he lists

---

1   Hebrew: *epikoros* (heretic), *min* (sectarian), and *kofer* (denier). By "heretic" I mean a person who is thought to be excluded from the world to come by virtue of his or her beliefs. In this essay I shall distinguish "heresy" from "unbelief" or "misbelief". By these two latter terms I mean heterodox belief which is not thought to cost one one's share in the world to come. One of the points I wish to make here is that this is a distinction with a difference, a claim denied by Isaac Abravanel with respect to all of the beliefs of Judaism and by Maimonides at least

thirteen beliefs the acceptance of all of which defines a person as a Jew. After listing and discussing his principles, Maimonides writes:

> When all these foundations are perfectly understood and believed in by a person, he is within the community of Israel and one is obligated to love and pity him and to act towards him in all the ways in which the Creator has commanded that one should act towards his brother, with love and fraternity. Even were he to commit every possible transgression, because of lust and because of being overpowered by the evil inclination, he will be punished according to his rebelliousness, but he has a portion [of the world to come]; he is one of the sinners of Israel. But if a man doubts any of these foundations, he leaves the community [of Israel], denies the fundamental, and is called a sectarian, *epikoros,* and one who 'cuts among the plantings'. One is required to hate him and destroy him. About such a person it was said, *Do I not hate them, O Lord, who hate thee?* (Ps. 139: 21).

As noted above in ch. 5, "Heresy and the Nature of Faith," it is clear from this and parallel texts that Maimonides defined the concept "principle of faith" as what we today would call a dogma. Maimonides' principles are quite clearly (a) beliefs laid down by supreme religious authority (God's word as expressed in the Torah) – Maimonides introduces them as the "foundations of the Torah" and supports them with citations from Scripture; (b) necessary (and sufficient!) conditions for membership in the religious community (of Israel); and, finally, (c) necessary (and sufficient!) conditions for enjoying a share in the world to come.

It should not surprise us to discover that if Maimonides had a strict understanding of what a "foundation of the Torah" is, he also had a strict understanding of what heresy is. Put simply, heresy consists of questioning (let alone denying) anyone of the principles as they were formulated by Maimonides. A person who questions anyone of the principles excludes himself or herself from the community of Israel and thus forfeits his share in the world to come.

---

with respect to his Thirteen Principles. Although Maimonides uses the three terms cited here in different ways, (see, for examples, "Laws of Repentance" III) the issue need not detain one here. It is discussed at length in the first chapter of my *Dogma*.

On Maimonides' account, then, it is easy to determine who a heretic is: it is any person who questions one of the principles of the Torah. Maimonides makes the job of identifying heretics even easier for us by conveniently and succinctly summarizing those principles which a Jew must be careful to accept, on pain of being condemned for heresy.

It should be emphasized that Maimonides' statements here in his Mishnah commentary, and in a parallel text in the *Mishneh Torah*,[2] do not interest themselves at all in the question of *why* a person questions the principles of faith. In order to be considered a heretic it is sufficient simply to question the principles for any reason. Maimonides makes no distinction between the adoption of incorrect beliefs intentionally (i.e., rejecting beliefs one knows are taught by the Torah or adopting beliefs one knows are denied by the Torah) and the adoption of incorrect beliefs unintentionally (i.e., rejecting beliefs one incorrectly thinks are rejected by the Torah or adopting one incorrectly thinks are taught by the Torah).[3]

This interpretation of Maimonides is supported by Rabad of Posquieres (c. 1125 - 1198). In "Laws of Repentance," III.7 Maimonides codifies as halakhah the assertion that one who believes God has a body is a sectarian [*min*] and has no share in the world to come. In his gloss to the halakhah Rabad comments:

> Why has he called such a person a sectarian? There are many people greater than and superior to him who adhere to such a belief on the basis of what they have seen in verses of Scripture and even more in the words of those *aggadot* which corrupt right opinion about religious matters.[4]

Rabad was not, of course, seeking to validate belief in the corporeality of God.[5] It was his point, rather, that even though God was incorporeal, a simple soul might be led by the highly anthropomorphic accounts of God in the Bible and in the midrashim to believe that God had a body. Such a person whose misbelief, as we might call it, was occasioned by an honest mistake, and who

---

2   "Laws of Repentance," III.

3   I am referring here to the two categories *mezid* ("intentional sinner") and *shogeg* ("unintentional sinner").

4   I cite the gloss as translated by Twersky in his *Rabad*, p. 282.

5   See Twersky, pp. 282-286.

thought that he or she believed what the Torah taught, ought not to be considered a heretic. It does not follow from this that Rabad thought that misbelief about principles of faith was excusable –after all, he may not even have held that belief in God's incorporeality was a principle (if he indeed held that the Torah had principles)– but it does follow from this that according to Rabad Maimonides did not allow for the possibility of innocent mistakes (*shegagah*) with respect to his principles.

Maimonides' position on heresy did not go unchallenged in the Middle Ages. He was criticized from two perspectives: Some scholars faulted him for being too liberal while others sought to restrict the concept of heresy in ways in which Maimonides would surely have condemned as being too liberal.

Rabbi Isaac Abravanel (1437-1508) is an example of the first tendency. He agreed with Maimonides that the Torah had principles of faith. He was unwilling, however, to admit that there principles could be reduced to the number thirteen, and insisted that every teaching of the Torah was a principle, the questioning of which constituted heresy:

> There is no need to lay down principles for the Torah of God which ought to be believed by every Israelite in order to merit life in the world to come as Maimonides and those who follow after him wrote, for the entire Torah, and every single verse, word, and letter in it is a principle and which ought to be believed.[6]

No only is every teaching of the Torah a principle, which must be accepted in order to merit life in the world to come, according to Abravanel, but the proper interpretation of the principles must be accepted. He continues:

> …for a false opinion about any one of the principles faith turns the soul from its true felicity and will not bring one to life in the world to come, even if the opinion is held without intention to rebel. This must be so, for were it otherwise, even one who unintentionally denies every principle will acquire a portion in the world to come… It would be possible, according to this, to find a man who does not believe in any of the principles or beliefs of the Torah and

---

6   See Abravanel's *Principles*, chapter 24 (p. 205).

yet who should not be called a sectarian or heretic if he were brought to this blind foolishness by his failure to understand the meaning of the Torah.[7]

It is hard to find fault with the logic of Abravanel's argument. Once we accept the claim that all of the teachings of the Torah are not only true, but that each and every one of them is a principle of faith, we cannot allow for mistakes with respect to any Torah beliefs. This is so even if the questioning is not intended as heresy: if a person could mistakenly reject a Torah belief on the grounds that he thought the Torah required it of him and not thereby be called a heretic, and since all the Torah beliefs are equivalent in the sense that they have the same dogmatic status, it would follow that a person who in good faith rejected all of the teachings of the Torah thinking that the Torah required this of him would have to be considered a good and pious Jew!

For the sake of convenience we may characterize the Maimonides/Abravanel position (for all the differences between them) as "hard line". This position, with its demand for absolute, uncompromising orthodoxy, dominated discussions of heresy in medieval Judaism. But it was not the only position adopted.

Rabbi Shimon ben Zemah Duran (1361-1444), the eminent halakhist, rejected Maimonides' position. He quoted Rabad's gloss with approval, citing him as an authority for his own rejection of the hard-line position.[8] Duran analyzed Maimonides' Thirteen Principles in his *Ohev Mishpat*, proposing that they could be reduced to three. In the final analysis, however, he maintained that formulating specific principles of faith was not fundamentally important:

Know this, O Reader, that the great principle in all this is to believe what the Torah included in these matters. He who denied what was included in the To-

---

7 *Principles*, chapter 12 (p. 122).

8 Rabad's gloss in Duran's version reads as follows: "[Even though] the essence of the belief [*ikkar ha-emunah ken hu*] is like this, if one believes that God has a body because he understands the words of the midrashim literally, one ought not therefore be called a sectarian." See Duran, *Ohev Mishpat* (Venice, 1580), chapter 9 (p. 15a); this passage appears on p. 89 of my *Dogma*. There is some room for dispute concerning Rabad's meaning in this version of his gloss: the phrase I translate as "the essence of the belief" could also be translated as "article of faith." This latter understanding of the phrase would be more congenial to Duran since then Rabad would be holding that even though belief in God's incorporeality is an article of faith, if one makes a mistake concerning it, one is not thereby a heretic.

rah –knowing that it was the teaching of the Torah– is a denier and is excluded from Israel.[9]

Duran here modifies Maimonides' strict position with respect to heresy. One is not considered to be a heretic simply for holding false beliefs. In order to be a heretic one must adopt beliefs which one knows to be rejected by the Torah or reject beliefs which one knows to be taught by the Torah. Duran makes this clear a bit further on:

> You also ought to know that one who has properly accepted the roots of the Torah but who was moved to deviate from them by the depth of his speculation and who thereby believed concerning one of the branches of the faith the opposite of what has been accepted as what one ought to believe and tries to explain the verses of Scripture according to his belief, even though he errs, is no denier. For he was not brought to this deviation by heresy at all and if he found a tradition from the Sages to the effect that he ought to turn from the position he adopted, he would do so. He only holds that belief because he thinks that it is the intention of the Torah. Therefore, even though he errs he is not a heretic according to what is agreed upon by our people since he accepted the roots of our Torah as he should.

Duran's position is precisely the opposite of Abravanel's. For Abravanel, deviation from any Torah teaching, whether intentional or not, constitutes heresy. For Duran, there is no teaching so basic that if one makes any honest mistake about it, one is thereby condemned as a heretic.[10]

Duran's teaching in this regard did not find many sympathetic listeners in the late Middle Ages. It was explicitly criticized by Abraham Bibago[11] and Isaac Abravanel[12] (although they both attributed the position to Rabad, ignoring Duran altogether) and Joseph Albo could not make up his mind about it.[13]

---

9   *Ohev Mishpat*, p. 15a.

10 This, at least, is Duran's expressed position. Whether he would be willing to stick to it in all cases, is another question altogether.

11 See Bibago, *Derekh Emunah*, III.5 (p. 102c).

12 See *Principles*, chapter 12 (p. 113).

13 See Albo's *Sefer ha-Ikkarim* I.1-2. I argue for the claim of Albo's ambivalence on this issue in the fifth chapter of my *Dogma*.

One could easily get the impression that Duran and possibly Rabad were alone in resisting the hard line on heresy in the Jewish Middle Ages. I think that this impression may be mistaken; a careful reading of Hasdai Crescas' (1340-1410) comments in the matter of belief suggests that he may have held a position similar in important respects to that of Rabad and Duran.

This proposal of mine concerning Crescas may appear surprising in light of the fact that Crescas explicitly states that if a person denies even one of the beliefs which he lists as principles than that person is a sectarian.[14] Crescas does not state that such disbelief must be intended as heresy in order to count as heresy. Despite all this, a close examination of Crescas' analysis of the possibility of *commanding* belief in God opens up the possibility that he may have allowed for non-heretical disbelief, even concerning the principles of the Torah.

Maimonides had asserted that belief in God was not only a "foundation of the Torah"[15] but that it was also the first and most fundamental of the commandments.[16] But "he who counted belief in God's existence as a positive commandment," Crescas insisted, "committed a notorious error."[17] Crescas presents a number of arguments against Maimonides' claim that belief in God could be counted as a commandment. He phrases the second of these arguments as follows:

> It will be seen from the meaning and definition of the term 'commandment' that it may be used only of things subject to will and choice. If [putative] commandments applied to beliefs and teachings-which are not subject to will and choice – the meaning of the term 'commandment' could not apply to them. This is one of the subjects we will investigate in what follows, with God's help.[18]

Crescas' argument may be rephrased as follows: William James to the contrary, we cannot will to believe things. But the very concept of a command-

---

14 Crescas, *Or Ha-Shem*, II, Introduction (Vienna, 1859, p. 61a; in the edition of Shlomo Fisher, p. 123). On Crescas, see Lasker, "Chasdai Crescas." This article contains a useful and up to date bibliography.

15 In the first of his Thirteen Principles.

16 "Laws of the Foundation of the Torah," I.1.

17 See *Or Ha-Shem*, preface (p. 3a; Fisher ed., pp. 9-12).

18 *Ibid.*

ment makes sense only in the context of will and choice: we cannot fairly be commanded to do things which we cannot choose to do or refrain from doing. So we cannot fairly be commanded to believe anything.

Crescas promises, we have just seen, to investigate further the issue of will and choice with respect to commandments. This he does in *Or ha-Shem* II.v.5. Crescas, it is well-known, maintained a doctrine of strict physical determinism.[19] In the chapter under discussion he raises the question, how is it possible to reconcile God's justice in reward and punishment with a position that holds that all of our acts are determined in accord with the laws of causality before they are done?

Crescas introduces the distinction between "determinism accompanied by a feeling of compulsion and necessity" and determinism unaccompanied by a feeling of compulsion and necessity."[20] We are subject to "determinism accompanied by a feeling of compulsion and necessity" when we are aware of the fact that we act, not freely, but in accordance with or as a result of causes over which we have no control; that is to say, we *feel* compelled, not free. It might be urged on this basis that reward and punishment justly apply in cases where we are not aware of the fact that our actions are determined. Crescas rejects this approach on the grounds that reward and punishment cannot depend upon whether or not we *feel* determined, because, in point of fact, we *are* determined.[21]

Crescas rejects this approach on the further grounds that it makes it impossible to account for the fact that we are rewarded and punished for our beliefs. How so? Well, for one thing, will and choice play no role in beliefs (i.e., we cannot choose to believe or disbelieve) and we are aware of the fact that our beliefs are determined. That is to say, we all realize full well, Crescas maintains, that we cannot choose to believe or disbelieve. Therefore, if the *feeling* of being free played some role in making just reward and punishment possible, we could not be rewarded for our beliefs since we do not even feel that we are free to accept them or reject them.

---

19 For discussion of this issue see Feldman, "Theological Determinism." Aviezer Ravitzky reproduces the text of chapters 5 and 6 in his article, "Development," from which they will be cited below.

20 *Or Ha-Shem* II.v; Ravitzky, p. 450.

21 *Ibid.*

Well, then, if our actions are determined, and if our awareness or lack of awareness of that determination plays no role in the justice of rewarding and punishing us for actions over which we have no control, how can we then be rewarded for observing the commandments and punished for violating them? Crescas' answer is simple. Actions are subject to choice and will and that –as opposed to the physical/causal *freedom* of our choice and will– is the criterion that makes them fit objects of reward and punishment.

Fine and good; but what about beliefs? They are not subject to choice and will.[22] Here the main issue in Crescas' discussion comes into play: we are not rewarded for holding certain beliefs, but for the pleasure and joy we feel in holding them. This joy, Crescas holds, is the result of choice and will. There is also a further point to be noted: we can choose to hasten the process of adopting a belief (through study and reflection, it seems[23]) and for this we can also be rewarded.

We may now revert to the question of inadvertent heresy. In order to understand what might be Crescas' position here it will be helpful to distinguish among the following cases:

(a) a person commits a crime –let us say murder– in the mistaken belief that he is commanded by the Torah so to act.

(b) a person knows that the Torah teaches a certain belief strives to adopt that belief, does not succeed in adopting it, and feels anguish over the fact.

(c) a person mistakenly thinks that the Torah teaches a certain belief (e.g., God's corporeality), holds that, belief, and feels joy over the fact that he holds a Torah belief.

In each of these cases the Torah is being violated unintentionally. What can Crescas say about them? These are not cases with which he explicitly deals, but perhaps we can extrapolate from what he does say to what he might or

---

22 As Crescas proves to his own satisfaction in II.v.5.

23 This, at least, is the way Crescas is interpreted by Isaac Abravanel. See *Principles* chapter 11 (pp. 108-109) and chapter 17 (pp. 154-155).

ought to say. With respect to the first case we may make the following comments. According to Crescas we are rewarded and punished for our *actions*.[24] Murder is an action and it is reasonable to assume that Crescas would hold in this case that the murderer would be punished. But, according to Crescas, we are also rewarded for our *intentions*.[25] Thus, one might expect him to say that the proper intention with which the murder was done, while not a cause for reward, perhaps, should at least mitigate the severity of the punishment. But on the other hand, Torah and tradition are quite clear on what ought and ought not to be done. There seems, therefore, to be little room for mitigation here.

With respect to the second case, that of the anguished non-believer, it would seem that consistency would demand that if we are rewarded for the joy we feel in holding correct beliefs, perhaps we ought also to be rewarded for the anguish we feel when we are unable to hold those correct beliefs. This may be going a bit far but it is certainly reasonable to suggest that Crescas would see the anguish as exculpating the sin of the person in question at least to some degree and quite properly mitigating the severity of his punishment.

The third case is that of the inadvertent or well-intentioned misbeliever. This is the misbeliever condemned by Maimonides and Abravanel and exonerated by Duran (and, at least in the case of corporeality, by Rabad). Crescas says nothing about such a case. We can, however, attempt to construct a position which is consistent with and perhaps derived from other statements of Crescas'.

We ought to take note of the following facts. Crescas himself admits that the basic teachings of the Torah are not as well-known as they should be. In the Introduction to the *Or ha-Shem* he writes:

> And yet one more, for it is great: concerning the fundaments of belief and the foundations of the Law and the principles of its roots. Until the completion of the Talmud, there never occurred any division of opinion with regard to them, but they were well-known and agreed-upon among the sages of our nation–with the exception of the secrets of the Law, including the Account of Creation and the Account of the Chariot, which were in the hands of the exceptional

---

24 At II.v.3. (Vienna, p. 48a; Fisher, p. 213) Crescas argues that punishment is a consequence of sin in the same way that burning is a consequence of approaching too closely to a fire.

25 See *Or Ha-Shem* II.v.5 (Ravitzky, p. 452).

individuals, the modest ones, and the modest ones transmitted them to their disciples at certain times and under certain conditions. However, when the generations became weak, and the hands of those who held the received Oral Law and the concealed things of its mysteries and secrets became feeble, the wisdom of our wise men perished and the understanding of our prudent men became hidden.[26]

Confusion and ignorance surround the principles of the Torah so much that, according to Crescas, even Maimonides strayed from the truth:

And many among the sons of our people exalted themselves to interpret [true prophetic] visions and shut up the sealed words of prophecy by means of dreams and vanities and by means of the children of strangers. It came to the extent that some of the greatest of our sages were drawn after their words, and they prettified themselves with their discourses and adorned themselves with their proofs. And among them at their head was the great master, our Rabbi Moses ben Maimon of blessed memory, who even with the greatness of his intellect, the extraordinarily encompassing scope of his Talmudic knowledge, and the breadth of his mind, when he meditated upon the books and discourses of the philosophers, they seduced him and he was seduced! From their weak premises, he made columns and foundations to the mysteries of the Law, in his book which he called *Guide of the Perplexed*.[27]

Maimonides may have been mistaken, but at least his mistakes were prompted by the best of intentions. Such was not the case with those who arose after him, claiming to be his students:

Now, whereas the intent of the Master in this was desirable, there have arisen today rebellious servants, and they have turned into heresy the words of the living God. They mutilated holy sacrifices. They inflicted upon the words of the Master blemish in the place of beauty.[28]

---

26 *Or Ha-Shem*, Introduction (Vienna, p. 2b; Fisher ed., p. 7). I quote from the translation provided in W. Harvey's dissertation, "Hasdai Crescas' Critique," pp. 361-362.

27 *Or Ha-Shem*, Introduction (Vienna, p. 2b; Fisher ed., p. 8); Harvey dissertation, pp. 362-363.

28 *Ibid.*

From these passages we learn a number of suggestive facts. First, confusion and ignorance dominate discussions of the principles of Judaism. From this we might expect that Crescas would exonerate a person whose belief was not occasioned by rebelliousness. This leads to our second point: Crescas does exactly that. He exonerates Maimonides for his mistaken approach to the basic teachings of the Torah, since his intentions were pure. Crescas condemns those who claim to follow Maimonides, and this is our third point, on the grounds that their deviations from Torah teachings were not well-intentioned. In other words, Maimonides may actually have been guilty of misbelief but since (a) his misbelief was well-intentioned and (b) he had reason to be confused about the basic teachings of Judaism, his misbelief can be excused.

This is fine and good with respect to Maimonides. Can we assume that unintentional misbelief on the part of all Jews would also be excusable? I think that the probable answer to that question is yes. As noted above, Crescas maintains that one is rewarded for the joy one feels at holding Torah teachings. In particular, he says:

> Chapter Six: an explanation that what has been established here speculatively accords with the doctrine of the sages. This is so for two matters have been established here. The first is that the belief concerning doctrines is acquired without will and the second is that reward and punishment are connected to the will, whether we have reference to the reward for the desire for, labor invested in, and, happiness at being of this religious sect, or if we have reference to the punishment for the opposite.[29]

What particular joy is it, then, which merits reward? The joy of holding a Torah teaching which makes one "of this religious sect." This joy is contrasted with the cause of punishment which is the opposite of the feeling of joy at membership in "this religious sect." From this it seems we are punished for our *conscious* rejection of "this religious sect." What then can we say of a person who holds a certain belief because he thinks it is taught by the Torah (when in fact it is not), thereby identifying himself with the Jewish "religious sect," and feels great joy at the holding of that belief and that identification with Judaism? The

---

29 Ravitzky, p. 452.

very strictest consistency would seem to demand that such a person actually be rewarded. Demanding such consistency of Crescas may be asking too much of him. But, given his comments quoted above from the Introduction to the *Or ha-Shemi* and his emphatic assertion that the reward for beliefs depends upon the joy with which they are held, it seems not altogether unlikely that were Crescas confronted with a Jew who held mistaken beliefs concerning the principles of Judaism but held these beliefs because he thought that they were Torah teachings, and felt joy at thus fulfilling his obligations as a Jew, that he (Crescas) might very well admit that, at the very least, this mistaken but well-intentioned Jew would not be punished for what, objectively speaking, is heresy. In other words, it seems that on the issue of unintentional sinning with respect to heresy, Crescas might side with Duran and not with Maimonides and Abravanel.

There are a number of reasons for suspecting that Crescas might not find this consequence of his position at all upsetting. We noted above that Maimonides presented his principles as "foundations of the Torah," supporting them with verses drawn from Scripture. He furthermore makes attaining a portion in the world to come dependent upon acceptance of his principles and defines a Jew by that acceptance. In his discussion, we may thus say, Maimonides was asking a religious or theological question: what beliefs does the Torah demand that Jews accept as fundamental? Rejecting the principles involves the violation of Torah commands. Thus it is not surprising that Maimonides repeatedly decries as heretics those who question or reject his principles and condemns them to exclusion from the world to come.

Crescas, on the other hand, was not asking a religious question so much as a logical or structural one: what beliefs must a Jew accept as fundamental in order to be consistent? And, where Maimonides emphasizes the centrality of the question of salvation (asking, what principles must one accept in order to merit a share in the world to come?), the question barely comes up in Crescas at all.[30] This may be some indication that Crescas had no compelling interest in excluding from the fold (and from the world to come) Jews who did not accept the principles as he promulgated them, especially if they did not mean thereby to rebel against the Torah.

---

30 At II.v.5 (Ravitzky, p. 450) Crescas notes that the Sages exclude heretics from the world to come. This is the only reference to such exclusion that I have encountered in Crescas.

We ought to note further that the Maimonides-Abravanel "hard-line" position ignores the category of unintentional transgression altogether. It seems odd that Halakhah should allow that category to obtain with respect to actions but not with respect to belief.[31] This point brings us to another reason why Crescas might have been happy with the position I have imputed to him in this essay.

Speaking in the very broadest of terms we may say that when Maimonides posited his principles of faith (an act for which he had no clear-cut precedent within the Jewish tradition) he give expression to a conception of faith radically at variance with Biblical-Talmudic usage. Judaism, for the Bible and Talmud, was not a series of propositions which could be either affirmed or denied. The Torah and Sages do not demand belief *that* certain propositions are true or false; they do demand belief *in* God. The Bible and Talmud do not conceive of Judaism as a science – affirming propositions which could be true or false.[32]

We may express this in other terms. The Bible and Talmud present God as primarily free, undetermined will and as the source of moral imperatives. This God is mysterious and transcendent; He can be encountered, but He cannot be described. A religion conceived of in these terms has little place for theological systematization, has little place for theology at all. It does, however, have plenty of room for *faith*, so long as that faith is defined more in terms of dispositions and states of mind, rather than in terms of statements which can be proven.

Speaking generally, in Greek thought the term belief (*pistis*) was ordinarily conceived more in propositional terms (i.e., that one accepts or rejects certain propositions) than in terms of trust or faith. This is, perhaps, a reflection of or related to the fact that in Greek thought by and large God is conceived of as the source or guarantor of order (cosmological order for the pre-Socratics, moral order for Plato, and physical and metaphysical order for Aristotle). Christianity from its inception, and Islam from at least the time of the Kalam onward both seem to define faith in Greek, rather than in Biblical and rabbinic terms; that is, in terms of the specific propositional content of faith. Formal systems of dogma are a logical outgrowth of such a conception of faith. In laying down

---

31 Compare Crescas' comments at the end of II.v.5 (Ravitzky, p. 452).

32 This distinction between belief *in* and belief *that* is subjected to a sophisticated philosophical analysis in Seeskin, "Faith." My indebtedness to Seeskin's discussion will be obvious to anyone who reads his paper. I revisit this issue in the first chapter of *Must*.

his principles Maimonides gave expression to the fact that by his day Jews, too, had begun to understand their religion in propositional terms.

The Rabbis, who understood faith in terms of trust in God, i.e., in terms of the way in which the believer related to God, could allow for error with respect to the specific beliefs of the Torah, since their main concern was not the niceties of theological formulations, but to see to it "that man does justice, loves mercy, and walks humbly with the Lord."

Maimonides, on the other hand, defining faith in terms of its specific propositional content would have good reason to be upset if the propositions held were incorrect. Whereas an attitude of trust in God is not necessarily compromised if some of one's specific conceptions about God are mistaken, if one's faith in God is defined in terms of certain specific propositions about God then that faith is certainly defective if one affirms incorrect propositions. Thus, there is little room for Maimonides to allow for error with respect to beliefs.

Where does Crescas fit into this picture? There is no doubt that many of the same forces which forced other Jewish thinkers to adopt basically alien categories of thought in their own understanding of Judaism were operative in Crescas' case. It is unlikely that any medieval Jew was aware of the ways in which his conception of Judaism differed from that of the Bible and Talmud. It is only our 20-20 hindsight which makes that possible. But there are indications that Crescas, more self-consciously than any other medieval Jewish thinker, resisted the hellenization of Jewish thought, one of the clearest expressions of which was Maimonides' creed.

Among these indications, we may note, in addition to Crescas' explicit comments in the Introduction to the *Or ha-Shem*, the fact that for Maimonides human perfection, human felicity in the greatest measure possible and the purpose of the Torah were all one and the same: intellectual perfection. This is as it should be: if Torah faith is defined as a series of propositions then the more perfectly one adheres to the Torah the more perfect is one's acquisition of the truths contained in those propositions.

Crescas subjects this conception of human perfection and the purpose of the Torah to devastating criticism.[33] To the Maimonidean ideal Crescas opposes another, one far-removed from a conception of faith understood in

---

33 See Harvey, "Crescas' of Critique of Philosophic Happiness."

propositional terms and much closer to classic rabbinic conceptions of man's proper relationship to God: love. The end of human existence, the purpose of the Torah (and of creation), and the greatest felicity to which a human being can aspire is the love of God –not the intellectual love of Maimonides, attainable only by the philosopher, but warm, passionate love, the route to which was the observance of the commandments; love not of the intellect but of the emotions, love attainable by all who worship God through the commandments.

If I am correct in seeing Crescas' analysis of the end of humanity and of the Torah as an attempt to resist Greek categories of thought and revert to a more pristinely Jewish approach, and if I am further correct in suggesting that this second approach was by its very nature open to the concept of unintentional sinning with respect to misbelief, then we have further grounds for accepting the interpretation of Crescas offered above and may more safely assert that in the question of what we may call inadvertent heresy the logic of his position forces him to stand with Duran in opposition to Maimonides and Abravanel.

This said, it ought to be emphasized, to avoid misunderstanding, that the position attributed here to Duran and probably to Crescas –that one who rejects a Torah belief by mistake and with no intention to rebel against God is neither cut off from the community of Israel nor excluded from the world to come– is not a position of theological anarchy. This position does not maintain that there are no correct beliefs (i.e., it does not deny the concept of orthodoxy); rather, it maintains that the criterion of true orthodoxy is not the rigid acceptance of certain carefully formulated, catechismal beliefs so much as the general acceptance of the Torah and trust in God.

It ought to be further noted that the position attributed here to Duran and probably to Crescas does not maintain that a person who mistakenly rejects a belief taught by the Torah, or a person who mistakenly accepts a belief rejected by the Torah, ought to be allowed to persist in the mistake. Such a person must be corrected, but ought not to be castigated as an unbeliever and condemned to perdition.

POSTSCRIPT:

This brings to an end my attempt to contribute something to our better understanding of the debate concerning heresy among medieval Jewish thinkers. I want now to build upon the analysis presented here in an attempt to answer the question with which this paper opened: for a Jew today who is committed to Halakhah, what is heresy?

Before turning to offer an answer to this question I think that I must first justify the very fact of raising it. Of what possible use, it may be objected, is the category of heresy? Does it not serve only to divide Jew from Jew, ruling some to be in the fold, and others out of Jewish discourse, why unearth it?

Despite the initial plausibility of this objection, I think that ultimately it is based upon assumptions which are, at least, open to question. In the first place, the category of heresy is now dead. Any Jew seriously committed to Halakhah cannot ignore the sorts of judgments quoted above at the beginning of this essay: if it is forbidden to associate with heretics, then it is important to know who heretics are. In the second place, the objection is based, it seems, upon a view which sees Judaism as fundamentally a pluralistic faith and which sees Jews as fundamentally tied together by cultural and ethnic as opposed to religious ties. If these views are rejected the objection loses much of its force.

We may now return to our question. How ought a traditionally observant Jew respond to another Jew who deviates from the tradition as he understands it, but whose deviation is motivated not by rebelliousness or rejection, but by a different understanding of what the Torah is and demands? Maimonides' answer is clear: the deviating Jew must be condemned outright as a heretic. He or she is condemned to perdition. But Duran and (probably) Crescas might respond differently, or at least they provide us with a model which makes a different response possible. Such a response would involve, not the acceptance of the position of the deviating Jew, but the acceptance of the deviating Jew as a person whose position has to be corrected. There would be no need on this approach to condemn the deviating Jew as a heretic and none of the laws which apply to heretics would apply to him.

Such a response, it must be emphasized, is not truly a pluralistic response in any serious sense since it does not recognize the deviant position as legitimate. Such recognition would indeed involve the theological anarchy feared by Abravanel. It must be further noted that it was much easier for Duran to adopt such a position in the Middle Ages than it would be to do so today: in the vast majority of cases even persons who deviated from orthodox beliefs did not deviate from orthodox practice.

But there are good reasons for urging an halakhic Jew today to adopt a Duranian as opposed to Maimonidean position on the question of heresy. In the first place, such a position is inclusive as opposed to exclusive, and makes serious theological discourse among religiously committed Jews of various persuasions possible. In the second place, it can be argued that such a position is closer to the spirit and practice of classical Judaism than is the position of Maimonides, reflecting as it does the influence of alien categories of thought. The Duranian position, allowing as it does for unintentional, exculpable sin with respect to beliefs, is consistent with rabbinic conceptions of unintentional sin while the Maimonidean position ignores this category altogether in connection with beliefs.

What is heresy, then? Heresy is the conscious, purposful rejection of faith in God and His Torah. It is not the rejection of traditional Torah beliefs by individuals who repose faith in God and in His Torah.

CHAPTER SEVEN
Maimonides' Thirteen Principles
and the Structure of the *Guide of the Perplexed*

A mong the many enigmas associated with Maimonides's *Guide of the Perplexed* there are two that are usually ignored, but deserve attention, and ought to be seen as related. First, why did Maimonides divide the *Guide* into three parts? Second, why did Maimonides not mention in the *Guide* his "Thirteen Principles of Faith" which he had promulgated in his earliest major work, the *Commentary on the Mishnah*? Why did Maimonides divide the *Guide* into three parts? He himself never addresses this question directly, although he insists that he wrote the work with great care and that "nothing has been mentioned out of its place, save with a view to explaining some matter in its proper place."[1] It may be assumed, therefore, that Maimonides's tripartite division of his book was not accidental. The question of the structure of the *Guide* is complicated by the fact that Maimonides informs his readers that he wrote his book in such a fashion as to confuse the vulgar and hide his true opinions from them. Maimonides intimates that one of the keys to the understanding of these true opinions is the understanding of the interconnection of the chapters in the *Guide:* "If you wish to grasp the totality of what this treatise contains you must connect its chapters one with another" (p. 15).

A number of modern scholars have sought to connect the *Guide*'s chapters one with another, and mention ought to be made of the studies of Rawidowicz, Strauss, and Berman.[2] On the question of the tripartite division of the *Guide*

---

1   *Guide*, Introduction, p. 15.

2   See Strauss, "How to Begin," and Berman, "Structure." Even though not directly relevant to the question of the tri-partite structure of the *Guide*, note should be made of Jospe, "Garden," an important study of the chapter divisions of the work.

Rawidowicz concluded that Part I contains a critique of erroneous views and serves to introduce Part II, concerning theory, and Part III, concerning practice.[3] Strauss divides the work into seven sections, ignoring Maimonides's own division of three parts. Berman, following Rawidowicz and to some extent Strauss, argues that Part I deals with "the imagination and its perils," Part II with "the domain of the theoretical intellect," and Part III with "the relationship between theory and practice." In my view, the analyses of Rawidowicz, Strauss, and Berman, while clarifying many aspects of the *Guide's* structure, do not succeed in fully accounting for its tripartite division.

Why did Maimonides fail to mention the Thirteen Principles in the *Guide*?[4] First put forward in the *Commentary on the Mishnah*, these principles were reiterated by Maimonides with almost no changes in the *Mishneh Torah*.[5] Both these works were written before the *Guide*. In his *Treatise on Resurrection*, written after the *Guide*, he intimates that he still considered the Thirteen Principles as the definitive statement of his views on the subject.[6] We also find references to the principles in Maimonides's *Medical Aphorisms*.[7] Furthermore, at the end of his life Maimonides still considered the principles important enough to be worthy of revision and improvement.[8] Given the importance the Thirteen Principles evidently had for Maimonides, both before and after he composed the *Guide*, why, then, did he fail to mention them in that work? The proposal I shall develop here is that the Thirteen Principles *are* present implicitly in the *Guide*. More precisely, I suggest that the overall structure of

---

3   Rawidowicz, "Structure."

4   Isaac Husik raises this issue without, however, proposing an explanation for it; *History*, p. 407.

5   In "Laws of Repentance," III. 6-8. On the differences between the two versions, see my *Dogma*, pp. 21-24.

6   Maimonides, *Iggerot* (Kafih), p. 72.

7   In Kafih, *Iggerot*, pp. 148-167, esp. p. 159. Berman understands this text, in which Maimonides makes reference to his composition on the *usul al-din* ("principles of religion") as referring to the *Guide*. If this is correct, then we have here a case of Maimonides himself referring to the *Guide* as a work concerning the principles of religion. Kafih on the other hand (*Iggerot*, pp. 148n., 159n.), maintains that the text was written before the *Guide* and refers to the *Mishneh Torah* and *Commentary on the Mishnah*. If he is correct, then we have further evidence supporting the claim that Maimonides considered the Thirteen Principles as important and authoritative throughout his life. See further, Berman, "Disciple" and Twersky, *Introduction*, p. 361n.

8   *Dogma*, pp. 53-61. Marc Shapiro published a letter from Rabbi Kafih to me on the subject. See Shapiro, *Studies*, p. 25 (Hebrew pagination).

the *Guide* – at least with respect to its gross anatomy –and especially with regard to its tripartite division, may be understood as reflecting the tripartite
structure of the Thirteen Principles.

Maimonides presents his Thirteen Principles in the context of a commentary on the following text (Mishnah Sanhedrin X.1):

> All Israelites have a share in the world to come, as it states, *Thy people are all*
> *righteous, they shall inherit the land forever* (Isaiah 60:21). But the following
> have no share in the world to come: he who says there is no resurrection taught
> in the Torah, that the Torah is not from heaven, and the *epikoros*. Rabbi Akiva
> says: "Even he who reads in the external books, and he who whispers over a
> wound, saying, *I will put none of the diseases upon thee, which I have put upon*
> *the Egyptians; for I am the Lord that healeth thee* (Exodus 15:26)." Abba Saul
> says: "Even he who pronounces the name according to its letters."

Maimonides lists those beliefs a person must hold in order to be counted
as an "Israelite." They may be summarized as follows: (1) that God exists, (2)
that God is one, (3) that God is incorporeal, (4) that God is eternal, (5) that
God alone may be worshipped, (6) that prophecy exists, (7) that the prophecy of Moses is superior to all other prophecy, (8) that the Torah was divinely
revealed, (9) that the Torah is immutable, (10) that God knows the deeds of
men, (11) that God rewards the righteous and punishes the wicked,(12) that
the Messiah will come, (13) that the dead will be resurrected. One of the earliest scholars to comment on these principles was R. Shimon ben Zemah Duran (1361-1444). Duran divides Maimonides's thirteen principles into three
groups: principles 1-5 deal with God, principles 6-9 deal with the Torah, and
principles 10-13 deal with retribution.[9] Duran also links the three groups to
terms in the mishnah *(Sanhedrin* X.1) cited just above: the *epikoros* denies the
principles dealing with God, "Torah from heaven" refers to the second group of
principles, and "resurrection" to the third. Once stated, Duran's tripartite division of the principles, and the relation of each part to a term in the mishnah,
is so obvious that it is difficult to believe that Maimonides did not intend it.
Could we rely on the argument of *consensus gentium,* the case would be estab-

---

9   For details, see *Dogma,* ch.3.

lished: almost all subsequent scholars, from Joseph Albo in the fifteenth century to Arthur Hyman in our own day,[10] have followed Duran's suggestions.

It is my contention that an important parallelism obtains between the subject matter of each part of the *Guide* and the subject matter of each group of principles as divided (if not necessarily as named) by Duran. The subject matter of the first group of principles is God: this is clearly the subject matter of the first part of the *Guide.* The subject matter of the second group of principles is prophecy in general and Mosaic (revelatory) prophecy in particular. This, I will argue below, is the subject matter of the second part of the *Guide.* The subject matter of the third group of principles is reward and punishment, and in particular the reward and punishment attendant upon the observance or nonobservance of the Torah of Moses. *Guide* Part III similarly concerns the rewards and punishments attendant upon the Torah of Moses and, like the third group of principles, deals with the questions of God's knowledge and providence, both of which are intimately connected with the question of reward and punishment.

The first part of the *Guide* is devoted to the following subjects; interpretations of Biblical terms that seem to impute corporeality to God (I. 1-50); divine attributes (I. 51-60); the divine names (I. 61-70); and Kalam proofs for the existence, unity, and incorporeality of God (I. 71-76). The first three principles, God's existence, unity, and incorporeality, are explicitly and exhaustively taken up here. The fourth principle, God's eternity (i.e., God's ontic priority) is discussed explicitly in I. 35, where all the first five principles are discussed and where their interrelated character is made clear, and in chapters 57, 68, 70, and 72. The fifth principle, that God alone may be worshipped, is in addition discussed and its importance emphasized in I. 36. While no one is likely to contest the claim that the first part of the *Guide* deals almost exclusively with the subject of God, the truth of my thesis concerning the parallelism between groups two and three of the principles and Parts II and III of the *Guide* is less immediately obvious and will have to be shown in greater detail.

In the second part of the *Guide,* we find the following major subjects: Aristotelian premises necessary for the proof of God's existence, unity, and incorporeality (introduction); Aristotelian proofs of God's existence, unity, and

---

10 Hyman, "Principles."

cy (II.1); the Separate Intellects (II. 2-12); creation (II. 13-31); and
pr.   (II. 32-48).

According to the scheme proposed here the introduction and first chapter of Part II seems to belong in the first part of the *Guide,* dealing as they do
with God, while the discussions of the Separate Intellects and creation would
seem to be out of place as well, and perhaps better off in Part I. The connection between these two discussions and prophecy, however, is not difficult to
discover. Maimonides, as he himself points out in II. 25, had to posit creation
in order to make Mosaic prophecy (the revelation of the Torah) possible.
Furthermore, he explicitly linked prophecy and creation at the beginning of
II. 32, saying that "the opinions of people concerning prophecy are like their
opinions concerning the eternity of the world or its creation in time" (p. 360).[11]
Maimonides' discussion of the Separate Intellects is basically an analysis of the
divine "overflow" (emanation) that is the basis for prophecy (and other phenomena). But what of Maimonides's Aristotelian proofs of God's existence,
unity, and incorporeality, with which he opens Part II? In the first instance it
ought to be pointed out that these proofs serve as the beginning and basis for
the analysis of the divine "overflow," which itself is a prerequisite for the discussion of prophecy. They are thus entirely germane to the subjects of prophecy
and revelation. Furthermore, without God, prophecy as anything more than a
psychological phenomenon becomes impossible. It might further be suggested
that Maimonides included this material here in order to demonstrate to the
philosophic Jew that accepting the basic premises of Aristotelianism, even to
the extent of being able to prove God's existence, unity, and incorporeality
thereby, does not commit one to belief in the eternity of the world. Belief in
eternity, in turn, would involve belief in the necessary existence of the world,
making it impossible to interpret revelation and prophecy in any other than
a wholly naturalistic fashion.[12] Be this last as it may, there can be little doubt

---

11 The question of how to relate the three positions on creation with the three positions
    on prophecy has become a crux of Maimonidean interpretation. Almost every possible
    correlation has been suggested. See Kaplan, "Miraculous Element," Davidson, "Secret
    Position," Harvey, "Third Approach," and Malino, "Aritotle on Eternity."

12 As Herbert Davidson points out ("Secret Position," p. 18), Maimonides, following Aristotle,
    held eternity and necessity to imply each other. This being so, were the world eternal, it could
    not have been created by God's free will. In an eternal, necessarily existent world, revelation
    can be interpreted only as a purely natural phenomenon. This reduces it to nothing other than

that the focus of Part II is the epistemology of the phenomenon of prophecy in general (corresponding to Principle 6), and of the unique legislative prophecy of Moses in particular (corresponding to Principles 7-9).

There are five major subjects dealt with in Part III of the *Guide*: explanation of Ezekiel's vision (*ma'aseh merkavah*) (III.1-7); evil (III.8-12); providence and God's knowledge (III. 13-24); rational explanation of the commandments (III.25-50); and human perfection (III. 51-54).

Certain correspondences between the third group of principles and this part of the *Guide* are immediately obvious. Principle 10 asserts that God knows the deeds of human beings, and Principle 11 asserts that God rewards the righteous and punishes the wicked. These principles clearly correspond to the discussions in the *Guide* of God's knowledge and providence. The discussion of evil is a necessary prerequisite for Maimonides's analyses of both providence and God's knowledge. The explanation of Ezekiel's vision (*ma'aseh merkavah*) – which Maimonides construes as "divine science" or metaphysics – concerns God's control of the world, just as the driver controls the chariot. This clearly relates to the issues of God's knowledge and reward and punishment.

We may also understand the essential correspondence between the last group of principles and the last part of the *Guide* in another fashion if we follow up and supplement an interpretation of the principles suggested by Arthur Hyman. In his study of the principles Hyman ("Principles," pp. 142-143) asserts that the second group of principles "is meant to guarantee the validity of the law [Torah]" (which is certainly what Maimonides is trying to do in the *Guide*, Part II), while the third group of principles is "required for instilling obedience to the Law." And that, I submit, is exactly what Maimonides sought to do in the third part of the *Guide*. The objective of the third group of principles, in Hyman's analysis, was to instill obedience to the Torah in simple Jews. The third part of the *Guide* sought to encourage obedience to the Torah in philosophically sophisticated Jews; hence its philosophic accounts of evil, providence, and especially, the rational explanation of the commandments. We may express the correspondence between the third group of principles and the third part of the *Guide* in another way, one that supplements rather than

---

a consequence of Moses' perfection and makes impossible its claim to immutability, for why could not another Moses arise?

---

contradicts the position just staked out. Both the third group of principles, and the third part of the *Guide* are meant to lead society[13] (as expressed in Principle 12, concerning the Messiah) and the individual (as expressed in Principle 13, concerning resurrection) to perfection and excellence. Principles 12 and 13 spell out in detail the claim of Principle 11 (divine reward and punishment), which in turn is based upon Principle 10 (God's knowledge).

I have shown the essential congruence between the third group of principles and the third part of the *Guide*; both deal with the rewards and punishments attendant upon obedience or disobedience of the Torah. This is true whether or not we accept Hyman's interpretation of the principles. But the argument may be pushed yet further. Principles 10 and 11, as noted above, are explicitly discussed in Part III. But what about messiah and resurrection? How also can we explain the connection between the concluding chapters of the *Guide* (III. 51-54) and the last group of principles?

In the first instance we may point out that the messianic era is alluded to in III. 11 and that it is by no means implausible to suggest that in effect the focus of Part III of the *Guide* is at least in part messianic: observance of the Torah leads man to true knowledge, which in turn abolishes enmity (see III. 11, p. 441) and thus brings about the messianic era.

A suggestion made by David Hartman, in his *Maimonides: Torah and Philosophic Quest*, points the way toward a further solution of these difficulties. Hartman (pp. 65-86) argues that according to Maimonides, the simple Jew, motivated by *yir'ah* (awe, reverence, fear of God), focuses his or her eschatological hopes on messianism (and its concomitant, resurrection). The more perfected (philosophic) Jew, on the other hand, motivated by *ahavah* (love of God), focuses his or her eschatological hopes on *olam ha-ba* (the world to come) with its uninterrupted apprehension of God.

Although I think that Hartman's suggestion is clearly wrong on the issue of messianism (we have just noted the messianic tone of *Guide* III), his overall thesis may be helpful in further understanding the relationship between the third group of the principles and *Guide* III. The third group of principles is aimed at the simple Jew. It encourages obedience to the Torah by positing that God knows of one's activities and by holding out the hope of a reward (res-

---

13 See *Guide*, III. 27.

urrection) that the simple Jew can understand. The third part of the *Guide* is intended to do the same thing with respect to the philosophic Jew. It justifies belief in God's providence and knowledge of individuals; it explains that the seemingly irrational laws of the Torah are susceptible of rational explanation (and hence worthy of obedience) and holds out the hope of a reward attractive to the philosophic Jew, *olam ha-ba*. This latter is the subject matter of *Guide* III. 51-54, both in terms of a future life and in terms of how the commitment to love of God and *olam ha-ba* are manifested in the philosophic Jew's life in this world.[14]

In sum, the first group of principles and the first part of the *Guide* deal with God, the second group of principles and the second part of the Guide deal with Torah and prophecy, while the third group of principles and the third part of the *Guide* both concern God's knowledge of the world, the goals of his Torah, and the reward and punishment attendant upon its observance or nonobservance.

We may now answer the questions with which I opened this discussion. I have shown why Maimonides divided the *Guide* into three parts and have shown that, far from failing to mention his thirteen principles in the *Guide*, Maimonides actually structures the whole work upon them. I do not mean to imply that every chapter and subject of the *Guide* may and ought to be understood in the light of this proposal; nor do I mean to imply that other proposals advanced concerning the structure of the *Guide* (such as those of Rawidowicz, Berman, and Strauss) are necessarily incorrect. I submit, rather, that one of Maimonides's aims in writing the *Guide of the Perplexed* was to explain in philosophic terms the truths taught in popular terms in his Thirteen Principles and that the overall structure of the *Guide* was determined by and reflects that aim.

Assuming that I am correct, what are the implications of this proposal? In the first place, I think it means that we must take Maimonides's Thirteen Principles very seriously as popular statements of his own philosophic positions. Second, if correct, my proposal, as much as it builds upon, also supports the "integrationist-harmonistic" view of Maimonides, which maintains

---

14 Hartman., pp. 81-82. Note especially Hartman's comments concerning the this-worldly effect on the philosopher of his or her striving for *alam ha-ba*.

the fundamental identity of the halakhic Maimonides and the philosophic Maimonides.

One more question begs to be addressed. If all that I have said here is correct, then why does not Maimonides explicitly appeal to the Thirteen Principles in the *Guide*? A possible answer to this question lies in the fact that the *Guide* is, as Maimonides announced in his introduction and as Leo Strauss forcefully reminded us, an esoteric book. One of the "secret" teachings of the *Guide*, I suggest, is that the teachings of philosophy, properly understood (i.e., as adumbrated in the *Guide*), do not conflict with the Torah, properly understood (i.e., as adumbrated in the *Guide*). This is a dangerous teaching in the hands of the philosophically unsophisticated: not understanding philosophy properly (e.g., by slavishly following Aristotle even when – as with creation, according to Maimonides – he is wrong), they might be led to give up important beliefs of the Torah. Had he openly advertised his claim concerning philosophy and Torah by exoterically structuring the *Guide* on the Thirteen Principles of Faith, Maimonides might have led philosophically unsophisticated persons astray. They might have used his authority to justify an extensive allegorization of Scripture in their attempt to make it accord with the "truths" they mistakenly thought that philosophy teaches. Subsequent developments, especially in Provence, show how realistic this fear was.

The Thirteen Principles of Faith, then, fall rather naturally into three groups; so naturally, in fact, that it is difficult to maintain that Maimonides himself did not realize it. The subject matters of these three groups parallel the subject matters of the three parts of the *Guide* and determine its structure. The upshot of this new interpretation of the structure of the *Guide* is that what Maimonides sought to teach the simple Jew in the principles he sought to teach the philosophic Jew in the *Guide*. In short, Maimonides was not schizophrenic.

CHAPTER EIGHT
Maimonides, Crescas, and Abravanel on Ex. 20:2: A Medieval Jewish Exegetical Dispute

Rosh Amanah (*Principles of Faith*) by Don Isaac Abravanel (1437-1508) is justly celebrated as the *locus classicus* for the view that Judaism has no dogmas as such.[1] In it he insists that every one of the beliefs, commandments, and narratives of Judaism is as true as all the others. One may not distinguish any one of them as being more fundamental than the others. Surprisingly, Abravanel makes this claim at the conclusion of a sustained defense of Moses Maimonides' enumeration of the thirteen basic principles of Judaism. Indeed, the book was written, as Abravanel informs the reader in the book's introduction, for no other purpose than to defend Maimonides from his critics, notably R. Hasdai Crescas (1340-1410) and the latter's student, R. Joseph Albo (15th century).

Rosh Amanah, however, is important for reasons beyond its argument concerning the place of dogma in Judaism. Abravanel, among other things, makes an important contribution to one of the best-known Jewish exegetical disputes in the Middle Ages, that between Maimonides and Crescas on the proper understanding of Ex. 20:2, the opening verse of the Decalogue. Abravanel's discussion takes up all of chapter eighteen of the *Rosh Amanah*.[2]

The questions raised in this dispute relate not only to the proper understanding of the Biblical verse, in particular to the question of whether or not it

---

1 For writings by and about Abravanel, see Lawee "Achievement," Lawee, "Biblical Scholarship," and J. Kellner, "Bibliography."

2 When this article was first published, I included an annotated translation of that chapter. In the interim, *Principles* has been published and there is no need to reproduce the translation here.

constitutes a commandment, but also to the enumeration of the Biblical laws which Jewish tradition claims to number six hundred and thirteen.[3]

In the Tractate Makkot of the Babylonian Talmud (23b-24a) we read:

> R. Simlai when preaching said: Six hundred and thirteen precepts were communicated to Moses, three hundred and sixty-five negative, corresponding to the number of solar days (in the year), and two hundred and forty-eight positive, corresponding to the number of the members of man's body. Said R. Hamnuna: What is the (authentic) text for this? It is, *Moses commanded us Torah, an inheritance of the congregation of Jacob* (Dt. 33:4), 'Torah' being numerically equal to six hundred and eleven,[4] *I am* (Ex. 20:2) and *Thou shalt have no* (Ex. 20:3) (not being reckoned, because) we have heard (them) from the mouth of the Almighty.

This idea that the Torah contained exactly six hundred and thirteen commandments became widely accepted in the Jewish tradition and gave rise to a whole genre of literature dedicated to identifying and enumerating the six hundred and thirteen commandments. One of the first books actually to contain such a list is the *Halakhot Gedolot*, attributed to Simeon Kayyara (9th century Babylonia). Scores of liturgical poems, known as *azharot*, were composed during the Middle Ages, all of them embodying enumerations of the six hundred and thirteen commandments.[5] These poems were meant to be recited on the Festival of Weeks, (*shavu'ot*), traditionally regarded as the anniversary of the revelation at Sinai. One of the most important attempts to enumerate the six hundred and thirteen commandments is that of Moses Maimonides. In his *Book of Commandments* he lists and explains the principles which guided him in his choice of precepts for inclusion in his list.[6]

Maimonides opens the *Book of Commandments* with positive commandment number one:

---

3 For a discussion of this tradition in the context of Maimonides, see Davidson, "First Two."

4 Each letter of the Hebrew alphabet has a numerical equivalent. The sum of the numerical equivalents of the letters in the word 'Torah' is six hundred and eleven.

5 On the *azharot* see Idelson, *Jewish Liturgy*, pp. 42, 197. It is interesting to note that the numerical value of the word *azharot*, written defectively, is six hundred and thirteen.

6 See Friedberg, "Enumeration."

GOD EXISTENCE.[7] By this injunction we are commanded to know God, that is to say, to know that there is a Supreme Cause which is the Creator of everything in existence. It is contained in His words (–exalted be He–) *I am the Lord thy God, who brought thee out of the land of Egypt*, etc. (Ex. 20:2). At the end of Tractate Makkot it is said: "Six hundred and thirteen commandments were declared unto Moses at Sinai, as it is said, *Moses commanded us a law [Torah]* (Dt. 33:4)," that is to say, he commanded us to observe as many commandments as are signified by the sum of the numerical values of the letters of TORAH. To this it was objected that the numerical value of the word Torah is only six hundred and eleven; to which the reply was: "The two commandments, *I am the Lord thy God, etc.* and *Thou shalt have no other gods before Me* we have heard from the Almighty Himself." Thus it has been made clear to you that the verse *I am the Lord thy God*, etc., is one of the 613 Commandments, and is that whereby we are commanded to know, as we have explained.

Maimonides reiterates this position at the very beginning of his great law-code, the *Mishneh Torah*:

The basic principle of all basic principles and the pillar of all sciences is the realization that there is a First Being who has brought every existing thing into being. All existing things, whether celestial, terrestrial, or belonging to an intermediate class, exist only through His true existence.... To acknowledge the truth of this is an affirmative precept, as it is said, I am the Lord thy God. And whosoever permits the thought to enter his mind that there is another deity besides this God, violates a prohibition, as it is said, *Thou shalt have no other gods before Me*, and denies the essence of religion, this doctrine being the great principle on which everything depends.[8]

Maimonides makes the same claim, that *I am the Lord thy God* expresses a positive commandment, in his Commentary on the Mishnah, where he enumerates the basic principles of Judaism:

---

7   Chavel has "Believing in God." I have emended his translation here following the Arabic source and Hebrew translation in Kafih's edition. For a discussion of the difference between "knowledge" and "belief" in this context, see pp. 353-358 in Manekin, "Hebrew Philosophy."

8   'Foundations of the Torah," I.I and I.6, pp. 34a, 34b.

The first foundation is the existence of the Creator, may He be praised, to wit that there exists a Being in the most perfect type of existence and that It is the cause of the existence of all other beings. He is the cause of all existence. ... This first foundation is attested to by the verse, *I am the Lord thy God.*

These texts clearly demonstrate that Maimonides understood Ex. 20:2, *I am the Lord thy God*, to express a commandment. It is logically the first positive commandment in the Torah and "the great principle on which everything depends."

Maimonides' position here can be explained in terms of a statement he makes in the *Guide of the Perplexed* (II. 33, p. 364):

This is their dictum: "*They heard I am and Thou shalt have no* from the mouth of the Almighty." They mean that these words reached them just as they reached Moses our master, and that it was not Moses our master who communicated them to them. For these two principles, I mean the existence of the Deity and His being one, are knowable by human speculation alone. Now with regard to everything that can be known by demonstration, the status of the prophet and that of everyone who knows it are equal; there is no superiority of one over the other. Thus these two principles are not known through prophecy alone. The text of the Torah says *Unto thee it was shown*, and so on (Dt. 4:35). As for the other commandments, they belong to the class of generally accepted opinions and those adopted by virtue of tradition, not to the class of the intellects.

It is Maimonides' claim, therefore, that God's existence and unity are rationally demonstrable and that human beings may, in principle, be commanded to accept their truth. This reflects Maimonides' general position concerning the relationship between faith and reason – he sought to integrate halakhah and philosophy.[9] The first two statements of the Decalogue, the content of God's unmediated revelation to the people of Israel, the first of which is the foundation of all foundations of the Jewish faith, are presented as rationally demonstrable philosophic teachings. This issue is the crux of the philosophic dispute between Maimonides and Crescas. Crescas wanted to divorce religion

---

9   David Hartman presents a statement of this reading of Maimonides in *Maimonides*. See chapts. 1 and 3 in particular, and with reference to the present context, p. 49 especially. In greater detail, see Twersky, *Introduction*, ch. 6.

from philosophy and to establish the former on purely dogmatic grounds. Indeed, in its overall structure his *magnum opus*, the *Or ha-Shem (Light of the Lord)*, is nothing other than a statement and explication of the basic dogmas of Judaism. Crescas therefore claims that *I am the Lord thy God* and *Thou shalt have no other gods before Me* are not commandments. Halakhah (Jewish law) in particular, and Jewish religion in general, he can be understood as saying, are not grounded in philosophy (are not rationally demonstrable statements about God's existence and unity).[10] This distinction, as Warren Zev Harvey points out,[11] was symbolized in Crescas' projected two-part work, *Ner Elohim (Lamp of God)*, of which the *Or ha-Shem* was to have been the first part. The second part, *Ner Mizvah (Light of the Commandment)* was never written. It was meant to be a strictly halakhic work, one which its author hoped would supersede Maimonides' code, the Mishneh Torah.

The argument between Maimonides and Crescas, therefore, is of far-reaching philosophical and theological significance and relates to a basic question concerning the very nature of Judaism. At the risk of oversimplification, the question may be stated as follows: Is Judaism ultimately a religion of reason or a religion of faith?

The dispute between Maimonides and Crescas, however, was not carried on in terms of the actual issues which divided them. Rather, as is so often the case in similar matters, it was expressed on another plane altogether through their different understanding of Ex. 20:2, *I am the Lord thy God*. Maimonides' understanding of this verse was subjected to vociferous criticism by Hasdai Crescas in the preface (*haza'ah*) to his *Or ha-Shem*.[12] Crescas leveled three arguments against Maimonides' position, and the third of these relates directly to the question of the proper exegesis of Ex. 20:2.[13] He wrote:

---

10 Schweid, *Crescas*, p. 23.

11 In his article on Crescas' philosophy in the *Encyclopaedia Judaica*, V, 1081.

12 The text of the *Or ha-Shem* is notoriously corrupt; see H. A. Wolfson, *Crescas' Critique*, pp. 703-05. In the translation that follows I have followed the text of the Vienna, 1859, edition.

13 The arguments are paraphrased by Abravanel in chapter 4 of *Rosh Amanah*. The first argument points out that a commandment presupposes a commander. The idea of a commandment to believe in the existence of the commander of that very commandment is logically incoherent. The second argument depends upon Crescas' analysis of the terms "will" and "choice" (*Or ha Shem*, treatise II, principle ii, chapter 5). Commandments, Crescas says, make sense only in contexts where will and choice obtain, and since one cannot will (or choose) to believe in something, there can be no commandments about beliefs. It should

He who counted it a positive commandment to believe in the existence of God committed a notorious error .... [Maimonides was] brought to this, that is, to counting this root as a commandment, by the dictum at the end of Gemara Makkot which says...[14] [Maimonides concluded from this dictum] that *I am* and *Thou shalt have no* were two commandments, and therefore counted belief in the existence of God as a commandment. It is clear that this does not follow, for what was intended there [in the passage in Makkot] is that the God who is called thus is the Deity and Guide who had brought us out of the land of Egypt.[15] Maimonides properly followed this understanding in his *Book of Commandments*, in which he counted the first commandment as involving belief in the Divinity: "By this injunction we are commanded to believe in God: that is to say, to believe that there is a Supreme Cause which is the Creator of everything in existence. It is contained in His words –exalted be He– *I am the Lord thy God.*" 25 He thus explained God's divinity in terms of His having created all existent beings. Because of this God said, *Who brought thee out of the land of Egypt* (Ex. 20:2), by way of proving this belief: from it we come to understand God's power, and that all existent beings are, when compared to Him, *as clay in the potter's hand* (Jer. 18:6).[16]

On this account the commandment relates to the belief that it was God who had brought us out of the land of Egypt. But this way of understanding the verse is in itself clearly false. This is so because the reference to *I am* and *Thou*

---

be pointed out here that Jewish commentators find many more than ten commandments in the Decalogue. They see it as a group of ten utterances or speeches, not a single listing of ten discrete commandments. Abravanel, in his Commentary on the Torah (Jerusalem, 1964), II, 178-186 (commentary on the Decalogue) provides an exhaustive analysis of the opinions of his major predecessors on this subject.

14 I omit the passage from Makkot here. It is cited above.

15 This is the view of Nahmanides (1194-1270) as expressed in his commentary on Ex. 20:2. As will be seen below, Crescas was strongly influenced by Nahmanides in his understanding of the verse.

16 In *Rosh Amanah*, ch. 7 Abravanel analyzes this passage of Crescas' and concludes that Crescas held that Maimonides contradicted himself. Abravanel writes: "This scholar thus thought that Maimonides' statements in these two places, i.e., the *Book of Knowledge* and *the Book of Commandments*, were not in agreement. He thought that in the *Book of Knowledge* [Maimonides held] that the first commandment is simply that God exists, while he thought that in the *Book of Commandments* [Maimonides held] that the first commandment is belief that God is the Cause of the world and its Creator."

shalt have no [in the passage from Makkot] may readily be seen to include all of the utterance which continues through . .. *of them that love Me and keep My commandments* (Ex. 20:6). Since both these utterances are spoken in the first person, as it is said, *I am the Lord . . . who brought thee out* (Ex. 20:2), *before Me* (20: 3), *for I the Lord thy God* (20:5), and *of them that love Me and keep My commandments* (20:6); and since the rest of the utterances are spoken in the third person, as it is said, *for the Lord will not hold him guiltless* (20:7), *for in six days the Lord made* (20:11), and *on the seventh day He ceased from work and rested*,[17] (the Sages therefore) held that *I am* and *Thou shalt have no* (were heard) from the mouth of the Almighty. All of the authors who enumerate *azharot* saw fit to count *Thou shalt not make unto thee a graven image* (20:4) and *Thou shalt not bow down to them* (20:5) as two [separate] admonitions; this is the truth itself.

Were we to count *I am* as a commandment, there would then be three commandments which we heard from the mouth of the Almighty[18] and [the total number of commandments] would then rise to 614.[19] If we consider *Thou shalt have no other gods* (20:3) as an admonition not "to believe in, or ascribe deity to, anyone but Him," as Maimonides wrote,[20] [then the number of commandments] would rise to 615. It is therefore appropriate that we say that it was not the intention of those who said "*I am* and *Thou shalt have no [other gods]* we have heard from the mouth of Almighty" that each [verse] be considered a commandment. Rather, they explained that we have heard them from the mouth of the Almighty because both were spoken in the first person, as [said] above. It follows that the two admonitions which we have heard from the mouth of the Almighty in the utterance *Thou shalt have no* were *Thou shalt not make unto thee a graven image, nor any manner of likeness* (20:4) and thou

---

17 Ex. 31:17. I have no idea why this verse, which is not in the Decalogue, appears here. As will be seen below, Abravanel also cites it in his summary of Crescas' argument.

18 Namely, not to make a graven image (v. 4), not to bow down to such an image (v. 5), and to affirm the existence of God (v. 2).

19 On the assumption that Moses taught six hundred eleven commandments, but none of those contained in the portion of the Decalogue (verses 2-6) in which God is presented as speaking in the first person

20 *Book of Commandments*, negative commandment 1.

shalt not bow down unto them (20:5). These, with the 611 we have heard from the mouth of Moses, add up to 613.

All that remains to be explained is why they[21] did not count *Thou shalt have no other gods before Me* as an admonition which would then make three admonitions in that utterance. This is easily explained. If will and choice did not apply to beliefs, the term "admonition" could not be applied to them. But if the term "admonition" is withal applied to them, the explanation of *Thou shalt have no* would be that one should not accept any other thing as God. [Indeed,] it has been established in the Tractate Sanhedrin [56b] that one who does so is guilty of a capital offense. But they did not see fit to consider *Thou shalt have no* and *Thou shalt not bow down unto them* as two [separate commandments], for the root of them both is one, viz., the acceptance of the Divinity. But *Thou shalt not make unto thee a graven image* (20:4) [applies] even if one did not worship [the image] or accept it as divine. They were therefore counted as two [separate commandments]. But it never occurred to them to consider *I am the Lord thy God as a commandment*, since it is the root and presupposition of all the commandments, as (stated) above.[22]

As noted above, Abravanel wrote *Rosh Amanah* in order to defend Maimonides from the criticisms leveled at his enumeration of the principles of Judaism by Hasdai Crescas and Joseph Albo. Following his practice in most of his philosophical and exegetical works, Abravanel lists all of the objections he can find to Maimonides in the writings of Crescas and Albo (and adds eight of his own) before turning to the defense proper. He summarizes Crescas' argument in chapter four of *Rosh Amanah*, paraphrasing it very closely.[23] He does

---

21 Those who count the *azharot*, and of course Crescas himself. As will be seen below, Abravanel seizes on this question to argue that Crescas himself thought that his argument was weak.

22 By way of summarizing the issue, it may be helpful to point out that both Crescas and Maimonides agree that Ex. 20:2-6 constitutes the first two utterances of the Decalogue. According to Crescas, these utterances contain two commandments: the commandment prohibiting the worship of idols and the one prohibiting the bowing down to idols. According to Maimonides, the two utterances contain five commandments: (a) to affirm that God exists (v. 2); (b) not to have other gods (v. 3); (c) not to make images for the purpose of worship (v. 4); (d) not to bow down before, or serve, idols (v. 5); and (e) not to worship idols (v. 5). These are, in Maimonides' *Book of Commandments*, positive commandment 1 and negative commandments 1, 2, 5 and 6.

23 Even to the extent of including the curious citation from Ex. 31:17 (as noted above).

not, however, respond to the argument itself until he gets to chapter eighteen. In that context he points out that Crescas' argument is strongly influenced by the argument of Moses Nahmanides found in his glosses to Maimonides' *Book of Commandments*. Nahmanides introduces the exegetical argument in his gloss to the first positive commandment in order to support the opinion of the author of the *Halakhot Gedolot* who did not count *I am the Lord thy God* as a commandment. But Nahmanides himself concludes (in his gloss to the first negative commandment), "But what is good in my sight (1 Sam. 29:6) in this matter is that we count *I am the Lord thy God* as a commandment, in accordance with the opinion of Maimonides." This accords with Nahmanides' statement in his commentary to Ex. 20:2, "This divine utterance constitutes a positive commandment."[24]

We may now turn to Abravanel's defense of Maimonides as presented in chapter eighteen of his *Rosh Amanah*. Abravanel begins the chapter with a brief summary of Crescas' exegetical objection to Maimonides, and then opens his defense by pointing out that there are many places where the Bible presents Moses as speaking in God's name. The fact that Ex. 20: 3-6 is presented in the first person does not therefore make it impossible that it was spoken by Moses. Abravanel then proceeds to attack Crescas' position. He points out that even if we do not count *I am the Lord thy God* and *Thou shalt have no other gods before Me* as commandments, there are still three commandments –and this is the opinion of all who enumerate the commandments– in the passage which Crescas says the Israelites had heard directly from God. But adding these to the six hundred and eleven taught by Moses, the total would come to six hundred and fourteen! Abravanel thereupon goes on to adduce Biblical and Rabbinic support for Maimonides' interpretation of Ex. 20:2.

Having answered the criticisms of Crescas, Abravanel introduces a new critique of Maimonides, one set forth by certain unidentified "contemporary scholars." They claim to find support for the assertion that Ex. 20:2 is not a commandment in two passages from rabbinic literature, one in the Midrash

---

24 Crescas' argument here may be explicated as follows: commandments are not a matter of belief (because one cannot will or choose to believe something); if *Thou shalt have no other gods before Me* is a commandment, it must be given an actional interpretation, such as forbidding the worship of other gods. But in such a case, *Thou shalt have no other gods before Me* becomes equivalent to *Thou shalt not bow down unto them*.

(Mekhilta) and one in the Talmud (Tractate Horayot). Abravanel responds by showing how each passage can be understood in a way consistent with the views of Maimonides. He also adduces interpretations of the passages (by Nahmanides in the case of the Mekhilta passage, and by Rashi in the case of the passage from Horayot) which agree with his own, and thus are consistent with Maimonides' position. Abravanel then goes again on the offensive, using the very weapon introduced by the "contemporary scholars" – citations from Rabbinic literature. He introduces two midrashic texts which support Maimonides' position, and concludes the chapter with a brief critique of the putative position of the author of the *Halakhot Gedolot*.

We must now point out something that is really quite remarkable: notwithstanding his extended defense of Maimonides' position concerning the status of Ex. 20:2 in *Rosh Amanah*, Abravanel in the end adopts Crescas' interpretation! In his commentary on the Decalogue Abravanel writes:

> I have already mentioned in the question[25] that R. Hasdai has proved that the term "commandment," according to its [proper] definition, does not apply to beliefs. His arguments are strong. Therefore, the words of the author of the *Halakhot Gedolot* are best in my eyes (cf. 1 Sam. 29:6), since he did not count *I am the Lord your God* as a commandment. It is his opinion that the six hundred and thirteen commandments are all God's decrees in which He has declared how we should act or refrain from acting. But the belief in His existence He made known to us through signs and demonstrations[26] and the revelation of the Divine Presence. It is the principle and root from which the commandments are derived, but is not counted in their number.[27]

Abravanel himself drew attention to the blatant contradiction between his positions in the Commentary and in *Rosh Amanah*. A little further in the same passage he wrote: "I have already discussed this issue in the eighteenth chapter

---

25 Abravanel's commentary on the Decalogue takes the form of an extended essay. It begins with thirteen questions, the seventh of which (p. 179b) deals with our issue.

26 I.e., miracles, especially the deliverance from Egypt.

27 Abravanel, Commentary on Exodus, p. 185a. It is entirely possible that Abravanel's usage of 1 Sam. 29:6 was prompted by Nahmanides' use of the verse in his gloss to the first negative commandment in Maimonides' *Book of Commandments*, quoted above. Nahmanides' position was "good in his eyes"; Abravanel's position, however, was "best in his eyes."

of the treatise *Rosh Amanah* which I wrote. There I defended the opinion of Maimonides, while here I spoke *as it was in my heart* (Josh. 14:7); there is no contradiction in this." There is no contradiction in this, because, as Abravanel made abundantly clear in chapter 22 of *Rosh Amanah*, while he wrote the book to defend Maimonides, he did not subscribe to the latter's views concerning the principles of Judaism. Whatever prompted Abravanel to defend Maimonides from the criticisms of Crescas and Albo, it was not his agreement with him. The case here, however, is not exactly parallel to that of chapter 22 of *Rosh Amanah*. There Abravanel disagrees with Maimonides but does not express agreement with the views of his critics. Here in the Commentary, however, Abravanel rejects Maimonides' view in favor of that of Crescas, apparently on the strength of Crescas' arguments! The contradiction here –which, to the best of my knowledge, has never been noted before– is thus particularly glaring.

This whole issue, however, deserves separate and extended treatment. Abravanel's final personal position does not affect the debate between Maimonides and Crescas on the exegesis of Ex. 20:2 or Abravanel's defense of the Maimonidean position as presented in Rosh Amanah, ch. eighteen. Despite his ultimate disagreement with Maimonides, Abravanel offers a spirited defense of his position, and it is with that defense which we are concerned here. Abravanel's argument is of interest not only for the light it sheds on the respective positions of Maimonides and Crescas (if ultimately not that of Abravanel) with respect to the proper understanding of Ex. 20:2, but also for the way in which it shows how an exegetical problem is used by two opponents in a philosophical dispute to bolster their respective cases.

CHAPTER NINE
Could Maimonides Get into Rambam's Heaven?

Once a religion specifies the distinct beliefs that constitute its theology, a new question must be answered: are all these beliefs equal in significance? Moses Maimonides was the first Jew to raise this question, and his answer is explicit: there are thirteen specific teachings of the Torah which stand on a plane all their own.

Rambam[1] makes this claim in his commentary on the mishnaic text which opens with the words, "All Israelites have a share in the world to come..."[2] Rambam thus makes clear that he views that text as a presentation of the dogmas of Judaism. Rambam lays down thirteen discrete beliefs as the dogmatic foundation of the Jewish faith. These were summarized above in ch. 7, "Maimonides 'Thirteen Principles and the Structure of the *Guide of the Perplexed.*

Rambam does not himself present a catechism but a discussion of these ideas. He cites proof-texts from the Written Torah and in some cases sketches the outlines of a philosophic proof of the truth of the dogma. The entire discussion is a lengthy essay written originally in Arabic. Rambam's principles are better known in the Jewish world in the form of two poetic summaries: *Yigdal* and *Ani Ma'amin*, found in most prayer books. The first of these has become part of the liturgy in many Jewish communities.[3]

After he finishes presenting his principles, Rambam makes the surprising statement quoted above near the beginning of ch. 5, "Heresy and the Nature

---

1   Ordinarily I refer to R. Moses ben Maimon as Maimonides; since the point of this article is to emphasize the differences between his more popular and more strictly philosophical persona, I use the name Rambam for the former, Maimonides for the latter.

2   The full text is found above in ch. 7 "Maimonides 'Thirteen Principles and the Structure of the *Guide of the Perplexed.*

3   For details on texts and translations, see *Dogma*, pp. 218-220.

of Faith." Rambam's statement of his principles occurs at the end of a passage in which he defines the terms appearing in Mishnah Sanhedrin X.1 ("All Israelites have a share in the world to come..."). One term alone remains undefined: "Israelite." He appears to have posited his principles here at least in part in order to define the term "Israelite." An Israelite is a person who affirms the thirteen principles.[4]

The text with which Rambam closes his statement of the principles of the Torah, turns out on close examination to be quite remarkable. In the first instance, we see that Rambam defines a Jew in terms of his or her acceptance of the principles, "When all these foundations are perfectly understood and believed in by a person he enters the community of Israel... ." That Rambam took this theological question "who is a Jew?" seriously is evidenced by the fact that he immediately attaches to the acceptance of his principles the halakhic rights which Jews may demand of their fellows – to be treated with love, pity, and fraternity – and by the further fact that he here makes one's portion in the world to come (i.e., one's personal salvation) dependent upon the acceptance of the thirteen principles. Further, Rambam makes admittance to the world to come conditional solely on the acceptance of his principles, explicitly divorcing halakhic obedience from the equation ("even were he to commit every possible transgression...").

It should be emphasized that Rambam here makes unambiguous, conscious acceptance of the principles not only a *necessary* condition for being Jewish and enjoying a share in the world to come but also a *sufficient* condition. In other words, in order to be counted as part of Israel, it is necessary that one accept the principles; that is also *enough*. If we take Rambam at his word here, one need not do anything further.

Second, if one simply casts doubt upon any of the principles (i.e., does not overtly deny them), one excludes oneself from the people of Israel. Such an individual must be hated and destroyed and loses his or her share in the world to come.

---

4   This interpretation was first proposed by Isaac Abravanel (1437-1508) in his *Rosh Amanah*, ch. 6. Hebrew, p. 68, English, pp. 82-84. The implications of this interpretation are analyzed in *Confrontation*, ch. 7.

Third, Rambam makes absolutely no provision for the possibility of inadvertence playing an exculpatory role when it comes to doubting or denying principles of faith. Even if one denies a principle of faith because one thinks mistakenly that one is following the teaching of the Torah, one has excluded oneself from the Jewish community and lost one's share in the world to come.

Fourth, Rambam presents his thirteen principles as dogmas in the strictest sense of the term. They are laid down as beliefs taught by the Torah (the highest ecclesiastical authority in Judaism), acceptance of which is a necessary (and sufficient) condition for being considered a part of the House of Israel and for attaining a share in the world to come.[5]

Rambam thus makes a number of claims about the status of dogma in Judaism:

Judaism has dogmas in the strict sense of the term

Acceptance of these dogmas makes one a Jew and guarantees one a share in the world to come

Doubts or mistakes (not even outright rejection) concerning one of these dogmas is sufficient to exclude one from the Jewish people and cost one his or her share in the world to come

Rambam distinguishes between *knowledge* and *belief* and imposes an halakhic obligation to know and not just believe (i.e., accept on traditional authority) that God exists, is one, and is incorporeal.[6]

When presented in this fashion, Rambam's position is seen be revolutionary. How are we to understand this? Rambam, it seems, understands the verse from Habakkuk, *the righteous shall live by his faith*, as teaching that the righteous person is defined as righteous by his or her faith. He furthermore seems to understand the term *live* in the verse as referring to life in the world to come. He also conflates the terms *Israel* and *righteous* (as the Mishnah itself did, justifying the claim that "all Israelites have a share in the world to come" by appealing to the verse, *thy people are all righteous...*). Finally, Rambam un-

---

5   Further on this, see Kellner, "Suggestion."

6   For full discussion of this point, see *Must*, ch. 1.

derstands the faith which defines the righteous Israelite and through which he or she earns a share in the world to come in terms of thirteen discrete beliefs which constitute that faith.[7]

One of the most striking elements in Rambam's formulation is his apparent unwillingness to accept inadvertence as exculpatory.[8] I mean by this that for Rambam a person who makes a mistake about matters of dogma is in no better shape than one who consciously and knowingly rejects one of the thirteen principles. Such a person is simply a heretic. This may not surprise all my readers: after all, if you are stopped for speeding, telling the police officer that you did not know that speeding was illegal is not going to get you very far. In Western legal systems, ignorance of the law is not generally considered a legitimate excuse for violating it.

Judaism, however, does recognize the category of *shegagah,* inadvertence, as mitigating guilt or even in some cases excusing it altogether. In matters of belief, however, Rambam leaves no room for *shegagah.*

Why does Rambam do this? He actually has no choice. Rambam was locked into this position by a number of his previous decisions. If we interpret Habakkuk as defining the righteous in terms of faith and further define faith in terms of its propositional content, as Rambam clearly does through his thirteen principles, then if one affirms an incorrect doctrine or denies a correct doctrine *for any reason,* one's faith is in fact deficient, and therefore, so is one's righteousness. If righteousness is a criterion for being member of the House of Israel and for enjoying a share in the world to come, then the mistaken believer is, however sweet, and good, and pious in the conventional sense, *not* righteous and thus not a Jew and not a candidate for a share in the world to come.

Rambam not only understood religious belief in terms of its intellectual, propositional content, he was convinced that the beliefs of Judaism, at least, were basically equivalent to the teachings of true philosophy. This underlying approach to religious faith comes out clearly in the very first sentence of Rambam's *Mishneh Torah,* his great and unprecedented law code. "The foundation of all [religious] foundations and pillar of [all] the sciences," Rambam

---

7   These points are further developed in *Confrontation,* ch. 7.

8   For proof that Rambam does not, in fact, distinguish the purposeful heretic from the inadvertent, see ch. 6, "What is Heresy," *Dogma,* 18-19, and *Must,* p. 83.

writes, "is to *know* that there exists a Prime Existent." Remember, please, that this is the first sentence of a systematic exposition of halakhah, Jewish law. In this sentence, Rambam teaches that religion and science share a common axiom: God's existence.[9]

This may sound odd to contemporary ears, but the science Rambam was dealing with Aristotelian; the most foundational of all the sciences for any Aristotelian was metaphysics, and the fundamental teaching of metaphysics was God's existence. Thus, one who was confused on that issue was confused at the very basic level of scientific truth.

The basic axiom of all the sciences is God's existence; the basic axiom of religious faith is God's existence. At their very heart, then, religion and science do not teach the same thing, they *are* the same thing.[10]

Science must be based on *knowledge*, not "blind" faith (the very opposite of Maimonidean faith!) or wishful thinking. Thus, one must be able to know scientifically that God exists. Since such knowledge is possible, Rambam can make it the first of his thirteen principles; he can also make it the first *commandment*: "knowledge of this [God's unconditional existence, uniqueness, and mastery of the cosmos] is a positive commandment."

Thus, "the foundation of all foundations and the pillar of [all] the sciences is to know" that God exists. In Maimonidean terms, to know something means to be able to show why it is so, in other words, to offer rational proof for it.[11] For Rambam, therefore, to fulfill the very first commandment, to accept the first principle of faith, one must be sufficiently sophisticated to prove God's existence.

The importance of scientific knowledge to religious faith is further underscored by Rambam in the four chapters following his emphatic opening assertion concerning the identity of the basic axioms of religion and of science. In these chapters, Rambam gives a quick course in two sciences, physics (includ-

---

9 In interpreting this sentence, I follow Isaac Abravanel. See *Rosh Amanah*, ch.5 (Hebrew, 63; English, 76).

10 Further on this point, see Kellner, "Conception of Torah", and "Maimonides and Gersonides on Astronomy." This latter article is to be republished in the companion volume to this one.

11 To know something, for any Aristotelian, is to know it with its causes. See, for example, *Physics* ii.3, 194b.

ing astronomy) and metaphysics, maintaining that it is through the study of these sciences that one can be brought to the love and fear of God.

Rambam does not specify in his statement of the "Thirteen Principles" whether they are to be *known* or simply *believed* (i.e., accepted on the basis of traditional authority without necessarily understanding why they are and must be true). But in his parallel statement in "Laws of the Foundations of the Torah," he clearly states that it is *knowledge* of God's existence which is the "foundation of all foundations." He further states there that *knowing* that God exists is the first of all the commandments of the Torah. It makes considerable sense, therefore, to interpret the "Thirteen Principles" (at least the first five of them, which deal with God) as involving knowledge rather than belief.

Rambam, as it happens, cannot be interpreted in any other fashion. For Rambam as for all other philosophers, the distinction between knowing and believing is crucial. Knowledge, as Rambam understands it, corresponds to reality and must, therefore, be true (the expression "true knowledge" is thus redundant). Belief is what we represent to ourselves as corresponding to reality, whether or not in fact it actually does so correspond. Human beings are distinguished from all other creatures on earth by their ability to achieve knowledge. In fact, being born with human potential means being born with that ability; becoming truly human means realizing that ability to one extent or another.

Note carefully what I have just written: the child of human parents is born as a potential human; only that potential human being who achieves knowledge actually becomes a full-fledged human being. Immortality, a share in the world to come, is something to which only humans can aspire. It is Rambam's settled doctrine that only human beings, i.e., only those individuals born to human parents who have also achieved knowledge ("perfection of the intellect" in the sort of language Rambam used) have shares in the world to come. This is a position which grates painfully on the ears of many people today, but there is no point in pretending that it isn't there. It is a position which Rambam adopts and which, in fact, he must adopt given his understanding of human psychology.[12]

What sort of knowledge must we acquire in order to establish our humanity and thereby earn a share in the world to come? On this the medievals were

---

12 On Rambam's psychology, see my *Judaism*, 9 -15 and Frank, "Heart and Soul."

divided with some saying all knowledge counted others said only knowledge of God and the angels counted.[13] In the language of the Middle Ages, the question was "does knowing mathematics and the physical sciences get one into the world to come, or must one also know metaphysics?" Rambam comes down heavily for the second alternative. To become an actual human being, to earn a share in the world to come, one must acquire *knowledge* of metaphysical matters — namely, God and the angels.

One must acquire *knowledge*: it is not enough to be able to recite things by heart like a parrot. One must be able to understand what one is saying. For Rambam, then, one cannot even fulfill the first of the 613 commandments until one can properly prove to oneself that God exists. Furthermore, since acceptance of the "Thirteen Principles" is a key to enjoying a share in the world to come and only those who have achieved knowledge gain entry into that world, it follows that *believing* the "Thirteen Principles" is not enough: one must *know* that God exists, is one, is incorporeal, etc.

We are now in a position better to understand why Rambam cannot allow for *shegagah* with respect to his principles. Well-intentioned but poor philosophers do not achieve knowledge; their mistakes exclude them from the ranks of actual (as opposed to potential) humans and thus keep them out of the world to come. Similarly, for well-intentioned but confused or mistaken Jews, their mistakes in metaphysics (i.e., mistakes concerning at least the first five of Rambam's principles) exclude them from membership in Israel and from the world to come.

I earlier noted that *shegagah* with respect to matters of religious belief renders that belief incorrect and thus not really belief at all as far as Rambam is concerned. I said that this reflected Rambam's claim that *emunah* is defined in terms of intellectual affirmations. Now we can understand why. Rambam defines belief in this fashion because of his theory of knowledge. If one holds incorrect beliefs (i.e., makes mistakes in metaphysics), then one has not achieved one's humanity and is thus not even a candidate for admission to the world to come.

---

13 On this, see Harvey, "Crescas and his Critique of Philosophic Happiness," and Kellner, "Gersonides on the Active Intellect." This latter article is to be republished in the companion volume to this one.

There is at least one way in which Rambam appears to be inconsistent with respect to the application of his principles. This has to do with his attitudes towards Karaites. Karaites reject part of the seventh principle in that they deny the divine origin of the Oral Torah. With respect to all the other principles, they are fully "orthodox."[14] In his first public statement concerning the Karaites in his *Commentary on the Mishnah*, Rambam considers them heretics and calls for their execution where possible. In the course of time, Rambam moderated his stance, distinguishing between the founders of Karaism and rabbinite Jews who join them, on the one hand, from their descendants on the other hand. Descendants of Karaites, Rambam avers in the *Mishneh Torah*,

> misguided by their parents [and] raised among the Karaites and trained in their views, are like a child taken captive by them and raised in their religion, whose status is that of an *anus* [one who abjures the Jewish religion under duress], who, although he later learns that he is a Jew, meets Jews, observes them practice their religion, is nevertheless to be regarded as an *anus*, since he was raised in the erroneous ways of his fathers. Thus it is with those who adhere to the practices of their Karaite parents. Therefore efforts should be made to bring them back in repentance, to draw them near by friendly relations, so that they may return to the strength-giving source, i.e., the Torah.[15]

Let us recall that acceptance of principles of faith is supposed to lead to a share in the world to come. This acceptance, I pointed out above, involves more than parroting the principles; it involves some level of understanding them. This is so because Rambam, on his own philosophical grounds, can only get people into heaven, so to speak, if they have made themselves full human beings, individuals with a certain amount of intellectual perfection. One achieves that level of perfection only through an understanding of basic metaphysical teachings. Correct knowledge concerning God, therefore, is the only key to immortality. Essential elements in this knowledge are taught *and explained* in the first five principles.

---

14 On Maimonides and Karaism see Lasker, *From Judah Hadassi*, pp. 155-189.

15 The passage from the *Mishneh Torah* is from "Laws of Rebellious Elders," III.3. Some mss. and some early editions omit the word "Karaites" from the text, replacing it with *to'im*, "those who are mistaken." This textual issue is of no significance for us here, since the mistake in question is the rejection of the Oral Torah.

Rambam's first five principles, therefore, teach metaphysical truths. Understanding those truths constitutes enough intellectual perfection to guarantee a share in the world to come. The other principles teach truths, of course, but of a type different from the first group. These latter truths relate to certain historical events (concerning the giving of the Torah), to the way God relates to us, and to certain future events (Messiah and resurrection). Rejection of these truths excludes one from that community constituted by their acceptance (the community of Israel) but does not and cannot in and of itself lead to exclusion from the world to come.

Rambam's claim, therefore, that *all* his principles are dogmas in the strict sense that perfect acceptance of them is a necessary and sufficient condition for being part of the House of Israel and having a share in the world to come is thus seen to be exaggerated: the first five principles are dogmas in that sense. No mistakes can be tolerated concerning them, and none are. Innocent mistakes concerning the other principles can be tolerated to the extent that those who make these mistakes need not be treated with the full rigor of the laws concerning heretics. The treatment of Karaite descendents in Rambam's writings proves this claim.

But is it indeed the case that Rambam distinguishes between the first five principles and all the others as I here claim? It turns out (luckily for my case!) that he makes the point more or less explicitly in the *Guide of the Perplexed*, part I, chapters 35 and 36. In these chapters, Rambam distinguishes infidelity from ignorance, allowing a certain latitude for the latter but absolutely none for the former. Infidelity relates to proper beliefs concerning God, ignorance to the other teachings of the Torah.[16]

Karaites did not reject God's existence, unity, or incorporeality; they did not reject God's creation of the Universe; and they did not pray to intermediaries. Persons raised as Karaites, in other words, are not "infidels" in the sense described here by Rambam. They reject a true teaching concerning the Torah, but they do not misconstrue or misrepresent the nature of God. As such, they do not commit fatal metaphysical mistakes and are not, therefore, excluded willy-nilly from the world to come.

---

16 Further on Rambam's distinction between the first five principles and the last eight, see
   Confrontation, pp. 233-238.

The founders of Karaism (and rabbinite Jews who join it later) consciously rebelled against the authority of the *Sanhedrin*, a capital offence. Thus, they deserve death. Their descendents have not so rebelled and can, therefore, be treated with greater leniency. By maintaining correct beliefs about God, Karaite descendents remain within the essential fold of Judaism (if not within the Jewish community); their disagreement is largely about matters of "detail," so to speak.

Rambam, thus, attached cardinal importance to the first five of the "Thirteen Principles" and somewhat less importance to the others. Rejection of or mistakes concerning the first group truly exclude one from the community of Israel and from the world to come. Mistakes concerning the latter group do not actually exclude one from the community of Israel (we are, after all, bound to make efforts "to bring them back in repentance, to draw them near by friendly relations, so that they may return to the strength-giving source, i.e., the Torah") and certainly do not, in and of themselves, exclude one from the world to come.

We have before us an interesting example of the interplay between popular and philosophical religion. This interplay can be understood in two different ways. Maimonides' philosophic conception of the nature of faith forced Rambam the theologian to posit an unyielding approach to questions of dogma: faith is defined in terms of its cognitive content, which in turn can be given dogmatic expression. But Rambam the communal leader was interested in making it possible to draw Karaites back into the fold and had to diverge from the strictly "Maimonidean" character of his own dogmas. It might be thought that philosophical religion demands that Karaites or other misguided folk who reject the Oral Torah be excluded from the Jewish community in this world and altogether from the next while the needs of popular religion forced Rambam to he more flexible. That has been shown not to be the case: Karaites (and others like them) can be encouraged to return to the fold specifically because they do not violate the canons of philosophical religion the first five of Maimonides thirteen principles.

There is another way of approaching the same set of facts: philosophical religion "needs" the first five principles; the others are the requirements of popular religion. Furthermore, *shegagah*, with respect to only the first five, is disallowed by philosophical religion; the needs of a besieged community, which could not allow for a relaxed approach to matters of theology, forced Rambam the communal leader to posit a more unyielding attitude towards *shegagah* with respect to the other principles than his philosophical commitments actually demanded. On this approach it may be said with a measure of poetic license that Maimonides, who could allow for *shegagah* with respect to principles six – thirteen, could not get into Rambam's heaven, since the latter did not allow for such laxity.

CHAPTER TEN

Returning the Crown to its Ancient Glory: Marc Shapiro's *The Limits of Orthodox Theology: Maimonides' Thirteen Principles Reappraised*

The Littman Library of Jewish Civilization has published three books concerning Orthodox Jewish theology. These books are works of scholarship but also seek to raise discussion of theological issues in the public square of Orthodox Judaism to a higher level of reflective self-scrutiny. In 1999 my own *Must a Jew Believe Anything?* appeared (second edition, 2006); 2001 saw the publication of David Berger's *The Rebbe, the Messiah, and the Scandal of Orthodox Indifference*; we now have before us Marc Shapiro's *The Limits of Orthodox Theology: Maimonides' Thirteen Principles Reappraised*. Each of these books was written by a professional academic specializing in Judaic studies; the three authors are themselves personally observant Jews, roughly affiliated with what used to be called "modern Orthodoxy."

Of the three, Shapiro's book (which, like all of his work, combines remarkable erudition with clarity of vision) appears to be well on the way to creating the biggest stir in Orthodox circles, even though it is actually the most conservative of the three. In my own book I argued that, strictly speaking, Judaism has no dogmas and that Maimonides' attempt to establish Judaism on a firm dogmatic footing represented a *novum* in the history of Judaism.[1] Berger

---

1   It is important to bear in mind that at the conclusion of his presentation of the principles, Maimonides makes it clear that they are *dogmas* in the strict sense of the term: beliefs laid down as true by the highest religious authority (the Torah itself), and which are necessary *and* sufficient conditions both for being part of the Jewish community in this world and for achieving a share in the world to come. I have tried to keep footnotes here to a minimum. Readers interested in elaboration upon and documentation for the claims advanced here are invited to examine Kellner, *Dogma* and ch. 9, "Could Maimonides Get Into Rambam's Heaven?"

took an opposed position, arguing that Judaism surely has dogmas, that Maimonides' Thirteen Principles are the closest thing Judaism has to an official statement of creed, and that Habad fails the test of Orthodoxy because of its beliefs concerning the Rebbe's quasi-divine status and his status as a soon-to-be-resurrected Messiah. Shapiro accepts the notion that Judaism has dogmas (pp. 29-30, 32) but, building on a controversial article he wrote for *The Torah u-Madda Journal*, he here seeks to demonstrate that "even a cursory examination of Jewish literature reveals that, both before and after his time, Maimonides' Principles were not regarded as the last word in Jewish theology" (p. 4). This despite the fact that a long string of 19th and 20th century authorities cited by Shapiro (pp. 17, 22-24) have maintained that Maimonides' Thirteen Principles are "the bedrock of Orthodoxy".

So far as I can judge, my book was simply ignored in Orthodox circles (with the notable exception of a friendly if critical review by Berger in *Tradition*) while Berger's book has been met with an embarassed "Yes, but…" Shapiro's book, on the other hand, sparked lively discussion in newspapers and on e-mail discussion sites.

There is very little point in reviewing the detailed contents of Shapiro's book in this essay. There can be no doubt that he is right in every important claim he makes about the reception of Maimonides' principles. Shapiro's method in the book is straightfoward and crushingly effective. With respect to each of Maimonides' principles (with the obvious exclusion of the first, which affirms the existence of God), Shapiro adduces Jewish thinkers over the generations who have rejected the principles outright, or revised them in ways which would have been absolutely unacceptable to Maimonides. With an eye to his intended audience, Shapiro cites only authorities who pass what might be called the "Artscroll" test (pp. 27-29, 73n24): "frum" enough to be cited in an Artscroll publication. After reading Shapiro's book, no one can deny that Orthodoxy has historically been much more latitudinarian in matters of doctrine than is ordinarily thought to be the case today.

Why, then, the stir? One reason is that Shapiro's apparent aim is to encourage Orthodox Jews to expend less energy on sniffing out *epikorsut*, and more energy in finding ways to live with other Jews. This clearly goes against a major trend in contemporary Orthodox circles, a trend I will try to explain below.

Thus, while reading the book, I was reminded of the old story concerning a young woman forced to spend the night alone in a sinister Transylvanian castle. In the middle of the night a huge vampire bat enters her room. Jumping out of bed in terror, the girl flees through the castle corridors, the vampire hard upon her heels. Making her terrified way to the castle chapel the unfortunate woman grabs a crucifix from the chapel altar and shoves it in the face of the menacing bat. The vampire bat hovers in the air opposite her, shrugs its shoulders, and says, "Es vet gornisht helfen!"[2]

Es vet gornisht helfen: those Jews who in Shapiro's eyes appear to need his message most have been long since immunized against both the message and its author, a beardless academic, and who has written a "scandalous" work about R. Jehiel Weinberg (1878-1966) to boot. But that is not to say that Shapiro's efforts have been wasted. If his aim is to support those Orthodox Jews who are more interested in living with other Jews than in measuring their orthodoxy with a frumometer, then he will surely have succeeded admirably in this book, providing such people with important support for their views, all the stronger for its being drawn from impeccably Orthodox sources only.

Why, then the stir? In order to understand it, we must take a quick tour of recent Jewish history. Pre-emancipation Judaism was an unself-conscious amagam of religion and what came, in the 19th century, to be called nationality. With very few exceptions (the *anusim* of Iberia being the most prominent example) Jewish authorities never had to define who a Jew was, since the matter was clear, both to the Jews and especially to the Gentiles. When, after the French revolution, Jews were invited to participate in the world around them, they found a world in which religion had been largely "privatized," a world in which religion had been severed from nationality, a world in which there developed a confusing myriad of news ways of being Jewish. It was suddenly not so clear anymore who was a Jew, and it was certainly no longer clear who a "good" Jew was. In a world in which membership in good standing in the Jewish community was no longer determined by descent (since so many Jews by descent had ceased being Jewish by belief and practice, or were adopting new beliefs and practices, while still calling themselves "good" Jews), in a world in which membership in the Jewish community was no longer determined by

---

2   Yiddish for: "it won't help."

identity with a shared Jewish past and hopes for a shared Jewish future (since so many Jews who identified with the shared Jewish past hoped for a shared Jewish future defined primarily in national or cultural terms), Maimonides' Thirteen Principles, wholly ignored by *poskim* (decisors) since their publication, and ignored by theologians (with the exception of Iberia between 1391 and 1492), suddenly came into their own and were used, with increasing vigor, to define the line between "good" Jews and those who must be excluded, those with whom no religious cooperation may be permitted, those who, for the most lenient, are *tinokot she-nishbu*, (children, as it were, raised among heathens) and for the most stringent, are out-and-out heretics.

A consequence of all this, I believe, is the following interesting anomaly. While Orthodoxy strongly adheres to the notion of 'decline of the generations,'[3] it is actually the latest of authorities who really determine what Jewish orthodoxy is. This may be illustrated by the following story. A respected friend of mine teaches Bible in an Orthodox institution. In a class on Ecclesiastes, one of his students said, "But, Rebbe, there is a problem on [sic] this verse from a passage in Ramhal [R. Moses Haim Luzzatto]!" My friend gently pointed out to his student that if there is a problem it is "on" Luzzatto (1707-1746), and not "on" Ecclesiastes.[4]

Maimonides himself was deeply critical of many aspects of the Judaism of his day and expressed contempt for many contemporary rabbis. He clearly held that there were rabbis in the generations preceding his who failed the doctrinal test of the Thirteen Principles. Rabbis of his own and subsequent generations held that Maimonides himself (not to mention his disciples) held views that it is forbidden to hear. Today Maimonides may be beyond criticism in Orthodox circles, but in his own day his books were burned at the instigation of Jewish opponents, and, as we know from the evidence of Nahmanides, some of the Tosafists wanted to ban the *Guide of the Perplexed* and *Sefer Madda* of

---

3   On which, see Kellner, *Decline*.

4   This story, I hope, explains why the issue of *hilkheta ke-batra'ei* (raised by several friends to whom I showed this review) is irrelevant in the present context. According to this principle, later *poskim* trump earlier *poskim*. But the principle is not applied to allow *aharonim* to dispute with *rishonim*, *rishonim* to reject the opinions of *ge'onim*, *ge'onim* to ignore the decisions of *amoraim*, or *amoraim* to decide against the *psak* of *tannaim*. It is certainly not used to justify the views of R. Moses Haim Luzzatto when they appear to contradict verses from Ecclesiastes! See Ta-Shema, "*Hilkheta*."

the *Mishneh Torah*. But despite the accusations, to speak anachronistically, of "non-Orthodoxy" leveled by Maimonides and against him, no one in the middle ages suggested excluding such people from the public square of Judaism. Even Gersonides was let into the *Mikra'ot Gedolot* rabbinic bible.[5] Rather, the attitude appeared to be the relative tolerance of R. Isaac Abravanel, who is reputed to have ended lectures on Maimonides' philosophy with the words: "This is the opinion of Rabbenu Moshe [Rabbi Moses Maimonides], not of Moshe Rabbenu [Moses our Teacher]." Abravanel thought that Maimonides held views at variance with those taught in the Torah, but he still taught those views in public!

At some level, Orthodox leaders today realize that the relatively relaxed attitude towards dogma adopted by the *rishonim* is a function of the medieval situation and context. Modernity, as I described it above, has made new and unprecedented demands upon Jews and Judaism. Thus, while paying lip service to the notion that the *aharonim* (later authorities) are subordinate to the *rishonim* (early authorities), many Orthodox Jews and certainly their rabbis act as if the reverse is the case. Note well Shapiro's list of authorities who hold that the Thirteen Principles represent the bedrock creed of Judaism. It was not for want of trying that Shapiro could not find a single authority who lived before the 19th century who made that claim.

Shapiro's book is thus a call to "return the crown to its ancient glory." But this is a call which is deeply discomfiting to rabbinic leaders who have been trained to believe that what is good for the Jews according to *rishonim* is good for the Jews according to *aharonim*, even if in fact they do not behave that way. A person who points out such cognitive dissonance is not likely to make many friends.

Why then the stir? I want to tell two brief anecdotes to explain another aspect of Shapiro's accomplishment which is upsetting to contemporary Orthodoxy. A number of years ago I published an article arguing that in Maimonides' view, the distinction between Jew and Gentile would ultimately disappear in the messianic era, that indeed, the whole world will serve God *with one accord*

---

5   True, the decision to do this was made by a Gentile, Daniel Bomberg, and a Jew who was then or would soon be an apostate, Cornelius Adelkind, but that decision was a function of Gersonides' antecedent popularity in Jewish circles.

(Zeph. 3:9).[6] I gave the article to a respected friend in my synagogue in Haifa. He read it carefully and said that it was not possible that Maimonides held such views. I promised to write a second article, showing why Maimonides had to hold such views; that project turned into a book, *Maimonides on Judaism and the Jewish People*. I presented the book to my friend who took the trouble to read it carefully and then told me: "I find your arguments convincing, which means that I now have less regard for Maimonides as an authoritative spokesperson for Judaism."

The second anecdote relates to a course I taught once at the University of Haifa on Maimonides' philosophy, in which I had occasion to elaborate upon a point also made by Shapiro (p. 16). Attending the classes was the wife of a deeply learned and leading figure in the Haifa rabbinic establishment, a woman of (then) unusual Jewish learning in her own right, who went on to become one of Israel's first *to'enot rabbaniyot* (women authorized to represent clients in rabbinic courts). Meeting my student's husband at a community function once, I found myself accosted with the following "accusation": "The rebbitzen [i.e., his wife] tells me that his honor [i.e., me] taught that according to Maimonides divine providence does not extend equally to all Jews." I agreed that that was what I had taught. He objected that it was impossible for Maimonides to have held such a view, since such a view contradicted several rabbinic statements. I replied that the issue of how to relate to such aggadic statements in general and how Maimonides related to them in particular was too big a topic to go into at a dinner, but that Maimonides had certainly said precisely what I had imputed to him. He replied: "There are three possibilities here: (a) the translation of the *Guide of the Perplexed* being used was simply incorrect; (b) if the translation was correct then, in the course of the generations since the time of Maimonides, the text of the *Guide of the Perplexed* at this point had become corrupted; (c) his honor [i.e., me] did not understand Maimonides."

In his book Shapiro (correctly) imputes to Maimonides certain views that run counter to the mainstream of traditional Jewish thought, most prominently: (a) the theory of immortality implied by the doctrine of the acquired intellect (i.e., that the key to earning a share in the world to come is intellectual

---

6   Kellner, "Suggestion." This view is defended at length below, ch. 18, "Maimonides' *True Religion*."

perfection; obedience to the commandments in and of itself is not enough) (pp. 12, 46-47, and 70); (b) the distinction between necessary and true beliefs (i.e., that both the Torah and Maimonides teach as true certain doctrines which are actually false) (p. 119-121, 131); (c) that there is no punishment after death for the wicked (they simply cease to exist) (p. 137). These views, all held by Maimonides, were unacceptable to many Jews in his day (remember, his books were burned in Montepellier in 1232 by, or at the very least, at the instigation, of Jews who opposed his doctrines) and are certainly unacceptable to Orthodox Jews today.

What is to be done? The most intellectually honest approach is that taken by my friend from synagogue: Maimonides may have said these things, but all that means is that he was wrong about some important issues. The more widely adopted approach (on which, see p. 83) is likely to be that of my student's husband: "But it is not possible for Maimonides to have held such views!" It is not possible because these are views which, while tolerated by many *rishonim* (and even held by some of them) have been rejected by *aharonim* as heterodox. Since Maimonides cannot be heterodox (he is, after all, the authority upon whom all rely to define orthdodoxy) he could not have held these views, and anyone, such as Marc Shapiro, who imputes them to him must in the best case be a fool and in the worst case a knave. And, it will be said of the author, that he may call himself Orthodox, but that does not make it so. Es vet gornisht helfen.[7]

It will also be argued against Shapiro and my defense of him here that matters of theology are assimilable to halakhah. Whatever the *rishonim* may have "paskened," as it were, on specific details of theology, we are duty bound to follow the *psak* (Jewish legal decision) of the rabbis of our own day. This is a popular position, even though it is historically unsound and conceptually muddled.[8] With respect to the historical reality, Maimonides himself, accepted by all as the greatest *posek* (Jewish legal decisor) in matters of theology, explicitly rejected the assimilation of theology to halakhah. Shapiro (pp. 116-117, 141-142) cites three clear-cut statements to this effect made by Maimonides

---

7 Further on these issues, see Kellner, "Kotler."

8 Valuable insights on this issue may be found in J. Sacks, *One People*, pp. 99-100. For historical discussion, see Solomon, *Analytic Movement*, pp. 223-240.

(statements which the late Yeshayahu Leibowitz used to quote regularly) and carefully distinguished halakhah from aggadah (in which latter he included theology).[9] Conceptually, the notion that dogma can be determined in the same way as the *kashrut* of a chicken, leads to weird consequences, the weirdest of which is the idea that holding a certain belief at one time time could cause one to be excluded from the community of Israel and to lose his or her share in the world to come, while holding that belief at another time carries with it no such consequences. Dogmas, it must be recalled, are beliefs taught as true by the Torah; is the truth taught by the Torah historically conditioned?[10]

I know personally one of the rabbis who was quoted in the press as being highly critical of the theses so ably defended by Shapiro in his book. This person, a distinguished halakhist in his own right, is also intimately familiar with the literature of medieval Jewish philosophy. It is inconceivable to me that he actually believes some of the things he has been quoted as saying. Rather, I suspect, he is following in the footsteps of Maimonides himself, who sought to hide his true views for what he took to be the good of the community. It may be, to judge some of Shapiro's critics *le-khaf zekhut* (leniently), that they realize full well that he writes the truth, but believe that in our day and age certain truths are dangerous and must be hidden. If I am right about this, then Marc Shapiro is a true disciple of Maimonides in seeking to uncover the deepest truths about God's Torah, and his critics are also true disciples of Maimonides in seeking to hide aspects of that truth from the Jewish masses.

---

9 For details, see Twersky, *Introduction*, pp. 11-12, 46-48. There are, of course, statements about God which Maimonides requires Jews to know (not simply to believe); but these are, to his mind, provable with the tools of Aristotelian philosophy. For details, see ch. 9. "Could Maimonides..."

10 Other logical and psychological problems with the notion of assimilating dogma to halakhah were explored as long ago as the fifteenth century, in the writings of R. Hasdai Crescas (p. 10) and R. Isaac Abravanel (p. 33).

CHAPTER ELEVEN
The Virtue of Faith

I t is with apparent reference to the verse describing Abraham, *And he believed in the Lord and it was accounted to him as justice (zedakah)* (Gen. 15:6) that Philo, who may well be considered the "father of Neoplatonism," calls faith a virtue, indeed, the "queen of virtues."[1] In his study of Philo's philosophy, Harry Wolfson explains that by 'faith' Philo means "two things: (1) belief in the unity and providence of God as well as in all the truths revealed directly by God, and (2) trust in God.[2] That faith which Philo held to be a virtue has cognitive (acquiescence to certain propositions) and non-cognitive (trust in God) elements.

This reading of faith as a virtue appears to be new in Philo. Wolfson says (p. 216): "But in Greek philosophy prior to Philo neither faith in general nor faith in God in particular is spoken of as a virtue on a par with piety, the fear of God, and holiness." This estimation is shared by John Passmore: "The path to perfection, as Philo envisages it, begins with faith, a faith in God comparable to Abraham's. This is a point at which Philo breaks sharply with the Greek tradition. There is nowhere in Greek thought any suggestion that faith is a virtue, let alone that it is 'the queen of virtues,' to quote only one of Philo's ecstatic descriptions of it."[3]

Philo's distinctive outlook finds a surprising echo in the writings of Moses Maimonides. In *The Guide of the Perplexed* (III.53) Maimonides calls faith *(al-iman)* a virtue. I will explain why this is surprising and how an understanding of the claim that faith is a virtue can help us better to understand the place of faith and of ethics in Maimonides' thinking. Maimonides' claim about the

---

1   See Philo, *On Abraham*, 270, LCL, 6.133.

2   Wolfson, *Philo*, vol. 2, pp. 216-218.

3   Passmore, *Perfectibility*, p. 61.

virtue of faith comes up in the context of a discussion of three terms, *hesed* (loving-kindness), *mishpat* (judgment), and *zedakah* (righteousness). The last of these is defined as follows (p. 631):

> The word *zedakah* is derived from *zedek*, which means justice; justice being the granting to everyone who has a right to something, that which he has a right to and giving to every being that which corresponds to its merits. But in the books of the prophets, fulfilling the duties imposed upon you with regard to others is not called *zedakah* in conformity with the first sense. For if you give a hired man his wages or pay a debt, this is not called *zedakah.* On the other hand, the fulfilling of duties with regard to others imposed upon you on account of moral virtue, such as remedying the injuries of all those who are injured, is called *zedakah.* Therefore it says with reference to the returning of a pledge: *And it shall be zedakah unto you* (Dt. 24:13). For when you walk in the way of the moral virtues, you do justice unto your rational soul, giving her the due that is her right. And because every moral virtue is called *zedakah,* it says: *And he believed in the Lord, and it was accounted to him as zedakah* (Gen. 15:6). I refer to the virtue of faith. This applies likewise to his dictum, may he be exalted: *And it shall be zedakah unto us if we take care to observe, and so on* (Dt. 6:25).

Maimonides here offers two definitions of justice. The first is giving to each his due; the second definition is Biblical and involves more than giving each his due. It demands acting towards others in keeping with the requirements of the moral virtues.[4] Maimonides uses the example of curing the hurts of those whom one has not injured. He cites as a further example the Biblical obligation not to keep a pledge needed by its owner:

> *When thou dost lend thy neighbor any manner of loan, thou shall not go into his house to fetch his pledge. Thou shall stand without, and the man to whom thou*

---

4 Maimonides' distinction here is perhaps best summed up in the words of Steven Schwarzschild: "Jewish justice is different from the classic philosophic (Greek-Western) view of this concept. In the latter, justice is generally considered under the headings of 'distributive' and 'retributive.' These are, of course, also comprised in *zedakah,* but while 'distributive' and 'retributive' justice are essentially procedural principles (i.e., how to do things), Jewish justice is essentially substantive (i.e., what human life should be like)." See "Justice," col .476. Schwarzschild continues: "Substantive justice depends on an ultimate (i.e., messianic) value commitment."

dost lend shall bring forth the pledge without unto thee. And if he be a poor man
thou shall not sleep with his pledge; thou shall surely restore to him the pledge
when the sun goes down, that he may sleep in his garment and bless thee; and it
shall be zedakah unto thee before the Lord thy God (Dt. 24:10-13).[5]

Maimonides gives another reason for calling the behavior demanded by
moral virtue just: When we act morally we do justice to our rational soul,
giving it its due. Maimonides here appeals to the first definition of justice in
order to justify his second use of the term. But how does acting morally give
our rational soul its due? The answer, I believe, involves Maimonides' claim
that rational perfection cannot be attained without first achieving moral perfection.[6]

Maimonides now gives a third reason for calling moral behavior just: the
fact that moral virtues are called *zedakah*. As his example he cites the verse,
"And he believed in the Lord and it was accounted to him as *zedakah*." Realizing that this citation would not be transparent to his reader, Maimonides
explains by saying, "I refer to the virtue of faith." This, then, is the context of
Maimonides' claim that faith is a virtue.

The concordance shows that Maimonides did not have any other ready options if he needed a verse connecting a specific virtue with *zedakah*. But his
identification of faith as a virtue remains striking: when he deals with questions
of faith or belief it is almost always in what we would tend to call an intellectual
as distinguished from a moral context. For example, he says of "belief" that it
is not "the notion that is uttered, but the notion that is represented in the soul
when it has been averred of it that it in fact is just as it has been represented."[7]
Maimonides reaffirms the point a hit further along in the same passage: "For
there is no belief except after a representation: belief is the affirmation that

---

5   See Maimonides, *Book of Commandments,* positive commandment 199, negative
    commandment 139; *Mishneh Torah,* "Laws of Lender and Borrower," III 5.

6   See *Guide* I. 34 (pp. 76-77): "For it has been explained, or rather demonstrated, that the moral
    virtues are a preparation for the rational virtues, it being impossible to achieve true, rational
    acts – I mean perfect rationality – unless it be by a man thoroughly trained with respect
    to his morals and endowed with the qualities of tranquility and quiet. ... It is accordingly
    indubitable that preparatory moral training should be carried out before beginning with this
    science [metaphysics] so that man should be in a state of extreme uprightness and perfection."
    Further on this, see *Confrontation,* p. 63, note 71.

7   *Guide* I. 50, p. 111.

was been represented is outside the mind just as it has been represented to the mind." Belief, then, is not a matter of disposition, tendency, or relationship between persons. Rather it is the affirmation that what one represents to oneself does actually correspond to objective reality. Belief must then have specific cognitive content, and this content must be subject to proof or refutation. Put in other words, belief is the affirmation or denial of propositions which, at least in theory, must be such that they can be shown to be true or false.[8]

Maimonides in fact insists that the Torah commands the adoption of certain beliefs: first and foremost the existence of God. But all of the beliefs that Maimonides treats as commandments are matters which in his view are philosophically demonstrable.[9] So even in the area where Maimonides most strikingly affirms an obligation to believe, we see the concurrent assumption of the intellectual content of belief.

But if belief is a matter of the intellect, how can it also he a matter of moral virtue? Maimonides distinguishes the two realms and relates each to a different part of the soul. He subordinates the moral realm to the intellectual and insists that the sound morality is a prerequisite of intellectual perfection, but that the moral aspect of our personhood is less distinguished than the intellectual. He affirms that the importance of the moral side is primarily instrumental.

Maimonides uses two different Arabic terms, *al-iman* and *al-itiqad*, for what we call belief or faith. Avraham Nuriel has argued that Maimonides consistently distinguishes between them, reserving *al-iman* for what we would call "trust" and *al-itiqad* for intellectual acquiescence in the truth of a proposition.[10] In contemporary terms, we can say that Maimonides distinguishes between "belief in" and "belief that."[11]

Thus Maimonides' intellectualist definition of 'belief' in the *Guide* is a definition of *itiqad*, not of *iman*. In those Arabic texts where Maimonides commands belief, such as the first positive commandment in the *Book of*

---

8 See Wolfson, *Spinoza*, vol. 2, p.147 and his "Aristotelian Predicables," p. 163: "What Maimonides therefore means to say is that belief is that which can be expressed by a logical proposition."

9 See ch. 8, "Maimonides, Crescas, and Abravanel on Exodus 20:2," and my *Dogma*, pp. 38-49.

10 See Nuriel, "Faith."

11 See Seeskin, "Judaism and the Linguistic Interpretation" my *Dogma*, pp. 1-6, and my *Must*, pp. 11-25

Commandments, he uses variants of *itiqad,* and not of *iman.* In their Hebrew parallels, such as "Laws of the Foundations of the Torah," in the *Mishneh Torah,* he uses variants of the Hebrew *yedi'ah,* knowledge, and not *emunah,* faith or trust. But when Maimonides calls faith a virtue he uses the term *iman.*[12] The text which prompts this study is a perfect example and is cited as such by Nuriel.[13] That faith which is a moral virtue, then, trust in God.[14]

Turning now to 'virtue', we find that Maimonides takes up the issue in the first work he is known to have written, his treatise on logic.[15] He devotes the fourteenth chapter to the classification of the sciences,[16] among other sciences discussing political science, which he treats under four headings. Virtue is addressed under one of these, self-government:

> Man's governance of himself is the science which enables him to develop good qualities and to free himself from bad qualities, if he has already acquired them. Moral qualities are dispositions which gradually become more and more fixed in the soul until they are formed into a habit by which actions are determined. Philosophers describe moral qualities as either excellent or defective. Praiseworthy moral qualities are called virtues; blameworthy moral qualities are called vices. Actions resulting from praiseworthy qualities are called good; those resulting from blameworthy qualities are called bad. [Similarly philosophers describe] reasoning, the act of conceiving ideas, as either excellent or

---

12 Shalom Rosenberg claims that there are many examples or Maimonides' not distinguishing between *al-iman* and *al-itiqad,* but he mentions only one. See his "The Concept of *Emunah,*" p. 275. The present essay shows that in III.53 Maimonides does not use *al-iman* in the sense of intellectual acquiescence but in the sense of trust in God.

13 An interesting sidelight to this whole discussion is provided by a posthumous text of Rabbi J. Kafih's. He was usually consistent in translating *al-iman* as *emunah* (faith) and *al-itiqad* as *yediah* (knowledge), but failed to do so in his translation of Maimonides' commentary to Sanhedrin X, *Perek Helek.* But in two places in his own copy of his translation (in the seventh and eighth principles of faith), he added marginal notes, correcting variants of *al-itiqad* from variants of *emunah* to variants of *yediah.* See A. Kafih, "*Moreinu,*" p. 308.

14 For a discussion of rabbinic texts on religious faith as trust, see *Must,* pp. 26-43 and 140-146.

15 Known as *Millot ha-Higayon* in Hebrew, this text was composed in Arabic and translated three times into Hebrew in the Middle Ages. For details, and for the controversy over its authorship, see *Confrontation,* p. 57.

16 On this chapter see Wolfson, "Classification," and "Note"; Strauss, "Maimonides' Statement," and Berman, "Reexamination."

defective. We thus speak of intellectual virtues and vices. The philosophers have many books on the moral virtues.[17]

Maimonides here follows Aristotle's distinction of two kinds of virtues: moral and intellectual. Moral virtues are praiseworthy moral qualities which can be "fixed in the soul," that is, strengthened by exercise. They can become habits which determine our behavior. Trust certainly is more appropriately thought of as finding expression in behavior than is intellectual acquiescence. One cannot truly claim to trust one's spouse, for example, if one acts inconsistently with such trust, say hiring private detectives to catch the spouse in acts of infidelity. But in most cases acquiescing to the truth of a proposition (that the earth revolves around the sun, for example, or that there exists a prime mover) has little immediate impact upon our behavior (and should not if Hume is correct in saying that we cannot derive 'ought' from 'is'). Intellectual virtues relate not to dispositions which determine behavior, but to excellence in reasoning. They reflect either our skills in conceiving ideas or the soundness of the ideas we have conceived.

Maimonides affords more information about his conception of virtue in the second of his "Eight Chapters," where he analyzes the diseases of the soul. The title of the chapter is "On the Disobedience of the Soul's Powers and on Knowledge of the Part in which the Virtues and the Vices are Primarily Found." Once again, Maimonides distinguishes moral from intellectual virtue:

> As for the virtues, there are two kinds: moral virtues and rational virtues. Opposed to them are two kinds of vices. The rational virtues are found in the rational part [of the soul]. Among them are: (i) wisdom, which is knowledge of the remote and proximate causes and which comes after knowledge of the existence of the thing whose causes are being investigated; and (ii) intelligence, which includes (a) the theoretical intellect, I mean, the first intelligibles, which we have by nature; (b) the acquired intellect, but this is not the place for that; and (c) brilliance and excellent comprehension, that is, excellent grasp of a thing quickly, in no time, or in a very short time. The vices of this power are the contrary of these or their opposite. The moral virtues are

---

17 I follow Wolfson's translation, in "Note," pp. 538-39.

So al-Farabi's text settles nothing for us, and Ibn Tibbon's translation remains our only source for including faith in Maimonides' list of virtues in "Eight Chapters," a rather thin reed on which to support the reading.

What we do learn from the "Eight Chapters" as it stands is that the moral virtues pertain to the appetitive part of the soul and are to be connected with the ethics of the mean, developed both here and in "Laws of Moral Qualities," for the moral vices involve excess or deficiency. So if faith is a moral virtue it should pertain to the appetitive part of the soul and the vices corresponding to it would be excessive or deficient faith. But what would a religious thinker mean by too much faith? The answer is not hard to provide if we follow Nuriel in defining 'faith' (al-iman) as 'trust.' Jewish tradition clearly acknowledges that trust in God may be exaggerated and warns against such exaggeration.[25]

Our discussion here, I think, allows us to correct the widely accepted view of Maimonides as a pure intellectual who ultimately prized nothing in the world of ideas or in the world of religion but intellectual perfection.[26] By emphasizing that there is a kind of belief that does not involve the cognition of the intelligibilia and is, in its own way, desirable we show that the faith of the non-philosopher, so long, of course, as it is not actually based on falsehood, is of moral value. At the same time we find a basis for criticizing the view that the ultimate perfection of the individual who has achieved a maximally perfected intellect is moral behavior. For there is no doubt that Maimonides prizes knowledge of God over simple trust in Him.[27]

---

25 The prevalent Rabbinic view is encapsulated in the maxim, "One is not to rely upon miracles" (Pesahim 64b). See Werblowski, "Faith"; Jacobs, *Faith*, ch. 10. Cf. Sa'adiah's strictures against excessive reliance upon God in his *Book of Beliefs and Opinions* X. 15, Rosenblatt translation, pp. 395-97.

26 This interpretation can be traced back to Samuel ibn Tibbon, in his introduction to his Hebrew translation of Maimonides' Commentary on *Avot*. See my edition and analysis of that text in "Maimondes and Samuel ibn Tibbon" and the discussion in ch. 4 above, "Is Maimonides' Ideal Person."

27 Just what Maimonides understands by knowledge of God and how such knowledge can inform our practical behavior is the central question of my monograph, *Maimonides on Human Perfection*. The key texts are *Guide* III.27 and III.54.

PART THREE

INTRODUCTION TO PART THREE,
Science and Torah

As noted in Chapter Three of this collection, Maimonides opened his magisterial law code, *Mishneh Torah* with the following statement (here translated loosely):

> The most important principle of all the principles of the Torah, and the fundamental axiom of all the sciences is the same, to wit, to know that there exists a First Existent, that It gives existence to all that exists, and that all existent beings, from the heaven to the earth and what is between them, exist only due to the truth of Its existence.

Knowing this, Maimonides goes on to say, is a positive commandment – indeed the first positive commandment in his *Book of Commandments*, not to mention the first of the 'Thirteen Principles'.

In making these claims Maimonides imports science (in the guise of *ma'aseh bereshit*, Greek physics, and *ma'aseh merkavah*, Greek metaphysics) into the very heart of Torah. Indeed the Twentieth Century's leading Maimonidean, Rabbi Josef Kafih, went so far as to deny the possibility of secular studies (*limmudei hol*) for Maimonides: if a discipline yields truth, it is not secular.

Moreover, to know something, for Maimonides (following Aristotle), is to know it through or with its causes. The first commandment of the Torah is to *know* that God exists; and, as Maimonides makes clear in the Introduction to the *Guide of the Perplexed*, the only way to fulfill that commandment is through the study of physics and metaphysics.

The implications of this are vast:

The study of science becomes incumbent upon all Jews who want to fulfill even the first commandment of the Torah.

Psychoanalysis may be a Jewish science, as its opponents claimed, and Lysenko's biology was certainly socialist 'science', but surely no reader of this book would claim that there can be a *Jewish* physics or *Jewish* metaphysics. Thus, the science which Jews are commanded to study is precisely that science which is taught (for Maimonides) by uncircumcised Greeks and oppressive Muslims.

One who has mastered what Maimonides calls (in the Introduction to the *Guide of the Perplexed*) the legal science of the Torah (i.e., the Talmudist) is thus inferior to one who has mastered the secrets of the Torah, i.e., the person who understands physics and metaphysics. (It is no wonder that many who read Maimonides expostulate: "This is Greek to me!" and that medieval rabbis wanted to burn or at least excise the 51st chapter of the third part of the *Guide*.)

Truth is absolute and objective; there can thus be no such things as intellectual (or spiritual) authority per se. Statements are true irrespective of the standing of the person making them. Maimonides could thus have no patience for the sorts of claims to rabbinic authority which underlie the contemporary doctrine of *da'at Torah* (charismatic rabbinic authority) in its various permutations (on which, see: *Maimonides on the Decline of the Generations and the Nature of Rabbinic Authority* [Albany: SUNY Press, 1996] and "Rabbis in Politics: A Study in Medieval and Modern Jewish Political Theory," *Medinah ve-Hevrah* 3 [2003]: 673-698 [Hebrew].)

The chapters in this section all elucidate different aspects of these issues. The originally appeared in the following places:

"On the Status of the Astronomy and Physics in Maimonides' *Mishneh Torah*: A Chapter in the History of Science," *British Journal for the History of Science* 24 (1991): 453-63.

"Maimonides on the Science of the Mishneh Torah – Provisional or Permanent?" *AJS Review* 18 (1993): 169-94.

"Maimonides' Allegiances to Torah and Science," *Torah U Madda Journal* 7 (1997): 88-104.

The last chapter in this section has not been published before.

CHAPTER TWELVE
On the Status of the Astronomy and Physics in Maimonides' *Mishneh Torah* and *Guide of the Perplexed:* A Chapter in the History of Science

An interesting question arises in the context of the typically medieval description of the universe presented at the beginning of Maimonides' great law code, the *Mishneh Torah*. What was Maimonides' own attitude towards that account? Was it meant only as a statement of the best description of nature available at the time (and thus radically distinct from the *halakhic* matters which make up the bulk of the *Mishneh Torah)* or was it meant to be a description of the true nature of the universe as it really is, not subject to revision in the light of new paradigms or new models (and thus essentially similar to the *halakhic* matters in the text) ? Answering this question will lead us to a better understanding of Maimonides' understanding of the nature of science and of what I shall call, for lack of a better term, scientific progress. Maimonides will be shown to hold that while sublunar science can reach perfection and completion such is not possible for superlunar science and that to the extent that the scientific matters in the *Mishneh Torah* deal with the latter they could not have been presented as the final description of the universe as it truly is.

Maimonides' universe is described in the third and fourth chapters of "Laws of the Foundations of the Torah." It is a finite universe, composed of nine concentric spheres, with the Earth in the centre. The ninth and largest sphere "includes and encircles all things." Each of the eight internal spheres is divided into subspheres, "like the several layers of onions." These subspheres are contiguous, with no empty space between them at all. In addition to the concentric spheres which encompass the Earth, there are smaller spheres fixed in the larger spheres.

"Laws of the Foundations of the Torah," III closes with a transition to the sublunar realm: the reader is told of the four elements of Greek physics: earth, water, air and fire. These bodies, unlike those of the superlunar world, are lifeless, without souls or intelligence.

The sublunar realm is then described in the fourth chapter: it is the world of the four elements and of bodies composed of them. It is a world in which things strive always to return to their natural place. It is a world of constant generation and corruption, a world whose most fundamental principles are form and matter.

Maimonides' description of the universe is dramatically different from the world in which we live, work and play: ours is an infinite universe, in which material bodies exist in a vacuum; in our solar system, the Sun stands at the centre, the dead planets revolving around it. Gravity replaces the notion of 'natural place' and atomic physics the four elements.

In another context[1] I have argued that Maimonides presented the scientific matters in the text as simply the most up-to-date account of the universe available to him, subject to change, development and refinement. In support of this claim I adduced materials showing that Maimonides held that the rabbinic Sages could err when presenting evidence based on the sciences of their day, that individuals perfected enough to achieve some level of prophetic inspiration could err, that Aristotle could err in scientific matters, that he (Maimonides) could and did err in matters of *Halakhah,* and that he expected there to be further progress in scientific and spiritual matters. All this being the case, I argued that Maimonides could not have been wedded irretrievably to his account of natural matters as found in 'Laws of the Foundations of the Torah' at the beginning of the *Mishneh Torah.*

But, taking away with the left hand what I had just given with the right, I then pointed out that the issue was not so simple and straightforward. Maimonides, in his medieval fashion, accepted the fact that closure or perfection of the sciences was inevitable.

Furthermore, he held that the physical (sublunar) matters discussed in the *Mishneh Torah* represented physical science in its perfected, completed form. But if this is the case, then perhaps the conclusion that Maimonides would

---

1   Ch. 13, "Maimonides on the Science of the *Mishneh Torah.*"

admit that the description of the universe he presents in "'Laws of the Founda-tions of the Torah" is provisional (in the sense that it represents only the best and most up-to-date account of the sciences available to him) is incorrect. If the various branches of wisdom had reached perfection, then what Maimo-nides was presenting in the *Mishneh Torah* was not simply a report on the cur-rent status of our understanding of the universe, but the absolute codification of physical and metaphysical truth, once for all, just as the laws in the *Mishneh Torah* are the absolute codification of the commandments of Judaism (errors aside), once and for all time. On this basis we could construe Maimonides as saying that the Sages and Aristotle erred in scientific matters simply because they lived in times before the various sciences had reached their perfection; the fact that they erred, therefore, does not mean that he must err. Since prog-ress understood in this fashion is not open-ended, there is no problem with asserting both that human beings progress scientifically and spiritually and that the acme of this progress has been reached, or nearly reached.

The situation is not, however, so simple. All this would make excellent sense had Maimonides restricted his description of the physical universe to the sub-lunar realm. It was with respect to this realm that he wrote in the *Guide of the Perplexed* (II.19, p. 319):

> Everything that Aristotle has said about all that exists from beneath the sphere of the moon to the centre of the earth is indubitably correct, and no one will deviate from it unless he does not understand it or unless he has preconceived opinions that he wishes to defend or that lead him to a denial of a thing that is manifest.

The situation with respect to the superlunar world is very different:

> On the other hand, everything that Aristotle expounds with regard to the sphere of the moon and that which is above it is, except for certain things, something analogous to guessing and conjecturing. All the more does this ap-ply to what he says about the order of the intellcts and to some of the opinions regarding the divine that he believes; for the latter contain grave incongruities and perversities that manifestly and clearly appear as such to all the nations, that propagate evil, and that he cannot demonstrate.

Superlunar science had not reached perfection in the time of Aristotle. Indeed it had not yet reached perfection in the time of Maimonides: "It is possible that someone else will find a demonstration by means of which the true reality of what is obscure for me will become clear to him" (*Guide*, II.24, pp. 325-326).

If superlunar science had not reached perfection and closure by Maimonides' time, and if Maimonides expected further progress in such science, then perhaps the physics described in the *Mishneh Torah* was not presented after all as the final picture of the universe?

What exactly does Maimonides say about our knowledge of the heavens in the *Guide?* In the context of his discussion of the question of creation, Maimonides raises a number of problems with Aristotle's account of astronomy, in order to cast doubt upon the sufficiency of Aristotle's arguments for eternity and against creation. By way of introducing the discussion (II.23, p. 322) he explains:

> I have promised you a chapter in which I shall expound to you the grave doubts that would affect whoever thinks that man has acquired knowledge as to the arrangement of the motions of the sphere and as to their being natural things going on according to the law of necessity, things whose order and arrangement are clear.

The following chapter (II.24) is given over to an account of these 'grave doubts'. Maimonides first deals with the question of devising a theory to account for observational phenomena: "What you know already," he says, addressing directly Joseph ben Judah, the student for whom he wrote the *Guide*, "is that as far as the action of ordering the motions and making the course of the stars conform to what is seen is concerned, everything depends on two principles: either that of the epicycles or that of the eccentric spheres or on both of them" (p. 322). Maimonides then gives a detailed account of how epicycles and eccentric spheres both contradict the principles of Aristotelian natural science.[2]

---

2   On Maimonides' astronomy see Langermann, "Some Issues" and the studies cited there.

But if this is the case, and Aristotelian natural science is correct, and "there are no epicycles or eccentric circles and everything revolves around the centre of the earth," then how can we account for the various observed motions of the stars? "Is it in any way possible," Maimonides asks (II.24, pp. 325-326), " that motion should be on the one hand circular, uniform, and perfect, and that on the other hand the things that are observable should be observed in consequence of it, unless this be accounted for by making use of one of the two principles [epicycles and eccentricity] or both of them?"

Maimonides responds to this last question by rejecting it altogether (p. 326):

> However, I have already explained to you by word of mouth[3] that all this does not affect the astronomer. For his purpose is not to tell us in which way the spheres truly are, but to posit an astronomical system in which it would be possible for the motions to be circular and uniform and to correspond to what is apprehended through sight, regardless of whether or not things are thus in fact.

What is Maimondes talking about here? He seems to be saying that astronomers are not interested in what actually happens in the skies, only in our ability to provide a model of what happens and, one assumes, to predict astral phenomena. This is precisely Maimonides' position. In order to understand it, we must take a brief glance at a long-running debate over the nature of science in general and of astronomy in particular. Pierre Duhem focused attention on the question in his well-known monograph, *To Save the Phenomena*.[4] Duhem distinguishes between two approaches to astronomy in the ancient and medieval worlds, the formalistic and the realistic. The formalistic or instrumentalist, utilitarian approach follows Plato and Ptolemy. According to it, our models of planetary motions are nothing other than mathematical constructs designed to facilitate our calculations; they are not meant to describe the "real world" as such. The formalistic approach was interested only

---

3   i.e. in direct conversation.

4   Duhem, *To Save the Phenomena*. My attention was drawn to this issue by Freudenthal, "Human Felicity." My indebtedness to Freudenthal's sophisticated and fascinating discussion is considerable.

in "saving the phenomena" (i.e. describing and calculating the occurrence of specific phenomena). The second, or "realistic" approach followed Aristotle in affirming that our astronomy ought to reflect physical reality. [5]

On this issue Maimonides placed himself firmly in the formalist camp.[6] That is the brunt of the passage just quoted. Duhem points out that Maimonides was the only Arabic writer to adopt the Greek [Platonic] idea that astronomical hypotheses are not judgments bearing on the nature of things; that it is not necessary that they be deducible from the principles of physics, nor even that they be in harmony with these principles; that it is not necessary that they allow of representation by means of suitably arranged rigid bodies revolving one on the other, because, as geometric fictions they have no function except that of saving the appearances.

Duhem continues:

The idea that dominates all of Maimonides' astronomical discussions - a new idea within Semitic Peripateticism, and one which, in this milieu, surprises by its sagaciously sceptical tendencies is the one suggested by Ptolemy and developed by Proclus: The knowledge of heavenly things, in their essence and true nature, is beyond man's capacities; sublunary things alone are accessible to our feeble understanding.[7]

Maimonides expresses himself quite clearly on this in another passage:

Know with regard to the astronomical matters mentioned that if an exclusively mathematical minded man reads and understands them, he will think that they form a cogent demonstration that the form and number of the spheres is as stated. Now things are not like this, and this is not what is sought in the science of astronomy ... But there has been no demonstration whether the sun has an

---

5 As we shall see immediately, Duhem's distinction is very helpful for understanding Maimonides; that does not mean that he is necessarily correct in the way in which he applies it across the board through the entire history of ancient and medieval science. The debates over his interpretations of the history of science need not detain us here.

6 For a discussion of this issue, see Bechler, "Methodological Basis." I am not convinced by Bechler's claim that Maimonides' main intent here was to undermine the authority of Aristotle generally so as to make the conflict between Aristotelian philosophy and Judaism less severe. See further the various positions of Shlomo Pines as discussed by Langermann, "Some Issues."

7 Pp. 32-35.

eccentric sphere or an epicycle. Now the master of astronomy does not mind this, for the object of that science is to suppose as a hypothesis an astronomy that renders it possible for the motion of the star to be uniform and circular with no acceleration or deceleration or change in it and to have the inferences necessarily following from the assumption of that motion agree with what is observed.[8]

Why does Maimonides reject the realistic approach to astronomy? *The heavens are the heavens of the Lord,* Maimonides quotes from Psalms 115: 16, *"but the earth hath He given to the sons of man.* I mean thereby that the deity alone fully knows the true reality, the nature, the substance, the form, the motions, and the causes of the heavens ... For it is impossible for us to accede to the points starting from which conclusions may be drawn about the heavens; for the latter are too far away from us and too high in place and rank."[9]

As is well-known, Maimonides places severe limits on the extent of human knowledge.[10] Knowledge of the heavens is literally beyond our ken. This is not a matter of "sagacious skepticism," as Duhem would have it, but of central *religious* importance to Maimonides. Insisting on the limitations of human knowledge, and emphasizing the absolutely qualitatively different characters of divine and human knowledge, allows Maimonides to eat his cake and have it too with respect to any number of theological problems. Breaking with the school of Andalusian Aristotelianism on this matter was absolutely crucial to Maimonides.[11] It was more than simply criticizing Aristotle's celestial physics so as to make the refutation of his arguments for the eternity of the world

---

8   *Guide of the Perplexed*, II.11, pp. 273-4.

9   II.24, p. 327. Compare Duhem's explanation: "The beings with which the first of these two kinds of physics deals are regarded as of a nature infinitely higher than that with which the second physics deals; hence the inference that the former is incomparably more difficult than the latter. Proclus teaches that sublunary physics is accessible to man, whereas celestial physics passes his understanding and is reserved for the Divine. Maimonides shares this view of Proclus; celestial physics, according to him, is full of mysteries the knowledge of which God has kept unto Himself; but terrestrial physics, fully worked out, is available in the work of Aristotle." Duhem then makes the following interesting observation, "Yet, contrary to what the men of antiquity and the Middle Ages thought, the celestial physics they had constructed was singularly more advanced than their terrestrial physics" (p. 114).

10 The precise extent of those limits is a matter of scholarly debate. For a recent discussion, with references to earlier studies, see Stern, "Maimonides on the Growth of Knowledge."

11 I have explored this issue in detail in "Maimonides and Gersonides on Astronomy and Metaphysics." This essay is scheduled to be republished in the companion volume to this one.

easier; it was a central element in the edifice Maimonides was trying to construct, an edifice in which the "foundation of all [religious] foundations" was equivalent to the "pillar of all the [Greek/Arab] sciences."[12] In order to harmonize Torah and (Aristotelian) science Maimonides had to draw narrow limits around what we can in principle know. His formalistic astronomy is a further expression of this.

This has brought us rather far afield. Returning to the point under discussion, what does Maimonides' attempt to "save the phenomena" have to do with the question of his attitude towards the science he presents in the *Mishneh Torah?* We are now in the position to state categorically that superlunar science had not reached perfection or closure in Maimonides' day for the simple reason that he held that such science would never reach that stage: the full picture is beyond our abilities to apprehend.

But perhaps Maimonides' account, even if incomplete, represents the highest stage that human beings will ever achieve? There are two reasons for rejecting this hypothesis. The first is found in the continuation of the passage adduced above (*Guide* II.24, p. 327):

> And to fatigue the minds with notions that cannot be grasped by them and for the grasp of which they have no instrument, is a defect in one's inborn disposition or some sort of temptation. Let us then stop at a point that is within our capacity, and let us give over the things that cannot be grasped by reasoning to him who was reached by the mighty divine overflow so that it could be fittingly said of him: *With him do I speak mouth to mouth* (Numbers 12: 8). This is the end of what I have to say about this question. *It is possible that someone else may find a demonstration by means of which the true reality of what is obscure for me will become clear to him* [emphasis added].

Maimonides tells us two things here: that we must stop our inquiries before we overstep the bounds set for us by God and that his account of superlunar phenomena has not yet reached that boundary. It is possible that some other savant/philosopher will find a "demonstration by means of which the true reality of what is obscure for [Maimonides] will become clear to him." In other words,

---

12 "Laws of the Foundations of the Torah," I.1, as interpreted by Isaac Abravanel in his *Principles of Faith*, p. 76 (Chapter 5, 4th objection).

the account of the heavens presented in "'Laws of the Foundations of the Torah"' is not the fullest account possible in this inherently incompletable science.

The second reason for rejecting the claim that Maimonides saw his account of the heavens in the *Mishneh Torah* as complete has to do with two apparent contradictions between the *Mishneh Torah* and the *Guide* to which earlier commentators have not paid sufficient attention.

Both of these contradictions have to do with astronomical matters. Concerning the first, Maimonides maintains in *Guide* II.24 that "there are no epicycles." "Foundations of the Torah," III.5 however, affirms the existence of eight "small spheres" or epicycles.[13]

This does not seem to be a contradiction that can be papered over. What is going on here? I do not think that there is any esoteric doctrine at work. Rather, Maimonides' aim in "Foundations of the Torah," II-IV was to show some aspects of the wonders of God's creation in order to bring the reader to the fear and love of God. Maimonides would have been defeating his own purpose had he said in such a context something to the effect, "I would love to describe the superlunar realm to you, but astronomy properly understood is really nothing other than a mathematical construct, bearing no essential relationship to physical reality." Instead of defeating his purpose by being wholly honest with his readers Maimonides presented a fairly standard account of the structure of the heavens. This said, we now see that Maimonides' account of the heavens in the *Mishneh Torah* could by no stretch of the imagination be construed as having been presented as the final, complete and perfect account of astronomy.

The second contradiction has to do with the number and order of the spheres, not with their nature. In "Foundations of the Torah," III.1 Maimonides tells us that there are nine spheres in the following order: Moon, Mercury, Venus, Sun, Mars, Jupiter, Saturn, fixed stars, all-encompassing sphere. Turning to the *Guide of the Perplexed* (II.9, pp. 268-269) we find that Maimonides tells us that there are five spheres, not nine, and in the following order: Moon, Sun, five planets, fixed stars, all-encompassing sphere. In this chapter Maimonides

---

13 This contradiction is subjected to close examination by Langermann, "Perplexity." Langermann suggests ways of eliminating the contradiction. This attempt, however, does not take into account all of the issues raised in the present context and cannot be seen as wholly successful.

raises the question of the relationship between the Sun on the one hand, and Mercury and Venus on the other. Ancient astronomers, Maimonides tells us, held that Venus and Mercury were above the Sun; Ptolemy held them to be below the Sun (so that, Maimonides explains, the Sun would be in the middle, three planets below it, three above it); modern Andalusian astronomers held with the ancients; finally "the excellent philosopher" Abu Bakr ibn al-Saigh (i.e. ibn Bajjah) showed that this last view was improbable - Venus and Mercury, according to him, were below the Sun. Despite his evident admiration for ibn Bajjah, Maimonides reverts to the view of the ancients, placing Mercury and Venus (and the other planets) above the Sun.

We have here two contradictions between the astronomy of the *Mishneh Torah* and that of the *Guide:* according to the former there are nine spheres, and Mercury and Venus are below the Sun, while according to the *Guide* there are four spheres and (in consequence of this) Mercury and Venus are above the Sun.

One might wish to respond that these contradictions are of no great account: since, as we saw above, Maimonides himself says that spheres can be subdivided, perhaps the two systems are really one - the third sphere of the *Guide* can be subdivided into five subspheres (one for each of the planets), giving us the nine spheres of the *Mishneh Torah.*

There are two reasons why we cannot accept this solution. The first is straightforward: even subdividing the spheres in this fashion does not overcome the problem of the place of the Sun: in the *Guide,* all of the planets are *above* the Sun, while in the *Mishneh Torah* the Sun, following Ptolemy, is right in the middle of the six planets (Moon, Mercury and Venus below the Sun, Mars, Jupiter and Saturn above it).

The second reason has to do with the fact that for Maimonides in the *Guide* the fact that there are precisely *four* spheres beneath the all-encompassing sphere is a matter of considerable importance. It is so important that he devotes an entire chapter (II.10) to it.[14] In this chapter Maimonides presents the number of four as what Gad Freudenthal characterizes as a *constant* of nature.

---

14 On this chapter, see Freudenthal, "Maimonides' Stance" and "Maimonides' Four Heavenly Spheres."

Each of the four spheres is "especially assigned to one of the four elements" (p. 270). More importantly:

> It is likewise possible that the arrangement of the universe should be as fol-
> lows. The spheres are four; the elements moved by the spheres are four; and
> the forces proceeding from the spheres into that which exists are four, as we
> have made clear. Similarly, the causes of every motion belonging to the sphere
> are four: namely, the shape of the sphere – I mean its sphericity; its soul; and
> its intellect through which it has conceptions, as we have explained; and the
> separate intellect, which is its beloved. Understand this well (p. 271).

Maimonides continues further in the chapter (p. 272): "This number four is wondrous and should be an object of reflection." After showing its importance in various midrashim and prophetic passages, Maimonides concludes:

In this way will he who wants to understand the prophetic riddles understand them. And he will awaken from the sleep of negligence, be saved from
the sea of ignorance, and rise up toward the high ones. He, however, who is
pleased to swim in the seas of his ignorance and *comes down lower and lower*
[after Deut. 28:43] has no need to weary his body and heart. When he ceases
moving, he goes down to what is lowest in nature. Understand all that has been
mentioned and reflect on it.

Anyone familiar with Maimonides' account of immortality and the extinction of the wicked (i.e. the intellectually unperfected)[15] will immediately realize that he is here telling us that reflection on the number four and its significance in the cosmos leads to intellectual perfection and immortality. Maimonides' account of the five spheres in the *Guide,* then, is very important to him.

The astronomy in the *Mishneh Torah* is thus shown once more to be straightforwardly and conventionally Ptolemaic.[16] This accords with what I said above: Maimonides is there interested in presenting a non-problematic account of the heavens in order to impress upon his readers the magnitude of God's wisdom. In the *Guide of the Perplexed,* on the other hand, he was interested in presenting the truth. Whether this truth was known to him when

---

15 For details, see my *Perfection*, pp. 1-5.
16 I do not mean to imply that Maimonides never follows Ptolemy in the *Guide;* he does in
 III.14.

he wrote the *Mishneh Torah,* and hidden from his readers so as not to confuse them, or whether he hit upon it after completing the *Mishneh Torah* and before writing the *Guide,*[17] is irrelevant; either way, the astronomy he presents in the *Mishneh Torah* does not represent the most perfect possible exposition of that science available to him and most certainly, therefore, does not represent the highest stage that astronomy can reach.

Wisdom, what we would today call "science," was understood by Maimonides as a product, not as a process. Because wisdom was a product it had to be compared, contrasted, and brought into harmony with another product, the content of revelation. The various sciences were understood as the amassing and organizing of knowledge about finite matters; they could, both in theory and in practice, be brought to completion or perfection. There are two sciences, however, which will never be brought to completion: astronomy and metaphysics. Astronomy deals with the motions of the heavenly bodies while metaphysics deals with the nature of those incorporeal entities associated with the heavenly bodies, the separate intellects, and with God. It seems that our knowledge of astronomical matters will always be restricted if only because of our inability to accomplish the necessary observations. As noted above, this state of affairs is very convenient for Maimonides. Our metaphysical knowledge will always be restricted, not because of observational limitations, but because our minds are in principle incapable of achieving more than a very slight acquaintance with metaphysical truths. We can know that God and the Separate Intellects exist, but will never truly be able to understand the nature of their existence.

This being the case, Maimonides' claim that we will never achieve perfection or completion in astronomy and metaphysics does not by any means imply that he has broken out of a typically medieval world view into a modern one: at basis, astronomy and metaphysics are still matters of *Wissenschaft,* not of *Forschung.* Even the fact that our perfection, or a large part of it, lies in the ceaseless quest to achieve ever greater metaphysical insight does not change this.[18]

---

17 A less likely option: Maimonides constantly corrected the *Mishneh Torah* and had he changed his mind about such important matters as those raised here it is more than likely that he would have corrected the text.

18 I do not believe that for Maimonides the acquisition of metaphysical insight is the final rung in the ladder of perfection open to and demanded of human beings. On this see *Perfection.*

Summarizing, we opened our discussion with the question of the status of the scientific matters presented by Maimonides in his law code, the *Mishneh Torah*. Maimonides clearly held what would today be called a 'whiggish' view of scientific progress, and also held that the sciences could reach perfection or completion. That being the case, perhaps he held that the science in the *Mishneh Torah* was not simply the most up-to-date scientific information available to him, but the most perfect account of science that could ever be reached?

In rejecting this position I noted that Maimonides distinguished radically between sublunar and superlunar science: the former could reach completion, and in fact had been brought to completion; the latter was incomplete and would for ever remain so. It must remain incomplete and unperfected because *the heavens are the heavens of the Lord* and will always remain beyond our ken, both in terms of the actual motions of the heavenly bodies and in terms of what we can know about the incorporeal intellects associated with those bodies. In other words, the actual truth concerning celestial physics and concerning metaphysics lies beyond the limits of human knowledge. This position (which aids him in the solution of many theological problems) forces Maimonides to adopt an instrumentalist view of astronomy, according to which it is the goal of the astronomer to provide a mathematical model of the observed motions of the heavenly bodies ("to save the phenomena"), not to describe them as they actually are. Maimonides' instrumentalism, then, is a maidservant of his theology.

Admitting that metaphysics and celestial physics will never be brought to completion, perhaps in Maimonides' day they had reached the highest level they ever would reach? Were that the case, then perhaps the account of natural matters given in the *Mishneh Torah* really does represent the most complete possible picture and not simply the most up-to-date picture available to Maimonides. Two reasons were adduced for rejecting this hypothesis. First, Maimonides himself foresaw the possibility of progress in the understanding of superlunar phenomena. Secondly, the account of astronomical matters presented in the *Mishneh Torah* is simply incorrect on Maimonides' own terms and thus could not represent his view of the most perfect possible view of superlunar science.

At the end we are left with the following: as a true medieval thinker, one who saw science (including philosophy) first and foremost in terms of the product *(knowledge)* and not the process *(research),* as one who understood science to be a body of knowledge which could reach completion, and as a thinker who thought that most sciences had been brought to completion by his time, there is every reason to expect that Maimonides would hold that the science presented in the *Mishneh Torah* was perfect and complete, demanding the same sort of acquiescence as did the *Halakhah* presented in that text. That Maimonides did not in fact reach this conclusion is not a consequence of his having adopted a view of science as a never-ending quest; rather, it is a consequence of his philosophical theology which forced him to impose strict limits on what human beings can know.

CHAPTER THIRTEEN
Maimonides on the Science of the *Mishneh Torah:*
Provisional or Permanent?

W hat was Maimonides' attitude toward the typically medieval description of the universe presented at the beginning of his great law code, the *Mishneh Torah*? Was that account of the physical universe meant only as a statement of the best description of nature available at the time (and thus radically distinct from the halakhic matters which make up the bulk of the *Mishneh Torah*), or was it meant to be a description of the true nature of the universe as it really is, not subject to revision in the light of new paradigms or new models (and thus essentially similar to the halakhic matters in the text)?[1] I here make the following argument: Maimonides, as a man of his time, had many reasons to hold that the physics he presented in the *Mishneh Torah* was complete and perfected, sharing the epistemological status of the

---

1 It is difficult to write on this subject without falling into anachronistic usages. The closest medieval terms for what we mean by the modern expression "science" in the broad sense seem to be *hokhmah* ("wisdom") or *iyyun* ("looking into," "speculation"), both of which can be translated back into modern English more easily as "philosophy" than as "science." *Hokhmah*, however, can also mean a specific discipline, and as such is adequately captured by the modern term "science" when it refers to a specific scientific discipline. But here, too, the overlap in meaning is hardly isomorphic. (On the term and its use by Maimonides, see *Guide of the Perplexed* III.54 and Septimus, "*Madda*.") The main problem is that between the time of Maimonides and his contemporaries and our own day, the great scientific revolution of the sixteenth and seventeenth centuries took place and the term "science" began carrying with it a whole new range of sociological and epistemological meanings; furthermore, the term "scientist" was coined, a usage which has no place in discussions of medieval thought. Another notoriously problematic term is "progress," and where I am forced to use it I hope that I can avoid invoking wholly inappropriate connotations. It is hard to avoid using the term, however, since Maimonides and some of his contemporaries held a "whiggish" view of the history of natural sciences, according to which they had indeed progressed beyond the accomplishments of their predecessors. On whig interpretations of history generally, see Butterfield, *Whig* and Gould, *Times' Arrow*, pp. 4-5.

laws codified in that text.[2] I will show that Maimonides did not in fact adopt this view. In so doing light will be shed on Maimonides' views of rabbinic and scientific authority.[3] In two related studies, comparing the astronomy of the *Mishneh Torah* with that of the *Guide of the Perplexed*, I prove that Maimonides rejects the idea that astronomy and metaphysics can reach perfection,[4] and suggest that this rejection is based upon theological considerations crucial to him.[5] The conclusions of those studies will be relied upon at certain points in this discussion, and where appropriate I will summarize their results.

Maimonides opens the *Mishneh Torah* as follows: "The foundation of all foundations, and the pillar of all sciences, is to know that there exists a First Existent."[6] Maimonides continues, telling us that the Torah positively commands that we know that God exists (I.6).[7] The rest of the chapter is given over to a discussion of God's unity and incorporeality.

Maimonides opens the second chapter by telling us that Jews are commanded to love and fear God. "What is the way," Maimonides then asks in II.2, "that will lead to the love of Him and fear of Him?" The answer, Maimonides says, is the examination[8] of God's work of creation: "When a person contemplates His great and wondrous works and creatures and from them obtains a glimpse of His wisdom which is incomparable and infinite, he will straightaway love Him, glorify Him, and long with an exceeding longing to know his great name."[9] By way of helping his reader to fulfill the commandment to love

---

2 For different views of Maimonides' intention in writing the *Mishneh Torah* see Halbertal, "*Mishneh Torah*" and Kellner, "*Mishneh Torah* – Why?"

3 I discuss Maimonides' conception of intellectual authority generally above in ch. 1, "Reading Rambam" and, more fully, in *Decline*.

4 Ch. 12, "On the Status of Astronomy."

5 Ch. 14, "Maimonides' Allegiances."

6 "Laws of the Foundation of the Torah," I.1. This translation is my own. Isaac Abravanel suggested that Maimonides meant to say here that the basic dogma of religious belief is the basic axiom of all the sciences; i.e., that religious belief and science share the same starting point and hence must arrive at the same conclusions. Abravanel makes this claim in his *Rosh Amanah*, chap. 5 – *Principles*, p. 76. For an argument to the effect that Abravanel was correct in his assessment of Maimonides here, see my *Judaism*.

7 In Maimonides' book enumerating the commandments, *Sefer ha-Mizvot*, this is positive commandment no. 1.

8 Hebrew: *ke-she-yitbonen*. Maimonides does not mean simply looking at the natural world, but examining it using the power of understanding, *binah*.

9 The obligation to study God's works in order to know God to some extent is one of the

and fear God, Maimonides explains "some large, general aspects of the works of the Sovereign of the Universe." Maimonides continues the second chapter of "Laws of the Foundations of the Torah" with a cursory account of the Separate Intellects, or angels.[10] These two chapters, we are told indirectly, deal with metaphysics.[11] The third and fourth chapters present a brief summary of physical science:[12] the third is given over largely to superlunar matters, the fourth to sublunar affairs. Chapters III and IV, then, present an account of the physical universe as Maimonides saw it. It is a finite universe, composed of nine concentric spheres, with the earth in the center. The ninth and largest sphere "includes and encircles all things." Each of the eight internal spheres is divided into subspheres, "like the several layers of onions." These subspheres are contiguous, with no empty space between them at all. In addition to the concentric spheres which encompass the earth, there are smaller spheres fixed in the larger spheres. In a statement (III.5) which will be important for us below, Maimonides summarizes the situation:

> The number of all the spheres that revolve around the world is eighteen. The number of small spheres that do not so revolve is eight. And from the courses of the stars, from their known daily and hourly rate of movement, from their declination from the south towards the north and from the north towards the south, from their height about the earth and their approximation to it, the number of these spheres can be ascertained, as well as the lines of their movement and the courses they traverse. This forms the science of mathematical astronomy, on which the Greek sages composed many treatises.

Maimonides continues his description of the superlunar realm, making comments about the size of some of the planets, and their distance from the

---

recurring motifs of medieval Jewish philosophical thought. See, for example, S. Harvey, *Falaquera*, p. 88.

10 On Maimonides on angels, see *Confrontation*, chapt. 8, and the texts and studies cited there.

11 Maimonides says that these chapters deal with *ma'aseh merkavah* ("Account of [Ezekiel's vision of] the Chariot") in Foundations II.11. For the claim that *ma'aseh merkavah* means metaphysics, see Maimonides' commentary on Mishnah Hagigah 2.1, *Guide* 1, Introduction (p. 6), and my detailed discussion in *Judaism*, chapt. 8. For the Hagigah text, see my "Maimonides on Hagigah." Further on all this, see Kellner, "Kotler."

12 Maimonides says that these chapters deal with *ma'aseh bereshit* ("Account of Creation") in Foundations IV.10. For the claim that *ma'aseh bereshit* means physics, see the previous note.

earth. The spheres and stars, we are told, are living beings, possessed of souls and endowed with intelligence.

"Laws of the Foundations of the Torah" III closes with a transition to the sublunar realm; the reader is told of the four elements of Greek physics: earth, water, air, and fire. These bodies, unlike those of the superlunar world, are lifeless, without souls or intelligence. The sublunar realm is then described in the fourth chapter: it is the world of the four elements and of bodies composed of them. It is a world in which things strive always to return to their natural place. It is a world of constant generation and corruption, a world the most fundamental principles of which are form and matter.

Maimonides' description of the universe is dramatically different from the world in which we live, work, and play: ours is an infinite universe, in which material bodies exist in a vacuum; in our solar system, the sun stands at the center, the dead planets revolving around it. Gravity replaces the notion of "natural place," and atomic physics the four elements. Maimonides' pre-Copernican description would present no problem did it not appear in a law code, the *Mishneh Torah*, in a section called "*Laws of* the Foundations of the Torah." Maimonides composed his code in an apodictic fashion because he expected it to be exactly that: a code.[13] Furthermore, it was a work meant to translate the immutable Torah of God into a useful, manageable body of specific prescriptions. It was Maimonides' hope that the *Mishneh Torah* would be adopted as the binding code of Jewish law.[14]

Did Maimonides expect his vision of the physical universe to be as immutable as his codification of the laws, say, of theft? In other words, does the

13 For a detailed and nuanced discussion of Maimonides' statements on this matter, see Twersky, *Introduction*, pp. 97-187. See also Halbertal, "*Mishneh Torah.*"

14 As Maimonides states: "On these grounds I, Moses, the son of Maimon, the Sefardi, bestirred myself, and, relying on the help of God, Blessed be He, intently studied all these works, with the view of putting together the results obtained from them in regard to what is forbidden or permitted, clean or unclean, and the other rules of the Torah–all in plain language and terse style, so that thus the entire Oral Law might become systematically known to all ... [and so] that all the rules shall be acessible to young and old ... so that no other work should be needed for ascertaining any of the laws of Israel, but that this work might serve as a compendium of the entire Oral Law.... Hence, I have entitled this work *Mishneh Torah* (Repetition of the Law), for the reason that a person who first reads the Written Law and then this compilation, will know from it the whole of the Oral Law, without having occasion to consult any other book between them" (Hyamson, p. 4b). See further Kasher, "Study" and, once again, Halbertal, "*Mishneh Torah.*"

description of the universe presented in "Foundations of the Torah" have the same binding status as the commandments codified there and in other parts of the *Mishneh Torah*? Some interpreters of Maimonides think so. I once heard a lecture by a prominent physicist and Habad Hasid who argued that since Maimonides wrote his *Mishneh Torah* with divine assistance, we had to interpret our view of the universe to match his; we are not permitted to dismiss his understanding of the superlunar and sublunar worlds as expressions of now outmoded theories.[15] Was this Maimonides' own view? Did he, that is, consider the description of the physical universe presented in the *Mishneh Torah* as representing the final word on the subject, or was he prepared to entertain the possibility that our understanding of the universe might develop beyond the stage it had reached in his day? An analysis of this issue will help us further to understand Maimonides' conception of philosophy and its relationship to halakhah, his views concerning what we would today call progress, his own self-understanding as a student of physics and metaphysics, and the vast gulf which separates the world of Maimonides from our own.[16]

At this point another issue raises its head, one which cannot be wholly ignored. Maimonides' philosophy is based in very large measure on his physics and metaphysics. I will demonstrate below that Maimonides related to the description of the universe presented in the *Mishneh Torah* as provisional in the sense that it could be superseded by future developments. If the physics of the *Mishneh Torah* (both terrestrial and celestial) is mutable, can the meta-

---

15 Not every traditionalist interpreter of Maimonides takes this view. R. Meir Leibush Malbim, the nineteenth-century author of a popular and highly traditionalist commentary on the Bible, in his Commentary to Ezekiel (Vilna, 1911), p. 3a, rejects Maimonides' explanation of Ezekiel's Vision of the Chariot (*ma'aseh merkavah*) on the explicit grounds that "the foundations on which he built it have been refuted. The astronomy, natural science, and ancient philosophy which were the foundations and supports of his interpretation have been completely undermined and destroyed by the scientific research which has developed in recent generations." I cite this passage as it is brought by Fox, *Interpreting*, pp. 23-24.

16 The issue gains further importance in the light of a comment by Isadore Twersky to the effect that for Maimonides, "knowledge of the physical sciences is necessary for a correct understanding of halakhah." See Twersky, "Epistemology of Maimonides," p. 132. I am not competent to go into the question of the status of specific halakhic decisions (if any) in the *Mishneh Torah* which depend upon now rejected theories concerning the nature of the physical world. But if Twersky is correct in his assessment (and the evidence he adduces is most convincing), then the question of Maimonides' own understanding of the status of the physics and biology he presents in the *Mishneh Torah* should be of crucial interest and importance to historians of halakhah. Further on the issue of halakhah and science, see the remarks of Shalom Rosenberg, *Torah u-Madda*, pp. 58-62.

physics of the *Mishneh Torah* and of the *Guide of the Perplexed* be immutable? Since Maimonides argues that correct religious belief depends upon correct philosophical belief,[17] our question here becomes, how can a mutable account of the universe serve as the basis for religion? In part, the answer to this question depends upon the fact that Maimonides dramatically distinguishes the description of the cosmos in the *Mishneh Torah*, which is conventional and addressed to the rank and file of the Jewish people, from that of the *Guide of the Perplexed*, which is far more sophisticated and serves as a stable basis for the philosophical and religious edifice constructed upon it. But what of the "wisdom" (physics and metaphysics) of the *Guide*: can it change too? I think that Maimonides would have been surprised if sublunar physics changed, but not be unduly upset, since that physics is not crucial to his theology. And since he held that celestial physics, which is crucial to his theology, is basically beyond our knowing, he could, I think, envision basic changes in it with relative equanimity. In effect, the limitations Maimonides imposes upon the scope and content of metaphysics render his theology relatively independent of change, development, even revolution in the sciences.

There are good reasons to suppose that Maimonides would urge us to relate to his account of the universe in the *Mishneh Torah* as being nothing more than a statement of the best physics available in his day, not as an incontrovertible account of the world as it actually is, was, and always will be.

The strongest reason for understanding Maimonides in this fashion is his account of how we are to relate to the scientific pronouncements of the rabbinic sages. He sharply distinguishes their role as transmitters of the Sinaitic revelation from their role as individuals reporting on their own ideas and interpretations or on the best physical science of their day. Thus, in connection with questions concerning the messianic advent, Maimonides writes:

Some of our Sages say that the coming of Elijah will precede the advent of the Messiah. But no one is in a position to know the details of this and similar things until they have come to pass. They are not explicitly stated by the Prophets. Nor have the Rabbis any tradition with regard to these matters. They

---

17 See my *Dogma*, chapt. 1, and *Must*.

are guided solely by what the scriptural texts seem to imply. Hence there is a divergence of opinion upon the subject.[18]

The talmudic sages, when describing the messianic world, were not transmitting "Torah from Sinai." They were, rather, reporting on what today would be called "educated guesses."[19]

If, with respect to the interpretation of eschatological verses, the opinions of the Sages are not obligatory, how much more so should we expect this to be the case with respect to their reports of physics, astronomy, and biology![20] In a notorious passage in the *Guide of the Perplexed* Maimonides informs his readers that the sages indeed erred on such matters:

> One of the ancient opinions that are widespread among the philosophers and
> the general run of people consists in the belief that the motion of the spheres
> produces very fearful and mighty sounds.... This opinion also is generally
> known in our religious community. Do you not see that the sages [Pesahim
> 94b] describe the might of the sound produced by the sun when it every day

---

18 "Laws of Kings and Their Wars," XII.2. For Maimonides' attitude toward midrash in general, see the introduction to his commentary on Mishnah Sanhedrin, *Perek Helek*. The text is available in English in Twersky, *Reader*, pp. 401-423. Compare further Marvin Fox, "Nahmanides" and, in general, Lawee, *Stance*.

19 Further on this issue, see my discussion in *Judaism*, ch. 5, and in ch. 18 below, "Maimonides' True Religion."

20 It might be objected to the argument being developed here that showing that Maimonides held that some of the Sages could and did err proves nothing about his understanding of the epistemological status of his own science, since he may have held himself to be superior (in having reached a higher degree of intellectual perfection) to all or most of the Sages. This is not the place to go into a detailed refutation of this hypothesis. Here it should suffice to note that this objection rests upon the claim that Maimonides presented as what Pines called "a convenient fiction" his argument that the prophets and Sages had access to a philosophic tradition some of the elements of which he had succeeded in teasing out of the sources with enormous difficulty. This objection further rests on a reading of Maimonides which renders absurd his attempts to understand rabbinic allegories philosophically: if he held himself to be a better philosopher than all or most of the Sages, why bother reconstructing the philosophic meaning under their allegories? I reject this approach to reading Maimonides. This rejection finds detailed expression in two books of mine, *Perfection* and *Judaism*. In the latter, for example, I show that Maimonides adopted unusual positions on religious matters (providence, prophecy, immortality, messianism, the nature of the Jewish people, the nature of the Torah, and others) because of his antecedent adoption of an Aristotelian psychology. Were his philosophic and religious concerns as radically divorced as Pines maintains, he could have saved himself from much aggravation and calumny by simply adopting unexceptional, standard positions on these religious matters, even though such positions contradicted his "truly held" philosophical beliefs.

proceeds on its way in the sphere? ... Aristotle, however, does not accept this[21] and makes it clear that the heavenly bodies produce no sound. You should not find it blameworthy that the opinion of Aristotle disagrees with that of the sages.... [The sages themselves] in these astronomical matters preferred the opinion of the sages of the nations of the world to their own. For they explicitly say [Pesahim 94b], "The sages of the world have vanquished." And this is correct. For everyone who argues in speculative matters does this according to the conclusions to which he was led by his speculation. Hence the conclusion whose demonstration is correct is believed. (II.8, p. 267)

Truth is truth;[22] what is proved is proved. No matter who says the opposite, their view is not to be accepted. Maimonides often gives expression to this attitude:

It is my intention in this chapter to draw your attention to the ways of research and belief. If anybody tells you in order to support his opinion that he is in possession of proof and evidence and that he saw the thing with his own eyes, you have to doubt him, even if he is an authority accepted by great men, even if he is himself honest and virtuous. Inquire well into what he wants to prove to you. Do not allow your senses to be confused by his research and innovations [stories]. Think well, search, examine, and try to understand [the ways of nature] which he claims to know. Do not allow yourself to be influenced by the sayings that something is obvious, whether a single man is saying so or whether it is a common opinion, for the desire of power leads men to shameful things, particularly in the case of divided opinions.... I advise you to examine critically the opinions even of such an authority and prominent sage as Galen.[23]

One of the reasons that people are led astray by arguments to authority is because of their excessive veneration of the written word, especially when found in ancient works: "The great sickness and the grievous evil (Eccl. 5:12)

---

21 Pines cites *On the Heavens* ii.9.290b.12 ff.

22 And, as Maimonides says, "For only truth pleases Him, may He be exalted, and only that which is false angers Him" (II.48, p. 409).

23 *Medical Aphorisms*, ch. 25.

consists in this: that all the things that man finds written in books, he presumes to think of as true-and all the more so if the books are old."[24]

Maimonides rejects the approach; one must follow the argument where it leads, even if that means that one imputes error to one of the sages of the Talmud:

> I know that you may search and find sayings of some individual sages in the Talmud and Midrashoth whose words appear to maintain that at the moment of a man's birth, the stars will cause such and such a thing to happen to him. Do not regard this as a difficulty, for it is not fitting for a man to abandon the prevailing law and raise once again the counterarguments and replies [that preceded its enactment].[25] Similarly, it is not proper to abandon matters of reason that have already been verified by proofs, shake loose of them, and depend on the words of a single one of the sages from whom possibly the matter was hidden. Or there may be an allusion in those words; or they may have been said with a view to the times and business before him. ... A man should never cast his reason behind him, for the eyes are set in front, not in back.[26]

In another passage from the *Guide* Maimonides informs his readers that the sages erred on what we today call scientific matters and explicitly distinguishes the authority of the sages as transmitters of Torah from their authority as astronomers:

> Do not ask me to show that everything they [the sages] have said concerning astronomical matters conforms to the way things really are. For at that time mathematics was imperfect. They did not speak about this as transmitters of the dicta of the prophets,[27] but rather because in those times they were men of knowledge in those fields or because they had heard these dicta from the men of knowledge who lived in those times. (III.15, p. 459)

---

24 "Letter on Astrology" p. 229 (1972), p. 179 (2000). On this text, see Dienstag, "Astrology."

25 I.e., Maimonides had just proven that the rejection of astrology is "one of the roots of the religion of Moses our Master" – p. 234 (1972), p. 185 (2000).

26 "Letter on Astrology," p. 235 (1972), p. 186 (2000).

27 Compare the passage cited above from "Laws of Kings," XII.2.

If Maimonides thought that the sages could err when they relied on the best account of the universe with which they were familiar, would he not feel the same about his own reliance on the prevalent accounts of the universe in his day?[28]

But not only could the sages err in such matters, so, Maimonides apparently held, could individuals who reached a low level of prophecy. Exodus 24 begins as follows: *And unto Moses He said: 'Come up unto the Lord, thou, and Aaron, Nadab, Abihu, and seventy of the elders of Israel; and worship ye afar off'*. After sundry events, the passage continues (vv. 9-11): *Then went up Moses, and Aaron, Nadab, and Abihu, and seventy of the elders of Israel; and they saw the God of Israel; and there was under His feet the like of a paved work of sapphire stone, and the like of the very heaven for clearness. And upon the nobles of the children of Israel He laid not His hand; and they beheld God, and did eat and drink.*

These verses obviously raise all sorts of questions.[29] Let us focus here on one that troubled Maimonides: what does the reference to God's "feet" mean in this context? Just "seeing" God can be understood in purely intellectual terms;[30] but what could the reference to that which was under God's "feet"

---

28 This attitude of Maimonides' toward the Sages finds indirect expression in another source. In *Guide* II.9 (p. 268) Maimonides records the claim that there are nine spheres. But spheres can be counted in different ways (compare "Foundations of the Torah," III.2), and what one person counts as nine, another could count differently. "For this reason," Maimonides says, "you should not regard as blameworthy" a rabbinic dictum which seems to indicate that there are only two spheres. Relevant to our theme here is the unarticulated supposition that in astronomical matters rabbinic dicta have to be brought into line with those of the astronomers, not the other way around. It was the rabbinic dictum which might be thought to be "blameworthy," not that of the astronomers. Another indirect expression of Maimonides' idea that the Sages could err on matters of physics and metaphysics may be found in his use of the expression "Ben Zoma is still outside" in *Guide* III.51 (p. 619). As Marc Saperstein has shown in a remarkably sensitive reading of this passage in the Guide (*Decoding*, p. 18), Maimonides uses this text (from Hagigah 15a) to indicate that Ben Zoma, a mishnaic sage, failed to attain mastery over the physical sciences and thus failed to attain even a rudimentary knowledge of God. Maimonides clearly felt that he himself was, and the student to whom he addressed the *Guide* could be, superior to Ben Zoma in scientific (and hence religious) attainments. Ben Zoma, it should be recalled, was one of the three companions who sought to enter "Paradise" with R. Akiba (Hagigah 14b). Ben Zoma apparently lost his mind as a result of this experience, adding to the impression that he would not have been considered by Maimonides to be one of the leading Sages. On the Hagigah text, see the discussion in Scholem, *Jewish Gnosticism*, pp. 14-19 and Halperin, *Chariot* and *Merkabah*.

29 See Regev, "Vision," Levene, "Exegesis," and Diamond, "Theodicy."

30 The point of Maimonides' discussion in *Guide* I.4-5.

mean? Maimonides explains that it was "the nobles of the children of Israel," not Moses, who saw this (I.5, p. 30). Their apprehension of God was imperfect because they were "overhasty [and] strained their thoughts," and thus "corporeality entered into" their apprehension of God to some extent. Put simply, they made a mistake in their approach to the science of metaphysics. Now, who were the "nobles of the children of Israel"? From the biblical text it appears that they are the "elders of Israel" spoken of earlier in the passage. This is the interpretation of the standard Jewish commentators on the Bible, and, more important, it is clearly the interpretation of Maimonides, as his discussion in I.5 makes clear. Who, then, are the elders of Israel? As it turns out, they are individuals who, at least from time to time, reach a low level of prophecy. In Guide II.45 Maimonides distinguishes eleven degrees of prophecy. The second degree is composed of those "who speak through the Holy Spirit." The authors of Psalms, Proverbs, Ecclesiastes, Song of Songs, Daniel, Job, in short, of all of the Hagiographa, wrote their works having achieved this degree of prophetic inspiration. "It was to this group," Maimonides says, "that the 'seventy elders' belonged" (with reference to Numbers 11:25), as did Eldad and Medad, and as did all the high priests when they received oracular information through the *Urim* and *Tummim*. Returning to our issue, we see that Maimonides imputed scientific error, not only to the rabbinic sages, but even to individuals who were capable of achieving a low level of prophetic inspiration.[31] How much more so, it is safe to assume, would he be willing to impute the possibility of such error to himself!

Further support for this position is found in Maimonides' attitude toward Aristotle. In a well-known letter to Samuel ibn Tibbon, the translator of the *Guide*, Maimonides observes that there is no need for Samuel to study the writings of philosophers who preceded Aristotle, because "the works of the latter are sufficient by themselves and [superior] to all that were written before them.

---

31 Two points should be noted here. First, this means that the "nobles of the children of Israel" were superior in their intellectual attainments to Aristotle, who, as we shall see below, never achieved even the lowest level of prophetic inspiration; despite this they erred on an important metaphysical (and thus scientific) matter. Second, if Isaac Abravanel, Shalom Rosenberg, and W. Z. Harvey are all correct, then Maimonides even imputed scientific error to Ezekiel, who achieved the fifth degree of prophecy. For details, see Harvey, "How to Begin," pp. 21 23

His intellect,[32] Aristotle's, is the extreme limit of human intellect, apart from those upon whom the divine emanation has flowed forth to such an extent that they reach the level of prophecy,[33] there being no level higher.[34]

We must further note that in *Guide* 1.5 (p. 28) Maimonides calls Aristotle, "the chief of the philosophers."[35] Who were the philosophers of whom Aristotle is the chief? In his "Letter on Astrology," Maimonides writes that the *hakhamim*, or wise men, of Greece, who were philosophers and "who are genuinely wise,"[36] never dealt with astrology. In his commentary to Mishnah Avodah Zarah IV.7, Maimonides explains at length that the philosophers never dealt with astrology, which, as he explains both there and in "Laws of Idolatry," I.1, is the cause and root of idolatry. Aristotle, then, in his own right nearly reached the level of prophecy; he is 'chief' of the philosophers who attained to such an understanding of the universe on their own steam that they rejected astrology because it leads to idolatry. Put simply, Maimonides thought very highly of Aristotle. But not so highly that he thought that Aristotle could not err on matters of physics and metaphysics: it is well known that Maimonides at least claimed to reject Aristotle's assertion that the universe was uncreated. It was Maimonides' argument that Aristotle was wrong on his own terms: in thinking that he could prove the eternity of the universe, Aristotle was simply doing Aristotelian philosophy poorly.[37]

But Aristotle could err in other areas as well:

Everything that Aristotle has said about all that exists from beneath the sphere of the moon to the center of the earth is indubitably correct, and no one will

---

32 Hebrew (the Arabic original of the letter is lost): *da'ato*. Another possible translation is "his knowledge." On Maimonides' use of this term, see Septimus, "Madda."

33 Compare *Guide* II.32-48 and ch. 4, "Is Maimonides' Ideal Person Austerely Rationalist?"

34 Maimonides, *Iggerot* (Sheilat), vol. 2, p. 533. On this letter, see S. Harvey, "Letter" and the studies cited there.

35 See also II.23 (p. 332). Jose Faur plays down the significance of these passages, interpreting them so as to diminish Maimonides' admiration for Aristotle. See his *Iyyunim*, p. 7. I find Faur's interpretation forced, an estimation reinforced by the fact that Shem Tov ibn Falaquera, Maimonides' great thirteenth-century admirer, criticized the Master for his excessive admiration of Aristotle. See Malter, "Shem Tob," p. 492. In general, see Davidson, *Maimonides*, pp. 98-110.

36 P. 230 (1972), p. 181 (2000); I have slightly emended the translation.

37 This is the burden of Maimonides' refutation of Aristotle's thesis concerning the eternity of the world in *Guide* II.13-31; see especially ch. 17. For a recent and important discussion, see Seeskin, *Origin*.

---

deviate from it unless he does not understand it or unless he has preconceived opinions that he wishes to defend or that lead him to a denial of a thing that is manifest. On the other hand, everything that Aristotle expounds with regard to the sphere of the moon and that which is above it is, except for certain things, something analogous to guessing and conjecturing. All the more does this apply to what he says about the order of the intellects and to some of the opinions regarding the divine that he believes; for the latter contain grave incongruities and perversities that manifestly and clearly appear as such to all the nations, that propagate evil, and that he cannot demonstrate. (II.22, pp. 319-320)

Maimonides emphasizes this point by repeating it:

I shall repeat here what I have said before [II.22]. All that Aristotle states about that which is beneath the sphere of the moon is in accordance with reasoning; these are things that have a known cause, that follow one upon the other, and concerning which it is clear and manifest at what points wisdom and natural providence are effective. However, regarding all that is in the heavens, man grasps nothing but a small measure of what is mathematical; and you know what is in it. (II.24, p. 326)[38]

Why was Aristotle mistaken in this fashion? Maimonides explains: "However, as I have let you know, the science of astronomy was not in his [Aristotle's] time what it is today" (II.19, p. 308).[39]

Once again, if Aristotle can be mistaken about astronomical matters, would not Maimonides admit that he himself could be mistaken?[40] There is yet a further reason for thinking so and for thinking that Maimonides was not irretrievably wedded to the details of the account of the structure of the universe presented in the *Mishneh Torah*.[41] Maimonides, it turns out, for all his inter-

---

38 On this chapter, see the studies collected in *Aleph* vol 8 (2008).

39 Compare also II.3, p. 254. Here we have an example of Maimonides' "whig" interpretation of the history of science.

40 The argument here rests upon the assumption that Maimonides saw himself as part of an ongoing process of investigation into physics and metaphysics; if he thought that his own work (or generation) marked the capstone of all possible scientific development, then my argument clearly fails. That he did not so think is shown by the text I will cite immediately below from II.24 (p. 327).

41 I say "details of the account" because it is safe to say that Maimonides would be very surprised by Copernicus, Newton, and Einstein. Acceptance of some notion of development in the

est in presenting the *Mishneh Torah* in apodictic terms, was not even wedded irretrievably to the details of his account of halakhah presented there. He recognized that he could err, corrected mistakes which he caught himself, and admitted the fact when others found mistakes in the work.[42] It seems fairly clear that if Maimonides was willing to admit that in halakhic matters the *Mishneh Torah* was not necessarily the last word, he would even more be willing to admit that such was the case with his description of the physical universe.

There are further reasons for thinking that Maimonides presented his account of nature in the *Mishneh Torah* provisionally, as a statement of the best science available to him, and not as the final, absolute account of the universe as it truly is, was, and always will be. Maimonides held that human history was largely marked by a development away from falsehood and toward truth, in matters both philosophical and religious. May we not assume that he held that this would continue after his day as well? With respect to the ever greater approximation of truth in the various spheres of philosophy (what we would today call "science"), we just saw that Maimonides held that the mathematical sciences were incorrectly understood in Aristotle's day; in his own day they had reached a much higher level of perfection. This is true not only of the mathematical sciences, but also of anatomy: "[Galen] attained enormous success in anatomy, and things became clear to him in his time that were not apparent to anyone else. In addition, the activities and functions of organs, and their physiology, as well as conditions of the pulse which were not clear at the time of Aristotle [were understood and explained by Galen]."[43] Finally, with respect to astronomical matters Maimonides thought that his own knowledge might be superseded: "It is possible that someone else will find a demonstration by means of which the true reality of what is obscure for me will become clear to him" (*Guide* II.24, p. 327). Without getting into the vexed question of when the idea of progress entered Western culture, we can see here that Maimonides admitted the fact of scientific development and even anticipated that science

---

understanding of the universe in the Middle Ages cannot be equated with our modern expectation that just as the Newtonian universe was replaced by the Einsteinian, the Einsteinian universe may very well be replaced by another vision of the structure of the cosmos. Compare Ch. 14 below, "Maimonides' Allegiances."

42 Marx, *Studies*, p. 52. See now Shapiro, *Studies*.

43 *Medical Aphorisms*, vol. 2, p. 205.

would develop beyond what he himself, or, more accurately, his generation, had been able to accomplish in it.[44]

In terms of what we can call "spiritual progress," Maimonides indicates that human beings grow and develop from generation to generation, both as individuals and as a race. As individuals, Maimonides maintained in one of the most notorious passages in the Guide, the generation of the Exodus were unable to worship God in a truly mature fashion and needed a sacrificial cult.

> For a sudden transition from one opposite to another is impossible. And therefore man, according to his nature, is not capable of abandoning suddenly all to which he was accustomed ... and as at that time the way of life generally accepted and customary in the whole world and the universal service upon which we were brought up consisted in offering various species of living beings in the temples ... His wisdom, may He be exalted, and His gracious ruse, which is manifest in regard to all His creatures did not require that He give us a Law prescribing the rejection, abandonment, and abolition of all these kinds of worship. ... At that time this would have been similar to the appearance of a prophet in these times who, calling upon the people to worship God, would say: "God has given you a Law forbidding you to pray to Him, to fast, to call upon Him for help in misfortune. Your worship should consist solely in meditation without any works at all." Therefore He, may He be exalted, suffered the above-mentioned kinds of worship to remain. (III.32, p. 526) [45]

Our forefathers may have been religious primitives; spiritual development had taken place since the days of the Exodus, however, and some Jews in Maimonides' day were ready to be told how to worship God truly. In III.51 Maimonides explains that in order to achieve true worship we must first strengthen the bond of intellect between ourselves and God. Having attained that apprehension, we can then truly love God ("love is proportionate to apprehension"). "After love of God, comes true worship: it consists in setting thought to work

---

44 Further on this point, see the discussion in Ch. 12 above, "On the Status of Astronomy."

45 On worship in Maimonides as philosophical meditation, see *Guide* III.51; for a comprehensive discussion of prayer in Maimonidean thought, see Blidstein, *Ha-Tefillah*; on Maimonides on sacrifices, see *Confrontation*, pp. 140-154.

on the first intelligible and to devoting oneself exclusively to this as far as this is within one's capacity" (p. 621).[46]

Individual human beings have developed spiritually to the point where they can truly worship God through intellectual meditation.[47] Eventually, all human beings will reach the point where they abandon idolatry and embrace Judaic monotheism: the Messiah "will prepare the whole world to serve the Lord with one accord, as it is written, *For then will I turn to the peoples a pure language, that they may all call upon the name of the Lord to serve Him with one consent* (Zeph. 3:9)."[48] Maimonides explains how this is going to come about in a remarkable text censored from the printed editions of the *Mishneh Torah*.

But if he does not meet with full success, or is slain, it is obvious that he is not the Messiah promised in the Torah. He is to be regarded like all the other wholehearted and worthy kings of the House of David who died and whom the Holy One, blessed be He, raised up to test the multitude, as it is written *And some of them that are wise shall stumble, to refine among them, and to purify, and to make white, even to the time of the end; for it is yet for the time appointed* (Daniel 11:35). Even of Jesus of Nazareth, who imagined that he was the Messiah, and was put to death by the court, Daniel had prophesied, as it is written *And the children of the violent among thy people shall lift themselves up to establish the vision: but they shall stumble* (Daniel 11:14). For has there ever been a greater stumbling than this? All the prophets affirmed that the Messiah would redeem Israel, save them, gather their dispersed, and confirm the commandments. But he [Jesus] caused Israel to be destroyed by the sword, their remnant to be dispersed and humiliated. He was instrumental in changing the Torah and causing the world to err and serve another beside God. But it is beyond the human mind to fathom the designs of the Creator; for our ways are not His ways, neither are our thoughts His thoughts. All these matters relating to Jesus of Nazareth and the Ishmaelite [Mohammed] who came

---

46 Further on the connection between knowledge of God and love of God, see the introduction to my translation of Maimonides, *Book of Love*, Lasker, "Love of God," and the discussion below in ch. 19, "Spirituality and a Life of Holiness."

47 This last point was suggested to me by J. J. Ross. See "Maimonides and Progress."

48 Laws of Kings XI.4. The text here is not without its problems, none of which, however, impinge upon our discussion. See ch. 18, "Maimonides' *True Religion*."

after him, only served to clear the way for King Messiah, to prepare the whole world to worship God with one accord, as it is written *For then will I turn to the peoples a pure language, that they all call upon the name of the Lord to serve Him with one consent* (Zeph. 3:9). Thus the messianic hope, the Torah, and the commandments have become familiar topics – topics of conversation (among the inhabitants) of the far isles and many people, uncircumcised of heart and flesh. They are discussing these matters and the commandments of the Torah. Some say, "Those commandments were true, but have lost their validity and are no longer binding"; others declare that they had an esoteric meaning and were not to be taken literally; that the Messiah has already come and revealed their occult significance. But when the true King Messiah will appear and succeed, be exalted and lifted up, they will forthwith recant and realize that they have inherited nothing but lies from their fathers, that their prophets and forbears led them astray.[49]

Thanks to the intervention of Christianity and Islam, then, the world is being slowly monotheized, thus making possible the eventual advent of the Messiah. With such human development possible, is it credible that Maimonides would have thought that the description of the universe presented in his *Mishneh Torah* would never become outdated?[50]

It will be useful to summarize the materials adduced to this point. Did Maimonides think that the picture of the universe presented in the *Mishneh Torah* was like the traditional halakhah codified in that text: a body of precepts that would stand for all time? Or did he present these matters in the text as simply the most up-to-date account of the cosmos available to him, subject to change, development, refinement, or even total rejection? In support of the latter hypothesis I have adduced texts showing that Maimonides held that the rabbinic

---

49 XI.4; for the discussion surrounding this text, see the studies cited by me in ch. 18, "Maimonides' *True Religion.*"

50 Lest it be objected that there is no necessary connection between spiritual and scientific improvement, let the following be noted: (a) true monotheism, for Maimonides, depends upon the correct intellectual apprehension of God; Maimonides' messianism, therefore, is based upon the assumption of universal intellectual (i.e., scientific) progress; (b) in general, and this is only to restate the previous point in broader terms, Maimonides did not view perfection as something which was radically divisible: true perfection in one area necessarily went hand in hand with true perfection in other areas; radical spiritual progress could not be absolutely divorced from radical intellectual (i.e., scientific) progress.

sages could err when led astray by the sciences of their day, that individuals capable of achieving a level of prophecy could make mistakes in fields such as physics, astronomy, and metaphysics, that Aristotle could so err, that he (Maimonides) himself could and did err in matters of halakhah, and that Maimonides recognized the fact of progress in scientific and spiritual spheres.

The question, however, is far from being as straightforward as I have made it appear to this point. In order fully to understand Maimonides' position on these matters, we will have to raise questions concerning the perfectibility of science and the role of astronomy.

The discussion to this point would strike a contemporary scientist as odd. Few working scientists today would claim that they could ever (practically, if not necessarily theoretically)[51] achieve a complete and once-for-all account of some aspect of science.[52] The reason for this has to do with modern conceptions of science as process (Forschung), not product (Wissenschaft),[53] and, overall, with the question of the perfectibility of science. These issues will be taken up in what follows.

Did Maimonides think that we could reach perfection in or closure of the sciences? In other words, did he think that we could reach a stage at which all that could be known in some particular science or other would be known? It seems that the answer to this question is both yes and no. Before explaining the answer, it may be useful to elaborate on the question. Citing a text by Gersonides (1288-1344) will be helpful in this connection. Having proved philosophically to his own satisfaction that the world was created, Gersonides adds the following consideration:

---

51 On this subject, see Rescher, *Limits*.

52 In modern philosophy of science this view has been particularly emphasized by Karl R. Popper, who called his autobiography, *Unended Quest*. See, for example, p. 131: "This is why the evolution of physics is likely to be an endless process of correction and better approximation. And even if one day we should reach a stage where our theories were no longer open to correction, since they were simply true, they would still not be complete – and we would know it. For Goedel's famous incompleteness theorem would come into play: in view of the mathematical background of physics, at best an infinite sequence of such true theories would be needed in order to answer the problems which in any given (formalized) theory would be undecidable." Stephen Hawking is notorious for holding the opposed view that we will soon achieve knowledge of all the fundamental equations of reality.

53 On this distinction with respect to the differences between medieval and modern philosophy, see Kellner, "Contemporary Jewish Philosophy."

That which adds publicity and perfection to what has been made clear concerning the creation of the world is that we find that all that has been written in the sciences[54] is new and recent. We find that the early [savants] said something about each science; afterwards each was perfected during the course of time. We find sciences which did not reach their perfection till Aristotle and others which did not reach their perfection till Galen. There is another science which we do not find perfectly in the work of any of the ancients; this is the science of astronomy. [All this shows that] a science which demands more time for its perfection because of what you must determine concerning it from the senses reaches its perfection later. Thus, the mathematical sciences, such as geometry and arithmetic, are found earlier than other sciences. Aristotle's predecessors already expressed them perfectly, according to what is told about them. Physical science, on the other hand, because of its greater need of the senses, reached its perfection later. Thus the art of medicine, which is more dependent upon the senses, especially with respect to what is learned in it from the senses and from dissection, reached perfection still later. But astronomy, which depends upon the senses in such a fashion that its perfection through them can come about only after a stupendously long time, reaches its perfection even later. Since these sciences bring a man along the route to perfection, and he naturally desires them, it cannot [therefore] be said [both] that the human race is uncreated and that these sciences were discovered by them recently, for were the matter so we would be faced with a possibility which only became actualized after the passage of an infinite period of time, despite the existence of many natural implements for bringing it into actuality, and of humankind's extremely strong natural desire to actualize it. This is clearly absurd.[55]

In this text we find an idea of scientific progress clearly expressed. Gersonides places a great deal of emphasis on the cooperative nature of the scientific enterprise: students of nature labor, generation after generation, to add to our knowledge.[56] Alongside this view of scientific progress we see the clearly

---

54 *Hokhmot*; plural of *hokhmah*.

55 Gersonides, *Wars of the Lord* VI.i.15, p. 356.

56 The idea is repeated frequently in Gersonides' commentary on Song of Songs. See, for example, the following comment on 1:2: "The third impediment – our ignorance of the way that leads to perfection – will also be overcome in this fashion. This is so because while each

expressed view that scientific progress is not an open-ended affair: the various sciences reach perfection or closure. The mathematical sciences were perfected by Aristotle's predecessors (contra Maimonides); Aristotle himself, it seems, brought physics to perfection; Galen brought medicine to perfection; astronomy, which depends upon a huge number of difficult observations, had not yet, by Gersonides' day, been brought to perfection.

This, then, is the notion of the perfectibility of science which I have in mind. The idea that sciences can be brought to closure or perfection in this manner depends upon a conception of science as being primarily a matter of the amassing of knowledge (Wissenschaft) as opposed to a matter of ongoing research (Forschung); on a conception of science, that is, as product and not process. On this view scientific progress is possible, but it is a closed-ended affair: given enough time, every science will be brought to perfection and closure.[57] Once that happens, the role of the student of nature is to preserve and teach what has been discovered; no longer does he or she investigate and conduct independent research.[58]

What is Maimonides' position on this question? On the basis of the texts already quoted, we can see clearly that Maimonides largely accepts the state of affairs described in the passage quoted from Gersonides above. The mathe-

---

of those who endeavor to achieve this apprehension by themselves will either apprehend nothing or very little, when what all of them have apprehended is gathered together, a worthy amount will have been gathered either by virtue of himself or by virtue of his directing those who see their words towards the achievement of the truth in this. Therefore, one must always be aided in one's research by the words of those who preceded him, especially when the truth in them has been revealed to those who preceded him, as was the case during the time of this sage, for the sciences were then greatly [perfected] in our nation. The matter being so, our perfected predecessors guide us in speculation in a way which brings us to perfection, either through their speech or writing, by virtue of the natural desire they have for proffering this influence, and will make known to us concerning each thing the way in which it should be researched, and what they have understood concerning it, together with the assistance [concerning it] which they have derived from their predecessors." In my edition of the Hebrew text this is found on pp. 76-77; in my English translation, it is found on p. 23.

57 The reason for this, I think, is that pre-Baconian science was largely deductive, not inductive. Starting out from a limited number of axioms, the number of useful and interesting theorems which can be deduced must be finite. Gersonides gives plenty of evidence that he conducted research into astronomy and even biology inductively, but his overall intellectual framework was deductive.

58 This is, as I understand it, the commonly accepted stereotype of pre-Galilean medieval science; for a discussion of the extent to which this stereotype matched reality, see Avi-Yonah, "Ptolemy." This is also the view of science held by the *ancien regime* in Isaac Asimov's *Foundation* series.

matical sciences, while not perfected in Aristotle's time, had ultimately reached or at least come close to perfection; Aristotle had brought the physics of the sublunar world to perfection and closure; Galen had brought anatomy to a state of great perfection.[59]

But if this is the case, then perhaps my conclusion above, that Maimonides would admit that the description of the universe he presents in Laws of the Foundations of the Torah is provisional in the sense that it represents only the best and most up-to-date account of the sciences available to him, was too hasty. If the various branches of wisdom had reached perfection, then what Maimonides was presenting in the *Mishneh Torah* was not simply a report on the current status of our understanding of the universe, but the absolute codification of physical and metaphysical truth, once for all, just as the laws in the *Mishneh Torah* are the absolute codification of the commandments of Judaism (minor errors aside), once and for all time. On this basis we could construe Maimonides as saying that the sages and Aristotle erred in scientific matters simply because they lived in times before the various sciences had reached their perfection; the fact that they erred, therefore, does not mean that he must err. Since progress understood in this fashion is not open-ended, there is no problem with asserting both that human beings progress scientifically and spiritually, and that the acme of this progress has been reached, or nearly reached.[60]

It turns out, however, that this is not Maimonides' position. I have demonstrated elsewhere that Maimonides distinguishes between the astronomy presented in the *Mishneh Torah* and in the *Guide*.[61] Maimonides' astronomy in the *Mishneh Torah* is straightforwardly and conventionally Ptolemaic. Maimonides is there interested in presenting a non-problematic account of the heavens in order to impress upon his readers the magnitude of God's wisdom. In the *Guide of the Perplexed*, on the other hand, he was interested in presenting the truth. The truth presented there is that astronomy and metaphysics

---

59 Progress in the sciences (in the Gersonidean sense of the term as we are using it here), it should be noted, was not always assumed by medieval thinkers. Maimonides' fellow Cordovan Averroes thought that humanity had regressed in astronomy from the time of Aristotle. See Kraemer, "Scientific Method," p. 81. See also Avi-Yonah, "Ptolemy," p. 125.

60 Maimonides asserts that he is living on the eve of the messianic era and may even have meant it. For details, see my "A Suggestion."

61 In Ch. 12, "On the Status of Astronomy."

are intrinsically uncompletable.[62] Whether this truth was known to him when he wrote the *Mishneh Torah*, and hidden from his readers so as not to confuse them, or whether he hit upon it after completing the *Mishneh Torah* and before writing the *Guide*, is irrelevant; either way, the astronomy he presents in the *Mishneh Torah* does not represent the most perfect possible exposition of that science available to him and most certainly, therefore, does not represent the highest stage that astronomy can reach.

I have argued here that Maimonides presented the scientific matters in the *Mishneh Torah* as simply the most up-to-date account of the universe available to him, subject to change, development, and refinement. In support of this claim I adduced materials showing that Maimonides held that the rabbinic sages could err when presenting evidence based on the sciences of their day, that individuals perfected enough to achieve some level of prophetic inspiration could err, that Aristotle could err in scientific matters, that he (Maimonides) could and did err in matters of halakhah, and that he expected there to be further progress in scientific and spiritual matters. All this being the case, I argued that Maimonides could not have been wedded irretrievably to his account of natural matters as found in Laws of the Foundations of the Torah at the beginning of the *Mishneh Torah*.

But, taking away with the left hand what I had just given with the right, I then pointed out that the issue was not so simple and straightforward. Maimonides, in his medieval fashion, accepted the fact that closure or perfection of

---

62 A "complete" science would be one which could be presented in the manner laid down by Aristotle in the *Posterior Analytics*: a finite number of axioms from which all true knowledge taught by that science could be derived. For the impact of this position on medieval Jewish philosophy, see, for example, Joseph Albo, *Sefer ha-Ikkarim* 1.17 and Isaac Abravanel, *Rosh Amanah*, chap. 23 (in my translation, p. 194); see further my discussion in "Conception of Torah." For Maimonides' reasons for reaching the conclusion that astronomy and metaphysics are uncompletable, see my "Maimonides and Gersonides on Astronomy" (to be republished in the companion volume to this collection). In that article I show that in order to make his synthesis of religion and philosophy possible, Maimonides was forced to claim that the science of astronomy can never be brought to perfection or closure. What humans can know of astronomical phenomena does not accord with the true (unknowable) facts; rather, astronomical knowledge is only a model which allows us to make predictions, while telling us nothing about the true state of the heavens. This instrumentalist stance in science, I further argue, is a consequence of Maimonides' theory of divine attributes, just as Gersonides' realism in science is connected to his theory of divine attributes. If astronomy, the science of the motions of the heavenly bodies, is uncompletable, then metaphysics, the science which, inter alia, deals with the incorporeal movers of the heavenly bodies, is *a fortiori* incompletable.

the sciences was inevitable. Furthermore, he held that the physical (sublunar) matters discussed in the *Mishneh Torah* represented physical science in its perfected, completed form.

But if this is the case, then perhaps it is incorrect to conclude that Maimonides would admit that the description of the universe he presents in Laws of the Foundations of the Torah is provisional in the sense that it represents only the best and most up-to-date account of the sciences available to him. If the various branches of wisdom had reached perfection, then what Maimonides was presenting in the *Mishneh Torah* was not simply a report on the current status of our understanding of the universe, but a permanent description of physical and metaphysical truth parallel to the laws in the *Mishneh Torah*; the latter are the absolute codification of the commandments of Judaism once and for all time; the former represents an unalterable description of physical reality. On this basis Maimonides could be construed as saying that the sages and Aristotle erred in their descriptions of the natural world simply because they lived in times before the various sciences had reached their perfection; that they erred, therefore, does not mean that he must err. This approach allows us a whig approach to progress, one which does not understand such progress as open-ended; thus Maimonides could assert that human beings progress scientifically and spiritually, and that the acme of this progress has been reached, or nearly reached.

But this in fact is not Maimonides' position. Astronomy and metaphysics had not reached perfection in his day, nor will they ever. The conclusion reached above stands: the astronomical science of the *Mishneh Torah* is not and cannot be the final, immutable statement of physical reality as it actually is.

CHAPTER FOURTEEN
Maimonides' Allegiances to Science and Judaism

I n the two preceding chapters[1] I argued that Maimonides presented the scientific matters in the first four chapters of the *Mishneh Torah* as the most up-to-date account of the structure of the physical and metaphysical universe available to him, and not as an absolute, ultimate account of nature as it really is, was, and always will be. I further showed that while Maimonides affirmed a "whig" view of progress in the sciences, according to which science progressed along a more or less straight line ever upward, he also maintained that the sciences could and most would reach a state of closure or perfection, where there was nothing new to be learned. Two sciences which had not reached perfection in his day, and *never* would, he felt, were astronomy and metaphysics. Further progress in astronomy was, of course, possible, but not beyond a certain limit. In addition I have argued, following Gad Freudenthal and against Tzvi Langermann, that Maimonides adopted a fictionalist, instrumentalist interpretation of the nature of astronomy.[2] In the above cited articles I not only showed that these claims about Maimonides were true, but also why he had to maintain them. In this essay I propose to discuss a problem these positions pose for him.

The problem can be stated briefly: astronomy (in the sense of the physics of the celestial spheres) is an important part of physics (as understood by Maimonides).[3] Physics and metaphysics undergird the commandments of the

---

1   And in "Maimonides and Gersonides on Astronomy."

2   See Freudenthal, "Felicity" and Langermann, "Perplexity." See now Freudenthal, "Instrumentalism and Realism"

3   This may easily be seen from the contents of "Laws of the Foundations fo the Torah," III-IV. These chapters, Maimonides tells us, are devoted to *maʿaseh bereshit*, which Maimonides identifies with physics. The issue is actually a bit more complicated than I allow here, since in most medieval classifications, astronomy is presented as part of mathematics, not as part of physics, although in some accounts it is thought to be that part of mathematics closest to

Torah. One cannot truly understand Torah, or even properly obey its commandments, without studying (and, of course, understanding, to the greatest extent possible) physics and metaphysics. The understanding of physics in the guise of astronomy can and likely will change; both physical and metaphysical knowledge is, after a certain point, unavailable to human beings.[4] Does this mean that as we better understand astronomy we better understand Torah?[5] In effect, as we better understand astronomy, does the Torah change, at least from our perspective? As we better understand astronomy, does our fulfillment of the commandments improve?

The eighth of Maimonides' "Thirteen Principles" states that "the Torah is from heaven; to wit, it [must] be believed that the whole of this Torah which is in our hands today is the Torah that was brought down to Moses...that all of it is from God..." The ninth principle deals with the immutability of the Torah, affirming "that this Torah of Moses, our Teacher, shall not be abrogated nor shall another Torah come from God...It may not be added to nor subtracted from-neither from its text nor from its explanation. . ." How can an immutable Torah be based upon foundations which are, at least from our perspective, mutable?[6]

Maimonides' philosophy of science commits him to the idea that sciences progress until they reach closure. His philosophical theology commits him to the idea that the individual commandments of the Torah in some significant

physics. For details, see Wolfson, "The Classification of Sciences." In general, mathematical astronomy in the tradition of the *Almagest* is part of mathematics; celestial physics in the tradition of *De Caelo* is part of physics.

4   For recent statements of the main elements in the debate around this issue, and for references to the main studies on it, see Ivry, "Getting to Know Thee," p. 150 and Stern, "Maimonides' Epistemology."

5   This possibility raises complicated questions concerning Maimonides' attitude towards the status and authority of earlier rabbinic figures. See Kellner, *Decline*. I should note that while through out this chapter I speak of "Torah," in most contexts I actually mean "the specific commandments of the Torah."

6   I refer readers who may (mistakenly) think that Maimonides did not hold the commandments of the Torah to be unalterable to Alfred Ivry's elegant statement of the issue. He writes that in his *Mishneh Torah*, Maimonides "gave his generation, and those after it, a definitive formulation of Mosaic cum rabbinic law, and he considered himself its supreme arbiter." See Ivry, "Ismaili Theology." Whatever one may want to say about Maimonides' understanding of how Torah and commandments developed to his day, he surely did not hold that they would change after the publication of the *Mishneh Torah*. For an even stronger claim, see Halbertal, "*Mishneh Torah*".

sense depend upon the sciences of physics and metaphysics, and that one cannot actually obey these commandments fully and properly until one has perfected oneself as fully as possible in these two disciplines. Maimonides' philosophy of *Halakhah* forces him to maintain that the Torah is static, in the sense that no change in it can occur. My question here is: can he consistently hold all these positions simultaneously? To rephrase the problem, once Maimonides affirmed that *ma'aseh bereshit* (i.e., the account of the creation of the world in the opening chapters of Genesis) and *ma'aseh merkavah* (i.e., the account of Ezekiel's vision of the chariot)[7] are roots and foundations of the Torah in general and of *Halakhah* in particular, can he consistently maintain his allegiance to the notions of dynamic science and static *Halakhah*?

Although this question relates to issues which Maimonides did not directly address, it is still valuable, I am convinced, to lay out the question in some detail, and show what answers were available to Maimonides.

I begin with an oft-cited but little-studied text, Maimonides' commentary to the first mishnah of the second chapter of tractate *Hagigah*. The mishnah states:

> One does not expound upon forbidden sexual relations in the presence of three, nor upon *ma'aseh bereshit* in the presence of two, nor upon the *merkavah* in the presence of one, unless that one were wise and understood upon his own. All who look upon four things, it were better had they not come into the world: what is above, what is below, what is in front, and what is behind. All who are not protective of the honor of their master, it were better had they not come into the world.

Maimonides' commentary on this passage is a dense and succinct statement of many of the basic themes of his philosophical theology and is worth citing in full. He writes:

> He said that it is forbidden to expound upon the "secrets of forbidden sexual relations"[8] unless those listening be fewer than three, the reason for this being

---

7 Ivry, p. 283 notes that for Maimonides *ma'aseh merkavah* means revelation. One of the implications of this insight is that on some important level, the content of revelation and the content of metaphysics are the same thing.

8 Kafiḥ, p 376. The term here is *sitrei 'arayot*, on which, see Idel, "*Sitrei 'Arayot*."

that were one of them to engage the teacher in discussion, the other two could engage in discussion between themselves, lose their concentration [on what the teacher taught] and thus not know the correct law concerning the "secrets of forbidden sexual relations." Given the great desire most humans have for this matter, they will not be sufficiently rigorous if a doubt should arise concerning what they heard from the teacher and they will decide the matter leniently.

He said, "nor upon *maaseh bereshit* in the presence of two" and certainly not if they be more.[9] They said: "*For ask now of the days past [which were before thee, since the day that God created man upon the earth, and from one end of heaven unto the other, whether there hath been any such thing as this great thing is, or hath been heard like it?]* (Dt. 4:32] - one asks, two do not ask."[10] We have already explained the reason for this in our Introduction to this composition:[11] it is that it is impossible for the masses to understand those matters, and they are [therefore] only transmitted from one individual to another with great care, for the masses understand very little of them. When a fool hears them his conviction[12] becomes undermined and he thinks that they contradict the truth, while they are [themselves, in reality] the truth.

But one does not expound upon *maaseh merkavah* at all, even to one individual unless he is, as it was said, "wise and understood upon his own," i.e., that he arouses himself to understand these matters on his own and does not need to have them explained to him. Rather he is given a hint, and he draws proper inferences on his own. This is the meaning of their statement, "they teach him chapter headings" [*Hagigah* 13a], [by which they mean] that these matters include issues which are impressed upon the souls of perfected human beings,

---

9 I.e., one may teach *maaseh bereshit* to, at most, one student.

10 *Hagigah* 11b. Maimonides is citing the talmudic explanation for the restriction against teaching *maaseh bereshit* to more than one student at a time: one person may ask concerning "the days past," not two people – the Hebrew in the verse is in the singular, not the plural.

11 Kafih, vol. 1, pp. 34ff. English translation, Rosner, p. 111.

12 Rabbi Kafih translates *emunato*, "his faith" (perhaps because Maimonides is here speaking about simple people). The Arabic is a variant of *itiqad*, which, when Maimonides translates himself from Arabic to Hebrew (as is the case with the first positive commandment in *Sefer ha-Mizvot* and the first *halakhah* in the *Mishneh Torah*), he renders as some variant of *daat*, "knowledge" or "understanding". For further discussion, see above, chs. 5, 6, and 9.

such that when they are explained in [straightforward] language or expressed in parables they lose their meaning and significance.

Listen to what has become clear to me according to my understanding on the basis of which I have studied in the words of the Sages; it is that they call *ma'aseh bereshit* the natural science and inquiry into the beginning of creation. By *ma'aseh merkavah* they mean the divine science, it being speech on existence as such[13] and on the existence of the Creator, His knowledge, His attributes, that all created things must necessarily have come from Him, the angels, the soul, the intellect which links with humans, and existence after death. Because of the importance of these two sciences, the natural and the divine – and they were justly considered important – they[14] warned against teaching them as the mathematical sciences are taught. It is known that each person by nature desires all the sciences,[15] whether he be an ignoramus or a sage. [It is further known] that it is impossible for a person to begin the study of these sciences, and direct his thought towards them, without the appropriate premises, and without entering the stages of science; they therefore forbade this and warned against it.[16] They sought to frighten one who directed his thought towards "the account of the beginning" without [appropriate] premises, as he said, "all who look upon four things…" They [also] sought to restrain one who would direct his thought towards and would examine divine matters with his unaided imagination, without ascending the rungs of the sciences and said, [with reference to such people,] "all who are not protective of the honor of their master [it were better had they not come into the world]."

"It were better had they not come into the world" – its meaning is that such a person is removed from the ranks of humanity, and classifying him in one of the other species of animal would be better for existence than his being a human because he wants to know something in an inappropriate manner and in

---

13 The main subject matter of metaphysics according to Aristotle.
14 I.e., the authors of the mishnaic text on which Maimonides is commenting here.
15 An obvious reference to the opening sentence of Aristotle's *Metaphysics*.
16 Compare the letter to his student with which Maimonides prefaces the *Guide of the Perplexed* (Pines, pp. 3-4).

a way that is unsuited to his nature, for only a person ignorant of the nature of existence would seek to imagine what is above or what is below. [17] When a man empty of all knowledge seeks to use his corrupt imagination in order to know what is above the heavens and below the earth, and imagines [reaching] them to be like ascending to the attic of a house, and also, [to know] what was before the creation of the heavens and what will be after they are no longer, he will certainly be brought to madness and desolation. Examine this wonderful expression, said with divine help, "all who are not protective of the honor of their master," the meaning of this being, all who are not protective of their intellects, for the intellect is the honor of God. [18] Since he does not know the value of this matter which was given him, he is abandoned into the hands of his desires, and becomes like an animal. [19] Thus, they said, "who is he who is not protective of the honor of his Master? – he who transgresses secretly" [*Hagigah* 16a; *Kiddushin* 40a]. They said elsewhere, "adulterers do not commit adultery until the spirit of madness enters them" [*Midrash Tanhuma*, Naso, 5]. This is the truth, for while one craves any of the desires, the intellect is not perfected. [20]

This matter is brought up here since above he said "these are the bodies of Torah [*gufei Torah*]," and thus here he cited matters which are the principles of "the bodies of Torah." The Talmud forbade teaching them publicly and expressly prohibited it and commanded that an individual teach them to himself and not pass them on to another and derived this [prohibition] from the parabolic statement of Solomon on this matter, *honey and milk are under thy tongue.* [21]

---

17 I.e., this person wants to attain knowledge the wrong way, via the imagination, which can only lead to harm. It would be better, therefore, were this person classified with the non-human animals; humans, after all, are distinguished by their intellects.

18 See the discussion of the term *kevod kono* in *Confrontation*, pp. 209-215.

19 This can only be understood in the context of Maimonides' Aristotelian comprehension of human beings as "rational animals"– humans become such only to the extent that they actualize their intellectual potential to some degree or other. For details, see ch. 4, "Is Maimonides' Ideal Person."

20 This should be understood in the light of Maimonides' stand that moral perfection is a prerequisite for intellectual perfection and that intellectual perfection is not like money in the bank (as Lenn Goodman once wisely observed to me); it is, rather, like vigor or "being in shape". To stay in shape, one must constantly exercise. It is like treading water: if you stop, you sink. Thus, Maimonides has a problem with the notion of a wicked philosopher. For more on the points raised in this note, see Kellner, *Perfection*, pp. 26-28 and above, ch. 11, "Virtue of Faith."

21 Song of Songs 4:11. On this, *Hagigah* 13a comments, "The things that are sweeter than

This text represents the first place in his writings where Maimonides clearly states that *maʾaseh bereshit* is the rabbinic name for that area of study called by the philosophers, "physics," and *maʾaseh merkavah* is the rabbinic name for that area of study called by the philosophers, "metaphysics". The ancient rabbis, he maintains, understood the true nature of *maʾaseh bereshit* and of *maʾaseh merkavah* and therefore tried to keep them hidden from the multitudes, who might be led astray and damaged were they to study physics and metaphysics improperly.[22]

At the very end of this passage Maimonides adds an apparently innocuous statement concerning the reason that the issue of the study of *maʾaseh bereshit* and *maʾaseh merkavah* is brought up here at all. He explains that the previous mishnah had ended by calling a whole variety of specific laws *gufei Torah* (literally, "bodies of the Torah").[23] Having mentioned "the bodies of Torah," the mishnah went on to cite "matters which are the principles of the bodies of Torah." Here, for the first time, we find Maimonides claiming that physics and metaphysics are the roots or foundations of the bodies of Torah, i.e., of the specific commandments of the Torah.[24]

The claims that *maʾaseh bereshit* and *maʾaseh merkavah* are physics and metaphysics, and that these two sciences represent the deepest level of the Torah upon which the specific laws depend, became, after the completion of the *Commentary on the Mishnah*, a standard trope in Maimonides' writings, and

---

honey and milk should be under they tongue," i.e., not taught expressly. My thanks to Y. Tzvi Langermann for his help with the translation of this passage. More on many of the issues raised in this text, see Kellner, "Kotler."

22 Maimonidean esotericism is a source of never-ending fascination to scholars. See Halbertal, *Concealment and Revelation*. My own view, for whatever it is worth (as my lamented teacher, Steven Schwarzschild used to love to say), is that Maimonidean esotericism is a function of both his elitism and a strong sense of *noblesse oblige*. See ch.1 above and *Confrontation*, pp. 15-17.

23 There is no doubt that by this expression Maimonides means "specific commandments." This is the sense of the term in the mishnaic text (*Hagigah* 1:8) to which Maimonides is referring here and it is the sense of the term in the two places in which he uses it in the *Mishneh Torah* ("Laws of Idolatry," II.5 and "Laws of the Sabbath," XII.8). The term occurs in the Jerusalem Talmud once (*Hagigah* 1:8) and six times in the Babylonian Talmud (*Berakbot* 63a, *Shabbat* 32b, *Hagigah* 10 and 11b, *Hullin* 60b, and *Kritot* 5a). In these passages as well, the sense of me term is clear: specific commandments of the Torah. The Soncino Talmud translates the term as "essentials of the Torah," which is misleading.

24 Isadore Twersky was the first to focus attention on this text. See his *Introduction*, p. 361. Twersky notes that all editions of the Mishnah before that of Rabbi Kafih mistakenly omitted the crucial phrase. See also Rabbi Kafih's notes to his edition/translation.

even served as the ideological substrate for the entire *Guide of the Perplexed*. It will be useful to illustrate this point in some detail.

In the *Mishneh Torah* (composed after the *Commentary on the Mishnah* and before the *Guide of the Perplexed*), we again find the equations, *maaseh bereshit* = physics and *maaseh merkavah* = metaphysics, but less explicitly. The first two chapters of "Laws of the Foundations of the Torah" expressly deal with *maaseh merkavah*, while the third and fourth chapters deal with *maaseh bereshit*. The subject matters raised in these four chapters are precisely those of metaphysics and physics. In light of the *Hagigah* commentary cited above, it is hardly surprising that a work devoted to "*gufei Torah*" (the *Mishneh Torah*) should open with a discussion of the "principles of the bodies of the Torah."

In the *Guide of the Perplexed* Maimonides explains that:

> It is not the purpose of this Treatise to make its totality understandable to the vulgar or beginners in speculation, nor to teach those who have not engaged in any study other than the science of the Torah - I mean the legalistic study of the laws [of the Torah].[25] For the purpose of this Treatise and all those like it is the science of the Torah in its true sense (p. 5).

This is not the place to go into the question of what Maimonides means by "the science of the Torah in the true sense." We may safely follow the unanimous opinion of his medieval commentators that the reference is to physics and metaphysics.[26]

Physics and metaphysics are expressly called "principles" of the specific commandments of Judaism in the *Hagigah* commentary. It is a safe assumption that in the *Guide of the Perplexed* they are presented as "the science of the Torah in the true sense." Metaphysics is on some important level unknowable;[27] physics (to the extent that it includes astronomy) is mutable. To return, then, once again, to our original question: is there not a problem with an unknowable science and a mutable science serving as "principles" for an immutable body of law?

---

25 On this expression see Schwarz, "al-Fiqh."

26 For details, see Kellner, "Conception of Torah."

27 God's existence, unity, and incorporeality are demonstrable; what is unknowable in metaphysics are other positive statements about God. For the considerable discussion surrounding this issue, see Ivry, "Getting to Know Thee," p. 150.

Maimonides expressly understood various sciences to have progressed to his day, and even expected further progress (at least in astronomy) in succeeding generations. This may be made clearer if we recall Maimonides' attitudes towards Aristotle. Aristotle was indeed the chief of the philosophers, and had indeed reached a level of human perfection just shy of prophecy, but he could still err on matters of physics and metaphysics. It is well-known that Maimonides at least claimed to reject Aristotle's assertion that the universe was uncreated. It was Maimonides' argument that Aristotle was wrong on his own terms; in thinking that he could prove the eternity of the universe, Aristotle exceeded the legitimate bounds of his science and made unwarranted claims.

Mathematical (Ptolemaic) astronomy, while not perfected in Aristotle's time, had ultimately reached or at least come close to perfection; Aristotle had brought the physics of the sublunar world to perfection and closure; Galen had brought anatomy to a state of great perfection. Maimonides thought very highly of Aristotle, so highly that he placed him on the scale of human excellence just beneath the prophets. But science had progressed since Aristotle's day, and human beings living in Maimonides' era (close to fifteen hundred years after Aristotle) knew much more than did the Stagirite.

We thus see that for Maimonides, science is dynamic and not static. But, if science changes, what does that do to the "bodies of Torah" which depend, in some sense, upon it?

Not only did Maimonides anticipate "progress" in the sciences, but he was convinced that certain scientific matters were better understood by Aristotle than by the Sages of the Talmud. Since Maimonides appears to agree with Aristotle on these matters, he appears therefore to hold that his own understanding of these scientific matters is superior to that of the Sages. We thus find him stating:

> One of the ancient opinions that is widespread among the philosophers and the general run of people consists in the belief that the motion of the spheres produces very fearful and mighty sounds. ... This opinion also is generally known in our religious community. Do you not see that the Sages describe the might of the sound produced by the sun when it every day proceeds on its way in the sphere? ...Aristotle, however, does not accept this and makes it clear

that the heavenly bodies produce no sound. You should not find it blamewor-thy that the opinion of Aristotle disagrees with that of the Sages.... [The Sages themselves] in these astronomical matters preferred the opinion of the sages of the nations of the world to their own. For they explicitly say, "The sages of the world have vanquished [us]." And this is correct. For everyone who argues in speculative matters does this according to the conclusions to which he was led by his speculation. Hence the conclusion whose demonstration is correct is believed (*Guide* II.8, p. 267).

Maimonides makes a similar claim elsewhere in the *Guide*:

Do not ask me to show that everything they [the Sages] have said concerning astronomical matters conforms to the way things really are. For at that time mathematics were imperfect. They did not speak about this as transmitters of the dicta of the prophets, but rather because in those times they were men of knowledge in those fields or because they had heard these dicta from the men of knowledge who lived in those times (III.l4, p. 459).[28]

The upshot of these two passages is that Jews (and non-Jews!) in Maimo-nides' time understood certain aspects of mathematics and astronomy better than did the Sages of the Talmud. Are we to say, then, that Maimonides' un-derstanding of the "foundations of the bodies of the law" was superior to that of (at least some of) the Sages of the Talmud?

It is difficult to ascribe to Maimonides (in an attempt to solve the problem raised in this chapter) the view that while the written Torah does not change, the Oral Torah does. For one thing, it ignores his express claim (quoted near the beginning of this chapter) to the effect that the Oral Torah is part of the immutable revelation at Sinai. In this connection, it should be remembered that Maimonides, unlike other commentators and decisors, drastically limits the extension of the term "Oral Torah"; for him it refers to a carefully circum-scribed subset of what is ordinarily thought of as Oral Torah. According to Mai-monides, it denotes "only the divine explanation of Scripture given explicitly at Sinai, which was to remain Oral. Subsequent intepretation and legislation are

---

28 For further discussion of these texts, see ch. 13 above and my *Decline*, pp. 55-59.

not termed Oral Law, though they may be treated as such in certain contexts."[29] Oral Torah is thus no less Sinaitic than the Written Torah, and no more given over to the possibility of change and new understandings. It is, moreover, not correct to see the sciences as part of Oral Torah as opposed to Written Torah; the Genesis account teaches physics[30] and the chariot vision of Ezekiel teaches (what can be taught about) metaphysics.[31] If science changes, we must still conclude that Torah (i.e., the commandments) changes.

But is this truly so? Let us now examine the relationship which Maimonides posits between science and Torah. Maimonides refers to physics and metaphysics (in a mixture of Arabic and Hebrew) as "usul gufei Torah," the "principles," "roots," or "foundations" of the "gufei Torah." What is the relationship which he thought obtained between physics and metaphysics on the one hand, and the specific commandments of the Torah on the other hand? He emphasizes the connection between the two in the Guide of the Perplexed:

> Do you not see the following fact? God, may His mention be exalted, wished us to be perfected and the state of our societies to be improved by His laws regarding actions. Now this can come about only after the adoption of intellectual beliefs, the first of which being His apprehension, may He be exalted, according to our capacity. This, in its turn, cannot come about except through divine science, and this divine science [metaphysics] cannot become actual except after a study of natural science [physics] (I. Introduction, p.9).

In the notes to his translation of the Guide of the Perplexed on this passage, Rabbi Kafih suggests that this means that the purpose of the Torah with respect to the commandments (that we be perfected and the state of our societies improved) can only be achieved if we adopt correct beliefs concerning God. This certainly seems to be what Maimonides is trying to say here, but the question

---

29 I quote from Blidstein, "'Oral Law.'"

30 *Guide*, Introduction, p. 9: "Hence God, may He be exalted, caused His book to open with the 'Account of the Beginning', which, as we have made clear, is natural science. And because of the greatness and importance of the subject and because our capacity falls short of apprehending the greatest of subjects as it really is, – which divine wisdom has deemed necessary to convey to us – we are told about these profound matters in parables and riddles and very obscure words."

31 *Guide* III,1-7.

of the precise way in which correct knowledge concerning God must precede perfected obedience to the commandments remains unclear.

Terminological considerations do not appear to be helpful. Maimonides uses the term "*usul*" in a wide variety of ways, often interchangeably with the term "*qawa'id*," and these various usages do not, I think, help us to understand his precise meaning here.[32]

However, we may, I think, understand Maimonides' point here as follows: the first commandment in the Book of Commandments, "the great principle upon which all depends" ("Laws of the Foundations of the Torah," I.6), the "foundation of all foundations and pillar of the sciences" (*ibid*. 1.1), is to know (not only believe) that God exists. Monothesim is the central axis around which the entire Torah revolves, denial of which is tantamount to denial of the Torah in its entirety.[33] Although Maimonides never says this explicitly, the consequence of holding a false conception of God is that every time one prays, or performs any act of religious devotion, one is actually committing idolatry.[34]

This being the case, only that person who truly *knows* that God is one and incorporeal can fulfill even the first of the commandments. All religiously

---

32 For details, see my *Dogma*, p. 17 and p. 53.

33 See *Guide of the Perplexed* III.29 (p. 521), III.30 (p. 523), and III.37 (p. 542 and p. 545) and, most especially, "Laws of Idolatry," II.4.

34 With respect to prayer, at least, the point is made clearly in *Guide* III.51, p. 620:

> As for someone who thinks and frequently mentions God without knowledge, following a mere imagining or following a belief adopted because of his reliance on the authority of someone else, he is, to my mind, outside the habitation and far away from it and does not in true reality mention or think about God.

Who are those "outside the habitation"? The answer, it appears to me, is on the previous page:

> Those who are within the city, but have turned their backs 'upon the ruler's habitation, are people who have opinions and are engaged in speculation, but who have adopted incorrect opinions either because of some great error that befell them in the course of their speculation or because of their following the traditional authority of one who has fallen into error. ... They are those concerning whom necessity at certain times impels killing them and blotting out the traces of their opinions lest they should lead astray the ways of others.

For Maimonides, prayer requires intention (*kavvanab*) – see "Laws of Prayer" IV.1 and IV.15 and Blidstein, *Ha-Tefillab*, pp. 77-122 – and prayer without intention is not prayer; one who directs prayer to a false god is thus committing idolatry. I have no proof for my wider claim that performance of any act of religious devotion while holding a corporealist conception of God is idolatry, although I am convinced that it is Maimonides' position. Abraham Maimonides seemed to agree with my interpretation of his father. See his *Milhamot Hashem*, pp. 52, 59, and 71.

obligatory practices are acts of devotion; for them to be done properly, the devotee must know that God is one and incorporeal.

This point needs expansion. In *Maimonides on Human Perfection* I argued that, for Maimonides, obedience to the commandments is the most effective route for human beings to prepare themselves to achieve intellectual perfection. Having achieved that perfection to the greatest extent possible, humans have reached the acme of their fulfillment as human beings, their *hazlahah*, or felicity. Jews, however, are commanded to take one further step and imitate God through obedience to the commandments. This fulfillment is, of course, qualitatively different from obedience to the same commandments before one has perfected oneself intellectually to the greatest extent possible. There is no further "reward" for this *imitatio Dei*; it is a pure act of worship. God performs "loving-kindess, judgment, and righteousness in the world" (*Guide*, III.51) for no self-benefit, so does the perfected worshipper of God fulfill the commandments, many of which lead to the betterment of society, for no self-benefit, not even the benefit of making oneself more perfected. One is called upon to obey the commandments on this understanding, in two radically different ways before and after having achieved as much intellectual perfection as one is going to achieve.

Thus far, metaphysics. Knowledge of physics is also a crucial pillar upon which religious observance depends for two reasons: it is a necessary prerequiste for studying metaphysics and it itself leads to knowledge of God to a certain extent. There is nothing which exists, says Maimonides in *Guide* I.34, but God and "the totality of things" made by God. These latter "are indicative of His existence, … and of what should be affirmed and denied with regard to Him." It is thus the case, Maimonides continues, that

> it is therefore indispensable to consider all beings as they really are so that we may obtain for all the kinds of being true and certain premises that would be useful to us in our researches pertaining to the divine science.... As for the matters pertaining to the astronomy of the spheres and to natural science, I do not consider that you should have any difficulty in grasping that those are matters necessary for the apprehension of the relation of the world to God's governance as this relation is in truth and not according to imaginings.[35]

---

35 P. 74. Compare also "Laws of the Foundations of the Torah," II.1.

Physics (including astronomy) is useful for what we can learn about God through an examination of the created world, for what we can learn about God's relationship to the world (providence), and as a stepping stone to metaphysics.

We are now in a position to answer the question posed at the beginning of this chapter. Does better understanding of astronomy result in a different relationship to Torah? In effect, as we better understand astronomy, does the Torah change, at least from our perspective? As we better understand astronomy, does our fulfillment of the commandments improve?

The answers to these questions, I think, are all negative. There are three unrelated reasons for this. First, Maimonides was convinced that Aristotle's description of the sublunar world accurately and adequately accounted for what needed and could be known in that realm. Terrestrial physics had reached closure. There was no danger of change there. By defining so much of metaphysics as largely unknowable, Maimonides insulated himself from problematic change in that realm as well. That leaves astronomy: unlike physics, it is subject to new knowledge and understanding, and, unlike metaphysics, it is to a considerable extent knowable. But what sort of knowledge? Maimonides' instrumentalist approach to astronomy, according to which we do not actually know anything about the heavenly bodies and their movements in and of themselves, but rely entirely on what today we would call models, largely insulates him from the danger of change there as well. Since we do not claim to have "real" knowledge of astronomical phenomena themselves, new models (necessitated by new developments and understanding) do not involve actual change in our understanding of the universe; that does not really change, only the models we use "to save the phenomena." Change in the science of astronomy should not, therefore, threaten the immutability of the commandments of the Torah.

Second, it must be recalled that even though Maimonides allowed for progress in celestial physics – "It is possible that someone else will find a demonstration by means of which the true reality of what is obscure for me will become clear to him" – he did not actually expect anything more than incremental changes in detail. There is no doubt that he did not anticipate the kind of revolution ushered in by Copernicus. In this sense, too, even though astronomy is one of the roots or foundations of the commandments, change in our astronomical knowledge represented no real challenge to the immutability of those commandments for Maimonides. This would be true even were Maimonides not a formalist in his approach to astronomy.

Our analysis above of the way in which Maimonides apparently saw the relationship between science and the commandments also provides a solution to our problem. If physics and astronomy are roots and principles of the commandments only in the sense that without them one cannot actually *know* that God exists, is one, and is incorporeal, progress in the sciences represents no threat to the commandments. Maimonides can not credibly be thought to have entertained the idea that science would some day undermine as opposed to support these three claims about God.

Science might undermine other claims about God: those concerning providence, for example, or the creation of the world. Such developments, however, would not undermine our obligation to obey the commandments. Maimonides links the Sabbath to the doctrine of the creation of the universe. Does that mean that if we could show the universe to be uncreated, we would be right in abandoning observance of the Sabbath? Maimonides' answer would be quite clearly, No.[36] But if we could, theoretically, refute God's existence, unity, and incorporeality, would that undermine our obligation to observe the Sabbath? The answer to that question is clearly, Yes. Commandments after all, must have commanders. But, clearly, there is no reason to suspect that Maimonides entertained the possibility of such a proof.

In short, as long as science does not refute the existence, unity, and incorporeality of God - and it appears that there is no way it could - progress in the sciences in no way threatens obedience to the commandments: science remains the root of the "bodies of Torah." In fact, I would go further and say that for Maimonides scientific progress, in bringing one closer to the truth, enables one better to observe the commandments.

Maimonides has one overarching allegiance: to truth. His attachments to both science and Judaism did not and could not contradict it.

---

36 Indeed, as my student Oded Horetzky never tires of reminding me, Maimonides does not claim to have proved the creation of the universe; no religious doctrine, therefore, can be based upon our *knowledge* that the cosmos is created.

CHAPTER FIFTEEN
Faith, Science, and Orthodoxy

How can an Orthodox Jew in today's world maintain faith in Torah in the face of the apparent challenges of natural science to that faith? I will here examine one historical solution to the problem, that of Moses Maimonides,[1] two contemporary solutions, those of Yeshayahu Leibowitz and Steven Schwarzschild, and then propose my own approach, one which relies upon reverting to what I understand as classic Jewish definitions of faith.

Before beginning I should like to note that I think that my task is relatively simple. Real challenges to Orthodoxy today do not come from the natural sciences but from literary criticism and history, which cast doubt upon the textual integrity of the Written Torah and upon Orthodox understandings of the nature of the Oral Torah;[2] from ethics, which challenges traditional Jewish understandings of the relationship of the sexes and of Jews and non-Jews, among other problems;[3] and from Enlightenment thought generally, which emphasizes the value of autonomy over faithful submission to God.[4]

How did Maimonides approach the reconciliation of Torah and science? He starts off by taking the text of the Torah as literally true in every case: "I believe every possible happening that is supported by a prophetic statement

---

1 Technically, Jewish orthodoxy is a modern phenomenon and Maimonides could thus not be Orthodox (even more so if my argument in ch. 9, "Could Maimonides Get into Rambam's Heaven?" is correct – as, of course, it is). I trust that the readers of this volume will be willing to grant some leeway here.

2 See Levy, "Orthodox Bible Study."

3 For a forthright statement of some of these problems by an Orthodox rabbi and scholar, see Solomon, "Intolerant Texts."

4 Important work in this regard has been done by the late Steven Schwarzschild. See the essays collected in *Pursuit*. See further the essays in Frank, *Autonomy and Judaism*. Extremely valuable in this connection is Sagi and Statman, "Divine Command Morality."

and do not strip it of its plain meaning."[5] But, there is an exception to this general rule: "I fall back on interpreting a statement [allegorically] only when its plain meaning is impossible, like the corporeality of God; the possible however remains as stated." What makes prophetic references to God as corporeal impossible to accept? Maimonides tells us in the *Guide of the Perplexed* (II.25, p. 328): "That the deity is not a body has been demonstrated; from this it follows necessarily that everything that in its plain meaning disagrees with this demonstration must be interpreted figuratively, for it is known that such texts are of necessity fit for figurative interpretation."

Maimonides' point is relatively straightforward: the Torah must be accepted as literally true in every case where its teachings do not contradict that which has been demonstrated to be true. By demonstration, Maimonides means "a syllogism both of whose premises are apodictic."[6]

Maimonides' position clearly makes demonstrated truth to be the criterion we use for determining which passages in the Torah we read literally, and which passages we read allegorically. If a scientific claim is demonstrably true, and the plain sense of Scripture contradicts it, we may not ignore or reinterpret the scientific claim; we must, rather, reinterpret Scripture. To all intents and purposes, science becomes our measure for understanding the Torah.[7]

Maimonides could be confident that this approach would cause him no problems since, at their deepest levels, Torah and science taught the same thing. Maimonides clearly states that *maaseh bereshit* is the rabbinic name for that area of study called by the philosophers, "physics," and *maaseh merkavah* is the rabbinic name for that area of study called by the philosophers, "metaphysics".[8]

Maimonides had further reason for calm: the sciences he was concerned with, physics and metaphysics, proved that which he wanted them to prove,

---

5   "Essay on Resurrection," in *Crisis and Leadership*, p. 228.

6   "Treatise on Logic," chapter 8, Efros trans., p. 48. By "apodictic," Maimonides explains there, he means knowledge derived from perception, axiomatic statements (literally, "first and second ideas"), and experience. Maimonides is relying here on the second chapter of the first book of Aristotle's *Posterior Analytics*. For a discussion of Maimonides' use of the term "demonstration" (Arabic: *burhan*; Hebrew: *mofet*) see Hyman, "Demonstrative."

7   For an explicit statement to this effect see the entire passage surrounding the sentences quoted from Maimonides in the last note to this essay.

8   See Ch. 15, "Maimonides' Allegiances to Science and Judaism."

that God exists, is one, and is incorporeal. It is acceptance of these three beliefs, as taught by science, that Maimonides construes as the first commandment, "the great principle upon which all depends" ("Laws of the Foundations of the Torah," I.6), the "foundation of all foundations and pillar of the sciences" (I.1). Monotheism is the central axis around which the entire Torah revolves, denial of which is tantamount to denial of the Torah in its entirety.

In short, as long as science does not refute the existence, unity, and incorporeality of God –and it appears that there is no way it could – progress in the sciences in no way threatens acceptance of the Torah and obedience to the commandments.

Thus far Maimonides, for whom natural science meant physics, who operated in a theistic universe, and for whom the greatest question posed by science was whether or not the world was created. What of contemporary thinkers, whose natural universe gets along quite well, thank you, without a final cause, confronted by the claims of geology, paleontology, and evolution, all of which demand far greater liberties with the "plain meaning" of Scripture than did Maimonides' naturalistic explanation of various miracles (but no greater liberty, I should note, than that demanded by his radically non-anthropomorphic reading of verses attributing corporeality to God)?[9] There are two contemporary Orthodox thinkers on whom I shall focus here: Yeshayahu Leibowitz (1903-1994) and Steven Schwarzschild (1924-1989).

Judaism, for Leibowitz, is a religion of commandments pure and simple. These commandments subserve no end beyond themselves and are to be performed simply because they are God's commands. If one "fulfills" them for any other reason, one has not fulfilled them at all: "For himself, a man has no more motivation for performing this act [wearing phylacteries] *and there could be no other motivation* than compliance with the will of God, who commanded the wearing of phylacteries."[10] There are no exceptions to this approach – even prayer must be undertaken as the fulfillment of the commandment to pray and for no other reason whatsoever. As Leibowitz says, "Only the prayer which one

---

9   I should also note that Maimonides worked with a deductive model of what science was all about, very different from the way in which the scientific enterprise is understood today. For details, see my "Gersonides on the Song of Songs and Science," to be republished in the companion volume to this one.

10 Leibowitz, *Judaism, Human Values*, p. 20 (emphasis added).

prays as the observance of a Mitzvah is religiously significant" (p. 31). It is not forbidden to turn to God out of joy or anguish, in praise, thanks, or supplication, it is just religiously irrelevant.

Leibowitz's extreme "orthopraxy" as presented here follows from his position that Judaism has no intellectual content as such. Religion, he insists, supplies no information: "Man's consciousness of standing before God has nothing to do with his knowledge of the world, which is understood scientifically" (p. 137).[11] If you want information about the world, go to science, not to the Torah. The two operate on wholly different planes, planes which do not intersect at all. Science deals with "is," Torah with "ought," and never the twain shall meet. Leibowitz understands clearly that medievals perceived things differently. For them, "Whether faith and science were intertwined, antagonistic, or supplementary, there was no doubt that they met on the same plane – that of perception of meaning." For us, however, "...science is no more than a matter of functional relationships which we [have] succeeded in discovering in factual data, [and thus] the world it describes does not express any specific meaning" (pp. 134-35).[12]

Leibowitz thinks that he has neatly solved the problems posed for religion by modern science. They cannot contradict each other, conflict with each other, undermine or support each other, since they never intersect or meet. "There is no [and can not be any] direct confrontation today between natural science and philosophy, between natural science and history, and least of all, between natural science and religion" (p. 136). Science makes no claims about how we ought to behave, religion makes no claims about what we ought to believe and thus the two cannot possibly come into conflict.

Underlying this unusual view of religion is Leibowitz's view of the nature of religious faith:

> I, however, do not regard religious faith as a conclusion. It is rather an *evaluative decision* that one makes, and, like all evaluations, it does not result from any information one has acquired, but is *a commitment to which one binds himself*. In other words, faith is not a form of cognition; it is a conative element of

11 See also p. 136.

12 Further: "Today we have no 'science' in the medieval sense, in which religion and science meet, either as mutually supportive or as conflicting. They are entirely alien to each other." (p. 138)

consciousness. Faith, therefore, cannot be taught. One can only present it in all its might and power (p. 37).

Such a conception of religious belief, of course, leaves no room for religious dogma, clearly defined obligatory beliefs.

Leibowitz buys "industrial peace" in the science/religion wars at the expense of making religion irrelevant to our intellectual selves and to our moral selves. This is a price which Steven Schwarzschild is absolutely unwilling to pay. Schwarzschild holds that Judaism is a consistent, rational system of teachings and actions, having an authoritative character.

Schwarzschild is convinced that normative, authoritative, halakhic Judaism is a consistent, rational system primarily characterized by the primacy it gives to ethical concerns. This system, he maintains, can be shown to have been given its canonical "secular" interpretation in the philosophy of Immanuel Kant as exposited by Hermann Cohen. Among the consequences of this position are that Judaism is systematizable, that non-Jews can, in effect, be "spiritually assimilated" into Judaism, and that there are religious and philosophical positions (Christianity on the one hand and Spinoza/Marx/Hegel on the other) absolutely antithetical to Judaism.

Schwarzschild is clear on the implications of this vision of Judaism:

> There is another implication in what has been said even so far. Hermann Cohen taught in word and practice that "the truth" that philosophy seeks is, in the first place, also the truth (*emeth*) toward which Judaism strives and, in the second place, decisively dependent upon Jewish monotheism... philosophy has to be ultimately Jewish in some real sense, and, indeed, Judaism is intellectually philosophical... I believe this.[13]

Thus, Schwarzschild writes, "'Judaism' (ideally, regulatively) = philosophical truth (ideally, regulatively)" (p. 257).[14] This conclusion is eminently Maimonidean.[15]

---

13 Schwarzschild, *Pursuit*, p. 252.

14 Or, as he put it (p. 110), philosophy and Judaism "turn out to be one and the same entity."

15 And, my friend Avram Montag adds, "any other conclusion distorts the message of the Bible and Talmud."

This notion of the "ideal," "regulative" character of Judaism, of ethics, of philosophy, even of science, which Schwarzschild took over from Hermann Cohen, is central in his thinking and deserves at least brief attention. Cohen's Kant, as presented by Schwarzschild, understands noumena "as constructs, which, while making possible and real the empirical universe, also show up its inadequacy by the standards of the noumenal, rationally constructed ideal model of a universe" (p. 109). It follows from this that, "the task of scientific and ethical man is then to bring the former [the real and empirical universe] increasingly into conformity with the latter [the rationally constructed ideal model of a universe]. Thus the 'ought' is the very presupposition of the 'is.' Both the ethics of science and the scientificity of ethics are thus grounded."

The differences between Schwarzschild and Leibowitz, it seems to me, can in large measure be traced to what might be called differences in philosophical anthropology. Schwarzschild has taken his place firmly in a philosophical tradition which stretches back to Aristotle and whose most emphatic Jewish exponent was Maimonides. According to this tradition humans are defined as rational animals. That which defines us as human, our specific difference, is our ability to think rationally. The moment a human is defined in those terms, rationality must play a key role in all that is essentially related to humanity, religion most emphatically included. It follows from this that for a thinker like Steven Schwarzschild nothing that is rational can be alien to Judaism. He takes this one step further: everything that is rational is, in the final analysis, Judaism – science most emphatically included.

The Aristotle/Maimonides/Schwarzschild position is, obviously, one-sided in its appreciation of human nature. Leibowitz, it appears to me, adopts an equally one-sided approach to the definition of humanity. So far as I understand him, that which makes us human is our *will*: faith for Leibowitz, as we saw above, is a decision, a commitment. It is not a matter of rational conviction and certainly not a matter of emotional or aesthetic response. The person of faith *chooses* to commit herself or himself to life lived before God.

With respect to the relationship between Torah and science, where Leibowitz seeks to separate them absolutely, Schwarzschild seeks to merge them absolutely. Torah and science, each in own way, seeks rationally to construct an ideal model of the universe. To the best of my knowledge Schwarzschild never directly addressed the question of possible contradictions between Torah and science but it seems clear that he would have said that when they do their jobs well they cannot conflict with each other. Such conflicts are the result of either bad Torah, or bad science, or both. If this is indeed Schwarzschild's position, then it is remarkably similar to that of Maimonides, who arrived at it without benefit of reading either Immanuel Kant or Hermann Cohen.[16]

Whether or not one accepts Schwarzschild's construction of Torah and of science, he at least does not seek to duck or finesse the issue of their relationship, as I take Leibowitz to be doing. Leibowitz, as I understand him, makes the central intellectual undertaking of our world, modern science, entirely irrelevant to Judaism. Schwarzschild, perhaps, makes it too relevant, but that, I think, is the lesser sin.

Maimonides, Leibowitz, and Schwarzschild offer us different ways of understanding science in the light of Torah, or Torah in the light of science. Maimonides' position, challenging as it is to many contemporary conceptions of Orthodoxy, relies for its cogency upon conceptions of demonstrative truth foreign to the present-day scientific enterprise. Since little that science teaches today is demonstrably true in Maimonides' sense, his position offers us no guidance on how to relate Torah and science in the contemporary world. Leibowitz insists that we deny that Judaism teaches any truths about the world. He has every right to make that claim normatively, of course, as his readers have every right to reject it (and well they should!); but he also seems to want to make it historically, claiming that this is what Judaism, properly understood, has always taught. That, of course, is nonsense. Accepting nonsense in order to allow science and Torah to live together in peace is a high a price to pay. For Schwarzschild's solution to work, we have to accept the entire structure of his Cohenian neo-Kantianism, and understand science as a radically instrumentalist, idealist enterprise, actually having precious little to do with the world in which we live. None of this is objectionable to me,[17] but I think that simpler, less "expensive" solutions are available to us.

---

16 I would assume that Schwarzschild's idealism would force him to be an instrumentalist, as opposed to realist, in his philosophy of science. If this is indeed the case, it would be another way in which his thought is similar to that of Maimonides, at least as I understand him. See ch. 14 above and my article, "Gersonides on the Song of Songs and Science," to be republished in the companion volume to this one.

17 Of course, it may be objectionable to living, breathing scientists.

Much of contemporary Orthodoxy has, it appears, backed itself into something of a corner with respect to the question of science and Torah. It has rather unreflectively adopted a kind of quasi-Maimonideanism according to which Judaism teaches truth in much the same way that science teaches truth. What brings Orthodoxy to adopt this stance? It makes two crucial assumptions, or, I should say, accepts two Maimonidean teachings which lock it into this position. The first concerns the "centrality of faith-commitments in Judaism" and the second the idea that Judaism recognizes a category of "commandments addressed to the intellect."[18]

Much of Orthodoxy today holds, in the words of Rabbi J. David Bleich, that "basic philosophical beliefs are not simply matters of intellectual curiosity but constitute a branch of Halakhah" and that matters of dogma are decided like other areas of Halakhah. Bleich has recently reiterated the same position: "matters of belief," he maintains, "are inherently matters of Halakhah. It is not at all surprising that disagreements exist with regard to substantive matters of belief, just as is the case with regard to other areas of Jewish law. Such matters are subject to the canons of halakhic decision-making no less than other questions of Jewish law."[19] This position invites conflicts between science and Torah since matters of belief include issues under the purview of the sciences. That is what Maimonides did; but how many of today's Orthodox Jews who agree with this position today would be willing to follow Maimonides in making "demonstration" (i.e., science) the arbiter of what the Torah means?[20]

There are a number of things which have to be said in response to this sort of position. First, I think that it misrepresents Maimonides: basic philosophi-

---

18 I quote, here and below, from Bleich, "Orthodoxy and the Non-Orthodox." I hasten to add that Rabbi Bleich is the last person I would accuse of doing anything unreflectively. I focus on some of his writings here because he has well articulated a position which I find characteristic of contemporary Orthodoxy.

19 See *Tradition* 30 (1966), p. 101. I must note that Rabbi Bleich's position is put forward in explicitly Maimonidean terms.

20 Fairness demands a few words of clarification here. My equation of science and demonstration is a bit too facile, since, as I noted above, Maimonidean science is demonstrative, but contemporary science is not demonstrative in the same way. But the point is still valid. Maimonides made science as he understood it the arbiter of how to understand the Torah. David Bleich's understanding of Judaism is explicitly based on his reading of Maimonides. He should be willing, it seems to me, to grant to contemporary science the same authority that Maimonides granted science in his day.

cal beliefs are *neither* simply matters of intellectual curiosity *nor* a branch of halakhah. They are attempts to understand the true nature of the universe to the greatest extent possible. *Ma'aseh bereshit* is the rabbinic term for what the Greeks called physics; *ma'aseh merkavah* is the rabbinic expression for what the Greeks called metaphysics – and these two are called the "roots" of the specific halakhot (*gufei Torah*).[21] Considering that these roots are either true or false absolutely, it is literally inconceivable that Maimonides could have held that their truth status depends upon rabbinic *psak* (decision), as would be the case were they matters of halakhah. This leads to my second point: can we seriously credit the idea that Maimonides would have held that before he "paskened" (decided halakhically) that Moses was superior to all the other prophets before and after him, for example, that the question was undecided in Judaism? Similarly, of course, with respect to the other twelve of the Thirteen Principles. Of course not. Third, even were this understanding of Maimonides correct, the latter's position is quite clearly a *innovation* in Judaism and it is simply incorrect to read it back into rabbinic texts.[22]

None of this is meant to minimize the contribution of Maimonides to Judaism. Maimonides' position that truth is objective and must be accepted whatever its source[23] and his willingness to understand the Torah such that it cannot conflict with the teachings of reason are two aspects of his thought that make it possible for many people today to remain faithful to Torah and Judaism without feeling that they must turn off their brains. These teachings concerning Judaism only make sense if we insist that the Torah addresses the intellect and not just the limbs.[24]

---

21 For details on all this and translations of the relevant texts, see ch. 14, "Maimonides' Allegiances to Science and Judaism."

22 Here of course, many would disagrees with me, holding Maimonides to be expressing Biblical and Talmudic teachings which were immanent in Judaism, just not explicitly stated before the 12th century. I, on the other hand, maintain that most Orthodox Jews today read Bible and Talmud through a Maimonidean glass (darkly). See my discussion with David Berger in the "Afterword" to *Must* and ch.10 above.

23 Most clearly stated in his Introduction to his "Eight Chapters:" "Hear the truth from whomever says it" (in the case at hand there, Aristotle and Alfarabi). See *Ethical Writings*, p. 60 in conjunction with Davidson, "Maimonides' *Shemonah Peraqim*."

24 In this Maimonides clearly follows Rabbenu Bahya in *Duties of the Heart* and is clearly not followed by Leibowitz.

But if the Torah contains the truth, why not command its acceptance, or at the very least, teach it in a very clear and unambiguous fashion? The reason is that for Bible and Talmud the translation of ultimate truth into clearly defined and manageable statements was less a pressing need than it was for Maimonides. Let me put this as follows: Maimonides and the Talmud agree that God's truth is embodied in the Torah. The Talmud finds pressing the need to determine the practical, this-worldly consequences of that truth, while Maimonides, in addition, finds its necessary to determine the specific, cognitive content of that truth. On one level, Maimonides is clearly right: Judaism does teach truth; but, on the other hand, his insistence on expressing that truth in specific teachings is an innovation in Judaism.

The point I am trying to make here comes out in the well-known talmudic story concerning the oven of Akhnai (Bava Mezia 59b). The Sages debated whether a particular kind of oven could become ritually impure. The text says:

> On that day R. Eliezer brought all the answers in the world [to support his position] but they were not accepted. He said to them: "If the halakhah accords with my opinion, let this carob tree prove it!" The carob tree uprooted itself and moved 100 amot [c. 50 yards] – some say, it was 400 amot. The [other] rabbis said to him: "One does not bring a proof from a carob tree." He continued, saying "If the halakhah accords with my opinion, let this pool of water prove it!" The water thereupon flowed backwards. They said to him: "One does not bring a proof from a pool of water." He continued, saying "If the halakhah accords with my opinion, let the walls of this house of study prove it!" The walls of the house of study thereupon began to fall inward. Rabbi Joshua reproved them [the walls]: "By what right do you interfere when Sages battle each other over halakhah?" The walls did not fall [all the way] out of respect for R. Joshua and did not stand upright [again] out of respect for R. Eliezer. To this day, they stand at an angle. He then said to them, "If the halakhah accords with my opinion, let it be proved by Heaven!" A voice from Heaven [immediately] spoke forth: "How do you disagree with R. Eliezer, when the halakhah accords with his opinion in every place?"[25] R. Joshua then stood upon his legs and said, *It is not in Heaven*! [Deut 30: 12]. [The Talmud then asks,] "What is the signifi-

---

25 This is hardly the case, but that is not an issue which we have to address here.

cance of *It is not in Heaven?*" R. Jeremiah said, "Since the Torah was given at Mt. Sinai we pay no attention to voices from Heaven [in determining halakhah] since You [i.e., God, the source of heavenly voices] have already written in the Torah at Mt. Sinai, *turn aside after a multitude* [Exodus 23:2]. R. Nathan met Elijah and said to him, "What did the Holy One, blessed be He, do when this happened?" Elijah replied: "He smiled and said, 'My children have defeated me! My children have defeated me!'"

Much can be (and has been!) said about this fascinating passage. Here it will suffice to quote an insightful comment of David Kraemer's: "Of course, we must assume that if the heavenly voice supported R. Eliezer's view, his view must have been closer to the 'truth.' Nevertheless, his truth is rejected, and the view of the sages, though objectively in error, is affirmed."[26] Judaism teaches truth, and that fact must never be forgotten. But the ultimate truth taught by the Torah need not necessarily be understood in its detailed specificity for us to live in the world in a decent fashion; while there is one objective "truth," the Talmud is interested in arriving at a halakhic determination, rather than at a determinate understanding of the final truth. We can safely put off determining the exact truth until *the earth be full of the knowledge of the Lord, as the waters cover the sea* (Isaiah 11:9);[27] but in the meantime we must know how to live.[28]

This talmudic position, I think, makes it possible for Jews to reach ever-greater understandings of the truth taught by the Torah and allows them to express that truth in language appropriate to each age. Had Judaism adopted a Maimonidean, as opposed to talmudic, understanding of the nature of our relation to the truth taught by the Torah, we would be forced to express our vision of the Universe in terms of the Neoplatonized Aristotelianism adopted by Maimonides. Our situation would be similar to that of Habad hasidim, who feel constrained to accept Maimonides' Ptolemaic description of the physical universe as "Torah from heaven," or to that of those Catholics who accept Thomism as normative and authoritative. But "the Torah is not in heaven" – it

---

26 Kraemer, *Mind of the Talmud*, p. 122.

27 Readers familiar with the last sentence of the *Mishneh Torah* will know that my use of this verse is no coincidence.

28 Daniel Statman points out that many readings of the Oven of Akhnai passage (including, he thinks, my own) are tendentious. See "Authority and Autonomy."

must be lived in this world, while the absolute truth which it embodies remains "from heaven," a constant challenge to our understanding, a constant critique of our tendency to intellectual complacency. The talmudic position, as hinted at in the story of the oven of Akhnai, allows Judaism to live and breathe in today's world as much as in yesterday's.

Maimonides, I have argued in a number of places, understood religious faith primarily in terms of propositions affirmed or denied. Bible and Talmud understood religious faith primarily in terms of trust and loyalty. This being so, "orthodoxy" is actually a misnomer, since Judaism, before Maimonides, knew no doctrines (=doxos) concerning which one absolutely had to be clearly and self-consciously "straight" (=ortho).[29]

It is further important to realize that even though classical Judaism does not understand the nature of *emunah* as Maimonides does, and therefore places little value and emphasis on precise theological formulations, there are limits to what one can affirm or deny and still remain within the Jewish community. Note my terminology here: there are limits to what one can affirm or deny and still remain with the Jewish *community*. Denying the unity of God, for example, or that the Torah is of divine origin in some significant sense, or affirming that the Messiah has already come, are claims which place one outside of the historical community of Israel.

Returning to the issue of "faith, science, and Orthodoxy," I am here proposing that we understand Jewish faith in terms of loyalty to God, Torah, and Israel, loyalty which finds expression in the fulfillment of the commandments and less as "commandments addressed to the intellect." It follows from this that the criterion for what we now call "Orthodoxy" should be construed less in terms of adherence to specific dogmas and more in terms of behavior which evinces trust in God. I further propose that we follow Maimonides in taking demonstrated truth to be the arbiter of how we understand Torah. But since we are not yet in the age of the Messiah, and the knowledge of the Lord does not yet cover the earth as the waters cover the sea, that means that we understand neither science nor Torah fully. One does not have to be a fan of Star Trek to know that we live in age in which we expect our scientific paradigms

---

29 These points are developed further in *Must* and in chapters 5-11 above.

to change. One can be a fully "Orthodox" Jew and maintain that, yes, the Torah teaches truth, but that we do not yet really understand that truth.

In concrete terms, I am calling for modesty, both as scientists and as believers. Modesty yes, a total suspension of belief/disbelief, no. To reject the claim that the earth is vastly old, for example, is not only to reject the science of geology, but the entire edifice of contemporary physics and chemistry. The cosmos simply cannot be 5769 years old. This, of course, is only a problem for the most stubborn of Biblical literalists. But how about Noah's flood? There is no geological or archeological evidence that the entire earth was once covered by water; nor is it possible for humanity, in its rich diversity, to have developed and spread over the globe in the roughly four and one half millennia which have passed since the time of Noah. In these and other matters, the Written Torah cannot be taken literally without rejecting the crushingly overwhelming weight of scientific evidence.

But in many other, and more important areas, we may not fully understand the Torah, but science has not yet had its last word either: on God's existence, the creation of the cosmos, Sinaitic revelation, providence, prophecy, miracles, efficacy of prayer, the special relationship of God to the Jewish people, divine retribution, etc., science seems to have little definite to say to us, and it appears to me, is not likely to have much to say in the foreseeable future.

In the final analysis, if we are really to use the eyes God gave us,[30] we can do no other but revert to a qualified Maimonideanism: the Torah cannot contradict that which has been *proven* scientifically but science often proves less than what some scientists think they have proven. We must live in a world of fewer absolutes than many thinkers (rabbis and scientists alike) would like: the Torah cannot teach what science rejects as false, but the evidence of science is not yet fully in, so we do not yet know what the Torah really teaches.

---

30 As Maimonides says in his letter to the Jews of Marseilles, "For is it not apparent that many statements of the Torah cannot be taken literally, but, as is clear from scientific evidence, require interpretation that will make them acceptable to rational thought. Our eyes are set in the front and not in the back. One should therefore look ahead of him and not behind him." Maimonides' next sentence is both revealing and touching: "I have thus revealed to you with these words my whole heart." I quote here from the English translation of Stitskin, *Letters of Maimonides*, p. 127. For the Hebrew text, see Sheilat, *Iggerot*, Vol. 2, p. 488.

PART FOUR

INTRODUCTION TO PART FOUR,
Universalism

One might expect that belief in one God Who created all human beings in the divine image should lead to a universalist ethic, according to which all human beings are –in principle – equal in the eyes of God and equally beloved by God. Maimonides, unlike many Jews, Christians, and Muslims over the last two millennia, actually accepts the universalist implications of the belief that humans are created in the image of God. But he couples that with acceptance of a hard-edged philosophical elitism. In his eyes, creation in the image of God is a challenge, not an endowment. Those who fail to rise to the challenge allow their potential for God-likeness to go to waste, and die as they were born, as only potentially human. Those who meet the challenge may be called the elect and are, in effect, "God-liked" (to use an expression Maimonides would himself never have used!).

In the history of Judaism very few figures were as consistently and emphatically universalist as Maimonides. The Torah is true, he held, and is certainly the most effective route to human perfection, but it is not the only route. It is the most effective route for the following reason. One cannot achieve perfection as a human being (i.e., deep understanding of the world created by God, and hence of God, to the extent that such understanding is possible) without first achieving a very high level of moral perfection. God, as our Creator, knows us best and knows what is best for us, and thus God's Torah is certainly the best way to achieve that perfection. But not the only way. An enthusiastic maimonidean such as Jacob Anatoli understood the implications of this clearly: a scientifically trained Gentile is superior to a punctilious Jew who has no scientific training (*Malmad ha-Talmidim*, Introduction, pp. 11-12 [unpaginated])

Maimonides was a rationalist, a universalist, an elitist, but also, in his own eyes, a proud Jew. The chapters in this section seek to illuminate the ways in which Maimonides at one and the same time adopted philosophical positions which made the notion of the election of Israel difficult to support while never rejecting it (even if he rarely mentions it).

The chapters in this section originally appeared in the following places:

"Chosenness, Not Chauvinism: Maimonides on the Chosen People," Daniel H. Frank (ed.), *A People Apart: Chosenness and Ritual in Jewish Philosophical Thought* (Albany: SUNY Press, 1993): 51-76, 85-89.

"Was Maimonides Truly Universalist?" *Trumah: Beitraege zur juedischen Philosophie* 11 (Festgabe zum 80. Geburtstag von Ze'ev Levy) (2001): 3-15.

"Maimonides' *True Religion* – for Jews, or All Humanity?" *Me'orot* [=*Edah Journal*] 7.1 (2008).

"Spiritual Life," in Kenneth Seeskin (ed.), *Cambridge Companion to Maimonides* (New York: Cambridge University Press, 2005): 273-299.

I should note that my books *Maimonides on Judaism and the Jewish People* (Albany: SUNY Press, 1991) (Serbian translation: *Maimonid O Judaizmu I Jevrejskom Narodu* [Belgrade, Pismo, 2000]) and *Maimonides' Confrontation With Mysticism* (London: Littman Library of Jewish Civilizaton, 2006) deal with the subject of this section as do the following essays, not reprinted here:

"On Universalism and Particularism in Judaism," *Da'at* 36 (1996): v-xv.

"Overcoming Chosenness," in Raphael Jospe, Truman Madsen, Seth Ward (eds.), *Covenant and Chosenness in Judaism and Mormonism* (Fairlawn: Associated University Presses, 2001): 147-172.

CHAPTER SIXTEEN
Chosenness, Not Chauvinism:
Maimonides on the Chosen People

I s it possible to articulate a Jewishly legitimate version the doctrine of the chosen people that does not lead to chauvinism? Three questions must immediately be posed: (1) What makes a doctrine Jewishly legitimate? (2) If affirming the doctrine of the chosen people raises problems, why not reject it? (It is, after all, an issue that appears so far from the central axis of the Jewish tradition that not one of the medievals who listed principles of faith included it in their lists.);[1] and (3) If, alternatively, it is important to affirm the doctrine, what is wrong with chauvinism?

I am going to sidestep the first issue; instead, I will simply affirm here that if a doctrine was held by Maimonides then it is Jewishly legitimate. That is not to say that Maimonides' holding a doctrine is the one criterion for Jewish legitimacy, nor is it to say that every doctrine that Maimonides held is correct[2] – or even well within the mainstream of the Jewish tradition as it had developed to his day. Rather, it is to say that if the "Great Eagle" gave his imprimatur to a position, we cannot reject that position as inconsistent with Judaism.

The issue of chosenness cannot be simply rejected, I think, because without it there is no way to justify adherence to Judaism in the face of adversity. As Emil Fackenehim has taught us, choosing to remain Jewish is not an ethically neutral act. It was the choice of many nineteenth-century Jews not to assimilate that led their descendents into Hitler's gas chambers. If, despite this, we choose to affirm our Judaism, we must have a good reason for it. The fact that God chose the Jews for some special purpose is the best possible reason

---

1   See Kellner *Dogma*, pp. 200-207.

2   A view that seems to be affirmed by Habad and that brings some of their spokespersons to interesting intellectual gymnastics.

of all, and the one historically most often affirmed for remaining Jewish. Even Mordecai Kaplan, who explicitly denied the existence of a choosing God, was forced, in his very last book, *The Religion of Ethical Nationhood,* to affirm the notion of chosenness in a sort of backhanded way: the Jews must remain distinct in order to save the world from a nuclear holocaust.

Well, then, why not simply affirm chosenness and, if necessary, chauvinism? This is the route chosen by many figures in Jewish intellectual history, and it seems especially widespread today. In his study, *The Jews in America,*[3] Arthur Hertzberg observes:

> When Jews were asked about their identity, it was possible for many of them to assert that their loyalty was to the Jewish people, and never mind faith in God. The sense of being one people, one family, as the seed of Abraham, had always been central in Jewish consciousness. This self-definition had become more pervasive in the 1950s, as American Jews increasingly identified with the new State of Israel. In Israel, all Jews belonged to the nation, even though many were indifferent to the Jewish religion.

Hertzberg shows how this approach gained steam and cites a 1983 study of the "Jewishness" of American Jewish leaders. The study found that despite a low level of synagogue affiliation and religious observance, 65 percent of the American Jewish community's leadership maintained that the Jews were God's chosen people. Hertzberg then observes:

> Such an assertion did not belong together with their usual rhetoric about ethnic pluralism. An ethnic group cannot assert "chosenness" without falling into chauvinism or worse. In a democratic society, only a religion dare use this term and only to describe believers who are committed to live spiritual lives. (p. 387)

Ethnic Jewish chauvinism may be inappropriate in the democratic societies of North America; when allied with strong religious belief in the state of Israel, it becomes downright dangerous. Chauvinists affirm the superiority of their group and the concomitant inferiority of other groups. It is views like this that

---

3   Hertzberg, *Jews*, p. 329.

underlie the common assumption in Israel that Arabs are in some way intrinsically different from Jews and inherently untrustworthy. Where Jews think of themselves as motivated by rational considerations of self-interest, Arabs are thought to be motivated by an irrational desire to drive every last Jew into the sea. Given the way in which the Germans in many cases sabotaged their war efforts towards the end of World War II in order to continue the destruction of the Jews, one cannot reject this fear of the Arabs as simple paranoia; but it certainly gets in the way of attempts to find out whether or not it is possible to arrive at some sort of *modus vivendi* with them. Theological positions that give "aid and comfort" to such approaches must be examined carefully, and, if possible, rejected or modified.

Thus, as a committed Jew, I must affirm chosenness; as an Israeli seeking peace with my neighbors I must reject chauvinism (there are, of course, other good reasons for rejecting chauvinism!) What can I do? Well, it turns out that Maimonides can be of assistance here. An examination of Maimonides' writings on the nature of the Jewish people in general and on the notion of chosenness in particular presents a Jewishly legitimate way of affirming chosenness without ethnic chauvinism.

That the Jews are distinct from the Gentiles is an axiom of Jewish faith and a lesson of Jewish history. But what is the basis of that distinction? Jacob Katz has pointed out that the distinction has been explained in two very different ways. One approach grounds it in theological terms and sees it as "a mere divergence in articles of creed."[4] Katz contrasts this to what we may call an "essentialist" view, one that traces "religious and historical differences to the dissimilar character of Jew and non-Jew respectively." On this view, "a qualitative difference was involved for which the individual was not responsible and which he [or she] could not change." There was, in other words, an *essential* difference between Jew and Gentile. Katz finds the origin of this view in Midrash, sees its development in Halevi, and explains its widespread acceptance among late medieval Jews to the impact of the *Zohar*.

I have written a monograph, *Maimonides on Judaism and the Jewish People*, in which I argue, *inter alia*, that Maimonides could not adopt an essentialist

---

4   See Katz, *Tradition*, p. 26. Subsequent citations from Katz are drawn from this page and the
    following one.

view of the nature of the Jewish people on the grounds that he was committed to an Aristotelian philosophical psychology.[5] The monograph is, I hope, a disinterested historical and philosophical study. That it has implications for current questions of Jewish ethics and policy is an expression of the fact that Jewish life, especially in Israel, cannot be divorced from questions of Jewish thought.

For Aristotle, the soul is the form of the body, that is, the animative principle whereby a human being is a human being. It is the soul that actualizes the potential given us by nature to be human beings.[6] But for Aristotle, form does not exist independently of the matter it actualizes. Contra Plato, there is no hint of preexistent souls "zapped" into the body at the moment of conception or birth. But if the soul does not preexist the body, can it, or some part of it, survive the death of the body? In Hellenistic and medieval times a theory was developed, elaborating on some ambiguous comments of Aristotle's, that accounted for the possibility that some humans, at least, would achieve immortality. For our purposes, the most important aspect of the Aristotelian theory, especially as it was developed by Aristotle's later interpreters, is that our rational capacities are not given to us fully formed. That part, element, or aspect of our souls that most truly distinguishes us from other living beings, that element through which human beings are truly human,[7] exists in us only as a capacity when we are born.

On this view, human beings are born, *contra* Plato, without innate knowledge, but with a capacity or potential to learn. This capacity is called, depending on the specific version of the theory that one encounters, "hylic intellect," "material intellect," or "potential intellect." If one takes advantage of one's capacity to learn (a process in which God or the Active Intellect plays a crucial role) and actualizes one's potential for study, then one will have acquired what Maimonides calls "an intellect *in actu*,"[8] often called the "acquired intellect." The question of how one must perfect one's intellect in order to acquire an intellect *in actu*, that is, the question of what one must master, was a matter of debate.

---

5   These views are developed and expanded in *Confrontation*, ch. 7.

6   *De Anima* 2.1 (412aff.). For some of the necessary qualifications, see Hyman, "Aristotle's Theory."

7   As Maimonides says: "through it [the conception of intelligibles which teaches true views concerning metaphysics] man is man" (*Guide* III.54, p. 635).

8   See, for example, *Guide* III.27, p. 511.

In the version of the theory often ascribed to Maimonides, one perfects one's intellect only through the apprehension of metaphysical truths. In the version of the theory adopted by Gersonides, the achievement of true knowledge in any discipline is sufficient to give one at least a measure of intellectual perfection.[9] To the extent that immortality is affirmed, it is the acquired intellect that is seen as immortal. Since one can actualize one's potential intellect to different degrees, it follows that one's perfection, and thus one's share of immortality, depends on the degree to which one perfects himself or herself intellectually.[10]

For our purposes, the crucial elements in this theory are the claims that (1) no human being is born with a fully developed soul –we are, rather, born with the *potential* to *acquire* what can be called a soul– and (2) the only way one can possibly actualize his or her potential to acquire a "soul" is through intellectual activity. On the one hand, this theory commits one to an extremely parochial position: only the intellectually gifted and energetic can ever fulfill themselves as human beings. This form of intellectual elitism leaves most of the human race out in the cold.[11] On the other hand, the theory also forces one to adopt a very nonparochial stance: anyone born with a measure of intelligence and a willingness to apply it to the exacting demands of intellectual labor can achieve some measure of perfection. Race, creed, sex, or national origin are simply not issues.

Consistent with his philosophical psychology, Maimonides develops a theory of ethics according to which human beings at birth are *tabulae rasae,* upon which education, training, and acculturation write out our moral characters. All humans are born with basically the same moral potential and the same absence of fully formed character traits. This being the case, moral qualities that we have acquired can be changed if we are willing to work at it,

---

9   See Harvey, "Crescas' Critique of Philosophic Happiness."

10 See Fakhry, "Contemplative Ideal," p. 139: "The whole process of human cognition thus becomes a gradual progression or ascent from the lowest condition of potentiality to the highest condition of actuality, or the apprehension of those intelligibles stored away in the active intellect. The name that ibn Sina and his successors gave to this progression is not union with, or even vision of, but rather conjunction or contact *(ittisal)* with the active intellect." For the theory of the acquired intellect in ibn Sina and al-Farabi, see Davidson, *Alfarabi.* The question of the nature of the contact with the active intellect became crucial in medieval Muslim and Jewish philosophy but need not detain us here.

11 Maimonides' notorious intellectual elitism is an expression of this. See ch. 4. "Is Maimonides' Ideal Person Austerely Rationalist?"

especially if we avail ourselves of the guidance of the wise, the "physicians of the souls." Obedience to the Torah leads to high moral virtue; in this sense Jews, Maimonides held, are morally superior to Gentiles. But that is a matter of education, not inborn character.

This philosophical psychology forces Maimonides to adopt a number of unusual positions on questions of a more narrowly religious or parochial nature. Among these are providence, prophecy, and immortality. In each case it is shown in my aforementioned monograph that, for Maimonides, the simple fact that one is a Jew plays no role in determining whether one will enjoy God's providence or prophecy or inhabit the world-to-come. In each case it is intellectual perfection that is crucial.

Another such issue is the question of the status of Gentiles in the messianic era. Many Jewish authorities assume that until the end of days the distinction between Jew and Gentile will remain; after the Messiah's coming, the Jews will rule the Gentiles, who at present rule them. Maimonides rejected this view, anticipating a time when all Gentiles would become Jews, either through formal conversion, as I believe, or because the distinction would cease to be relevant, as Ya'akov Blidstein maintains.[12] This position was made both possible and necessary by Maimonides' philosophical psychology. Since all human beings will devote themselves to the pursuit of the knowledge of God in the messianic era, that which truly distinguishes Gentiles from Jews will disappear.

Similarly with the question of conversion. While there are conflicting views within the tradition about proselytes, some very positive, some very negative, the rabbinic tradition has never encouraged proselytization. For Halevi, converts could become the equals of native Jews only after many generations of intermarriage between them. For certain strands of the Midrash and for the *Zohar,* conversion as such was not possible. Converts were actually persons of Gentile parentage into whom intrinsically Jewish souls happened to find their way. Conversion, then, was not so much the issue as was returning an errant soul to its proper place. Gentiles not having such souls could never truly convert to Judaism. Maimonides rejected these views altogether, welcomed sincere proselytes wholeheartedly, allowed for proselytization, and adopted a warmly positive attitude towards the whole issue of conversion. Given that we are at

---

12 See Blidstein, *Ekronot*, pp. 227ff.

root the same, and given that one day all humans would convert to Judaism, Maimonides had no reason to have reservations about sincere proselytes and may even have seen in the welcoming of proselytes an anticipation of the messianic era. Whether this last point may or may not ne true, Maimonides' views on this issue are a consequence of his philosophical psychology.

Maimonides' views on dogma were absolutely unprecedented in the Judaism which developed to his day. The essence of being and becoming a Jew, and of earning a place in the world-to-come, Maimonides teaches, involves the acceptance or rejection of certain views. Defining a Jew in terms of the views that he or she accepts goes hand in hand with a view of human nature that insists that all humans are at root alike, distinguished, to the extent that they are distinguished, only by the views they adopt. Thus, Maimonides' philosophical psychology plays a role in one of his religiously most unusual claims, that concerning the place and nature of dogma in Judaism.

What sort of views are those the adoption of which is crucial for being Jewish? These turn out to be the science of the Torah in its true sense, which, in turn, is *ma'aseh bereshit* and *ma'aseh merkavah,* physics and metaphysics. The body of knowledge to be mastered, then, if one wishes to become a Jew, or, if already a Jew, to become a perfect Jew, is difficult but not occult or esoteric. Any intelligent person can master it to one degree or another. One sees yet again the footprints of Maimonides' nonessentialist definition of what a Jew is, which, in turn, is a consequence of his philosophical psychology.

In my monograph, then, I prove that Maimonides adopts a variant of the theory of the acquired intellect and examine the consequences of that adoption for his positions on ethics, providence, prophecy, immortality, the place of Gentiles in the messianic era, the nature of proselytes, the definition of a Jew, and the nature of Torah. In this chapter I would like to examine Maimonides' conception of the nature of the Jewish people.

Maimonides' attitude towards the Jewish People ("Israel" in his terminology) was one of great national pride. He was convinced that the Jews, as a national group, were in every way superior to other national groups.[13] Unlike Halevi,

---

13 This comes out very clearly in many places. In his "Epistle to Yemen," for example, he speaks of the preeminence of the Jew (pp. 96-97) and of the "pure and undefiled lineage of Jacob" (p. 103); see also Laws of Repentance II.10.

however, he did not make an entire metaphysic out of this pride.[14] The superiority of the Jews derived from two sources: God's promise to Abraham that his progeny would enjoy special benefits and, most importantly, the Torah.

Maimonides' comments on the nature of the Jewish people mirror these two sources of Jewish superiority. The Jews are, on the one hand, a people defined by their descent from Abraham and, on the other hand, a community defined by the Torah. While both these understandings of the Jewish people find expression in Maimonides' writings, the latter is much more important than the former. It is my intent in this study to prove this last claim and explain its significance.

In order to make my discussion clearer, I will introduce a distinction that is not textually grounded in Maimonides' writings but that will help us keep in mind the twofold nature of his writings about the Jews. Those individuals constituted as a national group by their shared descent from Abraham I will call "Jews," while that religious group constituted by its adherence to the Torah I will call "Israel." Maimonides was not always careful to keep these two meanings distinct and may even have occasionally inadvertently fudged them. The distinction is in any event hard to keep sharp since in historical and halakhic terms "Jews" and "Israel" denote the same entity. Despite all this, ignoring the distinction makes understanding Maimonides very difficult.

Indirect but compelling evidence to the effect that Maimonides adopted the distinction here outlined can be found in "Laws of Kings," X.8:

> The Rabbis said that the sons of Keturah, who are of the seed of Abraham, who came after Ishmael and Isaac, are obligated to be circumcised. But since today the descendants of Ishmael have become intermingled with the descendants

---

14 Fairness to Halevi demands that we take note the special circumstances surrounding the adoption of his position and that we not accuse him of or blame him for twentieth-century racism. Halevi flourished in a place and time in which conflicting national and religious groupings each advanced their own claims to nobility and belittled the character of their opponent. Spanish Christians affirmed their superiority over Jews and Muslims; Muslims affirmed their superiority over Jews and Christians; Muslim Arabs affirmed their superiority over non Arab Muslims; Halevi affirmed the superiority of the Jews over the Christians, Arabs, and North Africans. Further on this, see Alloni, "Kuzari." Furthermore, as Rabbi Daniel Korobkin points out in the introduction to his English translation of the *Kuzari* (p. 12), the Talmud teaches that prophecy has ceased since early in the period of the Second Commonwealth; thus the superiority of Jews over Gentiles in Halevi's eyes is entirely theoretical, not actual.

of Keturah, all of them are obligated to be circumcised on the eighth day, but are not executed because of it.[15]

Here we have a *commandment,* not one of the seven Noahide laws, devolving upon a group of non-Jews because of their Abrahamic descent. The commandment of circumcision was given to Abraham and to his descendants (Gen. 17:9-14). Maimonides takes that literally and imposes upon the Ishmaelites (Muslims), who had married into the descendants of Abraham, the obligation to circumcise their children on the eighth day after birth (as mandated by Gen. 17:12). Can there be clearer proof to the effect that Maimonides distinguishes between Abrahamic descent on the one hand and membership in the people of Israel on the other hand?[16]

Just as Maimonides refuses to accept an essentialist definition of who an individual Israelite is, he also rejects essentialist definitions of Israel the people. Maimonides never denies, indeed he is eager to affirm, that the Jews should be proud of their Abrahamic descent and that this descent confers great benefits upon them. But, withal, Maimonides repeatedly affirms that what makes Israel, Israel is the Torah and not any inborn characteristic, inherent quality, or shared biological origin.

We can see this in many ways. First, in his letters to Obadiah the Proselyte, Maimonides emphasizes the importance of commitment to Torah over and above actual physical descent from Abraham: "Let not your lineage be base in your eyes, for if we link our lineage to Abraham, Isaac, and Jacob, you link your lineage to He Who spoke and the world came into being."[17]

Examining Maimonides' comments on the nature of the activities of Abraham himself is also illuminating. In "Laws of Idolatry," I.1-2 Maimonides explains how humankind, originally monotheist, fell into error (literally) and began to worship idols.

"The world moved on in this fashion," Maimonides says in II.2 (p. 66b),

---

15 I.e., if they neglect it.

16 Compare Isadore Twersky's more muted formulation of this point: "Maimonides' spiritual conception of Judaism, in which biological factors are rather insignificant." *Introduction,* p. 486. See also Kasher, "Circumcision."

17 See *Iggerot* (Sheilat ed.), p. 235. On this text see the important discussion of Diamond, *Converts,* ch. 1 and Kellner, "Farteitsht."

till that pillar of the world, the patriarch Abraham, was born. After he was weaned ... his mind began to reflect ... : "How is it possible that this sphere should continuously be guiding the world, and have no one to guide it and cause it to turn round; for it cannot be that it turns round of itself?" He had no teacher ... but his mind was busily working and reflecting till he had attained the way of truth and apprehended the correct line on the basis of his own correct intellect and knew that there is one God, that He guides the sphere, that He created everything, and that among all that exists there is no god beside Him.

Abraham, then, is presented as a natural philosopher who came to recognize that God exists, is one, and created the world, on the basis of his unaided reason.[18] What then did Abraham do? He tried to convince his neighbors, rationally, of their error (pp. 66b-67a):

He realized that the whole world was in error. ... Having attained this *knowledge* he began to *refute* the inhabitants of Ur of the Chaldees, *arguing* with them ... and commenced to instruct the people... When he prevailed over them with his *arguments,* the king sought to slay him ... When the people flocked to him and questioned him regarding his assertions, he would instruct each one according to his *intellect,* until he had returned them to the way of truth.

Abraham, having achieved philosophic certainty, sought to share his knowledge and certainty with others, by way of rational argumentation.

Maimonides presents a similar picture in the *Guide of thePerplexed* (I.63, pp. 153-154), although there the emphasis is on distinguishing the Patriarchs, who sought rationally to convince their fellows of the truths of God's existence, unity, and creation, from Moses, who brought the Torah, which includes these truths but also includes commandments and was sent by God. Moses was distinguished from the Patriarchs because he was able to "make a claim to prophecy on the ground that God had spoken to him and sent him on a mission." The Patriarchs, however, "were addressed in regard to their private affairs only; I mean only in regard to their perfection, their right guidance concerning their actions, and the good tidings for them concerning the position their descen-

---

18 Abraham, that is, came to knowledge of God through philosophic conviction, not religious faith. On this distinction, see *Confrontation*, pp. 77-79.

dants would attain." Unlike Moses, who came with commandments from God, the Patriarchs "addressed a call to the people by means of speculation and instruction." Once again we see that Abraham, Isaac, and Jacob[19] came to know God on the basis of rational, philosophical grounds and sought to share the truth thus discovered with their contemporaries. Thanks to this, God promised their descendants many benefits.

The same point is reiterated in *Guide* II.39. Protecting the uniqueness of the Torah, Maimonides asserts the uniqueness of Mosaic prophecy. No other prophet has ever said to a group of people, "God has sent me to you and commanded me to say to you such and such things; he has forbidden you to do such and such things and commanded you to do such and such things." Prophets other than Moses,

> who received a great overflow, as for instance Abraham, assembled the people
> and called them by way of teaching and instruction to adhere to the truth that
> he had grasped. Thus Abraham taught the people and *explained to them by
> means of speculative proofs* that the world has but one deity, that He has cre-
> ated the things that are other than Himself, and that none of the forms and no
> created thing in general ought to be worshipped.[20]

The founder of the Jewish nation, then, is presented in both the *Mishneh Torah* and the *Guide of the Perplexed* as a philosopher who achieved knowledge of God through rational examination of the world around him and sought rationally to convince others of the truths he had discovered. This is made clear here in this passage from the *Guide*. Abraham received an "overflow" (i.e., emanation) from God, such an emanation, as Maimonides explains in his chapters on prophecy (II.32-48), being a consequence of intellectual perfection. As a reward, Abraham was promised that special benefits would be conferred upon his progeny. The foundation of the Jewish people as an entity defined in terms of its Abrahamic descent is itself a consequence of a philosophic appreciation of God.

---

19 In the continuation of the text quoted above from Idolatry I.2, Maimonides makes clear that
    Isaac and Jacob were as motivated by philosophic considerations as was Abraham.
20 P. 379; emphasis added.

Maimonides' explanation of how the descendants of Abraham were constituted into the entity called "Israel" is particularly illuminating. Maimonides compares the creation of Israel with the process of conversion:

"With three things did Israel enter the covenant: circumcision, immersion, and sacrifice ... And so it is for all generations, when a Gentile wishes to enter the covenant and shelter [literally, "stand at the threshold of"] under the wings of the *Shekhinah,* and accept upon himself the yoke of Torah, he needs circumcision, immersion, and the bringing of a sacrifice."[21] Maimonides makes the essential element of conversion to be the acceptance of (philosophic) teachings concerning God.[22] I do not think that it is pressing the issue too much to impute to Maimonides the view that the philosophic acceptance of the existence and unity of God was no less essential to the mass "conversion" of the Jews from the tribe of Abraham to the people of Israel at Sinai than it is for the conversion of individuals through the ages.

This interpretation of Maimonides is strengthened by his account of the theophany at Sinai. Maimonides denies that all the Jews prophesied at Sinai,[23] but he does insist that the assembled people rationally understood the philosophic import of the first two statements in the Decalogue. "It is clear to me," Maimonides says, opening *Guide* II.33, "that at the gathering at Mt. Sinai, not everything that reached Moses also reached all Israel. Speech was addressed to Moses alone ... and he, peace upon him, went to the foot of the mountain and communicated to the people what he had heard" (pp. 363-64). The people of Israel did not then share Moses' prophetic apprehension. But in explaining the rabbinic dictum to the effect that Israel heard the first two statements of the Decalogue directly from the "mouth" of God,[24] Maimonides says,

They mean that these words reached them just as they reached Moses our Master and that it was not Moses our Master who communicated them to them. For these two principles, I mean the existence of the deity and his being one,[25]

---

21 "Laws of Forbidden Intercourse," XIII.1 (following Tractate Gerim).

22 See Kellner, *Judaism,* ch. 6; Kellner *Dogma,* pp. 19, 226-27.

23 Compare Halevi, *Kuzari* I.87.

24 *Makkot* 24a.

25 Precisely the principles of faith that Maimonides says must be taught to the prospective

are knowable by human speculation alone. Now with regard to everything that can be known by demonstration, the status of the prophet and that of everyone else who knows it are equal; there is no superiority of one over the other. These two principles are not known through prophecy alone. The text of the Torah says: *Unto thee it was shown*[26] [Dt. 4:35], As for the other commandments, they belong to the class of generally accepted opinions and those adopted in virtue of tradition, not to the class of the intellecta. (p. 364)

Here we are told by Maimonides that Israel at Sinai apprehended by philosophical demonstration the truth of precisely those two principles (God's existence and unity), which are taught to the convert and by virtue of the acceptance of which he or she becomes a proselyte to Judaism. Israel became Israel by virtue of its acceptance of these two principles. This is convincing proof of the congruence between the process of conversion and the creation of Israel. At the moment of its inception, therefore, Israel was constituted as such by the rational acceptance of true philosophic teachings concerning God. This is as far from an essentialist definition of Israel that one can get!

The same point becomes clear when we examine how individuals are excluded from *klal yisrael*, the community of Israel. At the end of his statement of the 'Thirteen Principles' Maimonides asserts that "anyone who destroys one of these foundations which I have explained to you [Maimonides' "Thirteen Principles"] has left the community of Torah adherents." Maimonides imposes harsh penalties on the heretic, sectarian, and *epikoros*. In "Laws of Repentance," III.7 Maimonides defines a sectarian as one who denies any of the first five of his thirteen principles of faith. In "Laws of Idolatry," II.5 he affirms that "Israelite sectarians are not like Israelites at all" and that it is forbidden to converse with them or return their greeting. He compares them to idolaters and says that even if they repent they are never accepted back into the community. The *epikoros* is defined in "Repentance," III.8 as one who denies prophecy, Mosaic prophecy, and God's knowledge. In "Laws of the Murderer," IX.10 and in "Laws of Mourning," I.10 Maimonides informs us that the

---

convert: "He should then be made acquainted with the principles of the faith, which are the oneness of God and the prohibition of idolatry. These matters should be discussed in great detail" ("Forbidden Intercourse," XIV.2).

26 I.e., proved.

epikoros is not considered part of the community of Israel; in the latter place we are bidden not to mourn them on their deaths. We are bidden to destroy them in "Laws of Idolatry," X.1 and are told that they are no better than informers, the lowest of the low in Jewish estimation. That the *epikoros* has no place in the world to come is the burden of *Laws of Testimony* XI.10; we are also informed there that it goes without saying that their testimony is not acceptable in a court, since they are not Israelites at all. In this paragraph we are bidden to kill the *epikoros*.[27] The parallelism here is compelling: one exits the community of Israel by *denying* certain teachings parallel to the way in which that community was constituted, namely, through the rational *acceptance* of certain (philosophic) teachings.[28]

Further evidence of Maimonides' nonessentialist understanding of the nature of the community of Israel can be found, of all places, in his "Epistle to Yemen." I say "of all places" because this text was written in order to bolster the confidence of a Jewish community suffering from Muslim persecution. Part of Maimonides' strategy here is to denigrate the Muslims and praise the Jews. That, at least, appears to be what he is doing at first glance. In actuality, he denigrates *Islam* and praises *Judaism*. Even in this context, then, his nonessentialist approach to the definition of Israel is apparent.

Maimonides begins that part of his discussion relevant to our concern by citing Dt. 10:15: *Yet it was to your fathers that the Lord was drawn in His love for them, so that He chose you, their lineal descendants, from among all the peoples.* That verse could be used to underline an essentialist definition of the nature

---

27 For more details, see Kellner, *Dogma*, pp. 251-253. Further on the need and obligation to kill heretics, see Halkin and Hartman, *Crisis and Leadership*, p. 114.

28 In ch. 9 above, "Could Maimonides Get Into Rambam's Heaven?" I show how the first five of Maimonides' thirteen principles, which are rationally demonstrable (actually, the first four are, while the fifth, not to worship any entity but God, is a consequence of them), are for him the most important and crucial of the thirteen. Our discussion on this point allows us to solve a puzzle. There are two areas in which Maimonides does not apply his strictures against the heretic, etc.: with respect to marriage and to the taking of interest. Why does he not inform us that a marriage entered into by a heretic is invalid (compare "Laws of Forbidden Intercourse," XIII.17 and "Laws of Marital Relations," IV.15), and why does he not inform us that we may take interest from a heretic? The reason, I submit, is as follows: The heretic, sectarian, and *epikoros* have excluded themselves from the community of Israel, but that does not change the brute biological fact that they are Jews by birth. Marriage restrictions are first and foremost a matter of lineage; Jews are forbidden to take interest from their *brother* (Lev. 25.35-37; Dt. 23.20-21); thus Maimonides did not and could not impose his strictures on theological deviants in these two cases.

of the Jewish people, distinguishing them from all other peoples by virtue of their lineal descent from Abraham. But Maimonides uses it for other purposes, explaining "that ours is the true and divine religion, revealed to us through Moses, chief of the former as well as the later prophets. By means of it, God has distinguished us from the rest of mankind."[29] This choice, Maimonides goes on to say after citing Dt. 10:15, "was not made thanks to our merits, but was rather an act of grace, on account of our ancestors who were *cognizant* of God and obedient to Him" (pp. 96-97).

Maimonides further emphasizes the point under discussion here: "... God has singled us out by His law and precepts, and our preeminence over the others was manifested in His rules and statutes" (p. 97). We are singled out by the Torah, not by anything inherent in our collective or individual character. We are indeed superior to other nations, not because of some inborn quality, but because of the rules and statutes of the Torah.

Maimonides' approach to the issue comes out even in his discussion of how other nations sought to attack the Jews. It was, according to him, not a matter of what we today would call anti-Semitism or Jew-hatred, but rather of anti-Torahism and anti-Judaism. Jealous of Jewish preeminence (a consequence of the Torah),

all the nations, instigated by envy and impiety, rose up against us in anger, and all the kings of the earth, motivated by injustice and enmity, applied themselves to persecute us. They wanted to thwart God, but He will not be thwarted. Ever since the time of revelation every despot or rebel ruler, be he violent or ignoble, *has made it his first aim and final purpose to destroy our Law and to vitiate our religion* by means of the sword, by violence, or by brute force. Such were Amalek, Sisera, Sennacherib, Nebuchadnezzar, Titus, Hadrian, and others like them.[30]

Attacks on the Jews, that is, are really attacks on Torah and Judaism.

---

29 Halkin and Hartman, *Crisis and Leadership*, p. 96. On this point, compare Saadia's well known dictum, "Our nation of the Children of Israel is only a nation by virtue of its laws." *Beliefs and Opinions*, III.7 (p. 158 in the Rosenblatt translation).

30 Halkin and Hartman, *Crisis and Leadership*, p. 97; emphasis added.

There is one place in the "Epistle to Yemen" where strong emphasis is placed on Abrahamic descent. It is also one of the few (perhaps only) places in his writings where Maimonides makes explicit reference to the notion of the chosen people: "When God spoke to Abraham He made it amply clear that all the blessings that He promised and all his children to whom He will reveal the Law and whom He will make the Chosen People – all this is meant only for the seed of Isaac. Ishmael is regarded as an adjunct and appendage in the blessings of Isaac."[31] Three points must be made. First, the immediate context of this passage, and the passage itself, make clear that Maimonides is primarily interested in refuting the Muslim claim that the favored son of Abraham was Ishmael, not Isaac. Second, it is reasonable to read this passage as saying that Israel will become the chosen people because of the fact that the Torah will be revealed to them, not because of some inherent essence or nature of the Jews. Third, it is true that the Jews did receive the Torah, and thus became constituted as the faith community of Israel, as a reward to Abraham; but this is no way implies that the Jews are such qualitatively different from other people.

There is one last place in the "Epistle to Yemen" that supports the reading of Maimonides offered here. Toward the end of the work Maimonides expresses a messianic wish. Referring to the Jews of Yemen, he says, "May God increase your numbers and hasten the day of gathering you with the entire *religious community*."[32] Even in the context of a prayer for the messianic ingathering, Maimonides makes reference to a *religious community* (defined, we have seen over and over, in terms of its having accepted the Torah) and not to a *people* defined in some essentialist fashion.

I noted above that Maimonides rarely makes reference to the notion of the chosen people. This alone is suggestive. While the Torah plays a central role in his thought and finds central expression in his "Thirteen Principles," the notion of the chosen people is almost entirely absent from his writings and plays no role whatsoever in the "Thirteen Principles" or in the "Laws of the

---

31 Ibid., p. 108.

32 P. 114; emphasis added. The Arabic for "religious community" is *milla*, which means exactly that, as opposed to *umma*, or "nation." See Stroumsa, "Sabians," p. 289.

Foundations of the Torah." Indeed, in that latter work, the term *Israel* shows up for the first time only at the end of chapter IV.[33]

Further illustration of this point can be had by examining Maimonides' use of biblical verses that form the basis for the notion of the chosen people. I examined a variety of these verses (Gen. 18:1, 18:18-19; Ex. 19:5-6; Dt. 7:6-8, 14:2, 18:5). Some of them Maimonides never discussed, and others are used in ways that throw no light on Maimonides' ideas concerning the nature of the Jewish people. Usages that are relevant, however, invariably support the interpretation of Maimonides here put forward (as is exemplified by his use of Dt. 1:15 in "Epistle to Yemen," discussed above). A number of examples will make clear. One of the earliest expressions of the idea of the chosen people is Gen. 18:18-19.

> And Abraham shall surely become a great and mighty nation, and all the nations of the earth shall be blessed in him. For I have known him, to the end that he may command his children and his household after him, that they may keep the way of the Lord, to do righteousness and justice; to the end that the Lord may bring upon Abraham that which He hath spoken of Him.

According to Rav Kafih's index of biblical citations in his works, Maimonides makes no reference at all to Gen. 18:18, while verse 19 is cited seven times. While some of these citations have nothing to do with the issue under discussion, others are most suggestive.

Thus, Maimonides opens the last chapter of "Laws of Gifts to the Poor" (X.1) by telling the reader that one must observe the commandment of charity more scrupulously than any other positive commandment, "for charity is the sign of the righteous seed of Abraham, our Father, as it says: *For I have known him, to the end that he may command his children ... to give charity*[34] and neither can the seat of Israel be firm nor the true religion stand without charity." Here we have the "righteous seed of Abraham" referred to and even distinguished by a special characteristic: charity. But Maimonides immediately explains that the seed of Abraham are not intrinsically charitable; rather, they are *commanded* to give charity; it was because they were going to receive that

---

33 For details, see Kaplan, "Singularity."

34 "To give charity" is an alternative translation for the word translated as "to do righteousness" in 18:19.

commandment that they became constituted as the "righteous seed of Abraham," and it is by fulfillment of that commandment that they are recognized as such. The persuasive nature of Maimonides' argument here is clear as well He is trying to encourage the Jews to give charity; if they do so naturally, due to some intrinsic character, the argument would be otiose.[35]

Our verse shows up four times in the *Guide*. In II.39 (p. 379) it is used to show that Abraham did not convey God's commandments to his household. In III.24 (p. 502) Maimonides cites the verse to support his claim that "Abraham our Father was the first to make known the belief in unity, to establish prophecy, and to perpetuate this opinion and draw people to it." In III.43 (p. 572) it is explained that the descendants of the Patriarchs enjoy benefits thanks to the promises God made to their forbears. These promises, in turn, were made because Abraham, Isaac, and Jacob "were perfect people in their opinions and their moral character." In the last citation of the verse in the *Guide* (III.51, p. 624) we are reminded that the Patriarchs sought "to bring into being a religious community[36] that would know and worship God" – a religious *community*, not a *people* defined by some essential characteristic, and a community defined by its mission: to know and to worship God.

Maimonides also cites the verse in his first letter to Obadiah the Proselyte.[37] That letter opposes any possibility of reading Maimonides as one who holds that the Jewish people have some inherent, essential characteristic that distinguishes them from other nations. In the particular context under discussion, Maimonides uses the verse to support his contention that all those who adopt Judaism are of the household of Abraham.

Our review of Maimonides' use of Gen. 18:19, then, confirms the thesis proposed above: Maimonides plays down the notion of the chosen people, denies that the Jews have any inherent, essential characteristic that distinguishes them *prima facie* from other nations, and emphasizes instead the importance of the community of Israel as constituted by the Torah, which in turn means the rational acceptance of the philosophical truths of God's existence and unity.

A further example is Ex. 19:5-6:

35 Further on this passage, see below, ch. 17, "Was Maimonides Truly Universalist?"

36 Arabic: *milla*

37 Maimonides, *Iggerot*, p. 234.

Now therefore if ye will hearken unto My voice indeed, and keep My covenant then ye shall be mine own treasure from among the peoples; for all the earth is Mine. And ye shall be unto me a kingdom of priests, and a holy nation.

Here is Maimonides' comment:

For a sudden transition from one opposite to another is impossible. And therefore man, according to his nature, is not capable of abandoning suddenly that to which he was accustomed. As therefore God sent Moses our Master to make out of us "a kingdom of priests and a holy nation" – *through the knowledge of Him.* (*Guide* III.32, p. 526, emphasis added)

Israel, then, is *made* into a holy a nation (i.e., it is not intrinsically or inherently holy) through its being taught by Moses correct knowledge concerning God. Here we see again that there is nothing inherently or essentially special or unique about Israel; it is the rational appropriation of metaphysical truths about God that constitutes Israel as a "kingdom of priests and a holy nation."

Other evidence for Maimonides' nonessentialist interpretation of the Jewish people is found in a text that seems, at first reading, to teach the opposite. At the end of a discussion of certain astronomical phenomena, and, more importantly and immediately, a discussion of the nature and activities of the separate intellects (*Guide* II.11, p. 276), Maimonides points out he has already explained that "all these views do not contradict anything said by our prophets and the sustainers of our Law. For our community[38] is a community that is full of knowledge and perfect, as He, may He be exalted, has made clear through the intermediary of the Master who made us perfect, saying: *Surely, this great nation[39] is a wise and understanding people* [Dt. 4:6]." Here we have a text in which Maimonides says that the Jewish nation or people is "full of knowledge and perfect." Does this not run counter to the reading of Maimonides urged here, according to which the Jewish people, in and of itself, as an ethnic entity, has no special, inherent, essential characteristics?

---

38 Arabic: *milla.* Pines translates this as "community," offering "nation" as an alternative. Since Maimonides immediately cites Dt. 4:6, where the term *am* (nation, people) appears, we have further evidence for our thesis: Maimonides in effect here translates the Hebrew *am* (nation, people) into the Arabic *milla* (religious community).

39 Hebrew: *am.* Pines renders this as "community," an odd translation of the Hebrew and one obviously influenced by Maimonides' use of the Arabic *milla.*

Not only does this text not run counter to my thesis, it strengthens it. When Maimonides says that the Jews are "full of knowledge and perfect," he means that they are full of knowledge and *therefore* perfect. This is proved by the sequel:

> However, when the wicked from among the ignorant nations ruined our good qualities, destroyed our words of wisdom and our compilations, and caused our men of knowledge to perish, so that we again became ignorant, as we had been threatened because of our sins – for it says: *And the wisdom of their wise men shall perish, and the understanding of their prudent men shall be hid* (Isaiah 29:14); when, furthermore, we mingled with these nations and their opinions were taken over by us, as were their morals and actions ... when, in consequence of all this, we grew up accustomed to the opinions of the ignorant, these philosophic views appeared to be, as it were, foreign to our Law, just as they are foreign to the opinions of the ignorant. However, matters are not like this.

We see here that the perfection of Israel is not an inborn characteristic but a consequence of their knowledge. When that knowledge is corrupted through assimilation to ignorant and immoral nations, the Jews behave as foolishly and wickedly as those who have influenced them. We further see here that it is the philosophic views embodied in the Torah that make us a "wise and understanding people." This is seen by the context of our discussion here in II.11 and by the conclusion of the passage just quoted: it is because Jews have grown accustomed to the opinions of the ignorant that the philosophic views discussed in II.11 appeared foreign to the Torah. Had the Jews understood that these views were not foreign to the Torah, they would still be a "wise and understanding people."

I have shown here that Maimonides, in effect, distinguishes the ethnic group, defined in the first instance through Abrahamic descent, from the faith community Israel, defined in the first instance by its acceptance of certain true philosophic views.[40] Texts discussed included Maimonides' letters to Obadiah the Proselyte, his discussions of Abraham the philosopher in both the *Mishneh Torah* and the *Guide of the Perplexed,* and Maimonides' argument to the effect that the Jews (the seed of Abraham) became Israel through a process of conversion that involved the acceptance of certain philosophic teachings. We

---

40 This distinction is expanded and deepened in *Confrontation*, ch. 7.

further saw that exclusion from Israel, like joining it, depends upon the holding of certain views (in this case, heretical ones). Maimonides' nonessentialist reading of the nature of the Jewish people was supported through an analysis of texts from his "Epistle to Yemen," his near total avoidance of the notion of the 'chosen people,' and his use of Gen. 18:19 and Ex. 19:56, verses easily interpreted as supporting an essentialist reading of the nature of Israel.

Maimonides' understanding of the nature of the people of Israel, like his understanding of ethics, prophecy, providence, and immortality, his conception of the place of Gentiles in the messianic era, his approach to proselytes and proselytization, his understanding of dogma, and his understanding of the nature of the Torah,[41] is a further consequence of his having adopted the psychological theory according to which human beings are born equally ignorant and equally capable of overcoming that ignorance.

Leaving the historical discussion and returning to the issues raised at the beginning of this chapter, we see that Maimonides has shown us a way to affirm chosenness and reject chauvinism: The Jews are God's chosen people because they have accepted the Torah. A Jew as such, that is, a descendant of Abraham, is in no way inherently superior to a non-Jew. The superiority of the Jew resides in the fact that he or she is also an Israelite, that is, a person who has accepted the Torah. Any human being can become such through the process of conversion, and, Maimonides holds, all human beings will become such in the messianic era. Gentiles, then, must be treated, not as second-class human beings, but as Israel *in potentia,* future partners in the messianic reformation of the world.

---

41 See Kellner, "Ante-Mundane Torah."

CHAPTER SEVENTEEN
Was Maimonides Truly Universalist?

Maimonides was among the most universalist of Jewish thinkers. This, at least, is the view of Maimonides held in academic circles.[1] According to this reading of Maimonides he rejected any understanding of the election of Israel which presented Jews as essentially distinct from Gentiles and superior to them.[2] Maimonides the universalist held Jews to be distinct from Gentiles only to the extent that they adhered to the Torah. In that he never doubted the divinity of the Torah, Maimonides also never doubted that true adherents of the Torah were, with very few exceptions, better people than those who did not adhere to it.[3]

Maimonides' universalism, it appears to me, is a reflection of a deeper issue in his thought. The late Isadore Twersky once noted laconically that "Maimonides' desacralization of language should seen as an expression of his consistent opposition to hypostasized entities endowed with intrinsic sanctity."[4] Twersky is surely correct. There is much to be learned from this about the character of the Judaism which Maimonides taught. To make the point very briefly here, Maimonides relates to distinctions fundamental to Judaism, such as holy/profane, ritually pure/ritually impure, permissible/impermissible as

---

1   For some important qualifications of this outrageous generalization, see Lasker, "Maimonides' Influence."

2   Maimonides' universalism, to be sure, was "horizontal," not "vertical." By that I mean that he was a thorough-going elitist, a point which comes up repeatedly in the chapters of this book.

3   I have sought to defend these generalizations in many of the other chapters of this book on universalism. I am not, of course, the first person to read Maimonides in this fashion. I was taught to read Maimonides by my teacher Steven Schwarzschild (1924-1989) whose approach to Maimonides was ultimately informed by the thought of the philosopher Hermann Cohen (1842-1918) and the talmudist Samuel Atlas (1899-1977).

4   Twersky, *Introduction*, p. 324n. In this Maimonides is the polar opposite of Judah Halevi. This difference is one of the foci of *Confrontation*.

institutional, sociological, and historical issues, and not as ontological matters. This applies also to his conception of the special nature of the Jewish People. In doing this Maimonides sought to dethrone a vision of Judaism which prevailed in his time and replace it with another vision altogether. This was a conscious project on his part, but one carried out without any explicit announcements. Maimonides was fighting what he took to be a debased and ultimately corrupt version of Judaism and appears to have thought that the best way to wage this war was by not declaring it.

In traditionalist Jewish circles, however, another view of Maimonides reigns. According to this view, Maimonides was much closer in his views to Judah Halevi, the great exponent of Jewish particularism, and he certainly did not diverge from the alleged mainstream of Jewish thinking according to which the election of Israel reflected or caused a reality in which Jews as such were essentially distinct from and superior to Gentiles as such.

I will here examine a number of texts which have been cited in support of the particularist reading of Maimonides. My point is to show that these texts do not in reality undermine the universalist reading of Maimonides.

But I must make three important preliminary points. First, Maimonides was proud of Judaism and of the Jews and certainly thought that in the world in which he lived Jews were in fact superior morally and spiritually to almost all contemporary Gentiles. He had no problems with preferring Jews to Gentiles in almost every way, and, as we shall see, had no problems with specific laws which discriminated against Gentiles. My point here is that for Maimonides the distinction between Jew and Gentile is, as my friend and colleague Professor Daniel J. Lasker puts it, a matter of software and not of hardware.[5] Second, I assume (for the sake of argument) that this claim that Jews are distinguished from Gentiles by software and not by hardware has been proven. Here, I will simply be examining some alleged counter-instances to that thesis. Third, Maimonides did not realize that he was a universalist – issues very important to 20th and 21st century Jews did not necessarily trouble the sleep of our medieval forbears.[6]

---

5   Lasker, "Proselyte Judaism."

6   This is the focus of Hoch and Kellner, "Voice."

What I have called here the universalist reading of Maimonides involves a large number of claims:

- that the election of Israel was not a fact built into the universe or its history from creation; rather, it was a consequence of the fact that Abraham, so to speak, chose God.[7]

- that the Torah is ultimately addressed to all human beings and not just to the descendents of the Biblical Patriarchs.

- that Jews share no special characteristic (be it a special soul, Halevi's *al-amr al-ilahi*, "das pintele Yid," or anything else) which is lacking in Gentiles.

- that proselytes are the equal of born Jews.

- that in the messianic era all human beings will worship the Lord from a stance of full spiritual equality.

- that while the Torah conveys a distinct advantage to its adherents, Jews *as such* have no advantage over Gentiles with respect to prophecy, providence, and immortality.

Maimonides holds each of these views. For most traditionalist Jews today that is a large mouthful, one that is too large to swallow. Most traditionalist Jews today have an image of what a normative Jewish thinker *must* believe. Everyone with claims to Jewish authority must fit into that mold. There is a tradition of Jewish particularism which flows from biblical and rabbinic sources through Judah Halevi and Nahmanides to Kabbalah and Hasidut and through the latter to contemporary Judaism. This stream has become so dominant in contemporary traditionalist Jewish thought that an alternative stream, flowing from biblical and rabbinic sources through Maimonides

---

7   There follow from this a number of far-reaching claims: that the history recorded in the Torah could have been different (had Abraham been a Navajo, for example) and that the commandments which reflect that history (the festivals, the sacrificial cult, etc.) could also have been different. From this there follows another claim: all texts which discuss the primordial character of the Torah must be read metaphorically. See Kellner, "Ante-Mundane Torah."

and Menahem ha-Meiri[8] to medieval and modern Jewish philosophers is barely recognized.

Confrontation with Maimonidean texts can be an unsettling experience for individuals convinced that (a) Maimonides is an authoritative Jewish teacher and (b) authoritative Jewish thinking is particularist. One way of solving this problem is to read Maimonides as a particularist. This is not an easy task, but there are about half a dozen passages in Maimonides' writings which led themselves to a particularist reading of the "Great Eagle" (as Maimonides has been known for generations). I shall analyze these texts closely here.

But first, a word about methodology: Maimonides, as is well known, wrote esoterically.[9] If he contradicts himself on the issue of universalism and particularism, why not see his universalist statements as exoteric window-dressing, which do not reflect his true views? Another way of putting this is, why insist, as I will be doing in this essay, on taking his universalist statements as basic and reading his particularist statements in their light? Why not do the reverse?

One ought to adopt, I think, the following methodology. First, it is crucial to read what Maimonides actually said, not what he *should* have said (according to the reader's preconceptions) – what Maimonides actually says in very many contexts is surprisingly universalist.[10]

Second, one must examine what options were really open to Maimonides (i.e., what ideas were really available to him). Available to Maimonides were not only the tradition of Greek-Arabic philosophy (with its implicit universalist thrust) but a tradition of Jewish biblical and rabbinic universalism as well.[11]

Third, one ought to adopt a method proposed by the philosopher Susan Haack (in the context of an argument against epistemological relativism) and see Maimonides' writings as a kind of crossword puzzle. At any given point in filling out a crossword puzzle, a number of different solutions might satisfy any given hint. But that does not make all solutions equally reasonable. As Haack notes, "How reasonable a crossword entry is depends on how well

---

8 1249-1316. See Halbertal, *Bein Torah*.

9 See the chapters in this book on how to read Maimonides.

10 Surprising not only to Jewish particularists, but also to anyone familiar with medieval culture generally. I think that it is fair to say that had Maimonides been a Christian or a Muslim his universalism would have been even more surprising.

11 See the other chapters in this section.

it is supported by its clue and any already completed entries; how reasonable these other entries are, independent of the entry in question; and how much of the crossword has been completed."[12] Reading Maimonides as a particularist demands the revision of a great many already completed entries in the Maimonidean crossword.

Let us turn to the texts themselves. There are a variety of passages in the *Mishneh Torah*, Maimonides' great law code, in which he seems to impute to Jews *qua* Jews certain moral characteristics absent from Gentiles *qua* Gentiles. They are:

1) "Laws of Repentance," II.10: "It is forbidden to be obdurate and not allow oneself to be appeased [when a person asks forgiveness for some trespass]. On the contrary, one should be easily pacified and find it difficult to become angry. And, when asked by an offender for forgiveness, one should forgive with a sincere mind and willing spirit… Forgiveness is natural to the seed of Israel, characteristic of their upright heart. Not so are the Gentiles[13] of uncircumcised heart [concerning whom it was said], *his resentment keeps forever* (Amos 1:11). Thus of the Gibeonites who did not forgive and refused to be appeased, it is said, *Now the Gibeonites were not of the children of Israel* (2 Sam. 21:2)."

2) "Laws of Forbidden Intercourse, XIX.17: "All families are presumed to be of valid descent and it is permitted to intermarry with them in the first instance. Nevertheless, should you see two families continually striving with one another, or a family which is constantly engaged in quarrels and altercations, or an individual who is exceedingly contentious with every-

---

12 Haack, "Staying," p. 12.

13 Hebrew: *goyyim*; as Ya'akov Blidstein notes, this term often means "idolaters" and not simply "non-Jews." See his "Status of the Resident Alien," pp. 44-45. In several contexts Maimonides distinguishes among non-Jews who are idolaters, non-Jews who are monotheists *but* have not accepted the seven Noachide commandments *because* they were given by God through Moses, and non-Jews who are monotheists *and* have accepted the seven Noachide commandments *because* they were given by God through Moses. All of these are to be distinguished from proselytes. See "Laws of Kings," VIII.10-11 and the discussion in *Confrontation*, pp. 238-250. In other contexts, Maimonides distinguishes between Jews and non-Jews simply, where the issue is obligations which Jews have one to the other on a fraternal basis, or on the basis of their being fellows (*re'im* and *amitim*). For relevant texts and useful discussion, see Halbertal, *Bein Torah* p. 83n.

one, and is excessively impudent, apprehension should be felt concerning them, and it is advisable to keep one's distance from them, for these traits are indicative of invalid descent…Similarly, if a person exhibits impudence, cruelty, or misanthropy, and never performs an act of kindness, one should strongly suspect that he is of Gibeonite descent, since the distinctive traits of Israel, the holy nation [ha-ummah ha-kedoshah], are modesty, mercy, and lovingkindess, while of the Gibeonites it is said, Now the Gibeonites were not of the children of Israel (2 Sam. 21:2), because they hardened their faces and refused to relent, showing no mercy to the sons of Saul, nor would they do a kindness unto the children of Israel, by forgiving the sons of their king, notwithstanding that Israel showed them grace at the beginning and spared their lives."

3) "Laws of Gifts to the Poor," X. 1-2: "It is our duty to be more careful in the performance of the commandment of charity [zedakah] than in that of any other positive commandment, for giving charity is the mark of righteous individuals who are of the seed of our father Abraham, as it is said, For I have known him, to the end that he may command his children … to do righteousness [zedakah] (Gen. 18:19). The throne of Israel cannot be established, nor true faith made to stand up, except through charity, as it is said, In righteousness [zedakah] shalt thou be established (Is. 54:14); nor will Israel be redeemed, except through the practice of charity, as it is said: Zion shall be redeemed with justice, and they that return of her with righteousness [zedakah] (Is. 1:27). No man is ever impoverished by giving charity, nor does evil or harm befall anyone by reason of it, as it is said, And the work of righteousness [zedakah] shall be peace (Is. 32:17). He who has compassion upon others, others will have compassion upon him, as it is said, That the Lord may… show thee mercy, and have compassion upon thee (Dt. 13:18). Whosoever is cruel and merciless lays himself open to suspicion as to his descent, for cruelty is found only among the Gentiles [goyyim], as it is said, They are cruel and have no compassion (Jer. 50:42). All Israelites and those who have attached themselves to them [ve-ha-nilvim aleihem] are to each other like brothers, as it is said, Ye are the children of the Lord your God (Dt.

14:1). If brother will show no compassion to brother, who will? And unto whom shall the poor of Israel raise their eyes? Unto the Gentiles who hate them and persecute them? Their eyes are therefore hanging solely upon their brethren."[14]

4) "Laws of Wounding and Damaging," V.10: "The injured person, however, is forbidden to be harsh and to withhold forgiveness, for such behavior does not become the seed of Israel."

5) "Laws of Slaves," IX.8: "It is permitted to work a heathen slave with rigor. Though such is the rule, it is the quality of piety [*hasidut*] and the way of wisdom that a man be merciful and pursue justice and not make his yoke heavy upon the slave or distress him, but give him to eat and to drink of all foods and drinks…Thus also the master should not disgrace them by hand or by word, because scriptural law has delivered them only unto slavery and not unto disgrace. Nor should he heap upon the slave oral abuse and anger, but should rather speak to him softly and listen to his claims. So it is also explained in the good paths of Job, in which he prided himself: *If I did despise the cause of my manservant, or of my maidservant when they contended with me…Did not He that made me in the womb make him? And did not One fashion us in the womb?* (Job 31:13,15). Cruelty and effrontery are not frequent except with the uncircumcised Gentiles.[15] The seed of our father Abraham, however, i.e., the Israelites, upon whom the Holy One, blessed be He, bestowed the favor of the Torah and laid upon them statutes and judgments, are merciful people who have mercy upon all. Thus also it is declared by the attributes of the Holy One, blessed be He, which we are enjoined to imitate: *And His mercies are over all His works* (Ps. 145:9). Furthermore, whoever has compassion will receive compassion, as it is said, *And He will show thee mercy, and have compassion upon thee, and multiply thee* (Dt. 13:18).

---

14 Slightly emended, following readings of the mss. cited in Shabtei Frankel's edition of the *Mishneh Torah*.

15 I follow the mss. and early editions here, and not the text found in most contemporary printed editions, "except with the Gentiles who worship idols." This latter reading appears to have been an attempt to appease Christian censors.

Before analyzing these passages seriatim, I think it fair to assert that a reasonable way of reading them is as normative, not descriptive, claims. Maimonides is not here describing how Jews actually behave, rather, he is prescribing how Jews ought to behave. Telling people that certain kinds of behavior casts doubt upon their pedigree is an effective way of getting them not to behave that way! This seems particularly clear to me in the third, fourth, and fifth passages above, but I think a fair-minded reading could see this applying to all five of the passages.

Now, to the first passage; in it Maimonides says that "forgiveness is natural to the seed of Israel, characteristic of their upright heart." Jews are contrasted here with "the Gentiles of uncircumcised heart." To read this text in a particularist fashion, one must make the following assumptions: the "seed of Israel" as such is characterized by uprightness of heart, while Gentiles as such have uncircumcised hearts. But the text may be as easily read in the following fashion: those Jews who have "upright hearts" are superior to those Gentiles who have "uncircumised hearts." This reading allows for the possibility of there being Jews with uncircumcised hearts and Gentiles with upright hearts, or, at the very least, of there being Gentiles with upright hearts. One reason for preferring this reading is Maimonides reference to Gibeonites here. The Gibeonites (J. Kid. IV.1) were said to embody the quality of cruelty. But, as we learn in our second passage, Maimonides did not think that *all* Gentiles were cruel by nature. On this basis, I think it fair to read our first passage as referring to cruel Gentiles, not all Gentiles as such. But there is another reason for reading our passage in this fashion. Maimonides clearly allowed for the possibility of there being wise Gentiles. Moral pefection is a pre-requisite for wisdom.[16] Thus, not all Gentiles can be immoral.[17] Given Maimonides' often ascerbic comments about his fellow Jews, it hardly needs saying that he did not think that all Jews had upright hearts.[18] Certainly worthy of note is the fact that term "uncircumcised hearts" derives from Jeremiah 9:25, where the referent is Jews, not Gentiles.

In the second passage, Maimonides, following the Talmud, associates impudence, cruelty, misanthropy, and failure to perform acts of lovingkindness with

---

16 See above, ch. 11, "The Virtue of Faith."

17 Given Maimonides' praise for Aristotle and other philosophers in his famous letter to Samuel ibn Tibbon, this point needs hardly to be made. For a valuable discussion of the letter, see S. Harvey, "Letter."

18 For one example among many, see the parable of the palace in *Guide* III.51.

Gibeonites specifically, not with Gentiles generally. Furthermore, Maimonides associates modesty, mercy, and lovingkindness[19] with the "holy nation" (*ha-ummah ha-kedoshah*) of Israel. Just as Maimonides here speaks not of Gentiles generally, but of Gibeonites in particular, so also, I think, it is legitimate to read the first passage, with its emphasis on Gibeonites. In this passage, Israel is called "the holy nation." It would take us very far afield here to analyze the notion of "holiness" as Maimonides uses it, but suffice it to say that holiness for Maimonides is a matter of halakhic status, not an intrinsic characteristic.[20] Thus, holiness is not a characteristic of Jews as such, but a status attained through consistent acts of "modesty, mercy, and lovingkindness."

In the third passage Maimonides associates charitableness with the "righteous individuals who are of the seed of our father Abraham" (*zadikei zera Avraham avinu*) – not all of the seed of Abraham is righteous, but those who are practice charity.[21] Being charitable, in other words, is not a matter of descent, but of righteousness, something Jews certainly should be, but not necessarily are. Cruelty, Maimonides goes on, is found only among the Gentiles (*goyyim*). Can this mean all non-Jews? In the first place the term "Gentile" in the *Mishneh Torah* usually means idolater.[22] Furthermore, we are told that those who attached themselves (*nilvim aleihem*[23]) to Israel[24] "are to each other like brothers" who are merciful towards each other. Clearly, we are speaking here of "Israel of the spirit" as opposed to "Israel of the flesh" (to adopt inappropriate language),

---

19 Modesty being the opposite of impudence, mercy the opposite of cruelty and misanthropy, and acting out of lovingkindness the opposite of never so acting.

20 See ch. 19 below, "Spirituality and a Life of Holiness."

21 Note that Ishmael also was descended from Abraham; there is nothing in this passage which might lead to one impute to Maimonides the claim that Arabs generally and Muslims in particular do not practice charity. Indeed, in that charity, as Maimonides do doubt knew, is one of the pillars of Islam, it is likely that Maimonides was directly familiar with acts of charity on the part of the Muslims among whom he lived.

22 See above, note 13.

23 The phrase derives from Isaiah 56:6 and Esther 9:27; in both places the reference appears to be to "fellow travellers" and not to converts. The use of the term by Maimonides in "Laws of Idolatry," I.3 and "Laws of the Murderer," XIII.14 is ambiguous on this issue.

24 In ch. 16 above, and in my *Judaism* I argue (pp. 81-96) that Maimonides distinguishes between "Israel," defined theologically and philosophically, from "the Jews," defined halakhically. Assuming the correctness of my arguments there would render further discussion here unnecessary. But the world has not yet reached that stage of perfection. These arguments are expanded and developed in *Confrontation*, ch. 7.

otherwise what sense does it make to include those who attach themselves to Israel among those who are merciful to each other? [25] To whom can poor Jews look for succor? Only to each other *and* to those who have attached themselves to the Torah; after all, Gentiles, i.e., idolaters, hate the Jews. What cannot be inferred from this passage, then, is that Maimonides holds that all Jews as such are merciful, that all non-Jews as such are cruel, and that all non-Jews as such hate the Jews. The persuasive, as opposed to descriptive, nature of this passage is clear. Maimonides cites seven different verses in order to impress upon the reader the importance of giving charity as an expression of compassion. Were Jews as such truly charitable by nature, Maimonides would not have to work so hard to convince them to give charity.[26]

Beyond all this, comparing what Maimonides writes here with his apparent source (Bezah 32b) is most instructive. He writes: "giving charity is the mark [*siman*] of righteous individuals who are of the seed of our father Abraham." The Talmud writes: "whoever is merciful to his fellow-men is certainly of the children of our father Abraham." Maimonides, as we have seen, connects *righteous* Jews to Abraham; the Talmud tells us that *anyone* who is merciful is certainly Jewish. Maimonides writes: "whosoever is cruel and merciless lays himself open to suspicion [*yesh la-hush*] as to his descent." The Talmud writes: "and whosoever is not merciful to his fellow-men is certainly not [*bi-yadu'a she-eno*] of the children of our father Abraham." The Talmud makes mercy a property of Jewishness and cruelty a proof of absence of Jewishness. Maimonides takes mercy as a sign of Jewishness and cruelty as a reason for suspecting the absence of Jewishness. The Talmud speaks in absolute terms, Maimonides in what might be called statistical terms.

The fourth passage is the easiest for me to deal with, since it most clearly makes a normative, prescriptive claim, not a descriptive one. Forgiveness is

---

25 I owe this point to Levinger, *Ha-Rambam*, p. 89.

26 For another example of persuasive writing on the part of Maimonides, see "Laws of Idolatry," XI.16: "These practices are all false and deceptive, and were means employed by the ancient idolaters to deceive the peoples of various countries and induce them to become their followers. It is not proper for Israelites who are highly intelligent [*hakhamim mehukamim*] to suffer themselves to be deluded by such inanities or imagine that there is anything in them..." (p. 80a). Maimonides certainly did not believe that all Jews were in fact highly intelligent! Anyone at all familiar with his writings can point to many places where he makes the opposite claim.

certainly appropriate to the seed of Israel (*derekh zera Yisrael*). The very fact that Maimonides has to make this claim (and all this others analyzed here) indicates that not all Jews behave as they should. Were all Jews *qua* Jews truly merciful, charitable, and forgiving, what would be the need for all these exhortations in what is allegedly a dry, halakhic compendium?

In the fifth passage Maimonides teaches that cruelty and effrontery are not frequent except among uncircumcised Gentiles. If we take him literally, he is exempting all Muslims from this charge. If we don't take him literally, then he is not drawing a literal distinction between Jews and Gentiles. And in this passage, from whom does Maimonides learn proper behavior? From Job, a non-Jew![27] Maimonides goes on to teach that "the seed of our father Abraham, however, i.e., the Israelites, upon whom the Holy One, blessed be He, bestowed the favor of the Torah and laid upon them statutes and judgments, are merciful people who have mercy upon all." Let us examine this sentence very carefully. A literal translation would read as follows: "But the seed of Abraham our father, they being that Israel upon whom the Holy One, blessed be He, emanated the boon of Torah and commanded them righteous statutes and judgments, have mercy upon all." In this case Maimonides explicitly distinguishes those who have been given the Torah from among all the seed of Abraham. The second clause of the sentence can be read in a number of ways. One is to read it as if Maimonides said simply that Israelites have mercy upon all. A second way of reading it is that the Torah, which includes righteous statutes and judgments, brings its adherents to merciful behavior. In the context of the clearly persuasive and prescriptive character of the whole paragraph (Maimonides is trying to wean his readers away from technically permissible behavior, working heathen slaves with rigor), this second reading makes more sense.[28]

---

27 Job, according to Maimonides, was not Jewish. See the text cited below from the Epistle to Yemen. It is interesting to note that in *Guide of the Perplexed* III.22 Maimonides mantains that Job was not an historical figure at all, and the whole story is a parable.

28 On this passage, Walter S. Wurzburger writes: "Maimonides pointed out that the deeply ingrained sense of pity and compassion and the resulting aversion to cruelty that [he thought] is characteristic of Jews can be traced back to the impact of the teachings of the Torah and of various historical experiences that engendered these character traits." See Wurzburger, *Ethics of Responsibility*, p. 23.

Clearly, I have been reading these paragraphs in a tendentious fashion, but no more tendentiously than those who want to use them as proof that Maimonides held that Jews *as such* are kind, merciful, etc. while non-Jews *as such* are not. Given the readings offered here, none of which are unfair to the Hebrew and none of which demand uprooting isolated passages from their contexts, it seems reasonable to say that the passages discussed here do not represent counter-instances to Maimonides' generally universalist stance, according to which that which distinguishes Jews from non-Jews is the Torah, and nothing inherent, inborn, metaphysical, ontological, or in any other way essentialist.

There is a passage in Maimonides' "Epistle to Yemen" which has been offered as proof that Maimonides (like Halevi, if for different reasons) held prophecy to be available only to Jews.[29] In a learned and penetrating essay, Rabbi Yizhak Sheilat, the translator of many of Maimonides' writings into modern Hebrew, has argued that Maimonides held prophecy to be in theory open to all but in practice (at least since the time of Moses[30]) to be found only among Jews since God miraculously withholds prophecy from otherwise qualified non-Jews.[31] Rabbi Sheilat is led to this (to my mind bizarre[32]) interpretation of Maimonides because of a text he found in the "Epistle to Yemen" which he reads as proving that Maimonides holds prophecy to be impossible for non-Jews.[33]

The passage in question reads as follows:

In order to comprehend the verse under discussion unequivocally: *The Lord Your God will raise up for you a prophet from among your own people like myself* (Dt. 18:15), it is necessary to ascertain its context...[Unlike the Gentiles]

---

29 For an argument that Maimonides thought prophecy a perfection available in principle to all human beings, see my *Judaism*, pp. 26-29.

30 Y. Sheilat (see next note, p. 281) has Maimonides adopt the position found in the Talmud (BB15b) that Moses beseeched God not to allow non-Jews to prophesy.

31 Sheilat, "Uniqueness of Israel."

32 If for no other reason it calls for God to perform otherwise unnecessary miracles. Rabbi Sheilat presents no evidence that Maimonides actually held this view.

33 To be entirely frank, I think it likely that Rabbi Sheilat was also led to adopt this interpretation because of an antecedent conviction that Maimonides *had to* be closer to Halevi than he is ordinarily thought to be. I have no proof of this, and may simply be expressing my own prejudices here.

you will arrive at a foreknowledge of the future from him [a true prophet like Moses], without recourse to augury, divination, astrology, and the like…Moreover, he conveys another notion, namely, that in addition to being near you and living in your midst, he will also be one of you, an Israelite. The obvious deduction is that you will be distinguished above all others by the sole possession of prophecy. The words *like myself* were specifically added to indicate that only the descendants of Jacob are meant…Our disbelief in the prophecies of Omar and Zeid is not due to the fact that they are non-Jews, as the unlettered folk imagine, and in consequence of it are compelled to establish their stand from the biblical phrase *from among your own people.* For Job, Zophar, Bildad, Eliphaz and Elihu are all considered prophets by us although they are not Israelites…But we give credence to a prophet or we disbelieve him because of what he preaches, not because of his descent, as I shall explain.[34]

R. Sheilat makes a great deal of the expression, "you will be distinguished above all others by the sole possession of prophecy." It is because of that phrase that R. Sheilat finds it necessary to find a way to maintain that Maimonides holds that non-Jews can prophesy in principle, but never in practice. I do not want to get involved in a philological discussion over whether Maimonides' words are best translated as above. I am willing to grant R. Sheilat that they should be. But whatever Maimonides means here,[35] it boggles the mind to think that Maimonides would tell us that only Jews can prophesy and then a few lines further on continue and explicitly say that non-Jews *can* prophecy.[36] Indeed, on the very next page of the "Epistle to Yemen" Maimonides writes (Halkin, p. 113):

---

34 I cite the translation of Halkin in *Crisis and Leadership*, pp. 110-112. For the Judeo-Arabic source and modern Hebrew translation, see Kafih, *Iggerot*, p. 36. For R. Sheilat's Hebrew translation, see his *Iggerot*, pp. 135-136.

35 Professor Lenn Evan Goodman suggested the following to me in a private communication: "The point of the distinction from the Gentiles here is that they, as a matter of culture, rely on divination, whereas Jews, as a matter of *mitzvah* do not. The Rambam is glossing "from among you" and "like myself" as a reference to this cultural difference. He does so precisely in order to exclude ethnocentric readings of the passage, since it has a Halakhic bearing (on the treatment of future claimants to prophecy) and a political one in his contemporaries' immediate situation, the situation that prompted their inquiry."

36 The entire discussion is in the present tense; for R. Sheilat's position to make sense, the entire discussion would have to refer to the pre-Mosaic period.

Now, if a Jewish or gentile prophet urges and encourages people to follow the religion of Moses without adding thereto or diminishing therefrom, like Isaiah, Jeremiah, and the others, we demand a miracle from him. If he performs it we recognize him and bestow upon him the honor due to a prophet, but if he fails to do so he is put to death.

Maimonides here explicitly allows for the possibility of non-Jewish prophecy *after* Moses. R. Sheilat's interpretation, it seems abundantly clear, is unsupportable.[37]

There are two further passages in Maimonides' writings which have been proffered as proof of his holding that Jews are in some innate way superior to non-Jews. In his commentary on the Mishnah (Bava Kamma IV.3) Maimonides writes:

I will explain to you how a case should be conducted if a Jew had a suit with a Gentile. If, according to their laws, we are vindicated, we judge them according to their laws say, "this is your law." But were it better for us to judge according to our laws, we judge them according to our laws and say, "this is our law." Let not this matter be hard in your eyes, nor be amazed at it, anymore than you are amazed at the slaughter of animals, even though they have done no wrong; for one in whom human characteristics have not been brought to perfection is not truly a human being and exits only to serve the purposes of the true human being. Explaining this matter would require a book of its own.

Maimonides repeats this law in two places in the *Mishneh Torah*:

In "Laws of Damage by Chattels," VIII.5, Maimonides codifies the issue dealt with in his commentary to Baba Kamma, but gives another reason for it:

If an ox belonging to a Jew gores an ox belonging to an alien [*nokhri*], the owner is exempt whether it is innocuous or forewarned, for Gentiles do not hold one responsible for damage caused by one's animals, and their own law is applied to them. However, if an ox belonging to an alien gores an ox belonging to a Jew, the owner must pay for the full damage caused whether his ox is innocuous or

---

37 R. Sheilat has a number of other texts in support of what I can only call his attempt to Halevi-ize Maimonides. With the exception of the text studied here, they are all either staples in the literature (and I discuss them in this essay) or are so forced as not to warrant detailed attention.

forewarned. This is a fine imposed upon Gentiles, being heedless of the scriptural commandments, they do not remove sources of damage. Accordingly, should they not be held liable for damage caused by their animals, they would not take care of them and thus would inflict loss on other people's property.

The law is the same as in the Mishnah commentary; Jews may take advantage of Gentiles in legal dealings, but the reason offered here is very different.

So, too, with the second place in which this law finds expression in the *Mishneh Torah*, "Laws of Kings and their Wars," X. 12:

> …In a suit involving a Jew and a Gentile, if the Jew can be vindicated by the law of the Gentiles, judgment is rendered according to the Gentile law, and the [Gentile] litigant is told: "This is your law." If the Jew can be vindicated by our law, the suit is decided according to Torah law and the [Gentile] litigant is told: "This is our law." … Even with respect to Gentiles,[38] the Rabbis bid us visit their sick, bury their dead along with the dead of Israel, and maintain their poor with the poor of Israel in the interests of peace, as it is written: *The Lord is good to all; and His tender mercies are over all His works* (Ps. 145:9). And it is also written, *Her ways are ways of pleasantness, and all her paths are peace* (Prov. 3:17).

The law in question is repeated here with no reason given, but in a context which makes it clear that Maimonides sees Gentiles as worthy of the mercy and goodness of God, and as people towards whom Jews ought to behave as they are commanded to behave towards their brethren.

In the first place in which this law is found (Commentary to BK IV.3) Maimonides either holds that Jews are inherently distinct from and superior to Gentiles, maintaining that Gentiles are not human beings, or is extremely elitist, maintaining that Gentiles "in whom human characteristics have not been brought to perfection" may, in effect, be treated like animals. The reason for this is that such a person "is not truly a human being and exits only to serve the purposes of the true human being."

This second reading may "save" Maimonides from the charge of proto-racism. But in so doing we have further confirmed that his definition of what it

---

38 As opposed to resident aliens, discussed in the passage skipped.

means to be a human is such that there are individuals born of human parents, raised among human beings, who look in many ways and act like human beings, who can give birth to human beings, but "in whom human characteristics have not been brought to perfection," and who therefore are not truly human. Such individuals exist in order to serve true human beings, in the same way in which animals exist in order to provide meat for the true human beings. Not a very attractive picture to us, of course, but one which was hardly is unusual among the Aristotelians.[39]

Even if this interpretation is rejected, I have no trouble admitting that in his early *Commentary on the Mishnah* Maimonides made an isolated statement which no one today (be they universalist or particularist in their reading of the Jewish tradition) can fail to regret. Maimonides himself apparently came to regret having made the statement, since he took two opportunities to correct it. In the first he repeats the law and also feels the need to explain it (as he did in the Mishnah commentary), offering an explanation which does not offend Gentiles at all, and certainly does not present them as being in any sense subhuman or essentially distinct from Jews. He goes further in the second place, implicitly pointing to God's mercy over Gentiles and their status as creatures of the Lord. Thus, if the juvenile Maimonides expressed the view that Gentiles are less than human, the mature Maimonides took two opportunities to correct himself.

The last passage which I would like to address is from the *Mishneh Torah* and for me is the hardest of them all. Chapter XII of "Laws of Forbidden Intercourse" deals with sexual congress between Jewish men and Gentile women. Paragraph 4 deals with the case of a Jewish man who has sexual relations with a Gentile woman (who is not the daughter of a resident alien) in public (in the presence of ten adult male Jews). Such a person may be attacked by zealots, and if brought before a court is to be flogged. In paragraph 6 we learn that if such a person escapes earthly punishment, he will suffer karet, "excision," at the hands of God. Maimonides goes on to tell us that "whosoever has intercourse with a Gentile woman is considered as though

---

39 Other treatments of these texts include Lifshutz, "Rules Governing Conflict," 179-189, who opines that Maimonides changed his mind. That is also the position of Lorberbaum, "Maimonides on *Imago Dei.*" Avi Sagi, *Yahadut*, pp. 170-171, reads Maimonides' commentary in elitist, as opposed to racist, terms. Sheilat, "Uniqueness of Israel," p. 294, on the other hand, reads Maimonides as holdng views which today would be called racist.

he had intermarried with an idol…and he is called one who has profaned the holiness of the Lord." Paragraph 7 continues emphasizing seriousness of the offence, while paragraph 8 explains why: "…such conduct causes one to cleave to idolaters from whom the Holy One, blessed be He, has separated us, to turn away from God, and to break faith with Him." Paragraph 9 discusses the fate of a Gentile man who cohabits with a Jewish woman. Paragraph 10 relates to the fate of a Gentile woman who has intercourse with a Jewish man and teaches the following:

> If, however, an Israelite has intercourse with a Gentile woman, whether she is a minor three years and one day old or an adult,[40] whether she is married or unmarried, even if the Israelite is only nine years and a day old, once he willfully has intercourse with her, she is liable to be put to death, because an offence has been committed by an Israelite through her, just as in the case of an animal.[41] This law is explicitly stated in the Torah,[42] *Behold, these caused the children of Israel, through the counsel of Balaam, to revolt, so as to break faith with the Lord … therefore kill every woman that has known man by lying with him* (Nu. 31:16-17).

I would feel immoral were I to try to defend Maimonides' decision and formulation in this paragraph.[43] Whatever motivated him, one thing should be clear: He is *not* saying that Gentile women are animals. In the case where a person has sexual relations with an animal, that animal is to be killed. The animal suffers death through no guilt of its own (obviously), but, apparently, because it was the tool through which a Jew performed a particularly odious transgression.[44] Similarly in a case the enormity of which Maimonides was at pains to emphasize (having intercourse with an idolater in the presence of ten adult male Jews), the person through which a Jew is thus brought "to marry"

---

40 In contrast to Yevamot 60b which restricts this law to an adult woman (*Maggid Mishneh*).

41 Sanhedrin 55b.

42 Maimonides has no known Talmudic warrant for deducing this law from this verse.

43 In his commentary on this passage, R. Joseph Kafih seeks to do so by reading the expression "once he willfully has intercourse with her," as applying to the woman as well; the only case in which she is executed is if she maliciously had intercourse with a Jew in public in an idolatrous context. He argues that this follows from Maimonides' citation of Nu. 31:16-17 and its reference to Midianite women who sought to entice the Jewish people into idolatry. But even R. Kafih has trouble explaining "just as in the case of an animal."

44 Lev. 18:23, 20:15-16; "Laws of Forbidden Intercourse," I.4.

idolatry must be put to death, even if she is only a three year old girl.[45] This may offend our sensibilities (it certainly offends mine!) but it does not mean that Maimonides considers non-Jews as such to be on a par with animals.

The texts analyzed in this chapter include all those which I have found which might be cited as "proving" that Maimonides held there be some intrinsic difference between Jews and non-Jews, to the obvious advantage of the former. As I understand him, Maimonides' true position is that Jews who obey the Torah are, because of that obedience and for no other reason, ethically superior to the general run of non-Jews. There is also no doubt that Maimonides held Judaism to be true, other religions false – he was no pluralist.[46] It may even be the case (although I know of no text of his in which he makes this claim) that he held that generations of Torah obedience lead to a people who are on the whole finer than the descendents of corrupt idolaters. What he clearly did not believe is that there is some essential, inborn, inherent, metaphysical distinction between Jews and Gentiles. People are people, all can be good, all can be bad, all can be righteous, all can be wicked.[47] It is God's Torah and nothing else which distinguishes Jews from Gentiles.[48]

---

45 It ought to be understood that this is a technicality; in Jewish law, a female under the age of three is considered incapable of intercourse.

46 See Kellner and Kellner, "Respectful Disagreement."

47 A point made explicitly by Maimonides about human beings (and not just Jews) in "Laws of Repentance," V.5. That Maimonides is there referrring to human beings as such, and not Jews, is not only clear from the context, but from his use of Gen. 3:22 (about Adam, progenitor of all human beings) as a proof-text.

48 Acceptance of that Torah does not make Jews ontologically distinct from Gentiles. This is made clear from the way in which Maimonides "defangs" a rabbinic passage which might otherwise be problematic for him. In *Guide of the Perplexed* II.30 (pp. 356-357) he writes:

Among the amazing dicta whose external meaning is exceedingly incongruous, but in which – when you obtain a true understanding of the chapters of this Treatise – you will admire the wisdom of the parables and their correspondence to what exists, is their statement [Shab. 145b-146a]: When the serpent came to Eve, it cast pollution into her. The pollution of [the sons of] Israel, who had been present at Mount Sinai, has come to an end. [As for] the pollution of the nations who had not been present at Mount Sinai, their pollution has not come to an end. This too you should follow up in your thought.

Maimonides makes it clear in the chapter from which this passage is taken that the pollution of the Gentiles is their reliance upon imagination instead of intellect. This, indeed, is the way in which his medieval and modern commentators understand him. For details, see Kellner, *Perfection*, p. 76, note 47.

CHAPTER EIGHTEEN
Maimonides' *True Religion* – for Jews, or All Humanity?

I n the first paragraph of the last chapter of the *Mishneh Torah*,[1] Maimonides writes:

> Let it not enter your mind that in the days of the Messiah any aspect of the regular order of the world will be abolished or some innovation will be introduced into nature; rather, the world follows its accustomed course. The verse in Isaiah, *The wolf shall dwell with the lamb, the leopard lie down with the kid* is an allegory and metaphor.[2] Its meaning is that Israel will dwell in security with the wicked nations of the earth which are allegorically represented as wolves and leopards, as it says (Jer. 5:6): *the wolf of the desert ravages them. A leopard lies in wait by their towns.* Those nations will all adopt the true religion [*dat ha-emet*]. They will neither rob not destroy; rather, they will eat permitted foods in peace and quiet as[3] Israelites, as it says, *the lion, like the ox, shall eat straw.* All similar things written about the Messiah are allegories, and in the days of the messianic king everyone will understand which matters were allegories, and also to what they refer.

What does the expression *dat-ha-emet* mean in this context? In a number of places I have argued that Maimonides means that in the messianic era (or, more accurately, by the time it reaches fruition since it is, after all, a process and not an event[4]) all human beings will worship God from a position of absolute

---

1   "Laws of Kings and Their Wars," XII.1.

2   Hebrew: *mashal ve-hiddah*. Sara Klein-Braslavy shows that Maimonides uses the Hebrew word *hiddah* as a synonym for *mashal*, allegory. See Klein-Braslavy, "Maimonides on Proverbs," p. 123 n.10.

3   Following Makbili's text; printed editions and some manuscripts read: "with."

4   This is an important point, not only because it makes Orthodox Zionism possible. While

spiritual equality.[5] Whether that means that all Gentiles will convert formally to Judaism,[6] that they will be absorbed into Israel in some other fashion, or that the distinction will become in some way less important than it is now[7] is open to question. What is clear, I maintain, is that the distinction between Jew and Gentile will disappear by the time that the messianic process has reached completion.[8] In making this claim, I stand opposed to those who interpret Maimonides in a more particularist fashion, according to whom even at the end of days for Maimonides the Jews will remain God's chosen people, especially beloved, and distinct from the mass of humanity. I also stand opposed to those who might want to read Maimonides in a pluralist fashion, as if he holds that in the messianic era many different paths will lead equally to God.[9] Rather, I read him as a messianic universalist.[10]

Maimonides rarely specifies the precise stages of the messianic process, reading him as if everything happens at once, *be-hese'ah ha-da'at* (Sanhedrin 97a), as it were, is radically to misunderstand him. He expects the messianic process to *unfold* within nature as we know it. Further on the connection between Maimonides' messianism and Orthodox Zionism, see my "Messianic Postures."

5 See *Judaism* and the other chapters in this section.

6 As I argue in *Judaism*, pp. 39-58. The term 'Judaism' sounds anachronistic – it is clearly a Nineteenth Century coinage. But it is clear from his writings that Maimonides had a conception of something that we now call Judaism as distinguished from what we now call Christianity and Islam, even if he did not use those precise terms. If nothing else, his use of the term *dat emet* instead of *Torat emet* is an indication of this. Maimonides may or may not have been the first Jewish thinker to use the term *dat* in the sense of 'religion' (as opposed to 'law', its Biblical meaning), but he certainly did so extensively. See also below, note 38.

7 Blidstein, *Ekronot*, pp. 245-248.

8 It is not clear to me that Maimonides himself addressed this question self-consciously; it may have been among the things he expected to be clarified after the coming of the Messiah – see "Laws of Kings," XII.1.

9 Raphael Jospe points to Netanel ibn al-Fayyumi (Yemen, c. 1165) as a medieval Jew who held a pluralist view of religious revelation. This is surely a case of an exception proving a rule. For sources and discussion, see the debate between Jospe on the one hand and Jolene and Menachem Kellner on the other in Eugene Korn (ed.), *Jewish Theology and the Other* (forthcoming). The philosopher cited by Halevi at the beginning of the Kuzari might be cited as an example of a medieval religious pluralist, but that is surely a mistake: his pluralism consists in saying that all religions but Judaism are equally false, not equally true.

10 There is no dearth of apologetic writing on Biblical and rabbinic universalism. Moshe Greenberg often (but not always) succeeds in going beyond apologetics; see his "*Atem Keruyim Adam*," "*Erekh Ha-Adam*," and "Mankind." In a wholly non-apologetic plane, for the Bible see Levenson, "Universal Horizon" and Kaminsky, *Yet I Loved Jacob*. For rabbinic Judaism, see Blidstein, "Rabbinic Missionizing," Hirshman, "Rabbinic Universalism, and Hirshman, *Torah Lekhol Ba'ei Olam*. For medieval views, see Kellner, *Confrontation*. For Maimonides' geonic background, see Sklare, "Are Gentiles" (and the other studies cited there).

This needs clarification. Let us distinguish between the Torah, as it were, of Noah, the Torah, as it were, of Abraham, and the Torah of Moses.[11] As I will point out below, the Torah of Noah includes neither the affirmation of God's existence nor the obligation to worship God. The Torah of Abraham can be seen as building on the Torah of Noah, but adding the affirmation of God's existence and the obligation (and, I would add, the privilege) of worshiping God. This Torah is meant for all human beings. The Torah of Moses can be seen as either a special boon to the Jewish people, or as a concession to their primitive character (as evidenced by the episode of the golden calf).[12] A radical reading of Maimonides would see him as envisioning a messianic era in which all humans, including the people of Israel, would observe the Torah of Abraham, and not the Torah of Moses. A more conservative but still universalist reading of Maimonides would see him as envisioning a messianic era in which all human beings observe the Torah of Moses. Particularist readings of Maimonides would have him envision a messianic era in which Jews observe the Torah of Moses and Gentiles observe either the Noachide laws or the Torah of Abraham. On my understanding, Maimonides is a conservative universalist: all humanity will accept and observe the Torah of Moses by the time that the messianic era reaches fruition.[13]

My friend and colleague, Rabbi Chaim Rappoport, is convinced that my understanding of Maimonides is mistaken. On his reading of the relevant texts, Maimonides holds that in the messianic era Jews will observe the Torah of Moses while Gentiles will observe the Noachide laws. Rabbi Rappoport

---

11 R. Joseph Albo may have been the first to posit a series of divine Torahs. See *Sefer ha-Ikkarim*, I, chaps. 13 and 14 On Albo's impact, see Melamed, "Natural, Human, Divine."

12 For sources which support this interpretation, see *Confrontation*, pp. 140-148 and 152-154.

13 It is certainly not inconceivable that Maimonides might have adopted the radical universalist view of the messianic era, in which all humanity observes "only" the Torah of Abraham. As I will note below, Nahmanides adopts a structurally similar view, according to which the Torah as we know it will not be observed in the messianic era. However, I take Maimonides' claims about the permanence of the Torah literally, not only because he says so, but because he holds that the Messianic era will someday end (Introduction to *Helek* [ed. Sheilat], pp. 138-139), at which point one assumes that the Torah of Moses will once again play a necessary role in the education of humanity. For arguments to the effect that Maimonides distinguished between the historical explanations of why commandments were given on the one hand, from their permanent validity on the other, see *Confrontation*, ch. 2, notes 21 and 125, chapt. 4, note 57, and chapt. 7, note 63. I have written a (Hebrew) essay in which I compare Maimonides and Nahmanides on the permanence of the commandments, proving (to my complete satisfaction) that Maimonides adopted a much more conservative stance than did Nahmanides. I hope to publish that essay soon.

paid me the compliment of writing a detailed refutation of my position and I would like now to offer my response to his critique.[14]

Rabbi Rappoport generously began his discussion by seeking to strengthen mine. I would like to repay his kindness by also trying to strengthen his position. His overall conclusion is that

> The expression "religion of truth" ("*dat ha-emet*") refers to the "religion of Moses," encompassing both "the Law of Israel" and the "Law of the Noahides"; both of them were "commanded by God in the Torah"—the one Torah—given to us through Moses our Teacher at Mount Sinai.

> The words "*dat ha-emet*" mean "the religion truly given by God" or "the religion that shows us the way of truth" or (combining the two) "the religion truly given by God, which shows us the way of truth." The words may also refer to the true belief, which is the foundation of religion.

> Whatever the case may be, the expression "*dat ha-emet*" is used to describe the entire Torah and all the commandments revealed by God through Moses our Teacher (parts of which had already been given via the prophets who preceded the giving of the Torah at Sinai). That religion includes "the ways of truth" (*darkhei ha-emet*) discovered by Abraham our Father and proclaimed by him throughout the world as well as the commandments issued to Adam, Noah, Abraham, Moses, etc.; and it is the religion that was bolstered by the righteous kings of the House of David over the years and that will be exalted by the King Messiah, may he speedily be revealed, may that be God's will.[15]

Rabbi Rappoport tells us that the term *dat ha-emet* in our text in the *Mishneh Torah* refers to true divine revelation. Such divine revelation encompasses two types of believers: Noachide Gentiles and Jews. The first group is bound to obey the Seven Noachide Laws, while the latter group is bound to obey the

---

14 After writing several drafts of this chapter, I had the pleasure of reading Kreisel, "Maimonides on Divine Religion," Professor Kreisel arrives at the same conclusion I do, although he largely takes a different route. I will cite this essay henceforth as "Kreisel."

15 Rappoport, "Dat ha-Emet."

Torah of Moses. In the messianic era *dat ha-emet* will be accepted universally but practiced in two different ways: by Jews through the 613 commandments of the Torah, and by Gentiles through the 7 Noachide Laws.[16]

This certainly seems to be a position congenial to Maimonides,[17] and accords with the broad outlines of his history of religions as outlined in the first chapter of "Laws of Idolatry."[18] On this account, Abraham taught monotheism to descendents of Noah, without imposing any commandments upon them.[19] The obligation of circumcision was, however, imposed upon Abraham and his descendents. The parallelism here is attractive: in the messianic era the descendents of Noah will 'practice' Abrahamic monotheism, while the descendents of Abraham will fulfill the commandments of the Torah.[20]

But, as much as I would like to help my friend Rabbi Rappoport (even if that involves showing that I am wrong in my interpretation of Maimonides), I fear that this suggestion is of little value in supporting his case. It ignores Maimonides' notorious claim to the effect that the Torah as we have it is a concession to the primitive character of the Israelites leaving Egypt.[21] On this view, Mosaic

---

16 Actually, Rabbi Rappoport himself in the end comes near to adopting my position. In his footnote 71 he writes: "While it is possible that some of them (and, over time, perhaps all of them) will convert, that is far from certain. It is one of those things about which Maimonides wrote 'no one is in a position to know the details of this and similar things until they have come to pass."

17 I suspect that some of the reasons that I find it congenial to Maimonides might appeal less to Rabbi Rappoport. Maimonides as I understand him sincerely held that the secrets of the Torah were pretty well captured in Aristotelian physics and metaphysics. Kabbalists, as I will have occasion to note below, agree with Maimonides that the Torah has a deeper meaning which underlies the commandments (and gives them much of their significance); they disagree with Maimonides about the nature of that deeper meaning.

18 For the text and discussion, see: *Confrontation*, pp. 77-83 and the sources cited there. See now also the very interesting discussion in Alex P. Jassen, "Reading Midrash."

19 Further on the distinction between Abraham and Moses, see *Guide of the Perplexed* II.39.

20 Often ignored in this context is the point that the obligation devolves upon all of Abraham's descendents (excluding Ishmael and Esau), including the offspring of Keturah who, according to Maimonides, are today's Arabs. See "Laws of Kings," X.8, ch. 16 above, and Kasher, "Circumcision." Thus, the Jews have 613 commandments, the Noachides 7, and the Arabs 8. This seems to weaken the parallelism between Abrahamic and messianic times I am trying to draw here in order to strengthen Rabbi Rappoport's thesis.

21 To traditional Jewish ears this positions sounds shocking. Indeed, Maimonides himself wrote about it: "I know that on thinking about this at first your soul will necessarily have a feeling of repugnance toward this notion and will feel aggrieved because of it" (*Guide*, III. 32, p. 527). But the fact of the matter is that in structural terms, Maimonides is making a claim very similar to that made by Kabbalists; only when they make it, it sounds very religious. When Maimonides makes it, it sounds shocking. There is an important strand in Kabbalah, expressed openly by Nahmanides, among others, that the Torah as we have it exists in its

legislation is a concession on God's part to the primitive, pagan nature of the Jews who left Egypt.[22] Taking Rabbi Rappoport's thesis to (admittedly) extreme lengths, one might even be led to suggest that Noachide monotheism is thus superior to Mosaic legislation, since it seems to follow that in the messianic era on this view the Noachides will follow a more refined religion than the Jews!

Further, the Torah of Moses may be a concession, but coming from God, it is also good for those to whom it was revealed (as Maimonides explains in detail in the latter half of the third part of the *Guide*), and will remain good for them in the messianic era. The Torah is a tool for perfecting us *as human beings;*[23] as such, how could it be restricted to descendents of Abraham only in the messianic era?

But perhaps the Torah is a tool for perfecting Jews only? This is a view certainly rejected by Maimonides and I will devote most of my efforts in this chapter to showing why this must be so. Here, I will present the point in a cursory fashion, developing it more fully below.

Maimonides' position is 'forced' upon him because, unlike Rabbi Shimon bar Yohai as reported in the Talmud,[24] and unlike a host of medieval interpreters of Judaism, Maimonides takes very seriously the implications of the Torah's unambiguous statement that all human beings are created in the image

---

corporeal form only because of the sin of Adam and Eve, and will cease to exist in the form in which we know it in the messianic era. I have a hard time understanding how that differs in structure from Maimonides' position (I realize that the music is very different.) Indeed, I wonder if Maimonides' insistence on the permanence of the Torah (in the ninth of the 'Thirteen Principles' and, in an explicitly messianic context, in "Laws of Kings," XI.2) might be aimed, not only at Christians and Muslims, but at what I have (in *Confrontation*) called proto-Kabbalists as well.

22 I have come to realize that Maimonides is not making an historical claim here, so much as explaining the human condition, just as his account of the Garden of Eden in *Guide of the Perplexed* I.2 is not meant to be taken as history; rather, it is an allegory explaining the nature of humanity. For support for this latter point from a traditionalist perspective, see Rabbi Kafih's commentary to "Laws of the Sabbath," V.3. I treat of the broader point in an article I am writing with my student and friend Oded Horetzky.

23 On the view (of the students of Rabbi Yishma'el) that the Torah is ultimately meant for all humanity (*kol ba'ei olam*) and not just for the Jews, it is obviously a tool for human, and not only Jewish, perfection. For details, see the book and article by Hirshman, cited above in note 10.

24 Taking literally R. Shimon bar Yohai's statement (Yevamot 60b-60a) that only Jews are called *adam*. This statement has generated a huge amount of commentary (starting with Tosafot *ad loc.*). Whether or not R. Shimon considered Gentiles as fully human, the Talmud reports several statements attributed to him which betray, to put it mildly, lack of sympathy for the Gentile world: Sifri Num 69; Shabbat 33b; Mekhilta Beshallah 2.

of God. Gentiles are no less created in God's image than Jews. There is simply no difference between Jews and Gentiles on the level of what Daniel J. Lasker calls 'hardware'.[25] Being facetious, on this issue we can call Maimonides a biblical fundamentalist. But at this point, another question must be addressed: in what way are humans created in the image of God? Maimonides adopts a definition of humanity most famously associated with Aristotle:[26] human beings are rational animals, and it is by virtue of our rationality, as Maimonides emphasizes in the opening chapters of the *Guide of the Perplexed*, that we are said to be created in God's image. Further in an Aristotelian vein, Maimonides saw rationality as a potential with which humans are endowed at birth. In his eyes, very few human beings (Jews – rabbis and laity – and Gentiles alike) convert that potentiality to actuality. Here Maimonides' notorious intellectualist elitism kicks in: God's image is present in all human beings, but to different degrees. Aha! says the reader – Maimonides can sneak preference for Jews over Gentiles into the equation in this fashion. Hardly: for Maimonides, thanks to the Torah, more Jews than Gentiles will actualize their humanity to the greatest extent possible. But that is a relative advantage: humans who live lives governed by the Torah *are more likely* to achieve intellectual perfection than those who don't. But still, a Gentile philosopher enjoys more divine providence than and has a greater share in the world to come than a saintly and learned Talmudist who knows no science.[27]

All this being so, and it most certainly is, on what grounds could Maimonides expect or want that the distinction between Jew and Gentile would have any relevance or significance in an era when, as he puts it in the very last paragraph of the *Mishneh Torah* ("Kings," XII.4),

---

25 Lasker, "Proselyte Judaism."

26 This view was already attributed to Aristotle in the ancient world, but my friend Moshe Grimberg and I have not been able to find any place where he actually says so in as many words. There can be little doubt that Aristotle actually agrees with the definition (see, for example, Nicomachean Ethics, X, viii, 1179a24-30), he just never actually stated it explicitly.

27 This is the way that the parable of the palace in *Guide* III.51 is usually read (see Shem Tov *ad loc.*); for my alternative interpretation, see *Perfection*, pp. 15-33. Further on this, see Profiat Duran's account of what medieval Jewish philosophers affirmed on pp. 770-774 of "Hakdamat 'Sefer Ma'aseh Ephod'." In *Perfection* I cited Duran as cited by Shem Tov in his commentary *ad loc.* In a private communication the late and lamented Isadore Twersky later made me aware of the original source.

there will be[28] neither famine nor war, neither jealousy nor strife. Good things will be abundant, and delicacies as common as dust. The one preoccupation of the whole world will be only to know the Lord. Hence [they][29] will be very wise, knowing things now unknown and will apprehend knowledge of their Creator to the utmost capacity of the human mind,[30] as it is written: *For the land[31] shall be full of the knowledge of the Lord, as the waters cover the sea[32]* (Isaiah 11:9).[33]

---

28 Hebrew: *lo yihiyeh sham*. This Arabism calls to mind the very first paragraph of the *Mishneh Torah*, a text addressed to all human beings.

29 On the textual issues here see: Schwarzfuchs, "Les lois royales." On pp. 81-82 Schwarzfuchs shows that many printed editions and manuscripts add the word 'Israel' here. Makbili has it in the first printing of his edition, with a note that Sheilat excludes the word from his text (*Ha-Rambam ha-Meduyak*). Makbili excluded it from the second edition. On literary grounds alone it appears clear that the word is an emendation since the prooftext from Isaiah speaks of the entire earth. See also the next note.

30 On this expression, and many of the issues raised here, see Ravitzky, "'To the Utmost.'" It must be recalled that in this context the intellectual perfection to which Maimonides refers here is relative, not absolute. Human beings, even in the messianic era, achieve intellectual perfection to different degrees. When Maimonides says here that humans will come to know God *kifi ko'ah ha-adam* he means, to translate him literally, "according to human abilities" and not "according to human ability." The latter reading would involve a miraculous change in human nature.

31 On the question of what this land is (and for more on the textual issues) see Blidstein, *Ekronot*, p. 246, n. 56. Radbaz (R. David ben Solomon ibn Abi Zimra, 15-16 century) to "Kings," XII.1 understands the term as referring only to the Land of Israel. Maimonides' use of the verse in *Guide* III.11 would seem to preclude Radbaz's reading. The text there reads:

> ...If there were knowledge, whose relation to the human form is like that of the faculty of sight to the eye, they would refrain from doing any harm to themselves and to others. For through cognition of the truth, enmity and hatred are removed and the inflicting of harm by people on one another is abolished. It holds out this promise, saying, The wolf shall dwell with the lamb, the leopard shall lie down with the kid, and so on. And the sucking child shall play, and so on (Isaiah 11:6-8). Then it gives the reason for this, saying that the cause of the abolition of these enmities, these discords, and these tyrannies, will the knowledge that men will then have concerning the true reality of the deity. For it says: *They shall not hurt nor destroy in all My holy mountain; for the earth shall be full of the knowledge of the Lord, as the waters cover the sea* (Isaiah 11:9). Know this.

Warren Ze'ev Harvey has pointed out (to my chagrin, since I thought that I had hit upon this idea myself) that this chapter of the *Guide* is a kind of poetic and philosophical rendition of the last paragraph of the *Mishneh Torah*, glossing it in the way Maimonides meant it to be read. See pp. 23-24 in Harvey, "Virtuous State." Pushing Harvey's insight one step further, I think that the next chapter in the *Guide* also glosses the last paragraph in the *Mishneh Torah*.

32 The verse from Isaiah recalls Genesis 6:13. I am tempted to say that just as that verse surely relates to humans simpliciter, and not to Jews, Maimonides uses the parallel verse from Isaiah in the same way. The prophet is surely alluding to the difference between the messianic and ante-diluvian eras through the use of the expression *ki mal'ah ha-aretz*; it is a safe bet that if I noticed it, Maimonides certainly did.

33 Rabbi Jeffrey Bienenfeld pointed out to me (modestly claiming that the idea was not his, but it is

---

Let us follow this a little bit further. Why should the distinction between Jew and Noachide be preserved in the messianic era? Why should not all humans be Noachides, or all followers of the Torah of Moses? If Maimonides were Judah Halevi, were he the author (or authors) of the *Zohar*, were he Maharal, were he the author of the *Tanya*, were he almost any post-medieval Jew, the answer would be simple: there is an ontological difference between Jews and Gentiles such that in one of many ways, it 'makes sense' for the Jews to fulfill the 613 commandments and makes no sense for Gentiles to do so. Since the distinction between Jew and Gentile is part of the very fabric of the universe, it will be maintained in the messianic era.

Maimonides, however, is not Judah Halevi, he did not write (or even know of) the *Zohar*, he is not Maharal, and he is certainly not the author of the *Tanya*! He denies that there is any ontological difference between Jew and Gentile. It is that denial which forms the basis of my discussion here.

As noted above, the expression in debate between Rabbi Rappoport and me is found in the first paragraph of the last chapter of the *Mishneh Torah*. In the *Mishneh Torah* Maimonides is usually the soul of precision. When translating the second volume of the *Mishneh Torah* into English,[34] I was struck by how rarely I came across ambiguous passages. But this paragraph is full of problems and ambiguities:

First, with whom will Israel dwell securely: the wicked *among* the nations of the earth, or are all the Gentile nations wicked? The latter seems to be the case, since the next sentence says "Those nations will *all* adopt the true religion," implying that *all* the Gentile nations are (or were?) wicked.

Second, what does *va-yahzeru* (translated here as 'adopt') mean?

Third, what does *dat ha-emet* mean?

Fourth, what are the "permitted foods" which the (erstwhile, according to me) Gentiles will eat? Does it mean kosher, tithed food as I maintain, or does it mean food permitted to Gentiles as Rabbi Rappoport maintains?

---

from him I heard it, so I shall cite it in his name, and, perhaps, bring the redemption that much closer) that the meaning of the word "sea" here is "seabed" and that just as water spreads to cover every part of any enclosure in which it is placed, seeping into every nook and cranny (as anyone who has had plumbing problems knows), so too will the knowledge of God extend to and seep into every nook and cranny of the world, and, hence, into the hearts of all human beings.

34 *Book of Love.*

Fifth, what does "as Israelites" mean?

I will paraphrase the paragraph, thereby expressing my interpretation of it, but before doing that, some linguistic issues must be addressed. First, the root *h-z-r* does not always mean 'return' or 'revert' in Maimonides' Hebrew; it often means 'change'.[35] For a good example of this usage, see "Laws of Repentance," III.9 where Maimonides explains that an apostate concerning the whole Torah is a person who *hozer* to Gentile[36] religions during a period of religious persecution.[37] It makes little sense to see this text as referring to a Jew who *reverts* to a Gentile religion; rather, its clear meaning is a Jew who opportunistically *changes* religions. The use of the term *datei* here confirms that. In Maimonidean usage the term *dat* usually means what we today would call 'religion'.[38] Thus, for example, we find Maimonides talking about the beautiful captive in the following fashion ("Laws of Kings," VIII.5):

> What is the law with regard to an Israelite and a captive woman? If after the first coition, while she is still a Gentile, she undertakes to enter under the wings of the Shekhinah, she is immediately immersed for the purpose of conversion. If she is unwilling, she remains in his house for thirty days, as it is said: *She shall bewail her father and mother a full month* (Deut. 21:13). She weeps also for her *religion* [*datah*] and he may not stop her.

I thus translate *h-z-r* in our passage as "adopt" and not as "revert" and translate *dat* as "religion." Having clarified these meanings, I can now paraphrase the text in dispute between Rabbi Rappoport and myself:

> Let it not enter your mind that in the days of the Messiah any aspect of the regular order of nature will be abolished or some innovation will be introduced into the world of nature; rather, the world follows its accustomed course. The

---

35 For details, see Friedman, *Ha-Rambam, Ha-Mashiah*, pp. 2 and 72. See also Blidstein, *Ekronot*, p. 247, note 60. I was not aware of this linguistic fact when I wrote *Judaism*, and thus my mistaken discussion on p. 35.

36 Although the term *goy* in the *Mishneh Torah* usually refers to idolaters, here the apparent meaning is any Gentile. See Blidstein, "Status of the Resident Alien," pp. 44-45.

37 *Ve-hameshummad lekhol ha-Torah, kegon ha-hozer ke-datei ha-goyyim be-sha'ah she-gozrin shemad...* . See also Responsum 149, cited below.

38 See Blidstein, *Ekronot*, p. 106, note 29, and Rabbi Rappoport's discussion of the term. Note also Diamond, *Converts*, p. 254 , note 32 and note 6 above.

verse in Isaiah, *The wolf shall dwell with the lamb, the leopard lie down with the kid* is an allegory and metaphor.[39] Its meaning is that Israel will dwell in security with [those who were] the wicked nations of the earth, which are allegorically represented as wolves and leopards, as it says (Jer. 5:6): *the wolf of the desert ravages them. A leopard lies in wait by their towns.* Those nations will all adopt the true religion. [In consequence,] they will neither rob not destroy; rather, they will eat permitted foods in peace and quiet as Israelites, as it says, *the lion, like the ox, shall eat straw.*[40] All similar things written about the Messiah are allegories, and in the days of the messianic king everyone will understand which matters were allegories, and also the meaning hinted at by them.

Rabbi Rappoport, on the other hand, would have to paraphrase it more or less as follows:

Let it not enter your mind that in the days of the Messiah any aspect of the regular order of nature will be abolished or some innovation will be introduced into the world of nature; rather, the world follows its accustomed course. The verse in Isaiah, *The wolf shall dwell with the lamb, the leopard lie down with the kid* is an allegory and metaphor. Its meaning is that Israel will dwell in security with the wicked nations of the earth, which are allegorically represented as wolves and leopards, as it says: (Jer. 5:6): *the wolf of the desert ravages them. A leopard lies in wait by their towns.* Those nations will all revert to the true [Noachide] religion. [In consequence,] they will neither rob not destroy; rather, they will eat foods permitted to Gentiles in peace and quiet as Israelites [will eat food permitted to them], as it says, *the lion, like the ox, shall eat straw.* All similar things written about the Messiah are allegories, and in the days of the messianic king everyone will understand which matters were allegories, and also the meaning hinted at by them.

These two paraphrases obviously express very different understandings of Maimonides' conception of the messianic era. Can one be shown to be textually superior to the other? I do not believe so. I obviously think that my interpreta-

---

39 As noted above, Klein-Braslavy shows that Maimonides uses the Hebrew word *hiddah* as a synoym for *mashal*, allegory.

40 Note that according to this prooftext, the lion and the ox eat the *same* food. But note Rabbi Rappoport's alternative reading of this at his note 79.

tion of the passage is closer to the meaning of the Hebrew original and closer to the spirit of Maimonides, but, as Rabbi Rappoport's spirited and learned analysis shows, I really can not prove that to be the case on textual grounds alone.

Let us turn now to an examination of the crucial term in this discussion, *dat ha-emet*. Maimonides is simply not consistent in his use of this term. Indeed, in one version of Maimonides' letter to Rabbi Obadiah the Proselyte, he uses it to mean the religion taught by Abraham, which is certainly not the Torah of Moses.[41] On the other hand, in one version of his "Letter on Astrology" to the rabbis of Marseilles, he explicitly refers to "adherents of the *dat ha-emet*, it being the religion of Moses our teacher (*dat Mosheh Rabbenu*)."[42]

One thing is pretty clear, however: the expression *dat ha-emet* in our passage from "Laws of Kings" can not mean the seven Noachide laws, as Rabbi Rappoport suggests, since the point of the messianic era, as Maimonides affirms towards the end of chapter XI, is to "correct[43] the whole world to worship the Lord with one accord, as it is written: *For then I will turn to the peoples a pure language, that they may all call upon the name of the Lord to serve Him with one consent* (Zeph. 3:9)." The worship of God is not one of the seven Noachide laws, as Maimonides makes clear in "Kings," IX.1, where he lists them, and in the same place states that Abraham, Isaac, and Jacob each added one prayer-service and one commandment to the seven Noachide laws, thus making clear that divine worship is not included in the Noachide laws.[44] On this technical ground alone, Rabbi Rappoport's reading must fail.

The fact that Rabbi Rappoport's specific reading of our passage is thus shown to fail does not mean that mine is correct. The real issue here, namely, what sort of messianic era Maimonides expected, can not be settled on textual grounds alone. But perhaps it can be settled on *contextual* grounds? As my friend Rabbi Shalomi Eldar pointed out to me, our text follows immediately

---

41 See "Laws of Character Traits," I.7, where the middle way between character extremes is called *derekh ha-shem* and is presented as the religion taught by Abraham.

42 This is the text as presented by Rabbi Sheilat on p. 485; other versions have: "*ve-anahnu, ba'alei ha-torah ha-amitit*." See Kellner, "Farteitsht."

43 *U-le-takken olam*; on this expression in Maimonides, see Lorberbaum, "Maimonides on Repair of the World."

44 This is noted by Blidstein, *Ekronot*, pp. 245-246. I hasten to explain that I am not equating worship with prayer (this is denied by Maimonides in *Guide*, III.32), only trying to show that there is no obligation of worship (or prayer) in the Noahide laws.

upon the notorious passage, censored from printed editions of the *Mishneh Torah*, in which Maimonides grants a messianic role to Christianity and Islam. At the conclusion of that passage, Maimonides writes:

> All these matters relating to Jesus of Nazareth and the Ishmaelite [Mohammed] who came after him, only served to clear the way for King Messiah, to prepare the whole world to worship God with one accord, as it is written, *For then will I turn to the peoples a pure language, that they all call upon the name of the Lord to serve Him with one consent* (Zeph. 3:9). Thus the messianic hope, the Torah, and the commandments have become familiar topics – topics of conversation (among the inhabitants) of the far isles and many people, uncircumcised of heart and flesh. They are discussing these matters and the commandments of the Torah. Some say, "Those commandments were true, but have lost their validity and are no longer binding"; others declare that they had an esoteric meaning and were not to be taken literally; that the Messiah has already come and revealed their occult significance. But when the true King Messiah will appear and succeed, be exalted and lifted up, they will forthwith recant and realize that they have inherited nothing but lies from their fathers, that their prophets and forbears led them astray.

Our passage follows immediately upon this text. Thanks to Christianity and Islam, Gentiles had become accustomed to discussing divine commandments, even if they now misunderstand and misrepresent them. But after the true King Messiah appears, succeeds, is exalted, and is lifted up, they will realize that they had been misled, and therefore "will all adopt the true religion," a true religion of commandments properly understood.

Contextualizing our passage in this fashion surely strengthens my interpretation of it. But context is a tricky thing – perhaps we should read our text in its larger context? My student David Gillis proposed that I do precisely that. What subjects are covered in "Laws of Kings" immediately before the last two, messianic chapters? Why the status of the Noachide laws in particular and of non-Jews in general in a Jewish state. Recalling that Maimonides insists: "Let it not enter your mind that in the days of the Messiah any aspect of the regular order of the world will be abolished or some innovation will be introduced into nature; rather, the world follows its accustomed course," we might be led to say that this is a contextual indication that there will be Noachides and perhaps also Gentiles in the messianic kingdom. Contextualizing our passage in this fashion supports Rabbi Rappoport's reading of it.

But context is a tricky thing – perhaps we should read our text in an even larger context? The *Mishneh Torah* opens with four chapters on physics and metaphysics, chapters addressed to all human beings (psychoanalysis may be a "Jewish science," but Aristotelian physics certainly is not!) and closes with two chapters on the messianic era, addressed, again I suggest, to all human beings. This way of looking at things is strengthened if we look at the exact mid-point of the *Mishneh Torah*, the famous text at the end of "Laws of the Sabbatical Year and the Jubilee."[45] In this passage Maimonides promises that any human being whatsoever who devotes himself or herself to God will become as sanctified as the holy of holies. Following immediately upon this text we find the eighth book of the *Mishneh Torah*, the "Book of [Temple] Service (*Avodah*)" which itself opens with "Laws of the Temple." The Temple, we have seen, will be rebuilt by the Messiah.[46] Contextualizing our passage in this fashion, it seems clear, supports my reading of it, not Rabbi Rappoport's.

Context is indeed a tricky thing. If we read our passage in light of the parallel discussion in the *Guide* (III.11),[47] my reading of Maimonides is strengthened, and Rabbi Rappoport's is weakened. Analyzing the afflictions from which humans suffer (most of which are self-inflicted, or inflicted by other humans), Maimonides discovers that the vast majority are the result of ignorance, ignorance which the prophet Isaiah promises will be overcome in the future. Let us recall the last sentence in the chapter:

> ...the cause of the abolition of these enmities, these discords, and these tyrannies, will the knowledge that men[48] will then have concerning the true reality of the deity. For it says: *They shall not hurt nor destroy in all My holy mountain; for the earth shall be full of the knowledge of the Lord, as the waters cover the sea* (Isaiah 11:9). Know this.

---

45 On my literal (and hence universalist) reading of this text see my: "Kotler."

46 See the fuller discussion of this point in *Judaism*, pp. 73-75.

47 I cite the text above, note 31.

48 The Arabic here is *al-nas*, which means human beings as such (cognate to the Hebrew *enosh*).

It is all human beings, and not just Jews, who will understand the truth of God's nature and who will therefore behave well on God's holy mountain; the whole world, and not just the Land of Israel, will be full of the knowledge of God. As I understand this passage, Maimonides teaches here that the whole Earth will be God's holy mountain. But, I must admit, Rabbi Rappoport could reply that one short chapter in the *Guide of the Perplexed* is not the appropriate context for determining the meaning of a passage in the *Mishneh Torah*. Alternatively, he might admit the relevance of the passage, while contesting my reading of it.[49]

Thus, seeking for a solution to the meaning of *dat ha-emet* in its context founders on the question of what that context is. We must look further to solve our problem.

It turns out that Rabbi Rappoport and I each 'darshan' (read midrashically) certain Maimonidean texts: he in one direction, me in another. This, I believe, is unavoidable. There *are* inconsistencies in Maimonides' writings.[50] The only

---

49 And, indeed, this seems to be the point of his footnote 70.

50 This is, of course, a huge issue. See my discussion in *Confrontation*, pp. xi and 15-16. Rabbi Yehonatan Simhah Blass, *Me-Nofet Zuf*, finds 136 contradictions in Maimonides' writings. Here, I do not have in mind the sorts of contradictions beloved of the Straussians, but, rather, contradictions of the following sort. The eleventh of Maimonides' 'Thirteen Principles' is divine reward and punishment. (Maimonides ignores this issue in his restatement of the Principles in the third chapter of "Laws of Repentance" but that is easily explained.) In every place but one, Maimonides' accounts of divine reward and punishment can be easily made to accord with the philosophical view, according to which there is no actual reward for the fulfillment of the commandments or actual punishment for their violation; rather, the only true reward is survival of the intellect after death, a consequence of intellectual perfection, not a reward for obedience to the commandments. For a discussion of this view, see my *Must*, pp. 149-164. But in one place, his commentary to the end of Tractate Makkot in the Mishnah (III.17), Maimonides explicitly states that it is a foundation of faith in the Torah that if one fulfills any single one of the six hundred thirteen commandments "appropriately, as they ought to be fulfilled, without associating with this fulfillment any this-worldly goal at all, but fulfilled the commandment for its own sake (*lishmah*), out of love, as I have explained to you," that person will merit a share in the world to come. Of course, I have no trouble interpreting this text according to the philosophic view (especially with its mention of obedience to commandments out of love, since love of God for Maimonides is a function of intellectual perfection), but it is still certainly a nonliteral interpretation which many will find forced. Another example of the sort of contradiction I have in mind is between *Guide* III.17 (and elsewhere), where providence is presented as attaching only to individuals and being consequent upon intellectual perfection, on the one hand, vs. *Treatise on Resurrection* (Sheilat, p. 370), the one place in his writings where Maimonides affirms special providence over the nation of Israel. A third example relates to the question of miracles in the messianic era: in "Laws of Kings" Maimonides denies that there will be any, in "Epistle to Yemen" he appears to affirm that there will be. As Maimonides tells in *Guide* II.25, the gates of interpretation are never closed, and one can certainly solve these contradictions, but it involves what I have

way to arrive at a consistent reading of his writings is to interpret some in the light of others. Thus, while admitting that in some places in Maimonides' writings the term *dat ha-emet* refers to 'Judaism' and while admitting that there are other medieval authorities who apparently support my universalist reading of Maimonides in "Laws of Kings,"[51] Rabbi Rappoport feels constrained to 'darshan' the passages in Maimonides' writings which do not accord with his understanding of what Maimonides must have meant to be teaching about the messianic era. In turn, I do the same thing, but in the opposite direction. As I have already stated, I do not believe that the issue can be settled textually. Rather, the question between us is not over how to read this that or the other specific text, but why it is that my Maimonides looks forward to a messianic era characterized by universalism and Rabbi Rappoport's Maimonides does not. I will not presume to answer on Rabbi Rappoport's behalf, and will devote the rest of this chapter to showing why it makes sense to read Maimonides as I do.

Maimonides is deadly serious when he defines human beings as rational animals and sees in their rationality that which makes them creatures made in God's image. In consequence of this definition, he is locked into a view of human perfection as intellectual.[52] This, in turn, forces him to accept the idea that the key to survival after death is cognition of the intelligibles. This view of what constitutes our humanity deeply affects Maimonides' understanding the nature of Torah and commandments. Jews are humans who happen to be descended from Abraham (biologically or spiritually)[53] while it is Abraham who happened to be the first human after the loss of world-wide monotheism during the time of Enosh who realized that the world had to have a Creator and Guide.[54] The Torah brought by Moses to Abraham's biological and spiritual descendents is ultimately meant for all humanity. [55] One consequence of

---

been calling the darshening of Maimonides' texts, in one direction or another.

51 The text cited by Rabbi Rappoport from RaN is particularly telling. Given his use of the verse from Zephaniah, which shows up in a crucial (and censored) point in Maimonides' discussion, it is likely that RaN interpreted Maimonides as I do.

52 Maimonides' position is actually more nuanced than often thought. For details, see ch. 4 above, "Is Maimonides' Ideal Person…"

53 For an important study of Maimonides' unusual attitude towards proselytes (spiritual descendents of Abraham), see Diamond, *Converts*, ch. 1.

54 "Laws of Idolatry," chapter one.

55 For rabbinic background to this idea, see the studies by Hirshman, above, note 10.

these positions is that Maimonides can have no reason for thinking that once all human beings have each achieved the highest level of understanding possible to them, that the distinction between Jew and Gentile will be preserved. That, in brief, is why I read his vision of the messianic era universally.

Let me make a number of assumptions clear. I assume that everyone reading this chapter is convinced that the cultural, ethnic, national, and linguistic matrices in which we are raised or with which we choose to identify are indissoluble parts of our personalities. It is hard for me to see how such an idea could have made sense to a twelfth-century neo-Platonically Aristotelian rabbi such as Maimonides. I also assume that most of the people reading this chapter can at least make sense of a pluralist notion of "different strokes for different folks" even in matters of religion. I am far from convinced that religious pluralism of any sort would make sense to Maimonides. For him, truth is one, unchanging, absolute and universal. While he would certainly understand a notion of different levels of understanding the one truth, I doubt that he would be happy with talk of different paths to that one truth.

There is any number of reasons why one might want to reject my universalistic approach to Maimonides:

- It takes his philosophical concerns seriously

- It commits us to reading the *Mishneh Torah* in the light of the philosophy Maimonides accepted

- It leads to imputing to him a thorough-going universalism, denying any essential difference between Jew and Gentile as such

- It leads to aligning him with Rabbi Yishma'el vs Rabbi Akiva on the question of to whom was the Torah given – to all humans, or just the Jews?

- It leads to imputing to him an instrumental view of the commandments; on this reading the commandments of the Torah are tools which enable us to reach our true perfection, which is constituted by understanding the cosmos and its Creator to the greatest extent possible

This in turn leads to the denial of any concrete reward for fulfillment of the commandments or punishment for violating them; the only true reward is survival of the intellect after the death of the body, but this is a *consequence* of certain actions, not a *reward* for them[56]

In a very real sense enjoying divine providence and surviving the death of the body on this view result from intellectual attainments, not from obedience to the commandments of the Torah in particular

It is a deeply elitist view

Let us assume for a moment that Maimonides indeed defines human beings as rational animals and that the various consequences listed above do indeed follow from that position. On what grounds might we reject the definition and the consequences that follow from it? We might, of course, simply say that no good rabbinic Jew could conceivably hold the positions here attributed to Maimonides and leave it at that.[57] We might take a more responsible approach and try to show how the texts on which these interpretations of Maimonides are based can and ought to be read differently.[58] We might propose that Maimonides says the things here attributed to them, but read him 'politically', i.e., affirm that he did not mean them.[59] We could say that Maimonides indeed defines human be-

---

56 Me'iri well understood this distinction. See his *Hibbur ha-Teshuvah* (New York, 5710) pp. 441 and 541. My thanks to Marc Shapiro for drawing my attention to these passages. For a full discussion of the issue, see my *Must*, pp. 149-163.

57 I am reminded here of a story my late father told me. In the 1930's he served as a rabbi in Miami, Florida, then a Jewish backwater. Unusual for an Orthodox rabbi, and under the influence of my American-born and raised mother my parents kept a pet dog. Their home in Miami was a small bungalow and my father told me that once he was sitting in the front room when a hungry yeshiva emissary, looking for a kosher meal, walked up to the door. My father told me that he overheard the following soliloquy: "I know this to be the home of Reb Avraham Kellner, whom I know to be an *ehrliche Yid* (an upright Jew). But I see sitting here on the front stoop, looking very much at home, what appears to be a dog, something which is inconceivable in the home of an *ehrliche Yid*. So, either Rabbi Kellner is not an *ehliche Yid*, or this is not a dog. But Rabbi Kellner is well known to be an *ehrliche Yid*, so this must not be a dog!" At which point our hungry emissary knocked on the door. Many people have said: "No *ehrliche Yid* could possibly hold the positions academics like Menachem Kellner attribute to Rambam; ergo, Rambam does not hold those positions."

58 Rabbi Yehonatan Blass (above, note 50) attempts to read Maimonides as if he fit well into the mainstream of what might be called standard contemporary rabbinic theology. To my mind, his attempt is, to put it mildly, unsuccessful.

59 This is basically the view I find in Responsum 45 of Rivash (Rabbi Isaac Bar Sheshet Perfet, 1326-1408). See Kellner, "Rabbi Isaac Bar Sheshet."

ings as rational animals, but that he was unaware of or uninterested in the consequences of that position. We might say that he was simply inconsistent.

For reasons which would take a book to explain,[60] I reject these various approaches to reading Rambam and insist that we pay him the courtesy of taking what he says seriously. What I mean is the following. We can decide that Maimonides fits seamlessly into the rabbinic tradition as it developed before him and continued to develop after him.[61] If we adopt this view, we will be forced to ignore or 'darshen' those passages in Maimonides which do not fit with the interpretation advanced here.[62] There is a sense in which for many Orthodox Jews this is the only possible approach to our issue: adopting what is essentially a static view of Torah,[63] they feel that it is somehow un-Orthodox to acknowledge that Jewish tradition has a history, that there are serious and profound debates about the nature of Torah within the tradition, and that great rabbis like Maimonides could have been influenced in their understanding of Torah by 'outsiders' like Aristotle and Alfarabi.[64] As I understand him, Maimonides played a pivotal role in effecting change in the history of the Jewish tradition (by placing it on a firm dogmatic footing); he rejected mystical understandings of the nature of Torah to the extent that he might have been tempted to agree with the late Yeshayahu Leibowitz and condemn as heretics all Kabbalists (including, emphatically, Nahmanides); and he preached a Torah influenced by Greeks and Muslims (not that he was aware of that – he was convinced that the Greeks and Muslims from whom he learned were teaching doctrines originally taught by the Torah and forgotten by the Jews).[65]

So, the task before me becomes to show:

- That Maimonides did define human beings as rational animals

---

60 Indeed, I wrote that book: *Confrontation*.

61 Of course what we take to be the main contours of that tradition is itself a matter of debate, as pointed out in the first and last chapters of *Confrontation*, but we can leave that aside for the moment.

62 There is, of course, a long history of that. See, for example, "Kotler."

63 On static vs. dynamic views of Torah in rabbinic thought, see Fisch, *Rational Rabbis* and Silman, *Kol Gadol*.

64 I cite these two in particular because of Maimonides' comments in his introduction to his 'Eight Chapters' as elucidated by Davidson in "Maimonides' *Shemonah Peraqim*.

65 For the history of this notion, see Melamed, *Al Kitfei Anakim*.

- That such a definition leads to the universalist positions I attribute to him

- That among these positions is the claim that all humans will worship God from a stance of complete religious equality by the time that the messianic era reaches its fruition

What does it mean to affirm that Maimonides defines human beings as rational animals? In terms of our genus, we are animals. Our specific difference, that which distinguishes us from all other members of the animal kingdom, is our rationality. Everything that is not a direct reflection of rational thought –hopes and fears, love and hates, desires, needs, passions– is a consequence of our animal nature. In his earliest work, *Treatise on Logic*, Maimonides wrote: "Rationality we call man's difference, because it divides and differentiates the human species from others; and this rationality, i.e. the faculty by which ideas are formed, constitutes the essence of man."[66] Thus, a person born of human parents is not human just by virtue of that birth; rather, "It behooves him who prefers to be a human being in truth, not a beast having the shape and configuration of a human being, to endeavor to diminish all the impulses of matter-- such as eating, drinking, copulation, anger, and all the habits consequent upon desire and anger, to be ashamed of them, and to set for them limits in his soul" (*Guide of the Perplexed*, III.8, pp 433-434).

The *Guide of the Perplexed* is full of consequences of this position. The very first chapters of the work make no sense unless one understands Maimonides as defining humans as rational animals. Humans are there said to have been created in the image of God only because of "the intellect that God made overflow unto man and that is the latter's ultimate perfection" (I.2, p. 24). It is consequence of this view of the nature of the divine image which humans can, through much effort, actualize in themselves[67] that Maimonides writes in I.51 that "being a rational animal is the essence and true reality of man" (p. 113).[68]

---

66 *Treatise on Logic*, pp. 51-52.

67 Maimonides thus sees being created in the image of God as a challenge, not an endowment.

68 See Michael Schwarz's note in his Hebrew translation of the *Guide*, p. 116, note 7. Tel Aviv University Press is to be commended for its decision to make this magnificent contribution to Jewish and human culture available on the internet [http://press.tau.ac.il/perplexed/]. See further *Guide* I.52 (pp. 114, 116), II.48 (p. 422), III.8 (p. 432), III.12 (p. 444), and III.14 (p. 458).

How does one do this? It consists in one's "knowing everything concerning all beings that it is within the capacity of man to know in accordance with his ultimate perfection" (III.27, p. 511). This perfection is purely intellectual; Maimonides continues: "It is clear that to this ultimate perfection there do not belong either actions or moral qualities..."[69]

Maimonides has little occasion in his non-philosophical writings explicitly to affirm the definition of human beings as rational animals.[70] But in these writings he consistently affirms an important consequence of that definition: to the extent that humans achieve immortality[71] this is due solely to their intellectual achievements.[72] All that survives death is what we have learned. This is a position that Maimonides espouses in all his major writings. The point is made in his commentary on the Mishnah,[73] in the *Mishneh Torah*,[74] and in the *Guide of the Perplexed*.[75] Viewing existence in the world to come in these terms, it is no surprise that Maimonides made fulfillment of the commandments of the Torah in particular and moral behavior in general only prerequisites for achieving a share in the world to come, not guarantors of it.[76] One

---

69 In that Maimonides defines humans as rational animals (i.e. humans belong to the genus 'animal', and to the species 'rational'), if language is a property by which humans are distinguished from all other animals, it must be intimately connected to rationality. Thus, it is no surprise that in Tibbonian Hebrew (following Arabic precedents) the term 'rational animal' is translated *hai medabber* (literally, speaking living being); see, for example, in Samuel ibn Tibbon's translation of the *Guide* I. 51, I. 52, III. 48, and III. 12. Ibn Tibbon makes this explicit in his *Perush hamilot hazarot, alef* (s.v. *ma'amorot–gader), heh* (s.v. *higayon*), and *kaf* (s.v. *ko'ah medaber*).

70 He does make the claim explicitly towards the end of the Introduction to his Commentary on the Mishnah. Sheilat, p. 57.

71 There is considerable debate among Maimonides' contemporary academic interpreters over whether or not humans can actually achieve immortality ("a share in the world to come") or not. For a recent contribution to the debate (with references to earlier studies), see Stern, "Maimonides' Epistemology ."

72 Other consequences of Maimonides' view of human perfection which find expression in the *Guide* are that providence and prophecy depend upon intellectual perfection. For discussion see my *Judaism*, ch. 4.

73 Sanhedrin, Introduction to *Perek Helek*. In the dual-language (Arabic/Hebrew) edition of Rabbi J. Kafih, vol. 4, p. 204.

74 "Laws of the Foundations of the Torah," IV.9, "Laws of Repentance," VIII.2-3, and "Laws of Phylacteries," VI.13.

75 I.30 (p. 63), I.40 (p. 90), I.41 (p. 91), I.70 (p. 174), I.72 (p. 193, implicitly), I. 74 (p. 220), III.8 (pp. 432-33), III.27 (p. 511), III.51 (p. 628), and III.54 (p. 635).

76 For Maimonides moral perfection is a necessary, but not sufficient, pre-requisite for intellectual perfection. See above, ch. 11, "The Virtue of Faith." Charles Manekin suggests the

must be a decent and disciplined human being in order to achieve any level of intellectual perfection. The Torah is the best, but not the only, route to achieve such decency and discipline.

Our issue is not entirely absent from Maimonides' rabbinic writings. The Talmud (Berakhot 17a) states: "In the world to come there is no eating, drinking, washing, anointing, or sexual intercourse; but the righteous sit with their crowns on their heads enjoying the radiance of the divine presence." Maimonides glosses this text on a number of occasions. In his commentary to *Helek* he explains: "The [rabbinic] expression, 'crowns on their heads' signifies the existence of the soul through the existence of that which it knows, in that they are the same thing, as the experts in philosophy have maintained..." He repeats the point in "Laws of Repentance" VIII.2 (pp. 90a-b). It is, I believe, worth citing the full text:

> In the world to come there is nothing corporeal, and no material substance; there are only the souls of the righteous without bodies, – like the ministering angels. And since in that world there are no bodies, there is neither eating there, nor drinking, nor aught that human beings need on earth. None of the conditions occur there which are incident to physical bodies in this world, such as sitting, standing, sleep, death, sadness, joy, etc. So the ancient sages said, "in the world to come there is no eating, drinking, washing, anointing, or sexual intercourse; but the righteous sit with their crowns on their heads enjoying the radiance of the divine presence" (Berakhot 17a). This passage clearly indicates that there is no corporeal existence there, since there is no eating or drinking there. The phrase, "the righteous sit" is allegorical and means that the souls of the righteous exist there without fatigue or labor. The phrase, "their crowns on

---

following analogy (in a letter which I paraphrase here): "To be a physicist one has to know math. Without knowing math, no matter how much physics one has managed to learn, one is not a physicist. And yet, knowing math is not part of being a physicist *per se*; it is not what distinguishes physicists from, say, mathematicians. In Maimonides' (and Gersonides') world, there can be no "Nazi scientists", although there can be Nazis who practice science. For true science entails morality. Morality is not something one can shed; if one does, one loses one's knowledge." My friend Avram Montag (a real physicist, as opposed to a metaphysicist) is uncomfortable with this analogy, since, he says, without knowing significant amounts of math, one can know very little physics. He prefers Jacob Bronowski's argument in *Knowledge and Imagination* that a certain level of honesty, integrity, and even morality is required if one is to make progress in science. Bronowski claims that nothing came out of the Nazi's horrible experiments on prisoners.

their heads" refers to the knowledge they know, by virtue of which they merited life in the world to come, which knowledge exists with them. This is their "crown"… And what is the meaning of "enjoying the radiance of the divine presence"? – that they know and apprehend of the truth of the Holy One, blessed be He, what they did not know when in their murky and lowly body.

Maimonides' point here is to insist that the world to come (i.e., the world that comes immediately after death to those who earn it) is entirely incorporeal. The righteous exist there without bodies, as do the angels;[77] there is therefore no eating or drinking in the world to come. Nothing that pertains to bodily existence, such as sitting, standing, sleeping, death, sadness or joy, occurs there; it is against that background that Maimonides cites the Talmud in Berakhot. The Talmud there cites the dictum as "a favorite saying of Rav," while Maimonides cites it in the name of the "Early Sages,"[78] conveying the impression that it is the generally accepted view of the Sages.[79] The text states:

In the future world there is no eating nor drinking nor propagation[80] [nor business nor jealousy nor hatred nor competition,][81] but the righteous sit with their crowns on their heads enjoying the radiance of the divine presence [as it says, *And they beheld God, and did eat and drink*].[82]

This text presents problems for Maimonides. First, the passage states that the righteous *sit* in the world to come. Maimonides explains that to mean that they exist without any effort. Second, the passage says that the righteous have

---

77 Maimonides' angels are a far cry from the common understanding of them. See *Confrontation*, ch. 8 and Diamond, *Converts*, pp. 214-218.

78 The standard term for *Hazal*, the Talmudic rabbis, in Maimonides' writings.

79 This is not the only place where Maimonides adopts this tactic; he does the same thing when he attributes to the generality of the Sages the view of the Amora Samuel that the only difference between this world and the next is political subjugation. Isaac Abravanel takes him to task for this in his *Yeshu'ot Meshiho*, Part II, *Iyyun* 3, Chapter 7, p. 157.

80 Maimonides has *tashmish*, our standard texts have *piryeh ve-reviyah*

81 These words are missing from Maimonides' text.

82 Ex 24:11. These words are missing from Maimonides' text. I follow the Soncino translation here, with minor emendations. Given Maimonides' attitude towards the Elders of Israel referred to in this verse, it is not surprising that he leaves out this part of the Talmudic text. See *Guide of the Perplexed* I.5, *Confrontation*, pp. 52-54, Regev, "Vision of the Nobles," and Levene, "Maimonides' Philosophical Exegesis." Isaac Abravanel wrote a whole book, *Ateret Zekenim*, defending the Elders from Maimonides' strictures.

crowns on their *heads*. This, Maimonides explains, means: the knowledge that they knew, *because of which* they merited life in the world to come, remains with them, and is their crown.

This passage is one of many examples from his rabbinic writings in which Maimonides accepts what came to be known as the theory of the acquired intellect. The technical philosophical issues need not detain us here; it is enough to say that according to this theory all human beings are born with a potential to know and that only those who actualize that potential are fully and truly human and achieve a share in the world to come.[83]

Defining human beings the way he does, Maimonides has no way of distinguishing Jews from Gentiles on any level but that of history, belief, and behavior. Since the middle ages various Jewish thinkers have sought ways to distinguish Jews from Gentiles in some ontologically significant way. Judah Halevi asserted that Jews only had what he called *al-amr al-ilahi*, which made it possible for native-born Jews alone to aspire to prophecy. The Zohar teaches that the souls of Jews derive from a higher, more spiritual level of the sefirot than do the souls of Gentiles.[84] The Maharal of Prague thought that with the giving of the Torah at Sinai the image of God in Gentiles was diminished.[85] The founder of Habad held that the souls of Gentiles were cruder than those of Jews.[86] One could multiply these unfortunate examples without end.[87]

As noted above, Maimonides will have none of this, and, given his philosophical anthropology (to use fancy language), he can have none of it.

We may now turn to the third point I promised to discuss above. Let us assume that all that I have written here is correct (and it is!). Why must that entail the claim that all humans will worship God from a stance of complete

---

83 For a fuller discussion see *Confrontation*, pp. 223-229. Isaac Abravanel and Shem Tov ibn Shem Tov, both opponents of the theory, had no problem attributing it to Maimonides; see *Confrontation*, p. 226, note 29.

84 See Hallamish, "Attitude to the Nations" and Wolfson, *Venturing Beyond*. Yehudah (Jerome) Gellman has recently examined the issue with sensitivity and sophistication in "Jewish Mysticism and Morality."

85 *Derekh ha-Haim* III.14 (end), *Gur Aryeh* on Ex. 19:22, and other places. See Kleinberger, *Ha-Mahshavah*, pp. 37-42.

86 *Tanya*, end of I.1.

87 Even Rabbi Samson Raphael Hirsch held that Jews occupy a higher rung of humanity than Gentiles. See Breuer, *Modernity Within Tradition*, p. 27, cited by Shapiro, "Torah im Derekh Erez." p. 96, note 15.

religious equality by the time that the messianic era reaches its fruition? In other words, why can not Maimonides define humans as rational animals, reject the notion that there is any essential difference between Jew and Gentile, and yet continue to maintain that Jew and Gentile will remain distinct in the messianic era? In principle, there is no reason why Maimonides could not maintain such a position. The position is not incoherent but, I suggest, it simply makes no sense in a world in which Jews and Gentiles are all ruled by the same wise and exalted king, a world in which there is no essential distinction between Jew and Gentile and that fact is acknowledged by all, a world in which Gentiles admit that the Torah is true and its commandments are divine, a world in which the closing peroration of the *Mishneh Torah* is realized:

> In that time there will be neither famine nor war, neither jealousy nor strife. Good things will be abundant, and delicacies as common as dust. The one preoccupation of the whole world will be only to know the Lord. Hence [they] will be very wise, knowing things now unknown and will apprehend knowledge of their Creator to the utmost capacity of the human mind, as it is written: *For the land shall be full of the knowledge of the Lord, as the waters cover the sea* (Isaiah 11:9).

In that world one can be a follower of the Torah,[88] the one full complete and true religion, or, according to Rabbi Rappoport, one can settle for a pale, thin, stripped-down and essentially spiritually empty[89] set of Noachide laws.[90] In a world in which all humans achieve knowledge of the Creator to the greatest extent possible to them, a world in which all humans live on God's holy mountain, a world in which evil and violence are banished because the knowledge of God fills the earth as the waters cover the sea, why would any person alive

---

88 I hesistate to use the word 'Judaism' here, not only because it may be anachronistic vis-à-vis Maimonides, but because of its intimate connection to the Jewish people. It is my claim here that in the messianic era the link between Torah as *dat ha-emet* and the Jewish people as ethnic entity will be severed – all humans, whatever their ethnos, will adopt the *dat ha-emet*.

89 Technically, as Kreisel points out (p. 161), a Noachide is forbidden perform idolatry, but need not even be a theist!

90 Consider further: the punishment for the violation of any of the Noachide laws is execution ("Laws of Kings," IX.14). On the view that messianic Gentiles will be Noachides we would have a situation in which a Jew who steals must return the stolen item and pay a fine while a Gentile who steals even something of trifling value will be executed! I take this one fact to be a *reductio ad absurdum* of the idea that in Maimonides' messianic world Gentiles will remain Noachides and not adopt the full range of the Torah.

settle for less than the true and complete *dat ha-emet*?[91] Let us also recall that Maimonides held an unusually positive attitude, not only towards proselytes, but even towards *proselytizing* (responsum 149).[92] In that light, one can assume that in the messianic world he would expect the Jews to mount missions to any remaining Gentiles, Gentiles, who, it will be recalled, accept the truth of Torah in any event.

As long as I have brought up the issue of conversion,[93] note should be taken of an issue to which I originally drew attention in my book, *Maimonides on Judaism and the Jewish People* (pp. 42-43). In two places (Yev. 24b and AZ 3b) the Talmud states:

> "Our Rabbis taught: proselytes are not accepted in the days of the Messiah, just as proselytes were not accepted either in the days of David or in the days of Solomon."

Maimonides relates to this in the *Mishneh Torah* as follows ("Laws of Forbidden Intercourse," 13:15):

> "Therefore, throughout the days of David and Solomon, the court accepted no converts – in David's time because [the convert] might have been motivated by fear, and in Solomon's time because [the convert] might have been motivated by the benefits and grandeur of the Israelite kingdom."

It is reasonable to suggest that in the messianic era, when the whole world will be ruled by King Messiah, and truth of the Torah will be evident to all, that one might be led to suspect the sincerity of converts. Despite that, Maimonides refuses to accept as authoritative a rabbinic statement ruling out the possibility of conversion to Judaism in the messianic era. My explanation for that is that he expected (all) Gentiles to convert during the messianic era.

---

91 Kreisel (p. 153) makes the same point very well: "Why would Gentiles settle for anything less than the one true divine legislation, if they have come to realize the true purpose of life, and the role played by Mosaic law in attaining that purpose…and finally have no other religious option, at least no other complete religious law that can be considered divine?"

92 See Diamond, *Converts*, ch. 1.

93 Actually, Rabbi Rapport brings it up in his footnote 71. He bases his discussion there on an alleged inconsistency in Maimonides. But, in point of fact, the inconsistency is not within Maimonides, but between Maimonides and the Talmud. I hope that the reader will find my discussion here more convincing than that of Rabbi Rappoport.

This brings up another point, to which Rabbi Hanan Balk of Cincinnati kindly drew my attention. The Talmud (Sanh. 58b-59a) teaches that a Gentile may not study Torah (other than the seven Noachide commandments) – on pain of death. Maimonides codifies this as law in "Laws of Kings," X.9. In his responsa (no. 149) he was asked if this is indeed the law, and that a Jew is forbidden to teach any but the seven Noachide commandments to a Gentile. He answered: "It is the law without a doubt. When the hand of Israel is uppermost over them, we restrain him from studying Torah until he converts, but he is not to be killed if he studied Torah…." And then, notoriously, Maimonides goes on to add: "It is permissible to teach the commandments to Christians and attract them to our religion, but none of this is permissible to Muslims." Maimonides explains that, unlike Muslims, Christians accept the divine origin of the Torah, and it is therefore more likely that they will turn to the good way (*yahzeru la-mutav*). The Talmud relates to the study of Torah by Gentiles in another context: Hagigah 13a teaches that it is forbidden for a Jew to teach Torah to a Gentile. Unlike the prohibition from Sanhedrin which Maimonides codifies as law, this prohibition is simply ignored in the *Mishneh Torah*. This odd state of affairs has led to considerable discussion on the part of Maimonides' traditionalist interpreters.[94]

Pulling together the points about conversion discussed here, it seems obvious that if Maimonides expected the Gentiles to convert in the messianic era, he could hardly have forbidden teaching them Torah now – and he could not very well forbid it now before the coming of the Messiah and permit it after his coming. That must be the reason why he permits teaching Torah to Christians in the pre-messianic world.

Further considerations support my claim that for Maimonides, all humanity in the messianic era would accept the Torah fully. Maimonides was severely criticized for his account of the reasons for the commandments, an account which boils down to the claim that the commandments of the Torah serve one of two ends: to improve moral and social relations, or to correct philosophical mistakes. Maimonides says this quite explicitly in *Guide*, III.27. The commandments of the Torah, therefore, have a relative, not absolute advantage over other systems of ethics and philosophy. But that relative advantage is great, since the commandments were ordained by God (Who obviously knows our

---

94 For discussion, see Novak, *Maimonides on Judaism*.

creaturely natures far better than any human legislator or philosopher).[95] Maimonides is also quite explicit in his repeated claims that one cannot achieve intellectual perfection unless one antecedently achieved a high level of moral perfection – no physicists like Einstein (who abandoned his first family) or (and I do not mean to equate the two) philosophers like Heidegger (who never expressed regret for his support of the Nazis) for Maimonides![96] One of the commandments which play a direct role in the achievement of moral perfection is circumcision.[97] As Maimonides says in *Guide*, III.49 (p. 609):

> Similarly with regard to *circumcision*, one of the reasons for it is, in my opinion, the wish to bring about a decrease in sexual intercourse and a weakening of the organ in question, so that this activity be diminished and the organ be in as quiet a state as possible. ... In fact this *commandment* has not been prescribed with a view to perfecting what is defective congenitally, but perfecting what is defective morally. ... violent concupiscence and lust that goes beyond what is needed are diminished.

If all humans are going to devote themselves to the knowledge of God when the messianic era reaches its fruition, how could Maimonides possibly expect that Gentiles would remain uncircumcised, and thus at a disadvantage in curbing their passions, which, in turn, leaves them at a disadvantage in seeking to know God?

Furthermore, circumcision for Maimonides is, as Shaye Cohen aptly puts it, "a sign of membership in the covenant of Abraham, the league of those who believe in the unity of God" (p. 152).[98] All humans in the messianic era will be members of that league – does it make sense to think that Maimonides would not expect them to bear the mark of that covenant? It should also be borne in mind in this context that in "Laws of Kings," X.7 Maimonides writes that "he alone is a descendent of Abraham who holds fast to his religion and honest way, and they alone are obligated to be circumcised." If Arabs in the

---

95 All these claims are supported in *Confrontation*, chapter two.

96 For texts and discussion, see *Confrontation*, p. 63, note 71.

97 See Stern, "Covenant of Circumcision," and "Parable of Circumcision." My thinking here was stimulated by reading S. Cohen's stimulating *Why Aren't Jewish Women Circumcised?* chapters 6 and 7.

98 See further, Kasher, " Circumcision."

---

pre-messianic world are obligated to perform circumcision, how much more so will all humanity in the messianic world be so obligated, a world in which all human beings will hold fast to Abrahamic monotheism?

As my friend and student Yisrael Ben-Simon pointed out to me, this argument ought to be generalized. The commandments of the Torah are the best way for human beings to achieve their full potential as human beings in that they are the best route to preparing us to perfect ourselves intellectually. It is simply inconceivable that in a world in which all human beings strive to perfect their knowledge of God (and thus reach the highest possible level of human perfection to which each person can separately aspire) that Gentiles would be left at the tremendous disadvantage of only being called upon to fulfill the Noachide commandments.

According to Maimonides all humanity will adopt *dat ha-emet* by the time the messianic era reaches fruition. The *dat* in question can refer either to the Torah of Noah, to the Torah of Abraham, or to the Torah of Moses. Rabbi Rappoport thinks it refers to the Torah of Noah; I am convinced that it refers to the Torah of Moses. He and I both agree that Maimonides did not mean the Torah of Abraham. Because text and context are not conclusive Rabbi Rappoport cannot prove his position textually any more that I can. Therefore, we must approach the issue philosophically and ask which position coheres best with Maimonides' overall view of Torah and humanity? I have shown here that Maimonides, who believed that *all* human beings are equally created in the image of God and that the part of us which is Godlike is our ability to reason, could not and would not hope for a messianic era in which Jews and Gentiles remain distinct.

I am very aware of the fact that according to this reading of Maimonides, all humans in the messianic era will obey the commandments of the Torah (including the festivals and holidays marking events in Jewish history) despite that most of them (at least in the first generation) will have no personal Jewish memory or identity. To rephrase this point in modern terms, for Maimonides Jewish ethnicity is accidental, not essential, to Judaism. Although this may sound surprising to some of my readers, it actually accords well with Maimonides' dogma-centered notion of what constitutes Jewish identity, and with the positions put forward in his letter to Obadiah the Proselyte. That Maimonides adopts surprising positions should not, after all, be surprising.

CHAPTER NINETEEN
Spirituality and a Life of Holiness –
How One Lives a Holy Life and Who Can Do It

'S pirituality" is a word for which there is no counterpart in classical Hebrew. *Ruhaniut*, the word in modern Hebrew, is itself a translation of the English term. *Ruhaniut* is derived from *ru'ah*, which means breath or wind, and, derivately, spirit. It's first occurrence is at the very beginning of the Torah:

When God began to create heaven and earth —the earth being unformed and void, with darkness over the surface of the deep and a wind [ru'ah] from God sweeping over the water— God said, "Let there be light"; and there was light.[1]

By Maimonides' time *ru'ah* had developed a wide range of uses, including, very importantly, *ru'ah ha-kodesh*, the spirit of holiness (or, as more usually translated, "the holy spirit"), and, very differently, *ru-ah tum'ah*, the spirit of ritual impurity (often used to mean demons). The one meaning the word does not have in classical or even medieval Hebrew is "spiritual" in the sense of "spiritual life." The closest one can come to this expression, I think, in classical Judaism is "holy life."

Maimonides might not know how to answer us if we asked him whether he thought a Jew ought to lead a spiritual life, but if asked how a Jew ought to lead a holy life, he would have an answer, an answer I shall elucidate here. Furthermore, the holy life, he would say, both makes possible and is itself made possible by true love of God. We shall, therefore, examine what Maimonides teaches on the inter-related questions of how to live the holy life, and how to love God.

---

1 Gen. 1:1-3. The relevant phrase (*a wind from God sweeping over the water*) is more traditionally translated as: *And the spirit of the Lord hovered over the face of the waters.*

At the outset it will be useful to distinguish three different views of holiness.[2] On one view, holiness is an essential feature of certain places, people, objects, or times; on this view, holiness is "hard-wired" into parts of the universe. Judah Halevi (d. 1141) held this view, at least with respect to the holiness of the Land of Israel, the holiness of the commandments, and with respect to the special character of the Jewish People, the "holy nation."

In addition to certain things being holy from the very moment of creation, Halevi also held that holiness can be conferred from without, but not on every person, place, thing, or time. This appears to be the brunt of the following passage from Halevi's *Kuzari* (III.53): "Actions [prescribed] by the religious Law," Halevi maintains, when properly performed, have actual, not "only" statuatory or institutional consequences:[3]

> when it has been completed in the proper way, and you see the heavenly fire, or discover another spirit within yourself, which you did not know [beforehand], or [you witness] veridical dreams and miracles, you know that they are the result of all you did before and of the mighty order with which you have come into contact and which you have [now actually] attained.[4]

Halevi holds that proper fulfillment of the commandments of the Torah thus brings about real change in the universe. On his view, holiness can inhere in certain things, not in others; just as non-Jews cannot prophesy, so not everything can be or become holy. The substrate makes a difference.

On a second view, the universe, as it were, starts out all of a piece, at least with respect to holiness. At various times God renders times, places, or objects holy. This is certainly one way of reading verses such as *And God blessed the seventh day and declared it holy, because on it God ceased from all the work of creation that He had done* (Gen. 2:3). A reasonable way of understanding this

---

2   I am deeply grateful to Prof. Joshua Golding for helping me to think through this issue; he is no way responsible for the use to which I put his insights here!

3   I put the word "only" in scare quotes to emphasize that on the view I find in Maimonides, holiness is, indeed, "only" institutional, but still extremely important; but as Halevi would understand him, Maimonides' view makes holiness *only* institutional, i.e., relatively unimportant.

4   I cite the translation of Barry Kogan, forthcoming in the Yale Judaica Series. I wish to thank Prof. Kogan for his collegial generosity in sharing the translation with me prior to publication.

and similar verses is that God took a day like every other day (the seventh) and rendered it sacred, changing its nature from that time on.

An example of the second view, it appears to me, may be found in the kabbalistic commentary of R. Hayyim ben Moses Attar (1696-1743) to the Torah, *Or Ha-Hayyim* (on Nu. 19:2). According to R. Hayyim, before receiving the Torah the Jews were like any other people; upon accepting the Torah they became ontologically distinct (my language, not his!) from all other nations. R. Hayyim writes: "The distinction by virtue of which the Jewish People were elevated above the other nations is the acceptance of the Torah, for without it, the House of Israel would be like all the other nations." In the sentences which follow R. Hayyim makes it very clear that the Jews are distinguished from non-Jews on a very basic, spiritually fundamental level. After Sinai, the Jews are ontologically distinct from Gentiles, even if before Sinai they were not.[5]

Both these views share in common the idea that however it becomes holy, a holy place, person, time, or object is, once holy, objectively different from profane places, persons, times, and objects. On both these views, holiness is real, it inheres in sacred places, etc., it is intrinsic to them; it is, one might say, part of their metaphysical make-up. I will characterize them both, therefore, as "ontological" or "essentialist" views of the nature of holiness. Holy places, persons, times, and objects are ontologically distinct from (and religiously superior to) profane places, persons, times, and objects. This distinction is part of the universe.

Let me try to make this point clearer with an analogy. Radioactivity existed before Geiger discovered a way to measure it. Similarly, holiness exists in holy places, persons, times, and objects, even though there is no way for us (presently) to measure it. It is "out there," a feature of the objectively real world, even if not part of the world susceptible to laboratory examination.

There is a third view of holiness in the thought of Moses Maimonides. On this view holiness cannot be characterized as ontological or essentialist since holy places, persons, times, and objects are in no objective way distinct from profane places, persons, times, and objects; holiness is a status, not a quality of existence. It is a challenge, not a given; normative, not descriptive. It is insti-

---

5 For a discussion of different views on the nature of the distinction between Jew and Gentile, see *Confrontation*, ch. 7.

tutional (in the sense of being part of a system of laws) and hence contingent. This sort of holiness does not reflect objective reality, it helps constitute social reality. On this view, holy places, persons, times, and objects are indubitably holy, and must be treated with all due respect, but they are, in and of themselves, like all other places, persons, times, and objects. What is different about them is the way in which the Torah commands that they be treated.

It will be useful to begin our analysis of Maimonides' views on holy living by glancing at the biblical and rabbinic evidence. What is called holy in the Torah? First and foremost, obviously, God. In a text which was to have profound influence on Jewish liturgy, the prophet Isaiah wrote (6:1-3):

> In the year that King Uzziah died, I beheld my Lord seated on a high and lofty throne; and the skirts of His robe filled the Temple. Seraphs stood in attendance on Him. Each of them had six wings: with two he covered his face, with two he covered his legs, and with two he would fly. And one would call to the other, "Holy, holy, holy! The Lord of Hosts! His glory fills all the earth!"

God is also called "the Holy One of Israel" some fifteen times in the Bible. God's being the Holy One *of* Israel has direct consequences (Lev. 11:44-45):

> For I the Lord am your God: you shall sanctify yourselves and be holy, for I am holy. You shall not make yourselves unclean through any swarming thing that moves upon the earth. For I the Lord am He who brought you up from the land of Egypt to be your God: you shall be holy, for I am holy.

Verses such as this, and others, like *Speak to the whole Israelite community and say to them: You shall be holy, for I, the Lord your God, am holy* (Lev. 19:2), admit, it seems to me, of very different interpretations. One of way of looking at them is to see them as teaching that God is holy and through the process of election Israel also becomes holy. Just as God's holiness is essentialist, so also is Israel's.

But these verses also admit of a different interpretation, the one held by Maimonides. On this interpretation, Israel is holy when it behaves in certain ways. Holiness on this view is a challenge, and not a gift.[6] I am not making

---

6   Even 2 Sam. ch. 6 and 1 Chron. ch. 13, often understood as teaching that the ark of the covenant had some sort of inherent and dangerous holiness, do not teach that. Uzzah's death was not an automatic consequence of his having touched the holy ark, but was a *punishment* by God for having done so. Similarly with the account in 1 Sam 5: the sufferings of the

any claims about the way in which the authors of the biblical books actually understood holiness; rather, I am pointing out that their words are ambiguous and not only can be but have been interpreted in very different ways.

The same ambiguity may be found in the language of the opening formula of blessings ordinarily recited before the fulfillment of any positive commandment (as established by the Talmudic rabbis): "Blessed are You, Lord our God, Who has sanctified us with His commandments and commanded us to…" Following R. Hayyim ben Moses Attar, one can understand this language as affirming that the imposition of the commandments has made Israel intrinsically holy, or, on the other hand, as affirming that holiness is a consequence of fulfilling the commandments and that it means nothing more than that. Again, I am making no claims about what the Talmudic Sages intended when they instituted this formula (assuming they all intended the same thing by it, which I consider unlikely), rather, I want to show how Maimonides understood it.

Maimonides' position appears to follows from his consistent nominalism and from his insistence on the absolute transcendence of God. With respect to the first, he writes:

> After what I have stated about providence singling out the human species alone among all the species of animals, I say that it is known that no species exists outside the mind, but that the species and the other universals are, as you know, mental notions and that every existent outside the mind is an individual or group of individuals.[7]

Philistines were *inflicted* by God as punishment and warning. There is nothing of Indiana Jones in the biblical text itself.

7   *Guide* III.18, p. 474. Maimonides repeats the point at the end of the same chapter (p. 476): "It would not be proper for us to say that providence watches over the species and not the individuals, as is the well-known opinion of some philosophic schools. For outside the mind nothing exists except the individuals; it is to these individuals that the divine intellect is united. Consequently providence watches only over these individuals." Maimonides immediately continues: "Consider this chapter as it ought to be considered; for through it all the fundamental principles of the Law will become safe for you and conformable for you to speculative philosophic opinions; disgraceful views will be abolished…." Elisheva Oberman and Josef Stern first drew my attention to these passages. Alfred Ivry comments perceptively: "Maimonides, as a good Aristotelian and would-be nominalist, would like to 'save the phenomena' and not add to them immaterial entities of a conjectural and ultimately redundant sort." See Ivry, "Strategies," p. 116. Maimonides' nominalism affects other aspects of his thought. See Silman, "Halakhic Determinations," and Kellner, "Rabbis."

The implications of this position for our purposes here are far-reaching. Holiness cannot inhere in the people of Israel, for example, in any essential fashion since there is no such *thing* as the people of Israel, there are only individual Jews.[8] There can furthermore be no such thing as holiness as such, at most there can be sacred objects, places, times, and perhaps individuals. Nor can there be ritual purity as such, only ritually pure or impure objects, places, and individuals.[9]

It must be emphasized: Maimonides' philosophical nominalism does not amount to conventionalism. He may think that the difference between a holy object and a profane object is to be found, not "out there" in the world, but "only" in legal (halakhic) institutions, but that does not mean that he holds the difference to be a matter of social convention and nothing more. For Maimonides, halakhic institutions are grounded in the Torah, revealed by God to Moses at Sinai, as opposed to reflecting some objective aspect of reality itself.

It must be further emphasized: Maimonides was convinced that the Torah reflects the wisdom of a beneficent God. Thus, to take a simple example, eating kosher food is an halakhic requirement; but it is *also* good for you. One should keep kosher because of the command, not because of the benefit, but that does not mean that the benefit will not accrue. The Land of Israel is holy *and* it is a pleasant land, flowing with milk and honey.

It is crucial to emphasize also: holiness may exist "only" at the level of halakhic institutions, but that does not mean that a person who holds this view must be insensitive to the numinous experience of encountering a place or thing or person which she or he holds sacred. There is no reason to think that Maimonides did not prize such experiences. In short, a nominalist can also have religious experiences!

With respect to my claim about God's transcendence: the Torah obligates Jews to be holy, because God is holy (Lev. 19:2). Were that interpreted to mean that Jews (or sacred objects, times, and places) are or can be essentially holy, we would be saying that God and certain created entities share a characteristic, namely, the characteristic of holiness. This is something which Maimonides

---

8   In *Judaism*, I argue that Maimonides maintained that Jews as such were in no way intrinsically different from any other people. I did not connect that issue to his nominalism, as I do here and in *Confrontation*.

9   I defend many of these assertions in *Confrontation*.

repeatedly disallows.[10] Holiness, it follows, must be institutional, a matter of halakhic definition, not ontological, somehow actually in the universe.

So much for theoretical considerations. What does Maimonides himself actually say on the topic of holiness generally? [11] There are a small number of texts in which he explicitly addresses the definition of holiness. The most important of these, I think, is found in *Guide of the Perplexed* III.47 (pp. 595-596):

> As for His dictum, may He be exalted, *Sanctify yourselves therefore and be ye holy, for I am holy* (Lev. 11:44), it does not apply at all to ritual impurity and purity. Sifra states literally: This concerns sanctification by the commandments. For this reason, transgression of the commandments is also called ritual impurity... The term ritual impurity is used equivocally in three different senses: It is used of disobedience and of transgression of commandments concerning action or opinion; it is used of dirt and filth...and it is used according to these fancied notions, I refer to touching or carrying certain things or being under the same roof with certain things.[12] With reference to this last sense, we say: "The words of the Torah are not subject to becoming impure."[13] Similarly, the term holiness is used equivocally in three senses opposed to those three senses.

"Holiness," therefore, can mean one of three things:

a) obedience to the commandments concerning action or opinion

b) physical cleanliness

c) ritual purity

With respect to the first and second, it is readily apparent that there is nothing "essentialist" or "ontological" at stake here. When one obeys the Torah,

---

10 See the second and third of Maimonides' 'Thirteen Principles', "Laws of the Foundations of the Torah," I.8, and *Guide* I.54.

11 My thinking on the question of holiness in Maimonides was enriched by Harvey, "Holiness," Seeskin, "Maimonides' Conception," Seeskin, *Searching*, pp. 93-109, 115-123, and 134; Kreisel, *Political Thought*, pp. 50-53 and 151-156; and Silman, "Introduction"

12 I.e., matters of ritual purity and impurity are "fancied notions," having no objective correlates in the "real" world.

13 Berakhot 22a.

when one holds true views, one has achieved a state of holiness. When one is physically clean, one may be called holy. With respect to the third, Maimonides explicitly teaches that matters of ritual purity and impurity are institutional, not ontological:

> It is plain and manifest that the laws about ritual impurity and purity are decrees laid down by Scripture[14] and not matters about which human understanding is capable of forming a judgment; for behold, they are included among the divine statutes [*hukkim*].[15] So, too, immersion as a means of freeing oneself from ritual impurity is included among the divine statutes. *Now "ritual impurity" is not mud or filth which water can remove, but is a matter of scriptural decree and dependent upon intention of the heart.* Therefore the Sages have said, If a man immerses himself, but without special intention, it is as though he has not immersed himself at all. Nevertheless we may find some indication of all this: just as one who sets his heart on becoming ritually pure becomes so as soon as he has immersed himself, *although nothing new has befallen his body,* so, too, one who sets his heart on purifying himself from the impurity that besets men's souls – namely, evil thoughts and wicked moral qualities[16]– becomes pure as soon as he consents in his heart to shun those counsels and brings his soul into the waters of pure reason. Behold, Scripture says, *I will sprinkle pure water upon you, and you shall be pure: I will purify you from all your ritual impurity and from all your fetishes* (Ezek. 36:25). May God, in His great mercy, purify us from every sin, iniquity, and guilt. Amen.[17]

Could we ask for a clearer statement? Matters of ritual purity and impurity are decrees of the Torah, having no objective correlation in the "real" world. These laws reflect no objective reality, on any level or in any dimension; rather, they create social/halakhic reality.

---

14 *Gezerat ha-katuv.* On this expression see the discussion in Stern, *Problems*, pp. 49-66.

15 This statement is interesting in light of the claim made by Maimonides in the *Guide* that the divine statutes (*hukkim*) can be understood. On the whole issue see Stern, *Problems*.

16 *Deʿot raʿot.* For many reasons I would prefer to follow Herbert Danby and translate this as "false convictions" but I fear that would be incorrect. On the expression *deʿah* as "moral quality" in Maimonides, see *Guide* III.35, p. 535. For discussion, see Septimus, "*Madda.*"

17 "Laws of Immersion Pools," XI.12 (emphasis added). For an extended discussion of this passage see *Confrontation*, pp. 148-152.

Thus, if we take Maimonides at his word in *Guide of the Perplexed* III.47 "holiness" is the term used by the Torah to characterize obedience, cleanliness, or ritual purity. It refers to nothing which can actually and objectively inhere in entities, persons, places, or times. Now that we understand the nature of holiness in general, we may finally get to the point of our discussion and characterize the holy life as understood by Maimonides.

The fifth of the fourteen volumes of the *Mishneh Torah* is *Sefer Kedushah*, the "Book of Holiness." This volume contains three sections: "Laws of Forbidden Intercourse," "Laws of Forbidden Foods," and "Laws of [Kosher] Slaughtering." What do these three issues have in common? Maimonides explains in *Guide of the Perplexed* III.35: the purpose of the laws of forbidden foods, he tells us there,

> as we have explained in the Commentary on the *Mishnah* in the Introduction to *Aboth*,[18] is to put an end to the lusts and licentiousness manifested in seeking what is most pleasurable and to taking the desire for food and drink as an end.

The laws of forbidden intercourse, he also explains there, are designed (p. 537):

> to bring about a decrease of sexual intercourse and to diminish the desire for mating as far as possible, so that it should not be taken as an end, as is done by the ignorant, according to what we have explained in the Commentary on *Tractate Aboth.*

Maimonides does not explicitly explain the purpose of the laws concerning ritual slaughter here (indeed, he does not mention them at all in this passage in the *Guide of the Perplexed*), but it is not hard to see how they would fit into the rubric of forbidden foods.

Indeed, Maimonides makes this tolerably clear in his introduction to the *Mishneh Torah*, where he describes "The Book of Holiness" as follows (p. 18b):

---

18 Maimonides prefaced his commentary to the mishnaic tractate *Aboth* with an introduction consisting of eight chapters. This text is generally known as "The Eight Chapters of Maimonides"; the reference here is to the fourth of them.

The Fifth Book. It includes in it precepts having reference to illicit sexual unions, and those that relate to forbidden foods; because in these two regards, the Omnipresent sanctified us and separated us from the nations, and of both classes of precepts it is said, *And I have set you apart from the peoples* (Lev. 20:26), ...*Who have set you apart from the peoples* (Lev. 20:24). I have called this book: The Book of Holiness.

One achieves holiness by refraining from forbidden food and from forbidden sex.[19] That is why the laws concerning forbidden foods and the laws concerning ritual slaughtering (which turn certain classes of edibles from forbidden to permitted) are classed together in the "Book of Holiness."

Maimonides derives this connection between holiness and refraining from forbidden activies from a midrashic passage cited in the fourth introductory principle to his *Book of Commandments* (vol. 2, pp. 380-381):

We are not to include charges which cover the whole body of the commandments of the Torah. There are injunctions and prohibitions in the Torah which do not pertain to any specific duty, but include all commandments... With respect to this principle other scholars have erred, counting *You shall be holy* (Lev. 19:2) as one of the positive commandments – not knowing that the verses, *You shall be holy* (Lev. 19:2) [and] *Sanctify yourselves, and be you holy* (Lev. 11:44) are charges to fulfill the whole Torah, as if He were saying: "Be holy by doing all that I have commanded you to do, and guard against all things I have enjoined you from doing." The Sifra says: "*You shall be holy*, keep apart;" that is to say, hold aloof from all the abominations against which I have admonished you. In the Mekhilta the Sages say: "*And you shall be holy men unto Me* (Ex. 22:30) – Issi the son of Yehudah says: with every new commandment the Holy One, blessed be He, issues to Israel He adds holiness to them." That is to say, this charge is not an independent one, but is connected with the commandments wherein they have been enjoined there, since whoever fulfills that charge is called holy. Now this being so, there is then no difference between His saying, *You shall be holy*, and, "Obey My commandments."... The Sifre says: "*And you be holy* (Nu. 15:40), this refers to the holiness of the commandments."

---

19 Further on this connection, see "Laws of Moral Qualities," V.4 and *Guide*, III.33 (p. 533). Relevant also is "Laws of Forbidden Intercourse," XXII.20.

Maimonides explains here that the Biblical statement, *You shall be holy*, is not to be counted as one of the six hundred thirteen commandments of the Torah since it encompasses the whole Torah. While doing so, Maimonides lets slip, as it were, a point crucial to our purposes: Jews are not made holy by having been given the commandments, rather, they become holy when they fulfill them. That does not mean that as one fulfills commandments one's ontological status changes from profane to holy; rather, it means that "holiness" is the way in which the Torah characterizes obedience to the commandments. As Maimonides says at the end of the passage, holiness refers to the holiness of [fulfilling] the commandments.

Returning to the exposition of this passage, Maimonides cites the explanation of Midrash *Sifra* to *You shall be holy*: keep yourself apart or separate yourself from illicit enjoyments (*perishut* ["renunciation"]). From what in particular must one refrain in order to achieve holiness? In the *Mishneh Torah* Maimonides explains: forbidden foods and forbidden sex.

Maimonides connects the *perishut* spoken of here with the *Perushim*, or Pharisees, in "Laws of Ritual Impurity of Foods," XVI.12:

> Although it is permissible to eat ritually impure foodstuffs and to drink ritually impure liquids, the pious of former times used to eat their common food in conditions of ritual purity, and all their days they were wary of every ritual impurity. And it is they who were called Pharisees, "separated ones," and this is a higher holiness. It is the way of piety that a man keep himself separate and go apart from the rest of the people and neither touch them nor eat and drink with them. For separation leads to the purification of the body from evil deeds, and the purification of the body leads to the hallowing of the soul from evil thoughts, and the hallowing of the soul leads to striving for imitation of the Shekhinah [divine presence]; for it is said, *Sanctify yourselves therefore and be ye holy* (Lev. 11:44), *for I the Lord Who sanctify you am holy* (Lev. 21:8).[20]

Acting like the Pharisees is a form of "higher holiness." It involves separating oneself from all forms of ritual impurity and from all people who are in a state

---

20 Compare *Guide* III.33, p. 533 and, on the connection between holiness and *perishut*, "Laws of the Foundations of the Torah," VII.1 (quoted below) and VII.7. See further Maimonides' Commentary on the Mishnah, Sotah III.3

of ritual impurity. This is not because there is anything intrinsically wrong with being ritually impure.[21] It is because such separation "leads to the purification of the body from evil deeds," which, in turn, "leads to the hallowing of the soul from evil thoughts," which itself "leads to striving for imitation of the Shekhinah."

I understand Maimonides to be saying here that the aim of holiness, of *perishut* (renunciation), is moral behavior (separation from evil deeds), which in turn makes possible intellectual perfection (separation from evil thoughts); that, in turn, brings one to strive for *imitatio Dei*.[22] This is to translate Maimonides' rabbinic vocabulary into the language of medieval Aristotelianism.[23] But one need not agree with this translation to see that on the evidence of the text here presented, holiness for Maimonides means the outcome of a kind of behavior. It is nothing which can be said to exist in and of itself, it is not some sort of superadded essence, it is nothing ontological. It is simply a name given to certain types of (extremely important, highly valued) behavior, and, by extension, to persons, places, times, and objects. It is, and this is a point which must be emphasized, something which is not given, but must be earned. Holiness is not an inheritable status.[24]

---

21 Maimonides writes in paragraph 9:

> Just as it is permissible to eat and drink common food that is ritually impure, so it is permissible to allow ritual impurity to befall common food in the Land of Israel; and ritual impurity may be imparted to common food that is at the outset in fit and proper condition. Similarly, it is permissible to touch any things that are ritually impure, and to incur ritual impurity from them, for Scripture warns none but the sons of Aaron and the Nazirite against incurring ritual impurity from a corpse, thereby implying that for all other people it is permissible, and that it is permissible even for priests and Nazirites to incur ritual impurity from other ritually impure things, except only the ritual impurity of corpses.

22 The point made here is well-stated by Kreisel, *Political Thought*, p. 156: "The dominant motif characterizing Maimonides' discussions of God is the negation of corporeality. His view of holiness as lying in the ethical virtues in general, and restraint of corporeal desires in particular, connects this notion with the negation of one's own corporeality. One must particularly negate that which is associated with the most corporeal of our senses." The literature on Maimonides' conception of human perfection is vast. Much of it is summarized and analyzed in my *Perfection*.

23 For a defense of this approach, see Kellner, *Must*, pp. 149-163.

24 In general, I agree with Avraham Nuriel's criticism of Yeshayahu Leibowitz's interpretation of Maimonides, to the effect that there is relatively little actually of Maimonides in Leibowitz's exposition of his thought; but on at least one important issue, I believe that Leibowitz was absolutely correct. As Leibowitz used to like to say in his many public lectures on Maimonides, the latter insisted that humans are given nothing on a silver platter; everything must be earned. It can be shown that for Maimonides this "everything" includes one's

It is important to note that for Maimonides holiness in this sense is not restricted to Jews. While I am not a devotee of the sort of Maimonidean numerology indulged in by Leo Strauss, sometimes it is simply too striking to be ignored. The *Mishneh Torah* comprises fourteen volumes. The precise midpoint, then, is the end of volume seven. Volume seven, devoted to laws relating to agricultural matters, ends with a section (the seventh) called "Laws of the Sabbatical Year and Jubilee."[25] This section is divided into thirteen chapters. The thirteenth chapter is divided into thirteen paragraphs.[26] The last of these paragraphs reads as follows:

> Not only the Tribe of Levi, but each and every individual human being,[27] whose
> spirit moves him and whose knowledge gives him understanding to set himself
> apart[28] in order to stand before the Lord, to serve Him, to worship Him, and to
> know Him, who walks upright as God created him to do,[29] and releases himself
> from the yoke of the many foolish considerations which trouble people – such
> an individual is as sanctified as the Holy of Holies, and his portion and inheri-
> tance shall be in the Lord forever and ever. The Lord will grant him adequate
> sustenance in this world, the same as He had granted to the priests and to the
> Levites. Thus indeed did David, peace upon him, say, *O Lord, the portion of*
> *mine inheritance and of my cup, Thou maintainest my lot* (Ps. 16:5).

---

humanity, one's status as a Jew, providence, prophecy, a share in the world to come, and, as I am arguing here, holiness. See Nuriel, "Faith."

25 For Maimonides, the re-institution of the Jubilee is intimately connected to the messianic era. See "Laws of Kings," XI.1. It not likely to be simply coincidental that the passage cited immediately below ends the first half of the *Mishneh Torah* and a discussion of messianism ends the second half.

26 At least in the printed editions; the mss. have inconsistent paragraphing in this chapter. The significance of the number thirteen in Judaism and for Maimonides (the author, it must be recalled of 'Thirteen Principles' of Judaism) is addressed by R. Isaac Abravanel in *Principles*, chapter 10. Abravanel missed an important source in this connection: "Laws of Circumcision," III.9.

27 *Kol ish va-ish me-kol ba'ei olam*. That Maimonides understands the expression to mean all human beings is made clear in parallel passages in the *Mishneh Torah*. See *Confrontation*, pp. 97-98 and 247.

28 *Le-hibbadel*. It would have been helpful for the argument being made here had Maimonides used some variant of *p-r-sh* (from which the word "Pharisee" is derived) in this passage, as he could have, but one must deal with texts as written, not as one would like them to have been written.

29 Perhaps a veiled attack on notions of original sin – found in Jewish as well as Christian sources?

Any human being (Jew or non-Jew) who sets herself apart from the foolishness of ordinary pursuits, behaves properly, worships God, and comes to know God,[30] is as sanctified as the Holy of Holies in the Temple in Jerusalem. Again, we see that holiness is a function of a kind of behavior; it is not an essentialist quality having ontological status. It is a *name*, not something really "out there" in the universe.

The universal character of holiness comes out in a second passage in the *Mishneh Torah*:

> It is among the foundations of religion to know that God causes human beings
> to prophesy, and that prophecy does not rest upon anyone but a sage great in
> wisdom, powerful with respect to his [moral] qualities –[i.e.] one whose pas-
> sions do not overpower him with respect to anything in the world, but, rather,
> through his intellect he always subdues his passions– and who has a very broad
> and well-established intellect. A person filled with all these qualities, sound of
> body, upon entering "pardes" and continuously dwelling upon those great and
> remote matters, and having an intellect prepared to understand and conceive
> them, and who continues to *sanctify* himself, by separating himself from the
> ways of most people who walk in the darkness of the times, and who zealously
> trains himself and teaches his mind not to have any thoughts concerning vain
> things, the nonsense of the time and its snares, but his mind is always directed
> above, bound under the throne in order to understand those sacred and pure
> forms, and who examines the entire wisdom of God from the first form till
> the navel of the world, learning from this God's greatness; the holy spirit im-
> mediately rests upon him, and at the time the spirit rests upon him, his soul
> mingles with the degree of the angels known as Ishim and he becomes another
> man, and understands through his intellect that he is not as he was, but has
> risen above the degree of other wise humans, as it says of Saul: *You will proph-
> esy and become another man* (1 Sam 10:6).[31]

---

30 By which I take Maimonides to mean that one can achieve intellectual perfection only after
    having achieved moral perfection [through performance of the commandments, at least
    where Jews are concerned]. I need not insist on this interpretation, however, in order to
    advance the argument being made here.

31 "Laws of the Foundations of the Torah," VII.1, emphasis added. On this passage, see ch. 3
    above, "Literary Character."

The sanctification spoken of here relates to the process of becoming a prophet. As is well-known, Maimonides teaches that prophecy is a natural, human quality.[32] All humans (Jew and Gentile) can, in principle, aspire to prophecy. One sanctifies oneself by separating oneself "from the ways of most people who walk in the darkness of the times." Becoming holy is a status open to all, and is achieved through certain kinds of elevated behavior. If anyone can aspire to holiness, and if achieving it is consequent upon behavior, holiness can hardly be ontological in any of the senses discussed above.

We may now return to our argument. In the *Mishneh Torah* Maimonides makes holiness mean refraining from forbidden foods and forbidden sex. In his *Book of Commandments* he in effect explains what that means by connecting holiness to *perishut* ("renunciation"). After explaining (again in the *Mishneh Torah*) that the Pharisees where called such because they strove for a higher level of holiness through separation from improper behavior and thoughts, Maimonides connects two distinct verses to make a single argument: *Sanctify yourselves therefore and be ye holy* (Lev. 11:44), *for I the Lord Who sanctify you am holy* (Lev. 21:8). Holiness, as defined here, leads to *imitatio Dei*.

The notion of *imitatio Dei*, in turn, is connected by Maimonides to holiness in a variety of interesting ways. In order to see this, we must look at the first text in which Maimonides discusses the imitation of God, *Book of Commandments*, positive commandment eight (vol. 1, pp. 12-13):

> Walking in God's ways. By this injunction we are commanded to be like God (praised be He) as far as it is in our power. This injunction is contained in His words, *And you shall walk in His ways* (Dt. 28:9), and also in an earlier verse in His words, *[What does the Lord require of you, but to fear the Lord your God,] to walk in all His ways?* (Dt. 10:2). On this latter verse the Sages comment as follows: "Just as the Holy One, blessed be He, is called merciful [*rahum*], so should you be merciful; just as He is called gracious [*hanun*], so should you be gracious; just as he is called righteous [*zaddik*], so should you be righteous; just as He is called saintly [*hasid*], so should you be saintly."[33] This injunction

---

32 *Guide*, II.32 and ch. 4 above, "Is Maimonides' Ideal Person Austerely Rationalist?"

33 Maimonides quotes here (in the original Hebrew, even though the *Book of Commandments* was written in Arabic) from *Sifri* Deuteronomy, *piska* 49, without the prooftexts found in the *Sifri*.

has already appeared in another form in His words, *After the Lord Your God shall you walk* (Dt. 13:5) which the Sages explain as meaning that we are to imitate the good deeds and lofty attributes by which the Lord (exalted be He) is described in a figurative way – He being immeasurably exalted above all such description.

One imitates God through merciful, gracious, righteous, and saintly behavior. The point is reiterated in the second text in which Maimonides deals with the imitation of God, *Mishneh Torah*, "Laws of Moral Qualities," 1.5-6 (pp. 47b-48a):

> …The ancient saints trained their dispositions away from the exact mean towards the extremes; in regard to one disposition in one direction, in regard to another in the opposite direction. This was supererogation. We are bidden to walk in the middle paths wich are the right and proper ways, as it is said, *and you shall walk in His ways* (Dt. 28:9). In explanation of the text just quoted, the sages taught, "Even as He is called gracious, so be you gracious; even as He is called merciful, so be you merciful; even as He is called holy, so be you holy." Thus too the the prophets described God by all the various attributes, "long suffering and abounding in kindness, rightous and upright, perfect, mighty, and powerful," and so forth, to teach us that these qualities are good and right and that a human being should cultivate them, and thus imitate God, as far as he can.

Maimonides changes his source here in interesting ways. The midrashic compilation *Sifri*, followed by Maimonides in the *Book of Commandments*, spoke of mercy, graciousness, righteousness, and saintliness. The text here speaks of graciousness, mercy and holiness. I will discuss the possible significance of this below, but here let it be noted that there is no known source for Maimonides' formulation. I have not examined all the known manuscripts of the *Sifri*, but in printed texts the first time that "holiness" is introduced into this discussion is here in "Laws of Moral Qualities."[34]

---

34 The *Sifri* passage is found, in various forms, in half a dozen places in rabbinic literature. While some of the traditionalist commentaries on the *Mishneh Torah* take note of the textual discrepancy, none seem to think it worthy of particular attention.

In the third text in which Maimonides discusses *imitatio Dei, Guide of the Perplexed* I.54 (p. 128) he reverts to the original formulation of the *Sifri*, or at least quotes part of it without the addition of holiness:

> For the utmost virtue of man is to become like unto Him, may He be exalted, as far as he is able; which means that we should make our actions like unto His, as the Sages made clear when interpreting the verse, *Ye shall be holy* (Lev. 19:2). They said: *He is gracious, so be you also gracious; He is merciful, so be you also merciful* (Sifre Dt. 10:12). The purpose of all this is to show that the attributes ascribed to Him are attributes of His actions and that they do not mean that He possesses qualities.

Becoming God-like, Maimonides makes very clear here, means behaving in a particular fashion. To achieve holiness, and thus to imitate God, one must act graciously and mercifully. Maimonides is not even willing to attribute holiness to God in any sort of essential or ontological fashion. *Holy, holy, holy! The Lord of Hosts! His glory fills all the earth!* said the prophet Isaiah, and what the prophet had to have meant, according to Maimonides, is that God's actions are gracious and merciful. If Maimonides is thus unwilling to attribute holiness to God in any sort of essential or ontological fashion, how much less so can he be willing to attribute it to any other entities, persons, places, and times.

It is very difficult to know what the addition of holiness to the passage from the *Sifri* in "Laws of Moral Qualities" signifies. It is possible that Maimonides had a different text in front of him, but I consider that highly unlikely, and that for a number of reasons. He quotes the received text in the *Book of Commandments* and repeats at least part of it in the *Guide of the Perplexed*. Second, it seems odd that only Maimonides should have had access to a version including holiness, one which is quoted in no other source. It seems more likely to me (as has been suggested by most of Maimonides' commentators) that he purposefully introduced into the passage from the *Sifri* a portion of another midrashic text, *Sifra* to Lev. 19:2. That verse reads, *You shall be holy, for I, the Lord your God, am holy* and on it the *Sifra* says: "As I am holy, so you be holy."[35]

---

35 This passage from the *Sifra* is quoted by Maimonides in the text from *Guide* III.47, cited above.

Is there any significance to this? In the context of our present discussion the following suggestion makes sense to me, but I must offer it tentatively, since there is no way to know if it is true. By introducing "holiness" into a passage talking of mercy and graciousness, Maimonides emphasizes the non-ontological character of holiness. Just as mercy and graciousness are matters of action and character, so also is holiness. It is just possible, in other words, that Maimonides alters the text of the *Sifri* in a way not likely to arouse comment in order to hint at his non-ontological understanding of the holiness of persons.

To this point, I have focussed on how a person achieves holiness for Maimonides. I have argued that for Maimonides holiness is not some sort of superadded essence; it is the way in which Judaism characterizes what we might call (in a very non-Maimonidean idiom), "God-liked" behavior. One achieves holiness, not by becoming like God (hardly a possibility for any creature), but by imitating God's attributes of action; by acting, as it were, like God.[36] This being so, it should not surprise us to discover that it is behavior also which brings about the opposite of holiness, profanation:

There are other things that are a profanation of the Name of God. When a man, great in the knowledge of Torah and reputed for his piety does things which cause people to talk about him, even if the acts are not express violations, he profanes the Name of God. As, for example, if such a person makes a purchase and does not pay promptly, provided that he has means and the creditors ask for payment and he puts them off; or if he indulges immoderately in jesting, eating or drinking, when he is staying with ignorant people or living among them; or if his mode of addressing people is not gentle, or he does not receive people affably, but is quarrelsome and irascible. The greater a man is the more scrupulous he should be in all such things, and do more than the strict letter of the law requires. And if a man has been scrupulous in his conduct, gentle in his conversation, pleasant towards his fellow-creatures, affable in manner when receiving them, not retorting, even when affronted, but showing courtesy to all, even to those who treat him with disdain, conducting his commercial affairs with integrity, not readily accepting the hospitality of the ignorant

---

36 In *Guide*, I.54 Maimonides explains that God may be known through His actions only, and not as He is, in and of Himself. For further details, see Seeskin, "Metaphysics."

nor frequenting their company, not seen at all times, but devoting himself to the study of Torah, wrapped in a prayer shawl and crowned with phylacteries, and doing more than his duty in all things, avoiding, however, extremes and exaggerations – such a man has sanctfied God, and concerning him, Scripture saith, *And He said unto me, 'Thou art My servant Israel, in whom I will be glorified'* (Is. 49:3).[37]

God's name can be sanctified or profaned: it depends entirely on how one behaves.

It is not just individuals who are expected to lead holy lives; the people of Israel as a whole is also expected to be holy. In what sense is Israel a holy nation? In a series of studies I have sought to defend the view that according to Maimonides Jews *as such* are in no way distinct from non-Jews. By this I mean that Maimonides rejected any understanding of the election of Israel which presented Jews as ontologically distinct from Gentiles and superior to them. That being the case, in whatever sense Israel may be called holy, it cannot be in ontological or essentialist terms. There must be something about the way in which the nation lives that makes it holy.

Maimonides held Jews to be distinct from Gentiles only to the extent that the former adhered to the Torah. In that he never doubted the divinity of the Torah, Maimonides also never doubted that true adherents of the Torah were, with very few exceptions, better people than those who did not adhere to it. I am not trying to say that Maimonides denied the idea of the election of Israel; that would be ridiculous. He held the idea, but in an unusual fashion.

Maimonides' conception of the election of Israel reflects other ideas of his. One of these is his adoption of the Aristotelian notions that human beings are rational animals[38] and that when born, humans are only potentially rational. Adopting on a useful analogy suggested by Professor Daniel J. Lasker,[39] all humans are born with the same hardware. What we do with that hardware (i.e., the software we run) determines the kind of people we become. Torah on this account is a challenge, not a gift, a demand, not an endowment.

---

37 "Laws of the Foundation of the Torah," V.11, pp. 41a-b.

38 Compare ch. 4 above, "Is Maimonides' Ideal Person Austerely Rationalist?"

39 In his article, "Proselyte Judaism."

Connected to all this is Maimonides' uncompromising and unprecedented inistence on strict doctrinal orthodoxy.[40] In effect, for Maimonides, in the final analysis, it is what we affirm (after we have learned to behave properly) which makes us what we are.

All this being so, it should come as no surprise that Maimonides does not count belief in the election of Israel as one of the dogmas of Judaism; indeed, to the best of my knowledge, he only mentions the doctrine explicitly once in all of his writings.[41] In fact, Maimonides' nominalism makes it impossible for him to attach any special qualities to the people of Israel as such (as opposed to individual Jews). "Israel" as a platonic idea, so to speak, cannot exist. The term can be no more than a a name, a convenient shorthand expression.

What, then, can we make of the holiness of the Jewish people? After all, the Torah itself teaches that the nation of Israel is holy (Ex. 19:5-6):

> Now then, if you will obey Me faithfully and keep My covenant, you shall be My treasured possession among all the peoples. Indeed, all the earth is Mine, but you shall be to Me a kingdom of priests and a holy nation. These are the words that you shall speak to the children of Israel.

and (Dt. 7:6):

> For you are a people consecrated to the Lord your God: of all the peoples on earth the Lord your God chose you to be His treasured people.

It seems clear to me that Maimonides must interpret passages such as these as normative and not descriptive. Indeed, this is precisely what he does with

---

40 For discussion, see the chapters in this collection on dogma.

41 "Laws of Idolatry," 1.3: "After Moses had begun prophesying and God chose Israel as an inheritance, He crowned them with commandments and taught them how to worship Him…" God sent Moses to save the Jews in Egypt from a total relapse into idolatry. This, Maimonides says, God did, "out of His love for us and in order to keep His oath to Abraham…" God loves the Jews, not because they are ontologically unlike other nations, but because of the love Abraham showed God and the oath He in consequence made to him. My thanks to Prof. Warren Zev Harvey for drawing this text to my attention. It is worth noting in this context that Maimonides rarely speaks of God's love for human beings. The passage quoted here is one of the rare exceptions to that generalization. This passage, I might further note, appears to be based upon Dt. 4:37, a verse nowhere cited explicitly by Maimonides.

the first of them (he nowhere mentions the second[42]) in his *Book of Commandments*, as we saw above.[43]

I have found two places in his writings, however, in which Maimonides might be thought to be attributing holiness to the people of Israel in a descriptive, as opposed to a prescriptive, fashion. The first of these is *Mishneh Torah*, "Laws of Forbidden Intercourse," XIX.17:

> All families are presumed to be of valid descent and it is permitted to intermarry with them in the first instance. Nevertheless, should you see two families continually striving with one another, or a family which is constantly engaged in quarrels and altercations, or an individual who is exceedingly contentious with everyone, and is excessively impudent, apprehension should be felt concerning them, and it is advisable to keep one's distance from them, for these traits are indicative of invalid descent...Similarly, if a person exhibits impudence, cruelty, or misanthropy, and never performs an act of kindness, one should strongly suspect that he is of Gibeonite descent, since the distinctive traits of Israel, the holy nation [*ha-ummah ha-kedoshah*], are modesty, mercy, and lovingkindess, while of the Gibeonites it is said, *Now the Gibeonites were not of the children of Israel* (2 Sam. 21:2), because they hardened their faces and refused to relent, showing no mercy to the sons of Saul, nor would they do a kindness unto the children of Israel, by forgiving the sons of their king, notwithstanding that Israel showed them grace at the beginning and spared their lives.

I think that it is fair to read Maimonides in this passage as writing persuasively. He wants to convince Jews to act with "modesty, mercy, and lovingkindness" *so as to be* a holy nation.[44] This is certainly consistent with the way in which Maimonides reads texts attributing holiness to (or, actually, demanding it of) individuals, as we saw above.

The second passage is from *Mishneh Torah*, "Laws of the Sanhedrin," XXV.1-2:

---

42 I rely here on Kafih, *Ha-Mikra*.

43 In *Guide*, II.35 (p. 368) Maimonides cites Ex. 19:6 to emphasize the greatness of Moses; he cites the verse in a clearly normative and prescriptive fashion in III.8 (p. 435) and so also in III.32 (p. 526).

44 See ch. 17 above, "Was Maimonides Truly Universalist?"

It is forbidden to lead the community in a domineering and arrogant manner. One should exercise one's authority in a spirit of humility and reverence. The man at the head of the congregation who arouses excessive fear in the hearts of the members thereof for any but a religious purpose will be punished. It will not be given to him have a son who is a scholar, as it is written: *Men do therefore fear him; he will not see any [sons] that are wise of heart* (Job 37:24). He is also forbidden to treat the people with disrespect, even if they are ignorant. He should not force his way through the holy people [*am ha-kodesh*][45] [to get to his seat].[46] For even if they be simple and lowly, they are the children of Abraham, Isaac, and Jacob, the hosts of God, brought forth out of Egypt with great power and with a mighty hand ...

In this passage Maimonides calls the Jewish people *am ha-kodesh*, "the holy people." The source of this expression is instructive: the prophet promises that the Jews will be called by a new name after the future redemption, *The Holy People, the Redeemed of the Lord.*[47] The prophet is not characterizing the Jews as a holy people in the present, he is prophesying that they will be so called after the redemption. The appelation is predictive, not descriptive. Further, given the point Maimonides is driving home in this passage, that leaders should be meek in their demeanor (like Moses, as he explains in the continuation), it makes excellent sense for him to emphasize the special character of those led. Isaiah's expression works well for him in that fashion. It would be a mistake, it appears to me, to read out of this isolated expression a retreat from Maimonides' repeated position that holiness in people is a matter of their behavior, not of their essence.

Maimonides may be understood in all this as teaching that the Torah engages in what might be called the construction of social reality. Religious reality is not a given, not something found in the universe. Torah, for Maimonides, seeks to inject religious meaning into human life, as opposed to finding it already present in reality. A life thus lived is "spiritual." This has important consequences for our understanding of Maimonides. He is ordinarily under-

---

45 See Isaiah, 62:12: *And they shall be called 'The Holy People, the Redeemed of the Lord'*...

46 Literally: "march over the heads of the holy people."

47 Malbim's commentary on this verse is exquisitely Maimonidean: the Jews will be *called* a holy nation thanks to the holiness of their actions and their righteousness.

stood as holding that only a life of philosophical examination of God is worth living. From our discussion here it is apparent that one can achieve a significant level of holiness, of spirituality, without philosophical perfection. Such a life is surely worthwhile, a life of meaning (even if it has no continuation in the world to come).[48]

Perishut, separation from moral impurity, may thus lead to a life of holiness, but it surely does not by itself lead to the best kind of spiritual life. To achieve that, one must go beyond separation from moral impurity to a life lived in the light of the love of God.

All Jews are commanded to love God: *You shall love the Lord your God with all your heart and with all your soul and with all your might* (Deut 6:5). Pious Jews recite this verse every morning and evening of every day of their lives. What is the nature of this love? Maimonides is often depicted as if he held love of God and knowledge of God to be identical.[49] This is not quite true.

Let us look at the texts in which Maimonides speaks of knowledge and love of God. He raises the issue explicitly first in "Laws of the Foundations of the Torah," II.1 (p. 35b):

> And what is the way that will lead to the love of Him and the fear of Him? When a person contemplates his great and wondrous works and creatures and from them obtains a glimpse of His wisdom which is incomparable and infinite, he will *immediately* love Him, praise Him, glorify Him, and long with an exceeding longing to know His great name...

Maimonides tells us here that love of God is an immediate consequence of knowing God; he does not reduce one to the other.

But there are other texts in which he seems more or less to equate the two: "One only loves God with the knowledge with which one knows him. According to the knowledge will be the love: if the former be little or much, so will the latter be little or much..."[50] What Maimonides actually says here is that the

---

48 For Maimonides, if there is any afterlife at all, it is only for those who have perfected their intellects. For details, see *Must*, pp. 149-163.

49 For recent studies of Maimonides on the love of God, see the introduction to my translation of the *Book of Love* and Lasker, "Love of God."

50 "Laws of Repentance," X.6, p. 92b.

more one knows God, the more one loves God. He does not say that love of God is nothing more than knowledge of God.

A passage in the *Guide of the Perplexed* (I.39, p. 89) seems to support both interpretations:

As for the dictum of Scripture: *And thou shalt love the Lord with all thy heart* (Dt. 6:5)–in my opinion its interpretation is: with all the forces of your heart; I mean to say, with all the forces of the body, for the principle of all of them derives from the heart. Accordingly the intended meaning is...that you should make His apprehension the end of all your actions.

On the one hand, we are told here that in order to fulfill the Scriptural command to love the Lord, one must use all the forces of one's body. On the other hand, we are further told here that the goal of using all the forces of one's body to love the Lord is make knowledge of God the end of all our actions. Everything we do should serve the end of furthering our knowledge of God.[51] The points made here are expressed again towards the end of the *Guide* (III.28, pp. 512-513):

...*with all thy heart, and with all thy soul, and with all thy might* (Dt. 6:5). We have already explained[52]... that this love becomes valid only through the apprehension of the whole of being as it is and through the consideration of His wisdom as it is manifested in it.

In this passage, Maimonides seems to present love of God as a consequence of knowledge of God, and not as the same thing. This makes excellent sense: love of God means not just the intellection of truths about God, but the direction of all one's actions and of all one's body towards that love.

Near the end of the *Guide* (III.51, p. 621), Maimonides reiterates the relationship of dependence between love and knowledge: "Now we have made it clear several times that love is proportionate to apprehension." The more we know God, the more we love God.

What is the nature of this love we are commanded to have for God? Maimonides tells us in *Mishneh Torah*, "Laws of Repentance," X.5 (p. 92b):

---

51 There are some passages where Maimonides makes this explicit. See "Laws of Character Traits," III.2 (p. 49b): "A man should direct all his thoughts and activities to the knowledge of God, alone." All one's activities, even cohabitation, should have thus ultimate end in view.

52 In "Laws of the Foundations of the Torah," II.1-2 and the fifth of the "Eight Chapters" among other places.

What is the love of God that is befitting? It is to love God with a great and exceeding love, so strong that one's soul shall be knit up with the love of God such that it is continually enraptured by it, like love-sick individuals whose minds are at no time free from passion for a particular woman, and are enraptured by her at all times...even intenser should be the love of God in the hearts of those who love Him; they should be enraptured by this love at all times...

Maimonides reiterates the point again in X.6, "It is known and certain that the love of God does not become closely knit in a man's heart till he is continuously and thoroughly possessed by it and gives up everything else in the world for it..." and makes much the same claim in the *Guide* (III.51, p. 627), defining the passionate love of God as "...an excess of love, so that no thought remains that is directed toward a thing other than the Beloved..."

Let us now look at the last passage in the *Guide* (III. 52, p. 630) in which the issue comes up explicitly:

You know to what extent the Torah lays stress upon love: *With all thy heart, and with all thy soul, and with all thy might* (Dt. 6:5). For these two ends, namely love and fear, are achieved through two things: love, through the opinions taught by the Law, which include the apprehension of His Being as He, may He be exalted, is in truth; while fear is achieved by means of all actions prescribed by the Law, as we have explained.

Maimonides' position here is tolerably clear: we achieve love of God through the apprehension of God's being to the greatest extent possible for humans. This does not mean that loving and apprehending God are the same.[53] Love of God means more than knowing God. True love of God involves knowledge of God, to be sure, but it also involves the direction of all one's heart, all one's soul, and all one's body to a life lived in the light of the love of God. The spiritual life for Maimonides, thus, has at least two crucial components: *perishut* from moral impurity and love of God.

Maimonides' conception of the nature of holy living is a valuable key for understanding the complicated interplay of religious and philosophical issues in

---

53 Compare further, Benor, *Worship*, pp. 56-58. For a very useful discussion of love and knowledge in Maimonides see Kaplan, "Rav Kook."

his thought and an invaluable key for unlocking his perception of the truly perfected (religious) life. As we have seen, philosophical ideas like nominalism and the transcendence of God led Maimonides to reject any notion of ontological holiness. This is connected in his thinking to two important and inter-related religious messages. The first has to do with a point emphasized by an important group of Maimonidean interpreters, in particular Hermann Cohen, Steven Schwarzschild, and Kenneth Seeskin: holiness is an ethical ideal. Holiness is not out there, waiting to be found, rather, it is made.

This has important implications: holiness is not the sort of notion which can be restricted to any particular person, nation, object, place, or time. In principle, any person, any nation, and object, any place, any time can be holy. Holiness as an ethical challenge is thus addressed to all people, not to Jews alone. This, I think, sums up Maimonides' conception of the messianic era.

The second religious message which grows out of Maimonides' conception of the holy life relates to his understanding that human beings are given nothing on a silver platter. We are given tools and a challenge, and it is then up to us to the earn what we receive. God plays more than fair: the tools with which we are endowed are all that we need to achieve our perfection: parents, health, ability to seek what is good for us, and intellectual abilities. It is then up to us to take advantage of all these and make something of our lives. In particular, it is up to us to make of our lives something holy, not something wasted. All this fits in well with Maimonides' overall approach: humanity, Judaism, divine providence, prophecy, immortality, none of these are given us as presents, rather, we can achieve them if we apply ourselves diligently. Maimonides' conception of holy living both contributes to and follows from his conception of Judaism as a religion of challenges, not of endowments.

Ultimately, and this perhaps explains why Maimonides' vision of Judaism has attracted so few adherents over the generations, his is a religion addressed to emotionally and spiritually mature human beings (not Jews specifically, human beings generally): it is a religion of challenges, not endowments; of demands, not bequests. It is, admittedly, the religion of an elite, but it is open to all willing to make the effort to join that elite, and it aims towards a (messianic) future when *all* will have joined that elite.

EPILOGUE

CHAPTER TWENTY
Epilogue[1]

Moses Maimonides expressed a vision of Judaism as a remarkably naturalist religion of radical responsibility. His Judaism is a religion in which concrete behavior serves the needs of abstract thought; abstract thought is the deepest layer of the Torah and, at least in Maimonides' day, could be most clearly and accurately expressed in the vocabulary of the Neoplatonized Aristotelianism that Maimonides accepted as one of the highest expressions of the human spirit. This Judaism was simultaneously deeply elitist and profoundly universalist. Maimonides crystallized and expressed his vision of Judaism because the Jewish world in his day was, in his view, debased and paganized.

Maimonides sought to transform the Judaism of his day, most notably the nature of halakhah, its distinctions between holy and profane, ritually pure and ritually impure, the character of the Hebrew language, the notion of "created light," the distinction between Jew and non-Jew, and the existence of angels as popularly understood, and to reform the curriculum of Jewish learning. In each of these areas Judaism continued to develop as if Maimonides had never existed and never written. The implications for modern Judaism are vast, yet hidden from view. Orthodoxy today is a Maimonidean antithesis, an enchanted world whose spirit guides provide indispensable intercession, rabbis as prophets and magicians. In short, it is a kabbalistic world.

There are indeed areas where Maimonides' influence has been decisive. Maimonides succeeded in convincing almost all Jews that the God of Judaism is entirely incorporeal. Given the dramatic anthropomorphism of the

---

1   This chapter, based upon *Confrontation*, "Afterword" was originally published as "Maimonides Agonist: Disenchantment and Reenchantment in Modern Judaism," *Covenant: Global Jewish Magazine* 1 (November, 2006 - article 9/9) [http://covenant.idc.ac.il/en/vol1/issue1/kellner.html]

Bible and rabbinic literature this was no mean feat. The project of creating comprehensive and logically organized codes of law, culminating in the publication of the *Shulhan Arukh*, must also be seen as at least a partial success of Maimonides'.

However, despite these achievements, his overall reform cannot be considered a success. Maimonides' attempted reform boomeranged badly: his attempt to 'demythologize' post-talmudic Judaism, to bring about the 'fall of myth in ritual', in the perceptive words of Josef Stern, led to the enthusiastic 'remythologization' of Judaism through Kabbalah. Whether or not the need to counter Maimonides was indeed a catalyst for the composition and publication of kabbalistic literature, there can be no doubt that its acceptance as normative by the rabbinic elite and by the rank and file of the Jewish people sounded the death knell for Maimonides' projected reforms. Of course, if Maimonides did indeed 'create an opposition' that might be construed as a form of success, since only a foolish general mobilizes his or her forces in the face of an inconsequential threat. Maimonides was not construed as an inconsequential threat.

An awareness of Maimonides' failures brings into focus what is at stake for modern Judaism, determining the fundamental substance of the Jewish tradition, defining the essence of a Jew's relationship to God, and finally, understanding the nature of God.

Many of Maimonides' writings are best understood not only as an attempt to harmonize Torah and what he considered to be science, but also as an attempt to counteract the influence of what I have called 'proto-kabbalistic' elements in pre-Maimonidean Judaism. In this, I believe (but cannot prove), Maimonides followed in the footsteps of those editors of the normative rabbinic writings who kept certain texts and allied literature out of the canon of Judaism. But the widespread acceptance of the *Zohar* as the work of the second-century CE Rabbi Simeon bar Yohai doomed this millennium-long attempt limiting the mystical elements of Judaism to failure.

For traditionally oriented Jews, an important religious issue rests upon a bibliographical question: who wrote the *Zohar*? If the *Zohar* represents the work of Rabbi Simeon bar Yohai and a circle of colleagues and students, then the teachings of the *Zohar* must be seen as part of the body of normative rabbinic Judaism, carrying at least as much authority as other midrashic compilations such as *Midrash Rabbah* and *Tanhuma*. No Jew today, believer or scholar, would think of claiming that the ideas and values of such midrashic compilations do not represent ideas and values at the heart of rabbinic Judaism. There may be questions about how to express these ideas and values in a modern idiom, how to understand them, and, for the most traditional, how to apply them, but there can be no doubt that they constitute an integral part of 'classical Judaism'.

If the *Zohar*, on the other hand, is the brilliant work of the Spanish kabbalist Moses de Leon (c. 1240-1305) and his friends, if the anonymous mystical work *Sefer Bahir*, attributed to first century sage Nehunyah Ben Ha-Kanah, is in fact a clumsy forgery, then the ideas and values embodied in these works have much less normative import for subsequent Judaism. Moses de Leon did indeed live during the period of the *rishonim* (early authorities), but had no particular credentials as halakhist or exegete that we know of.

So, putting the question rather tendentiously, is Judaism the sort of religion found in the Bible, Mishna, Talmud, and Maimonides, or is Judaism the sort of religion found in the Bible, Mishna, Talmud, and *Zohar*? These are very different sorts of religions and the answer to the question depends on the answers to the question, who wrote the *Zohar* and when?

To all intents and purposes the question has been settled in Jewish history if not by Jewish scholarship. Scholars such as Gershom Scholem accept that these works are the invention of Moses de Leon, but in traditionalist circles the *Zohar* is almost universally seen as the work of Rabbi Simeon bar Yohai, with all that implies. That being the case, it is no surprise that what might be called, anachronistically, Maimonides' anti-*Zohar*ic reform had little chance of success. In the rest of this chapter I want to indicate how very little of Maimonidean Judaism can be found in the contemporary Orthodox world.

If one follows 'Jewish politics', both in Israel and abroad, it is easy to come to the conclusion that Orthodox Judaism recognizes the authority of rabbis as such to make policy determinations. It is a staple of *haredi* politics in Israel that rabbinic leaders decide all matters. Indeed, one of the hallmarks of *haredi* parties is that each has a council of sages that determines all matters of policy for the party's representatives in the Knesset and government. Until recently, it was this reliance upon the *da'at torah* or Torah wisdom of prominent rabbis that distinguished *haredi* from Zionist Orthodox politics. In the old Mizrahi movement, and to an ever-diminishing extent in its offshoot, the religious Zionist party Mafdal, rabbis were respected and occasionally consulted, but on matters of policy the party leadership made its own decisions. In the 1970s young Turks in the party took advantage of the prominence of the late Rabbi Shlomo Goren (and of his own apparent desire for power and prestige) to involve rabbinic authorities in internal political disputes. Debates within the religious Zionist community over the Oslo peace process were often phrased in terms of acceptance or rejection of this or that *da'at torah*.

All observers agree that this phenomenon is gaining strength with each passing year. There must therefore be strong forces within Jewish Orthodoxy pushing in this direction. After all, an objective examination of the actual political record of rabbis is hardly encouraging. From the first rabbi whom we know to have actively involved himself in politics (Rabbi Akiva *vis-à-vis* Bar Kokhba) to the rabbis who counseled Jews not to flee Europe before the Holocaust, prominent rabbis as a class do not appear to have distinguished themselves by their political acumen.

Those elements in what is often called Modern Orthodoxy that seek to resist what they see as the 'creeping haredization' of Orthodoxy regard this issue as crucial. It is often phrased in terms of whether what *haredi* Orthodoxy calls *da'at torah* is a modern innovation or a venerable tradition. For years I have been convinced that the notion of *da'at torah* was a *haredi* innovation, a politically expedient if Jewishly questionable response to the challenges of modernity. However, I have been forced to change some of my cherished opinions. While it is clear that the term *da'at torah* is a late nineteenth-century innovation, the notion actually reflects forces that existed earlier in Judaism.

Elsewhere I have analyzed two opposed philosophies of halakhah, that of Judah Halevi and his successors, which tends towards the expansion of rabbinic authority into political spheres, and that of Maimonides, which tends to limit the authority of rabbis to what may be called technical matters of halakhah. In its narrowest form, the debate revolves around the question: what role do prophets as such have in the halakhic process? This issue has been studied at length, both within the tradition and by academic scholarship. But this debate reflects a much deeper and more profound difference of opinion. For religious thinkers like Halevi, the issue is not only that prophets have a role to play in the halakhic process, but that the very nature of halakhah makes it necessary that prophecy play a role in its determination. For religious thinkers like Maimonides, on the other hand, the nature of halakhah is such that prophets as prophets are irrelevant to the process.

This debate itself reflects an even deeper one, about the nature of God's relationship to the created cosmos. In many ways, the God of Halevi is more present in the world as we know it than is the God of Maimonides. The immanent God of Halevi, omnipresent if invisible, acts more directly on the world than does the transcendent and somewhat aloof God of Maimonides. Moreover, the immanent God is acted upon by inhabitants of that world in ways that would have scandalized Maimonides.

Can and ought there to be a 'separation of powers' in Judaism? Are there areas of life that are by definition outside the reach of rabbinic authority? Few questions have greater significance in contemporary Jewish life and politics, especially in Israel.

For Halevi, fulfilling the commandments actually does something in the world and accomplishes something which cannot be accomplished in any other fashion. I do not want to get into the question of whether or not Halevi's position constitutes full-blown theurgy as found in some streams of Kabbalah. For our purposes it is enough to note that, for Halevi, proper fulfilment of the commandments has actual consequences: when sacrifices are brought in the proper manner, the person bringing the sacrifice is brought closer to God. A sacrifice improperly brought brings no religious benefit to the person bringing the sacrifices.

How and why does this work? For Halevi, the commandments of the Torah reflect an antecedent reality, a kind of parallel universe of godliness and holiness accessible only to a holy few. Halakhic distinctions for Halevi reflect a reality which is really 'out there', an actual facet of the cosmos, even if it is a reality not accessible to our senses. Holiness, for example, is something that actually inheres in holy places, objects, people, and times. Were we able to invent a 'holiness counter' it would click every time its wand came near something holy, just as a Geiger counter clicks in the presence of radioactivity. Radioactivity, of course, is present in the physical universe, while holiness is present only in the metaphysical universe, as it were. But just as radioactivity can have effects, even though it is not apprehended by the senses, so also holiness can have effects, even though it cannot be apprehended by the senses–there really is something there, but not on the plane of existence accessible to people who lack contact with the *inyan ha-elohi*, the divine influence.

Maimonides saw the commandments of the Torah as creating a social reality, not as reflecting anything actually existing in the universe. Maimonides, as opposed to Halevi (and Nahmanides), sees halakhah as constituting institutional, social reality, not as reflecting an antecedent ontological reality. In further opposition to Halevi and Nahmanides, he distinguishes between mistakes in halakhic contexts, which have relatively modest consequences, and errors in scientific and dogmatic contexts, which have profound consequences. This reflects his perception of halakhah as a system of rules imposed upon reality. In further opposition to what I have been calling the Halevi-Nahmanides stance, Maimonides maintains that ritual purity and impurity are not states of objects in the 'real world', but descriptions of legal status only.

If halakhah reflects an antecedent reality, a reality which cannot be apprehended through normal tools of apprehension but only through an 'inner eye', enriched in some fashion by contact with the divine in some fashion, then people who can properly make halakhic decisions are people endowed with a power of apprehension which rises above the natural. That being the case, it makes sense to accept their leadership even in matters which many might think lie outside the four cubits of the law. Halevi's insistence on blurring the boundaries between halakhah and prophecy is thus seen as an outgrowth of his philosophy of halakhah. Deciding halakhic matters is not simply a matter of erudition, training, insight, and skill; it demands the ability to see things invisible to others.

Maimonides, on the other hand, sees halakhah as a social institution, ordained by God, of course, but an institution that creates social reality, not one that reflects antecedent metaphysical reality. Since he holds that so much of halakhah is historically contingent (i.e. it could have been otherwise), he could not have held otherwise. For Maimonides, halakhah does not 'work' in the way in which it 'works' for Halevi. Obedience to the commandments for

Maimonides is immensely important on all sorts of levels–personal, educational, moral, social–but accomplishes nothing outside the psychosocial realm of identity and community.

A good way to see the difference between Halevi and Maimonides is to focus on the following question. Can a non-Jew (or, for that matter, a future computer) determine halakhah? For Halevi the question is ridiculous. In order to determine the law a person must be a Jew who has perfected his contact with the *inyan ha-elohi* to the greatest extent possible. For Maimonides, the question is not ridiculous. I assume that for many reasons he would not want to see the halakhic decision of a non-Jew as authoritative but he would have to invoke arguments which do not reject the theoretical possibility of a non-Jew achieving sufficient familiarity with halakhic texts and canons of reasoning to formulate decisions which stand up to the most rigorous halakhic examination.

The modern doctrine of *da'at torah* is thus clearly Halevian and not Maimonidean. For Halevi, in order properly to determine halakhah one must tap into a kind of quasi-prophecy; for Maimonides, one must learn how to handle halakhic texts and procedures properly. If halakhah *creates* institutional reality, then, beyond technical competence (and, one hopes, personal integrity), the charismatic or other qualities of the individual halakhist are irrelevant to questions of authority; if, on the other hand, halakhah *reflects* antecedent ontological reality, then the only competent halakhist is the one who can tap into that reality, a function of divine inspiration, not personal ability or institutional standing.

No observer familiar with Jewish Orthodoxy today can doubt that Halevi's view of halakhah is paramount. It was adopted by the *Zohar* and its related literature and spread from there into almost every nook and cranny of halakhic thinking. Maimonides' attempt to move halakhah back from the realm of prophetic inspiration to the realm of institutions has not yet succeeded.

There is another point to be made here. Maimonides tells us what a law is, and how one determines what a law is. There is a real sense in which he wants to 'rationalize' the whole process, excluding from it appeals to *seyata deshemayah* ('help of heaven') or to *ruah hakodesh* ('holy spirit'). This, of course, is threatening to people whose authority rests upon their access to such sources.

I do not mean to accuse anti-Maimonideans of playing Machiavellian power politics, but it would be naïve to ignore this aspect of the matter.

Issues of sanctity and of ritual purity and impurity obviously relate to halakhah, but also, at least in the eyes of Maimonides' opponents, to the nature of the universe itself. Much of the discourse in contemporary Orthodoxy (both Zionist and *haredi*) about the Land of Israel relates to its ontological status as a land significantly unlike all other lands. I literally have no idea how Maimonides, were he to walk among us today, would react to the State of Israel, and to questions concerning territorial compromise. But I am certain that he would not phrase the question in terms of the ontological status of the Land of Israel.

With respect to the issue of ritual purity and impurity, one example taken from contemporary discourse will show how far Maimonides is from being representative today. Newly observant Jews in the *haredi* world invariably marry other newly observant Jews. One of the reasons for this is that such people were born to unobservant parents. That means that at the moment of conception their mothers were tainted by menstrual impurity, so that their offspring are in some sense also tainted. This taint in no way impinges upon their character, their chances for a share in the world to come, or the esteem in which they are held. But it is a taint nonetheless, a defect in *yihus*, or lineage. This whole approach is dramatically anti-Maimonidean.

Matters of holiness and ritual purity relate to the kind of world in which Maimonides wants us to live. It is a 'disenchanted' world, a world that can be understood and, so to speak, applied. It is a world which demands maturity of those who live in it, since nothing, not their humanity, not their Jewishness, is presented to them on a silver platter; everything must be earned. It is a world in which Jews are called upon to fulfill the commandments, not because failure to do so is metaphysically harmful, but because fulfilling them is the right thing to do. By making demands, imposing challenges, Maimonidean Judaism empowers Jews. Their fate is in their own hands, not in the hands of semi-divine intermediaries or in the hands of a rabbinic elite.

The world favored by Maimonides' opponents, on the other hand, is an 'enchanted' world. Many of Maimonides' opponents, in his day and ours, do indeed accept the efficacy of charms and amulets, and fear the harm of demons and the evil eye. But it is not in that sense alone that I maintain that they live in an enchanted world. Theirs is not a world that can be explained in terms of the unvarying workings of divinely ordained laws of nature; it is not a world that can be rationally understood. It is a world in which the notion of miracle loses all meaning, since everything that happens is a miracle. In such a world instructions from God, and contact with the divine in general, must be mediated by a religious elite who alone can see the true reality masked by nature. This is the opposite of an empowering religion, since it takes their fate out of the hands of Jews, and, in effect, puts it into the hands of rabbis. This is, in effect, the Jewish world we live in.

However, and this must be admitted, a disenchanted world may be empowering, but it is also frightening; in such a world, God can be approached, but rarely approaches. It is a world fit for a philosopher like Maimonides, but hard on a frightened person, who does not want the challenge of living by her wits (literally), but the comfort of God's love and the instructions of God's agents. We may admire those who think for themselves, but many are just as happy to have their thinking done for them. An enchanted world has many attractions! This indeed may be one of the reasons why Maimonides' attempted reforms aroused so much opposition.

Maimonides' Judaism demands much, and offers little. More precisely, it offers much, but few can take advantage of it. Even more precisely, Maimonides' Judaism offers much, but few can take advantage of it in the pre-messianic age. Seeking to help the few who could immediately benefit from his teachings and to minimize the damage to those who could not, he presented his views gingerly. The rage provoked by these views when they were understood proves the wisdom of his approach. Those, like me, who find in his views a vision of Judaism which is both attractive in its own right and true to Torah, can only regret that he has as yet not succeeded in winning over the vast bulk of Jews who study his writings with much devotion but little understanding. But, with Maimonides, I am optimistic that the day will come when *the earth will be full with the knowledge of the Lord as the waters cover the sea* (Is. 11: 9).

WORKS CITED

Works by Maimonides:

Book of Commandments, trans. Charles Chavel, 2 vols. (London: Soncino, 1967)

Commentary on the Mishnah, ed. and trans. from Arabic Joseph Kafih, 6 vols. (Jerusalem: Mosad Harav Kook, 1963-67). General Introduction translated by Fred Rosner in: *Commentary on the Mishnah: Intoduction to the Mishnah and Commentary on Tractate Berachoth* (New York: Feldheim, 1975). Introductions to various parts translated into Hebrew by Yizhak Sheilat in: *Hakdamot ha-Rambam le-Mishnah* (Jerusalem: Ma'aliyot, 1992).

Commentary to Mishnah Aboth, trans. Arthur David (New York: Bloch, 1968).

Epistle to Yemen, trans. in Abraham Halkin and David Hartman, *Epistles of Maimonides: Crisis and Leadership* (Philadelphia: Jewish Publication Society, 1985), 91-131.

Essay on Resurrection, trans. in Abraham Halkin and David Hartman, *Epistles of Maimonides: Crisis and Leadership* (Philadelphia: Jewish Publication Society, 1985), 209-233.

Ethical Writings of Maimonides, trans. Raymond Weiss and Charles Butterworth (New York: Dover, 1983).

Guide of the Perplexed, English trans. Shlomo Pines (Chicago: University of Chicago Press, 1963); Hebrew trans., J. Kafih (Jerusalem: Mosad Harav Kook, 1972); Hebrew trans., Michael Schwarz (Ramat Aviv: Tel Aviv University Press, 2002).

"Letter on Astrology" from Lerner and Mahdi (eds.), *Medieval Political Philosophy* and from Ralph Lerner, *Maimonides' Empire of Light*.

Letters of Maimonides [Iggerot], Hebrew trans. David Z. Baneth (Jerusalem: Magnes, 1985); Hebrew trans. J. Kafih (Jerusalem: Mosad Harav Kook, 1972); Hebrew trans. Y. Sheilat, 2 vols. (Jerusalem: Ma'aliyot, 1987); English trans. L. Stitskin (New York: Yeshiva University Press, 1977).

Medical Aphorisms of Maimonides, trans. Fred Rosner and Suessman Muntner, 2 vols. (New York: Yeshiva University Press, 1970).

Mishneh Torah, Translated into English as *The Code of Maimonides* (Yale Judaica Series) (New Haven: Yale University Press). *The Book of Knowledge* (Vol. 1 of the *Mishneh Torah*), trans. Moses Hyamson (Jerusalem: Feldheim, 1974). *Mishneh Torah, Hilchot Kri'at Shema – The Laws of Kri'at Shema*, trans. Boruch Kaplan (New York: Moznaim, 1989). *Mishneh Torah, Hilchot Tefilin UMezuzah, V'Sefer Torah – The Laws [Governing] Tefillin, Mezuzah, and Torah Scrolls*, trans. Eilyahu Tourger (New York: Moznaim, 1990).

Responsa of Maimonides. Hebrew trans. J. Blau, 3 vols. (Jerusalem: Mekize Nirdamim, 1960).

Treatise on Logic, trans. I. Efros (New York: American Academy for Jewish Research, 1938).

Translations from the Bible are taken from *Tanakh - the Holy Scriptures: The New JPS Translation According to the Traditional Hebrew Text*. Philadelphia: Jewish Publication Society, 1985. Translations from the Babylonian Talmud are from the Soncino Edition.

All translations have been silently emended where I thought it necessary or useful. Translations from the *Mishneh Torah* are taken from the Yale Judaica series translations (and from Hyamson's *Book of Knowledge*), heavily emended to make them more literal and to match the text in Yohai Makbili's one-volume edition of the work (Haifa: Or Ve-Yeshu'ah, 5765).

Abraham Maimuni, *Milhamot*	Abraham (ben Rambam) Maimuni. *Sefer Milhamot Ha-Shem*. Ed. Reuven Margoliot. Jerusalem: Mossad ha-Rav Kook, 1953.
Abravanel, *Principles*	Abravanel, Isaac. *Principles of Faith*. Translated by Menachem Kellner. London: Littman Library of Jewish Civilization, 1981.
Abravanel, *Rosh Amanah*	Abravanel, Isaac. *Rosh Amanah*. Edited by Menachem Kellner. Ramat-Gan: Bar-Ilan University Press, 1993.
Abravanel, *Yeshu'ot Meshiho*	Abravanel, Isaac. *Yeshu'ot Meshiho*. Bnei Brak: Me'orei Sefarad, 1993.
Adret, *Responsa*	Adret, Solomon ben Abraham. *Responsa*. Jerusalem: Mossad ha-Rav Kook, 1990.

Albo, *Ikkarim*	Albo, Joseph. *Sefer Ha-Ikkarim*. Translated by Isaac Husik. 5 vols. Philadephia: Jewish Publication Society, 1929.
Alloni, "Kuzari"	Alloni, Nehemiah. "Kuzari – Book of the Jewish War of Independence from the 'Arabiyya.'" *Eshel Beersheva* 2 (1980): 119-37 (Hebrew).
Altman, *Medieval and Renaissance Studies*	Altmann, Alexander ed. *Jewish Medieval and Renaissance Studies*. Cambridge: Harvard University Press, 1967.
Altmann, "Translator's Introduction"	Altmann, Alexander. "Introduction to Saadiah Gaon's 'Book of Doctrines and Beliefs.'" In *Three Jewish Philosophers*. New York: Atheneum, 1972.
Anatoli, *Malmad*	Anatoli, Ya'akov. *Malmad ha-Talmidim* (Lyck: Mekize Nirdamim, 1866).
Avi-Yonah, "Ptolemy"	Avi-Yonah, Reuven S. "Ptolemy vs. Al-Bitruji: A Study of Scientific- Decision Making in the Middle Ages." *Archives Internationales d'Histoire des Sciences* 35 (1985): 124-47.
Baneth, "Terminlogy"	Baneth, David. Z. "Maimonides' Philosophical Terminology." *Tarbiz* 6 (1935): (Hebrew)
Bechler, "Methodological Basis"	Bechler, Zvi. "The Methodological Basis of Maimonides' Attack on Aristotelian Physics." *Iyyun* 17 (1966): 34-41 (Hebrew).
Benor, *Worship*	Benor, Ehud. *Worship of the Heart: A Study in Maimonides' Philosophy of Religion*. Albany: SUNY Press, 1995.
Ben-Sasson, "Ha-Rambam"	Ben-Sasson, Haim Hillel. "*Ha-Rambam: Hanhagat Ish Ha-Ru'ah.*" In *Rezef U-Temurah*, edited by Joseph Hacker, 301-15. Tel Aviv: Am Oved, 1984.
Berger, *Rebbe*	Berger, David. *The Rebbe, the Messiah, and the Scandal of Orthodox Indifference*. London: Littman Library of Jewish Civilization, 2001.
Berman, "Disciple"	Berman, Lawrence. "Maimonides, the Disciple of Alfarabi." *Israel Oriental Studies* 4 (1974): 154-78.
Berman, "Political Interpretation"	Berman, Lawrence. "The Political Interpretation of the Maxim: The Purpose of Philosophy Is the Imitation of God." *Studia Islamica* 15 (1961): 53-61.

Berman,   Berman, Lawrence. "A Reexamination of Maimonides' 'Statement on
"Reexamination"   Political Science." *Journal of the American Oriental Society* 89 (1969):
                        106-11.

Berman,   Berman, Lawrence. "Some Remarks on the Arabic Text of
"Remarks"   Maimonides' 'Treatise on the Art of Logic." *Journal of the American
                        Oriental Society* 88 (1968): 340-42.

Bibago,   Abraham Bibago, *Derekh Emunah* (Constantinople, 1522). Selections
Derekh Emunah   edited by Chava Fraenkel-Goldschmidt (Jerusalem: Mossad Bialik,
                        1978).

Bland,   Bland, Kalman. *The Artless Jew: Medieval and Modern Affirmations
Artless Jew   and Denials of the Visual*. Princeton: Princeton University Press,
                        2000.

Bland,   Bland, Kalman. "Beauty, Maimonides, and Cultural Relativism in
"Beauty"   Medieval Jewish Thought," *Journal of Medieval and Early Modern
                        Studies* 26 (1996): 85-112.

Bland,   Bland, Kalman. "Medieval Jewish Aesthetics: Maimonides, Body, and
"Medieval Jewish   Scripture in Profiat Duran." *Journal of the History of Ideas* 54 (1993):
Aesthetics"   533-59.

Blass,   Blass, Yonatan. *Me-Nofet Zuf: Iyyunin Ba-Moreh Ha-Nevukhim*. 2
Me-Nofet Zuf   vols. Neveh Zuf: Kollel Ratzon Yehudah, 2006.

Bleich,   Bleich, J. David. "Orthodoxy and the Non-Orthodox: Prospects of
"Orthodoxy and the   Unity." In *Orthodoxy Confronts Modernity*, edited by J. Sacks, 97-108.
Non-Orthodox"   Hoboken: Ktav, 1991.

Blidstein,   Blidstein, Gerald. "Maimonides on 'Oral Law." *Jewish Law Annual* 1
"'Oral Law'"   (1978): 108-22.

Blidstein,   Blidstein, Gerald. "A Note on Rabbinic Missionizing." *Journal of
"Rabbinic   Theological Studies* 47, no. 2 (1996): 528-31.
Missionizing"

Blidstein,   Blidstein, Ya'akov. *Ekronot Mediniim Be-Mishnat Ha-Rambam*.
Ekronot   Ramat Gan: Bar Ilan University Press, 1983.

Blidstein,   Blidstein, Ya'akov. *Ha-Tefillah Be-Mishnato He-Hilkhatit Shel Ha-
Ha-Tefillah   Rambam*. Jerusalem: Mossad Bialik, 1994.

Blidstein, "Joy in Maimonides"	Blidstein, Ya'akov. "Joy in Maimonides' Ethical Teaching." *Eshel Beersheva* 2 (1980): 145-63 (Hebrew).
Blidstein, "Status of the Resident Alien"	Blidstein, Ya'akov. "On the Status of the Resident Alien in Maimonides' Thought." *Sinai* 101 (1988): 44-52 (Hebrew).
Blumenthal, *Philosophic Mysticism*	Blumenthal, David R. *Philosophic Mysticism: Studies in Rational Religion.* Ramat-Gan: Bar-Ilan University Press, 2006.
Breuer, *Modernity within Tradition*	Breuer, Mordechai. *Modernity within Tradition.* Translated by Elizabeth Petuchowski. New York: Columbia University Press, 1992.
Bronowski, *Knowledge and Imagination*	Bronowski, Jacob. *The Origins of Knowledge and Imagination* New Haven: Yale University Press, 1978.
Buber, *Two Types of Faith*	Buber, Martin. *Two Types of Faith: A Study of the Interpenetration of Judaism and Christianity.* New York: Harper Torchbooks, 1961.
Butterfield, *Whig*	Butterfield, Herbert. *The Whig Interpretation of History* London: Bell, 1963.
Cohen, *Jewish Women*	Cohen, Shaye J. D. *Why Aren't Jewish Women Circumcised? Gender and Covenant in Judaism.* Berkeley: University of California Press, 2005.
Crescas, *Or ha-Shem*	Crescas, Hasdai. *Or ha-Shem.* Vienna, 1959. Edited by Shlomo Fisher. Jerusalem: Sifrei Ramot, 1990.
Davidson, *Alfarabi*	Davidson, Herbert. *Alfarabi, Avicenna, and Averroes on Intellect.* New York: Oxford University Press, 1992.
Davidson, "First Two"	Davidson, Herbert. "The First Two Positive Commandments in Maimonides' List of the 613 Believed to Have Been Given to Moses at Sinai." In *Creation and Re-Creation in Jewish Thought: Festschrift in Honor of Joseph Dan on the Occasion of His Seventieth Birthday* edited by Rachel Elior and Peter Schaefer, 113-45. Tuebingen: Mohr Siebeck, 2005.
Davidson, *Maimonides*	Davidson, Herbert. *Moses Maimonides: The Man and His Works.* Oxford: Oxford University Press, 2005.

Davidson, "Material and Active Intellects"	Davidson, Herbert A. "Gersonides on the Material and Active Intellects." In *Studies on Gersonides: A Fourteenth-Century Jewish Philosopher-Scientist*, edited by Gad Freudenthal, 195-265. Leiden: Brill, 1992.
Davidson, "Secret"	Davidson, Herbert. "Maimonides' Secret Position on Creation." In *Studies in Medieval Jewish History and Literature*, edited by Isadore Twersky, 16-40. Cambridge: Harvard University Press, 1979.
Davidson, "Shemonah Perakim"	Davidson, Herbert. "Maimonides' *Shemonah Perakim* and Alfarabi's *Fusul Al-Madani.*" *Proceedings of the American Academy for Jewish Research* 31 (1963): 33-50.
Davies, *Torah*	Davies, W. D. "Torah and Dogma: A Comment." *Harvard Theological Review* 61 (1968): 87-105.
Diamond, "Biblical Monarch"	Diamond, James. "The Biblical Monarch as Anarchy Personified: Narrative Configuring Law." *Hebraic Political Studies* 2, no. 1 (2007): 20-45.
Diamond, *Converts*	Diamond, James. *Converts, Heretics, and Lepers: Maimonides and the Outsider.* Notre Dame: University of Notre Dame Press, 2007.
Diamond, "Theodicy"	Diamond, James. "The Failed Theodicy of a Rabbinic Pariah: A Maimonidean Recasting of Elisha Ben Abuyah." *Jewish Studies Quarterly* 9 (2002): 353-80.
Dienstag, "Astrology"	Dienstag, Jacob I. "Maimonides' Letter to the Sages of Southern France on Astrology – Bibliography of Editions, Translations, and Studies." *Kiryat Sefer* 61, no. 1 (1986-87): 147-58 (Hebrew).
Dienstag, "Gersonides and Maimonides"	Dienstag, Jacob I. "The Relationship of Gersonides to the Philosophy of Maimonides – Annotated Bibliography." *Da'at* 23 (1989): 5-13 (Hebrew).
Dienstag, "Providence"	Dienstag, Jacob I. "Maimonides and Providence – Bibliography." *Da'at* 20 (1988): 17-28 (Hebrew).
Dienstag, "Steinschneider"	Dienstag, Jacob I. "Moses Steinschneider as Maimonidean Scholar." *Sinai* 66 (1970): 347-66 (Hebrew).
Diesendruck, "Samuel and Moses ibn Tibbon"	Diesendruck, Zvi. "Samuel and Moses Ibn Tibbon on Maimonides' Theory of Providence." *Hebrew Union College Annual* 11 (1936): 341-66.

Duhem,
*To Save the
Phenomena*

Duhem, Pierre. *To Save the Phenomena: An Essay on the Idea of
Physical Theory from Plato to Galileo.* Translated by Edmund Doland
and Chaninah Maschler. Chicago: University of Chicago Press, 1969.

Duran,
*"Hakdamat Sefer
Ma'aseh Ephod"*

Duran, Profiat. "Introduction to *Ma'aseh Ephod* by Profiat Duran
Edited by Dov Rappel." *Sinai* 100 (1986-1987): 749-95 (Hebrew).

Duran,
Ohev Mishpat

Duran, Shimon ben Zemah. *Ohev Mishpat.* Tel Aviv: Zion, 1971
[Venice, 1590.].

Efros,
*"Maimonides'
Treatise"*

Efros, Israel. "Maimonides' *Treatise on Logic*: The New Arabic Text
and Its Light on the Hebrew Versions." *Jewish Quarterly Review* 53
(1962-63): 269-73.

Eisen, "Job"

Eisen, Robert. "Gersonides' *Commentary on the Book of Job.*" *The
Journal of Jewish Thought and Philosophy* 10 (2001): 239-88.

Eisen, *Providence*

Eisen, Robert. *Gersonides on Providence, Covenant, and the
Chosen People: A Study in Medieval Jewish Philosophy and Bible
Commentary.* Albany: SUNY Press, 1995.

Fakhry,
"Contemplative Ideal"

Fakhry, Majid. "The Contemplative Ideal in Islamic Philosophy:
Aristotle and Avicenna." *Journal of the History of Philosophy* 14
(1976): 137-45.

Farabi,
*Fusul al-Madani:
Aphorisms*

Farabi, Abu Nasser Muhammad. *Fusul Al-Madani: Aphorisms of
the Statesman.* Translated by D. M. Dunlop. Cambridge: Cambridge
University Press, 1961.

Faur,
Homo Mysticus

Faur, Jose. *Homo Mysticus: A Guide to Maimonides' Guide for the
Perplexed.* Syracuse: Syracuse University Press, 1999.

Faur,
Iyyunim

Faur, Jose. *Iyyunim Be-Mishneh Torah Li-Ha-Rambam.* Jerusalem:
Mossad ha-Rav Kook, 1978.

Faur,
Maimonides on
Imagination"

Faur, Jose. "Maimonides on Imagination: Towards a Theory of Jewish
Aesthetics." *The Solomon Goldman Lectures* 6 (1994): 89-104.

Feldman,
"Theological
Determinism"

Feldman, Seymour. "Crescas' Theological Determinism." *Da'at* 9
(1982): 3-28.

Feldman, "Universe" Feldman, Seymour. "The End of the Universe in Medieval Jewish Philosophy." *AJSReview* 11 (1986): 53-77.

Fisch, *Rational Rabbis* Fisch, Menachem. *Rational Rabbis: Science and Talmudic Culture.* Bloomington: Indiana University Press, 1997.

Fox, *Interpreting* Fox, Marvin. *Interpreting Maimonides: Studies in Methodology, Metaphysics, and Moral Philosophy.* Chicago: University of Chicago Press, 1990.

Fox, "Nahmanides" Fox, Marvin. "Nahmanides on the Status of Aggadot: Perspectives on the Disputation at Barcelona, 1263." *Journal of Jewish Studies* 40 (1989): 95-109.

Frank, "Heart and Soul" Frank, Daniel H. "'With All Your Heart and All Your Soul...': The Moral Psychology of the *Shemonah Perakim*." In *Maimonides and the Sciences,* edited by Robert S. Cohen and Hillel Levine, 25-34. Dordrecht: Kluwer, 2000.

Frank, *Autonomy and Judaism* Frank, Daniel H., ed. *Autonomy and Judaism.* Albany: SUNY Press, 1992.

Freudenthal, "Felicity" Freudenthal, Gad. "Human Felicity and Astronomy: Gersonides' Revolt against Ptolemy." *Da'at* 22 (1989): 55-72 (Hebrew).

Freudenthal, "Instrumentalism and Realism" Freudenthal, Gad. "'Instrumentalism' and 'Realism' as Categories in the History of Astronomy: Duhem Vs. Popper, Maimonides Vs. Gersonides." *Centaurus* 46 (2003): 227-48.

Freudenthal, "Maimonides' Four Heavenly Spheres" Freudenthal, Gad. "Maimonides' Four Heavenly Spheres: Four Comments (*Guide for the Perplexed*, II. 9-10)." In *Rambam: Shamranut, Radikaliut, Mahapkhanut,* edited by Aviezer Ravitzky, 499-527. Jerusalem: Merkaz Zalman Shazar, 2008 (Hebrew).

Freudenthal, "Maimonides' Stance" Freudenthal, Gad. "Maimonides' Stance on Astrology in Context: Cosmology, Physics, Medicine, and Providence." In *Moses Maimonides – Physician, Scientist, and Philosopher,* edited by Samuel Kottek and Fred Rosner, 77-90. Northvale: Jason Aronson, 1993.

Friedberg, "Enumeration" Friedberg, Albert Dov. "An Evaluation of Maimonides' Enumeration of the 613 Commandments, with Special Emphasis on the Positive Commandments." Ph. D. Dissertation, University of Toronto, 2008.

Friedman, *Ha-Rambam, Ha-Mashiah* Friedman, Mordechai Akiva. *Ha-Rambam, Ha-Mashiah Be-Teiman, Ve-Ha-Shemad.* Jerusalem: Yad Ben-Zvi, 2002.

Gellman, "Jewish Mysticism and Morality"	Gellman, Jerome. "Jewish Mysticism and Morality: Kabbalah and Its Ontological Dualities." *Archiv fuer Religionsgeschichte* 9 (2008): 23-35.
Gersonides, *Song of Songs*	Levi ben Gershom. *Commentary on Song of Songs*. Trans. Menachem Kellner. New Haven: Yale University Press, 1998.
Gersonides, *Shir ha-Shirim*	Levi ben Gershom. *Perush Shir ha-Shirim*. Ed. by Menachem Kellner. Ramat-Gan: Bar-Ilan University Press, 2001.
Gersonides, *Wars*	Levi ben Gerson. *Wars of the Lord [Milhamot ha-Shem]*. Leipzig, 1929.
Goodman, *Rambam*	Goodman, Lenn. *Rambam: Readings in the Philosophy of Moses Maimonides*. New York: Viking, 1976.
Gould, *Times' Arrow*	Gould, Stephen Jay. *Time's Arrow, Time's Cycle* Cambridge: Harvard University Press, 1987.
Greenberg, "Atem Keruyim Adam"	Greenberg, Moshe. "*Atem Keruyim Adam*." In *Al Ha-Mikra Ve-Al Ha-Yahadut: Kovetz Ketavim*, edited by Avraham Shapira, 55-67. Tel Aviv: Am Oved, 1984 (Hebrew).
Greenberg, "Erekh Ha-Adam"	Greenberg, Moshe. "*Erekh Ha-Adam Ba-Mikra*." In *Al Ha-Mikra Ve-Al Ha-Yahadut: Kovetz Ketavim*, edited by Avraham Shapira, 13-23. Tel Aviv: Am Oved, 1984 (Hebrew).
Greenberg, "Mankind"	Greenberg, Moshe. "Mankind, Israel, and the Nations in the Hebraic Heritage." In *No Man Is Alien: Essays on the Unity of Mankind*, edited by J. Robert Nelson, 15-40. Leiden: Brill, 1971.
Haack, "Staying for an Answer"	Haack, Susan. "Staying for an Answer: The Untidy Process of Groping for Truth." *Times Literary Supplement*, no. July 9, 1999 (1999): 12-14.
Halbertal, *Bein Torah*	Halbertal, Moshe. *Bein Torah Le-Hokhmah: R. Menachem Ha-Meiri U-Ba'alie Ha-Halakhah Ha-Maimunim'im Be-Provanz*. Jerusalem: Magnes, 2000.
Halbertal, *Concealment*	Halbertal, Moshe. *Concealment and Revelation: Esotericism in Jewish Thought and Its Philosophical Implications*. Translated by Jackie Feldman. Princeton: Princeton University Press, 2007.

Halbertal,
People of the Book

Halbertal, Moshe. *People of the Book: Canon, Meaning, and Authority*. Cambridge: Harvard University Press, 1997.

Halbertal,
"*Mishneh Torah*"

Halbertal, Moshe. "What Is the *Mishneh Torah*? On Codification and Ambivalence." In *Maimonides after 800 Years: Essays on Maimonides and His Influence*, edited by Jay Harris, 81-112. Cambridge: Harvard University Press, 2007.

Halevi,
Kuzari

Judah Halevi, *The Kuzari: In Defense of the Despised Faith*. Translated by N. Daniel Korobkin. Jerusalem: Feldheim, 2009.

Halkin and Hartman,
Crisis and Leadership

Halkin, Abraham S. and David Hartman *Crisis and Leadership: Epistles of Maimonides*. Philadelphia: Jewish Publication Society, 1985.

Hallamish,
"Attitude to the Nations"

Hallamish, Moshe. "The Kabbalists' Attitude to the Nations of the World." In *Joseph Baruch Sermonetta Memorial Volume (=Jerusalem Studies in Jewish Thought 14)*, edited by Aviezer Ravitzky, 289-312. Jerusalem: Jerusalem Studies in Jewish Thought, 1988 (Hebrew).

Halperin,
Chariot

Halperin, David J. *The Faces of the Chariot*. Tuebingen: J C B Mohr, 1988.

Halperin,
Merkabah

Halperin, David. *The Merkabah in Rabbinic Literature*. Leiden: Brill, 1980.

Hanley,
Is Data Human?

Hanley, Richard *Is Data Human? The Metaphysics of Star Trek*. New York: Basic Books, 1997.

Hartman,
Maimonides

Hartman, David. *Maimonides: Torah and Philosophic Quest*. Philadelphia: Jewish Publication Society, 1976.

Harvey,
"Crescas' Critique of Philosophic Happiness"

Harvey, Warren Zev. "R. Hasdai Crescas and His Critique of Philosophic Happiness." *Proceedings of the Sixth World Congress of Jewish Studies* 3 (1977): 143-49.

Harvey,
"Crescas vs Maimonides"

Harvey, Warren Zev. "Crescas vs Maimonides on Knowledge and Pleasure." In *A Straight Path: Studies in Medieval Philosophy and Culture*, edited by Ruth Link-Salinger, 113-23. Washington, DC: Catholic University of America Press, 1988.

Harvey,
"Hasdai Crescas' Critique"

Harvey, Warren Zev. "Hasdai Crescas' Critique of the Theory of the Acquired Intellect." Ph. D. Dissertation, Columbia University, 1973.

Harvey,
"Holiness"

Harvey, Warren Zev. "Holiness: A Command to Imitatio Dei."
Tradition 16 (1977): 7-28.

Harvey,
"How To"

Harvey, Warren Zev. "How to Begin to Study *The Guide of the
Perplexed*, I.1." *Daʾat* 21 (1988): 5-24 (Hebrew).

Harvey,
"Maimonides' First
Commandment"

Harvey, Warren Zev. "Maimonides' First Commandment, Physics,
and Doubt." In *Hazon Nahum: Studies ... Presented to Dr. Norman
Lamm*, edited by Yaakov Elman and Jeffrey S. Gurock, 149-62. New
York: Yeshiva University Press, 1997.

Harvey,
"Miriam the
Prophetess"

Harvey, Warren Zev. "The Heresy of the Prophetess Miriam in
Maimonides' Seventh Principle." In *Al Pi Ha-Beʾer: Mehkarim....
Mugashim Li-Yaʾakov Blidstein*, edited by Haim Kreisel Uri Ehrlich,
Daniel J. Lasker, 183-94. Beersheva: Ben-Gurion University Press,
2008.

Harvey,
"Return"

Harvey, Warren Zev. "The Return of Maimonideanism." *Journal of
Jewish Social Studies* 42 (1980): 249-68.

Harvey,
"Theories of
Imagination"

Harvey, Warren Zev. "Three Theories of the Imagination in 12th
Century Jewish Philosophy." In *Intellect and Imagination in Medieval
Philosophy*, edited by Maria Candida and Jose F. Meirinhos Pacheco,
287-301. Turnhout: Brepols, 2006.

Harvey,
"Third Approach"

Harvey, Warren Zev. "A Third Approach to Maimonides'
Cosmogony-Prophetology Puzzle." *Harvard Theological Review* 74
(1981): 287-301.

Harvey,
"Virtuous State"

Harvey, Warren Zev. "Averroes, Maimonides, and the Virtuous State."
In *Iyyunim Bi-Sugyot Philosophiot...Likhvod Shlomo Pines*, 19-31.
Jerusalem: Israel Academy of Sciences, 1992 (Hebrew).

Harvey, S.
Falaquera

Harvey, Steven. *Falaqueraʾs 'Epistle of the Debate'*. Cambridge:
Harvard University Press, 1987.

Harvey, S.
"Letter"

Harvey, Steven. "Did Maimonides' Letter to Samuel Ibn Tibbon
Determine Which Philosophers Would Be Studied by Later Jewish
Thinkers?" *Jewish Quarterly Review* 83 (1992): 51-70.

Harvey, S.
"Love"

Harvey, Steven. "The Meaning of Terms Designating Love in
Judaeo-Arabic Thought and Some Remarks on the Judaeo-Arabic
Interpretation of Maimonides." In *Judaeo-Arabic Studies*, edited
by Norman Golb, 175-96. Amsterdam: Harwood Academic
Publishers, 1997.

Harvey, S.
"New Islamic Source"
Harvey, Steven. "A New Islamic Source of *The Guide of the Perplexed*." *Maimonidean Studies* 2 (1991): 31-59.

Hertzberg,
Jews
Hertzberg, Arthur. *The Jews in America*. New York: Simon and Schuster, 1989.

Heschel,
Maimonides
Heschel, Abraham Joshua. *Maimonides: A Biography*. Translated by Joachim Neugroschel. New York: Fasrrar, Straus, and Giroux, 1982.

Heschel,
Search
Heschel, Abraham Joshua. *God in Search of Man*. New York: Farrar, Straus, and Giroux, 1977.

Hirshman,
"Rabbinic
Universalism"
Hirshman, Menachem (Marc). "Rabbinic Universalism in the Second and Third Centuries." *Harvard Theological Review* 93 (2000): 101-15.

Hirshman,
*Torah Lekhol
Ba'ei Olam*
Hirshman, Menachem (Marc). *Torah Lekhol Ba'ei Olam: Zerem Universali Be-Sifrut Ha-Tana'im Ve-Yahaso Le-Hokhmat He-Amim*. Tel Aviv: Ha-Kibbutz ha-Meuhad, 1999.

Hoch and Kellner,
"Voice"
Hoch, Liron and Menachem Kellner. "'The Voice is the Voice of Jacob, but the Hands are the Hands of Esau': Isaac Abravanel between Judah Halevi and Moses Maimonides," *Jewish History*, forthcoming.

Hon,
"Going Wrong"
Hon, Giora. "Going Wrong: To Make a Mistake, to Fall into Error." *Review of Metaphysics* 49 (1995): 3-20.

Husik,
History
Husik, Isaac. *A History of Mediaeval Jewish Philosophy*. New York: Atheneum, 1969.

Hyman,
"Aristotle's Theory"
Hyman, Arthur. "Aristotle's Theory of the Intellect and Its Interpretation by Averroes." *Studies in Philosophy and the History of Philosophy* 9 (1981): 161-91.

Hyman,
"Demonstrative"
Hyman, Arthur. "Demonstrative, Dialectical and Sophistic Arguments in the Philosophy of Moses Maimonides." *Studies in Philosophy and the History of Philosophy* 19 (1989): 35-51.

Hyman,
"Principles"
Hyman, Arthur. "Maimonides' 'Thirteen Principles.'" In *Jewish Medieval and Renaissance Studies*, edited by Alexander Altmann, 119-44. Cambridge: Harvard University Press, 1967.

Idel,   Idel, Moshe. "*Sitre 'Arayot* in Maimonides' Thought." In *Maimonides*
"*Sitrei 'Arayot*"   *and Philosophy,* edited by Shlomo Pines and Yirmiyahu Yovel, 79-91.
                        Dordrecht: Kluwer Academic, 1986.

Idelson,   Idelson, Abraham. Z. *Jewish Liturgy and Its Development.* New York:
Jewish Liturgy   Holt, 1972.

Ivry,   Ivry, Alfred. "Getting to Know Thee: Conjunction and Conformity
"Getting to Know   in Averroes' and Maimonides' Phiilosphy." In *Adaptations and*
Thee"   *Innovations: Studies ... Dedicated to Professor Joel L. Kraemer,* edited
                        by Y. Tzvi Langermann and Josef Stern, 143-56. Paris: Peeters, 2007.

Ivry,   Ivry, Alfred. "Isma'ili Theology and Maimonides' Philosophy." In *The*
"Ismaili Theology"   *Jews of Medieval Islam: Community, Society, and Identity,* edited by
                        Daniel Frank, 271-99. Leiden: Brill, 1995.

Ivry,   Ivry, Alfred. "The Logical and Scientific Premises of Maimonides'
"Logical and   Thought." In *Perspectives on Jewish Thought and Mysticism...*
Scientific Premises"   *Dedicated To...Alexander Altmann,* edited by Elliot Wolfson, Alfred
                        Ivry, Allan Arkush, 63-98. Amsterdam: Harwood Academic, 1998.

Ivry,   Ivry, Alfred. "Strategies of Interpretation in Maimonides' *Guide of the*
"Strategies"   *Perplexed." Jewish History 6 (= The Frank Talmage Memorial Volume,*
                        vol. 2), (1992): 113-30.

Jacobs,   Jacobs, Louis. *Faith.* New York: Basic Books, 1968.
Faith

Jacobs,   Jacobs, Louis. *Principles of the Jewish Faith.* New York: Behrman
Principles   House, 1974.

Jassen,   Jassen, Alex P. "Reading Midrash with Maimonides: An Inquiry
"Reading Midrash"   into the Sources of Maimonides' Account of the Origins of Idolatry."
                        Australian Journal of Jewish Studies 21 (2007): 170-200.

Jospe,   Jospe, Raphael. "'The Garden of Eden': On the Chapter Divisions
"Garden"   and Literary Structure of the *Guide of the Perplexed."* In Jospe, *Jewish*
                        Philosophy: Foundations and Extensions, Vol. 2: On Philosophers and
                        Their Thought, 65-78. Lanham, MD: University Press of America,
                        2008.

Kadish,   Kadish, Avi Seth. "The Book of Abraham: Rabbi Shimon Ben
"Duran"   Zamah Duran and the School of Rabbenu Nissim Gerondi," Ph. D.
                        Dissertation, University of Haifa, 2006.

Kafih, A.   Kafih, Amit. "Moreinu Ha-Rav Yosef Kafih's Glosses to His Edition
"*Moreinu*"   of the Commentary on the Mishnah." *Mesorah le-Yosef* 4 (2005): 298-
                        315 (Hebrew).

Kafih,
Ha-Mikra

Kafih, Yosef. *Ha-Mikra Be-Rambam*. Jerusalem: Mossad ha-Rav Kook, 1972.

Kafih,
Iggerot

Kafih, Yosef. *Iggerot Ha-Rambam*. Jerusalem: Mossad ha-Rav Kook, 1972.

Kaminsky,
Yet I Loved Jacob

Kaminsky, Joel S. *Yet I Loved Jacob: Reclaiming the Biblical Concept of Election*. Nashville: Abingdon, 2007.

Kanarfogel,
"Anthropomorphism"

Kanarfogel, Ephraim. "Varieties of Belief in Medieval Ashkenaz: The Case of Anthropomorphism." In *Rabbinic Culture and Its Critics: Jewish Authority, Dissent, and Heresy in Medieval and Early Modern Times* edited by Daniel Frank and Matt Goldish, 117-60. Detroit: Wayne State University Press, 2008.

Kanarfogel,
"Compensation"

Kanarfogel, Ephraim. "Compensation for the Study of Torah in Medieval Rabbinic Thought." In *Of Scholars, Savants, and Their Texts: Studies in Philosophy and Religious Thought: Essays in Honor of Arthur Hyman*, edited by Ruth Link-Salinger, 135-47. New York: Peter Lang, 1989.

Kaplan,
"Miraculous Element"

Kaplan, Lawrence. "Maimonides on the Miraculous Element in Prophecy." *Harvard Theological Review* 70 (1977): 230-56.

Kaplan,
"Rav Kook"

Kaplan, Lawrence. "Rav Kook and the Jewish Philosophical Tradition." In *Rabbi Abraham Isaac Kook and Jewish Spirituality*, edited by Lawrence Kaplan and David Shatz, 41-77. New York: New York University Press, 1995.

Kaplan,
"Singularity"

Kaplan, Lawrence. "Maimonides on the Singularity of the Jewish People." *Da'at* 15 (1985): v-xxvii.

Kasher,
"Circumcision"

Kasher, Hannah. "Maimonides' View of Circumcision as a Factor Uniting the Jewish and Muslim Communities." In *Studies in Muslim-Jewish Relations*, edited by Ronald L. Nettler, 103-08. Luxembourg: Harwood Academic Publishers, 1995.

Kasher,
"*Hakham*"

Kasher, Hannah. ""Hakham," "Hasid," And "Tov" In Maimonides' Writings – a Study in Terms and Their Reference." *Maimonidean Studies* 4 (2000): 81-105 (Hebrew)

Kasher,
"Job's Image"

Kasher, Hannah. "Job's Image and Opinions in Maimonides." *Da'at* 15 (1985): 81-88 (Hebrew).

Kasher, "Sufferings"	Kasher, Hannah. "Sufferings without Transgression." *Da'at* 26 (1991): 35-42 (Hebrew).
Kasher, "Talmud Torah"	Kasher, Hannah. "Talmud Torah as a Means of Apprehending God in Maimonides' Teachings." *Jerusalem Studies in Jewish Thought* 5 (1986): 71-81.
Kassirer and Glicksberg, Me-Sinai	Shlomo Kassirer and Shlomo Glicksberg, *Me-Sinai le-Lishkat ha-Gazit: Torah she-be'al Peh bi-Mishnatam shel ha-Rambam ve-ha-Ramban*. Ramat-Gan: Bar-Ilan University Jesselson Institute for Higher Torah Studies, 2008
Katz, Tradition	Katz, Jacob. *Tradition and Crisis: Jewish Society at the End of the Middle Ages*. New York: Schocken Books, 1971.
Kellner, J. "Bibliography"	Kellner, Jolene. "Academic Studies on and New Editions of Works by Isaac Abravanel: 2000-2008." *Jewish History* (in press).
Kellner and Kellner, "Respectful Disagreement"	Kellner, Jolene and Menachem Kellner, "Respectful Disagreement." In *Jewish Theology and the Other*, edited by Eugene Korn (in press).
Kellner, "Ante-Mundane Torah."	Kellner, Menachem. "An Ante-Mundane Torah? - A Maimonidean Study." *Da'at* 61 (2007): 83-96 (Hebrew).
Kellner, "Astronomy"	Kellner, Menachem. "On the Status of the Astronomy and Physics in Maimonides' *Mishneh Torah*: A Chapter in the History of Science." *British Journal for the History of Science* 24 (1991): 453-63.
Kellner, "Bibliographia Gersonideana"	Kellner, Menachem. "Bibliographia Gersonideana 1992-2002." *Aleph* 3 (2003): 343-74.
Kellner, "Conception of Torah"	Kellner, Menachem. "The Conception of Torah as a Deductive Science in Medieval Jewish Thought." *Revue des etudes juives* 146 (1987): 265-79.
Kellner, Confrontation	Kellner, Menachem. *Maimonides' Confrontation with Mysticism*. Oxford: Littman Library of Jewish Civilization, 2006.
Kellner, "Contemporary Jewish Philosophy"	Kellner, Menachem. "Is Contemporary Jewish Philosophy Possible?-No." In *Studies in Jewish Philosophy: Collected Essays of the Academy for Jewish Philosophy, 1980-1985*, edited by Norbert M. Samuelson, 17-28. Lanham, MD: University Press of America, 1987.

| Kellner, "Cultured Despisers" | Kellner, Menachem. "Gersonides and His Cultured Despisers: Arama and Abravanel." *Journal of Medieval and Renaissance Studies* 6 (1976): 269-96. |

| Kellner, Decline | Kellner, Menachem. *Maimonides on The "Decline of the Generations" And the Nature of Rabbinic Authority*. Albany: SUNY Press, 1996. |

| Kellner, Dogma | Kellner, Menachem. *Dogma in Medieval Jewish Thought: From Maimonides to Abravanel*. Oxford: Oxford University Press, 1986. |

| Kellner, "Farteitsht" | Kellner, Menachem. "Farteitsht Un Farbessert: Comments on Tendentious 'Corrections' in Maimonides' Writings." In *Be-Darkei Shalom: Iyyunim Be-Hagut Yehudit Mugashim Le-Shalom Rosenberg*, edited by Binyamin Ish-Shalom and Amihai Berholz, 255-63. Jerusalem: Bet Morashah, 2007 (Hebrew). English translation in *Me'orot* [=*Edah Journal*] 6.2 (2007). |

| Kellner, "Gersonides on the Active Intellect" | Kellner, Menachem. "Gersonides on the Role of the Active Intellect in Human Cognition. *HUCA* 65 (1994): 233-259. |

| Kellner, "Gersonides on the Song of Songs and Science" | Kellner, Menachem. "Gersonides on the Song of Songs and the Nature of Science." *Journal of Jewish Thought and Philosophy* 4 (1994): 1-21. |

| Kellner, Judaism | Kellner, Menachem. *Maimonides on Judaism and the Jewish People*. Albany: SUNY Press, 1991. |

| Kellner, "Kotler" | Kellner, Menachem. "Dor Dor Ve-Rambamav: Ha-Rambam Shel R. Aharon Kotler." In *Al Pi Ha-Be'er: Mehkarim....Mugashim Li-Ya'akov Blidstein*, edited by Haim Kreisel Uri Ehrlich, Daniel J. Lasker, 463-86. Beersheva: Ben-Gurion University Press, 2008. |

| Kellner, "Maimondes and Samuel ibn Tibbon" | Kellner, Menachem. "Maimonides and Samuel Ibn Tibbon on Jer. 9:22-23 and Human Perfection." In *Studies...Presented to Emanuel Rackman*, edited by M. Beer, 49-57. Ramat-Gan: Bar-Ilan University Press, 1994. |

| Kellner, "Maimonides' Allegiances" | Kellner, Menachem. "Maimonides' Allegiances to Torah and Science." *The Torah U-Madda Journal* 7 (1997): 88-104. |

| Kellner, "Maimonides and Gersonides on Astronomy" | Kellner, Menachem. "Maimonides and Gersonides on Astronomy and Metaphysics." In *Moses Maimonides: Physician, Scientist and Philosopher*, edited by Samuel Kottek and Fred Rosner, 91-96 and 249-51. Northvale NJ: Jason Aronson, 1993. |

Kellner, "Maimonides on Hagigah"	Kellner, Menachem. "Maimonides' Commentary on *Mishnah* *Hagigah* II.1: Translation and Commentary." In *From Strength to* *Strength: Lectures from Shearith Israel*, edited by Marc Angel, 101-11. New York: Sepher Hermon Press, 1998.
Kellner, "Messianic Postures"	Kellner, Menachem. "Messianic Postures in Israel Today." *Modern* *Judaism* 6, no. 2 (1986): 197-209.
Kellner, "Miracles"	"Gersonides on Miracles, the Messiah and Resurrection," *Da'at* 4 (1980): 5-34.
Kellner, "*Mishneh Torah –* Why?"	Kellner, Menachem. "*Mishneh Torah* - Why?" *Mesorah le-Yosef* 4 (2005): 316-29 (Hebrew).
Kellner, "Misogyny"	Kellner, Menachem. "Philosophical Misogyny in Medieval Jewish Thought: Gersonides Vs. Maimonides." In *Y. Sermonetta Memorial* *Volume*, edited by Aviezer Ravitzky, 113-28. Jerusalem: Magnes, 1998 (Hebrew).
Kellner, *Must*	Kellner, Menachem. *Must a Jew Believe Anything?* 2nd. ed. London: Littman Library of Jewish Civilization, 2006.
Kellner, *Perfection*	Kellner, Menachem. *Maimonides on Human Perfection*, Brown Judaic Studies 202. Atlanta: Scholars Press, 1990.
Kellner, "Philosophical Themes"	Kellner, Menachem. "Philosophical Themes in Maimonides' *Sefer* *Ahavah.*" In *Maimonides and His Heritage*, edited by Lenn Evan Goodman, Idit Dobbs-Weinstein, and James Grady, 13-35. Albany: SUNY Press, 2009.
Kellner, "Rabbi Isaac Bar Sheshet"	Kellner, Menachem. "Rabbi Isaac Bar Sheshet Perfet's Responsum Concerning the Study of Greek Philosophy." *Tradition* 15 (1975): 110-18.
Kellner, "Rabbis"	Kellner, Menachem. "Rabbis in Politics: A Study in Medieval and Modern Jewish Political Theory." *Medinah ve-Hevrah* 3 (2003): 673- 98 (Hebrew).
Kellner, "Reading"	Kellner, Menachem. "Reading Rambam: Approaches to the Interpretation of Maimonides." *Jewish History* 5 (1991): 73-93.
Kellner, "Religious Faith"	Kellner, Menachem. "Religious Faith in the Middle Ages and Today." In *Al Ha-Emunah*, edited by David Kurzweil Moshe Halbertal, and Avi Sagi, 312-27, 647-50. Jerusalem: Keter, 2005.

Kellner, "Status"	Kellner, Menachem. "On the Status of the Astronomy and Physics in Maimonides' Mishneh Torah: A Chapter in the History of Science." *British Journal for the History of Science* 24 (1991): 453-63.
Kellner, "Strauss' Maimonides"	Kellner, Menachem. "Strauss' Maimonides vs. Maimonides' Maimondes: Could Maimonides Have Been Both Englightened and Orthodox?" *Le'ela* December 2000, no. 50 (2000): 29-36.
Kellner, "Suggestion"	Kellner, Menachem. "A Suggestion Concerning Maimonides' Thirteen Principles and the Status of Gentiles in the Messianic Era." In Tura, *Oranim Studies in Jewish Thought: Simon Greenberg Jubilee Volume* edited by Meir Ayali, 249-60. Tel Aviv: Ha-Kibbutz Ha-Meuhad, 1988.
Kellner, "True Religion"	Kellner, Menachem. "Maimonides' True Religion – for Jews, or All Humanity?" *Me'orot Journal* 7 (2008).
Kellner, "Universalism"	Kellner, Menachem. "On Universalism and Particularism in Judaism." *Daat* 36 (1996): v-xv.
Kellner, "Virtue"	Kellner, Menachem. "The Virtue of Faith." In *Neoplatonism and Jewish Thought*, edited by Lenn Goodman, 195-205. Albany: SUNY Press, 1992.
Kleinberger, Ha-Mahshavah	Kleinberger, Aharon Fritz. *Ha-Mahshavah Ha-Pedagogit Shel Ha-Maharal Me-Prag.* Jerusalem: Magnes, 1962.
Klein-Braslavy, "Exoteric and Esoteric"	Klein-Braslavy, Sara. "Maimonides' Exoteric and Esoteric Biblical Interpretations in the *Guide of the Perplexed*." In *Study and Knowledge in Jewish Thought*, edited by Howard Kreisel, 137-64. Beersheva: Ben-Gurion University Press, 2006.
Klein-Braslavy, "Maimonides on	Klein-Braslavy, Sara. "Maimonides' Commentaries on Proverbs 1:6." In *Alei Shefer: Studies in Literature and Jewish Thought Presented to Rabbi Dr. Alexandre Safran*, edited by Moshe Hallamish, 121-32. Ramat-Gan: Bar-Ilan University Press, 1990 (Hebrew).
Klein-Braslavy, Shlomoh ha-Melekh	Klein-Braslavy, Sara. *Shlomo Ha-Melekh Ve-Ha-Ezoterizm Ha-Philosophi Be-Mishnat Ha-Rambam (King Solomon and Philosophical Esotericism in Maimonides).* Jerusalem: Magnes, 1996.
Kogan, "What Can We Know"	Kogan, Barry S. "'What Can We Know and When Can We Know It?' Maimonides on the Active Intelligence and Human Cognition." *Studies in Philosophy and the History of Philosophy 19* [= *Moses Maimonides and His Time*, edited by Eric L. Ormsby] (1989): 121-37.
Kraemer, "Opinions"	Kraemer, Joel. "Alfarabi's *Opinions of the Virtuous City* and Maimonides' Foundations of the Law." In *Studia Orientalia: Memoriae D. H. Baneth Dedicata*, edited by J. Blau et al., 107-53. Jerusalem: Magnes, 1979.

Kraemer, "Maimonides on Aristotle and Scientific Method"	Kraemer, Joel. "Maimonides on Aristotle and Scientific Method." *Studies in Philosophy and the History of Philosophy 19* [= *Moses Maimonides and His Time*, edited by Eric L. Ormsby] (1989): 53-88.
Kraemer, *Mind of Talmud*	Kraemer, David *The Mind of the Talmud: An Intellectual History of the Bavli*. New York: Oxford University Press, 1990.
Kreisel, "Maimonides on Divine Religion"	Kreisel, Howard. "Maimonides on Divine Religion." In *Maimonides after 800 Years: Essays on Maimonides and His Influence*, edited by Jay Harris, 151-66. Cambridge: Harvard University Press, 2007.
Kreisel, "Sage and Prophet"	Kreisel, Haim. "Sage and Prophet in the Thought of Maimonides and His School." *Eshel Beersheva* 3 (1986): 149-69 (Hebrew).
Kreisel, *Political Thought*	Kreisel, Haim. *Maimonides' Political Thought: Studies in Ethics, Law, and the Human Ideal*. Albany: SUNY Press, 1999.
Kreisel, *Prophecy*	Kreisel, Howard. *Prophecy: The History of an Idea in Medieval Jewish Philosophy*. Dordrecht: Kluwer, 2001.
Labendz, "Epicurean"	Labendz, Jenny R. "'Know What to Answer the Epicurean' - A Diachronic Study of the *Apikoros* in Rabbinic Literature." *HUCA* 74 (2003): 175-214.
Lamm, *Torah U-Madda*	Lamm, Norman. *Torah U-Madda: The Encounter of Religious Learning and Worldly Knowledge in the Jewish Tradition*. Northvale, NJ: Jason Aronson, 1990.
Langermann, "Letter of R. Shmuel"	Langermann, Y. Tzvi. "The Letter of R. Shmuel Ben Eli on Resurrection." *Kovetz al Yad* 15 (2000): 41-92 (Hebrew).
Langermann, "Perplexity"	Langermann, Y. Tzvi. "The 'True Perplexity': *The Guide of the Perplexed*, Part II, Chapter 24." In *Perspectives on Maimonides: Philosophical and Historical Studies*, edited by Joel Kraemer, 159-74. Oxford: Littman Library of Jewish Civilization, 1991.
Langermann, "Some Issues"	Langermann, Y. Tzvi. "Some Issues Relating to Astronomy in the Thought of Maimonides." *Da'at* 37 (1996): 107-18 (Hebrew).
Lasker, "Chasdai Crescas"	Lasker, Daniel J. "Chasdai Crescas." In *History of Jewish Philosophy*, edited by Daniel H. Frank and Oliver Leaman, 399-414. London: Routledge, 1997.

Lasker,
"Love of God"

Lasker, Daniel J. "Love of God and Knowledge of God in Maimonides' Philosophy." In *Ecriture Et Reecriture Des Textes Philosophiques Medievaux: Volume d'hommage Offert a Colette Sirat*, edited by J. Hamesse and O. Weijers, 329-45. Turnhout: Brepols, 2005.

Lasker,
"Maimonides and
Karaites"

Lasker, Daniel J. "Maimonides and the Karaites: From Critic to Cultural Hero." In *Maimonides Y Su Eoca*, edited by Carlos del Valle et al., 311-25. Madrid: Sociedad Estatal de Conmemoraciones Culturales, 2007.

Lasker,
"Maimonides'
Influence"

Lasker, Daniel J. "Maimonides' Influence on Israeli Politics." *Tarbut Demokratit* 2 (1999): 101-12.

Lasker,
"Proselyte Judaism"

Lasker, Daniel J. "Proselyte Judaism, Christianity, and Islam in the Thought of Judah Halevi." *Jewish Quarterly Review* 81 (1990): 75-91.

Lasker,
From Judah Hadassi

Lasker, Daniel J. *From Judah Hadassi to Elijah Bashyatchi: Studies in Late Medieval Karaite Philosophy*. Leiden: Brill, 2009.

Lawee,
"Achievement"

Lawee, Eric. "Isaac Abarbanel's Intellectual Achievement and Literary Legacy in Modern Scholarship: A Retrospective and Opportunity." In *Studies in Medieval Jewish History and Literature* III, edited by Isadore Twersky and Jay M. Harris, 214-45. Cambridge: Harvard University Press, 2000.

Lawee,
"Biblical Scholarship"

Lawee, Eric. "Isaac Abarbanel: From Medieval to Renaissance Jewish Biblical Scholarship." In *Hebrew Bible / Old Testament: The History of Its Interpretation*, edited by Magne Saebo, 190-214. Goettingen: Vandenhoeck and Ruprecht, 2008.

Lawee,
"Good"

Lawee, Eric. "'The Good We Accept and the Bad We Do Not': Aspects of Isaac Abarbanel's Stance Towards Maimonides." In *Be'erot Yitzhak: Studies in Memory of Isadore Twersky*, edited by Jay Harris, 119-60. Cambridge: Harvard University Press, 2005.

Lawee,
Stance

Lawee, Eric. *Isaac Abarbanel's Stance Towards Tradition: Defense, Dissent, and Dialogue*. Albany: SUNY Press, 2001.

Leibowitz,
Judaism,
Human Values

Leibowitz, Yeshayahu. *Judaism, Human Values, and the Jewish State*. Edited by Eliezer Goldman. Cambridge: Harvard University Press, 1992.

Lerner,   Lerner, Ralph. *Maimonides' Empire of Light: Popular Enlightenment*
Empire   *in an Age of Belief.* Chicago: University of Chicago Press, 2000.

Lerner and Mahdi,   Lerner, Ralph and Muhsin Mahdi, ed. *Medieval Political Philosophy:*
Medieval Political   *A Source Book.* Ithaca: Cornell University Press, 1972.
Philosophy

Levene,   Levene, Michelle. "Maimonides' Philosophical Exegesis of the
"Exegesis"   Nobles' Vision (Exodus 24): A Guide for the Pursuit of Knowledge."
                            Torah U-Madda Journal 11 (2003): 61-106.

Levenson,   Levenson, Jon D. "The Universal Horizon of Biblical Particularism."
"Universal Horizon"   In *Ethnicity and the Bible*, edited by Mark G. Brett, 143-69. Leiden:
                            Brill, 1996.

Levinger,   Levinger, Jacob. *Ha-Rambam Ke-Philosoph U-Ke-Posek (Maimonides*
Ha-Rambam   *as Philosopher and Codifier).* Jerusalem: Mossad Bialik, 1989.

Levy,   Levy, B. Barry. "The State and Directions of Orthodox Bible Study."
"Orthodox Bible   In *Modern Scholarship in the Study of Torah*, edited by Shalom
Study"   Carmy, 39-80. Northvale, NJ: Jason Aronson, 1997.

Lewis,   Lewis, C. S. *The Discarded Image.* Cambridge: Cambridge University
Discarded Image   Press, 1964.

Lichtenstein,   Lichtenstein, Aaron. "Torah and General Culture: Confluence and
"Torah and General   Conflict." In *Judaism's Encounter with Other Cultures: Rejection or*
Culture"   *Integration?*, edited by J. J. Schachter, Northvale: Jason Aronson,
                            1997.

Lifshutz,   Lifshutz, Berahyahu. "The Rules Governing Conflict of Laws
"Rules Governing   between a Jew and a Gentile According to Maimonides." In *Melanges*
Conflict"   *a La Memoire De Marcel-Henri Prevost*, 179-89. Paris: Presses
                            Universitaires de France, 1982.

Loewe,   Loewe, Raphael. "Credat Judaeus Appella?" *Journal of Jewish Studies*,
"Credat Judaeus   no. 50 (1999): 74-86.
Appella?"

Lorberbaum,   Lorberbaum, Menachem. "Maimonides on Repair of the World."
"Maimonides on   *Tarbiz* 64 (1995): 65-82 (Hebrew).
Repair of the World"

Lorberbaum,
"Maimonides on
Imago Dei"

Lorberbaum, Yair. "Maimonides on *Imago Dei*: Philosophy and
Law – the Felony of Murder, the Criminal Procedure, and Capital
Punishment." *Tarbiz* 68 (1999): 533-56 (Hebrew).

Malino,
"Aristotle on Eternity"

Malino, Jonathan. "Aristotle on Eternity: Does Maimonides Have
a Reply?" In *Maimonides and Philosophy*, edited by S. Pines and Y.
Yovel, 52-64. Dordrecht: Martinus Nijhoff, 1986.

Malter,
"Shem Tob"

Malter, Henry. "Shem Tob Ben Joseph Palquera II: His 'Treatise of
the Dream'." *Jewish Quarterly Review (OS)* 1 (1910-1911): 451-501.

Manekin,
"Hebrew Philosophy"

Manekin, Charles. "Hebrew Philosophy in the Fourteenth and
Fifteenth Centuries: An Overview." In *History of Jewish Philosophy*,
edited by Daniel H. Frank and Oliver Leaman, 350-78. London:
Routledge, 1997.

Manekin,
"Limited
Omniscience"

Manekin, Charles. "On the Limited-Omniscience Interpretation of
Gersonides' Theory of Divine Knowledge." In *Perspectives on Jewish
Thought and Mysticism*, edited by Alfred Ivry, 135-70. Amsterdam:
Harwood Academic Publishers, 1998.

Marx,
"Texts"

Marx, Alexander. "Texts by and About Maimonides." *Jewish
Quarterly Review* 25 (1934-35): 371-428.

Marx,
Studies

Marx, Alexander. *Studies in Jewish History and Booklore*. New York:
Jewish Theological Seminary, 1944.

Melamed,
"Natural, Human,
Divine"

Melamed, Abraham. "Natural, Human, Divine: Classification of the
Law among Some 15th and 16th Century Jewish Thinkers." *Italiah* 4
(1985): 59-93 (Hebrew).

Melamed,
"Maimonides on the
Political Character"

Melamed, Abraham. "Maimonides on the Political Character of
Human Beings – Needs and Obligations." In *Minhah Le-Sarah*,
edited by Moshe Idel et al., 292-333. Jerusalem: Magnes Press, 1994
(Hebrew).

Melamed,
Al Kitfei Anakim

Melamed, Abraham. *Al Kitfei Anakim: Toldot Ha-Pulmus Bein
Aharonim Le-Rishonim Be-Hagut Ha-Yehudit Bimei Ha-Benayim
U-Ve-Reshit Ha-Et Ha-Hadashah*. Ramat-Gan: Bar Ilan University
Press, 2003.

Melamed, Women	Melamed, Avraham. "Maimonides on Women: Formless Matter or Potential Prophet?" In *Perspectives on Jewish Thought and Mysticism...Dedicated To...Alexander Altmann*, edited by Elliot Wolfson, Alfred Ivry, Allan Arkush, 99-134. Amsterdam: Harwood Academic, 1998.
Newman, "Women, Saints, and Heretics"	Newman, Aryeh. "Women, Saints, and Heretics in Maimonides: The Challenge of Translating Judaica." *Conservative Judaism* 59 (1997): 75-84.
Novak, *Maimonides* *on Judaism*	Novak, David. *Maimonides on Judaism and Other Religions*. Cincinnati: Hebrew Union College Press, 1997.
Nuriel, "Faith"	Nuriel, Avraham. "The Concept 'Faith' in Maimonides." In *Galui Ve-Samui Ba-Philosophiah Ha-Yehudit Biynmei Ha-Benayim*, 78-82. Jerusalem: Magnes, 2000 (Hebrew).
Passmore, *Perfectibility*	Passmore, John. *The Perfectibility of Man*. London: Duckworth, 1970.
Philo, *On Abraham*	
Popper, *Unended Quest*	Popper, Karl. *Unended Quest*. LaSalle, IL: Open Court, 1976.
Ravven, "Spinoza and Maimonides"	Ravven, Heidi M. "Some Thoughts on What Spinoza Learned from Maimonides About the Prophetic Imagination. Part 1. Maimonides on Prophecy and the Imagination. Part Two: Spinoza's Maimonideanism." *Journal of the History of Philosophy* 39 (2001): 193-214, 385-406.
Raffel, "Providence"	Raffel, Charles. "Providence as Consequent Upon the Intellect: Maimonides' Theory of Providence " *AJS Review* 12 (1987): 25-71.
Rappoport, *Dat ha-Emet*"	Chaim Rappoport, "*Dat ha-Emet* in Maimonides' *Mishneh Torah*," *Me'orot* 7 (2008).
Ravitzky, "Development"	Ravitzky, Aviezer. "The Development of R. Hasdai Crescas' Views on Free Will." *Tarbiz* 51 (1982): 445-69 (Hebrew).
Ravitzky, "*Mishnato*"	Ravitzky, Aviezer. "Mishnato Shel R. Zerahiah Ben Shealtiel Hen." Ph. D. Dissertation, Hebrew University, 1978.

Ravitzky,
"Samuel ibn Tibbon"

Ravitzky, Aviezer. "Samuel Ibn Tibbon and the Esoteric
Interpretation of the *Guide of the Perplexed*." *AJS Review* 6 (1981):
87-123.

Ravitzky,
"To the Utmost"

Ravitzky, Aviezer. "'To the Utmost of Human Capacity': Maimonides
on the Days of the Messiah." In *Perspectives on Maimonides:
Philosophical and Historical Studies*, edited by Joel Kraemer, 221-56.
Oxford: Littman Library of Jewish Civilization, 1991.

Rawidowicz,
"Structure"

Rawidowicz, Shimon. "The Question of the Structure of the *Guide of
the Perplexed*." In *Iyyunim Be-Mahshevet Yisrael*, edited by Benjamin
Ravid, 237-96. Jerusalem: Reuven Mass, 1969 (Hebrew).

Regev,
"Vision of
the Nobles"

Regev, Shaul. "The Vision of the Nobles of Israel in the Jewish
Philosophy of the Middle Ages." *Jerusalem Studies in Jewish Thought*
4 (1984-85): 281-302 (Hebrew).

Rescher,
Limits

Rescher, Nicholas. *The Limits of Science*. Berkeley: University of
California Press, 1984.

Rosenberg,
"Emunah"

Rosenberg, Shalom. "The Concept of *Emunah* in Post-Maimonidean
Jewish Philosophy." In *Studies in Medieval Jewish History and
Literature*, edited by Isadore Twersky, 273-308. Cambridge: Harvard
University Press, 1984.

Rosenberg,
Torah u-Madda

Rosenberg, Shalom. *Torah U-Madda' Bi-Hagut Ha-Yehudit Ha-
Hadashah*. Jerusalem: Ministry of Education and Culture, 1988
(Hebrew).

Ross,
"Maimonides and
Progress"

Ross, Ya'akov. "Maimonides and Progress - Maimonides' Concept of
History." In *Hevrah Vi-Historiah*, edited by Yehezkel Cohen, 529-42.
Jerusalem: Ministry of Education and Culture, 1980 (Hebrew).

Rynhold,
"Good and Evil"

Rynhold, Daniel. "Good and Evil, Truth and Falsity: Maimonides
and Moral Cognitivism." *Trumah* 12 (2002): 163-82.

Sacks, J.
One People

Sacks, Jonathan. *One People? Tradition, Modernity and Jewish Unity*.
London: Littman Library of Jewish Civilization, 1993.

Sacks, O.
Anthropologist

Sacks, Oliver. *An Anthropologist on Mars*. New York: Knopf, 1995.

Sagi and Statman,
"Divine Command
Morality"

Sagi, Avi and Daniel Statman. "Divine Command Morality in Jewish
Tradition." *Journal of Religious Ethics* 25 (1995): 39-67.

Sagi,
Yahadut

Sagi, Avi. *Yahadut: Bein Dat Le-Musar*. Tel Aviv: Ha-Kibbutz ha-
Me'uhad, 1998.

Samuelson, *God's Knowledge*	Samuelson, Norbert. *Gersonides on God's Knowledge*. Toronto: Pontifical Institute of Medieval Studies, 1977.
Saperstein, "Conflict"	Saperstein, Marc. "The Conflict over the Rashba's Herem on Philosophical Study: A Political Perspective." *Jewish History* 1 (1986): 27-38.
Saperstein, *Decoding*	Saperstein, Marc. *Decoding the Rabbis : A Thirteenth-Century Commentary on the Aggadah*. Cambridge: Harvard University Press, 1980.
Schachter, "Rabbi Jacob Emden"	Schachter, Jacob. "Rabbi Jacob Emden's Iggeret Purim." In *Studies in Medieval Jewish History and Literature*, edited by Isadore Twersky, 441-46. Cambridge: Harvard University Press, 1984.
Scholem, "From Philosopher to Cabbalist"	Scholem, Gershom. "From Philosopher to Cabbalist (a Legend of the Cabbalists on Maimonides)." *Tarbiz* 6 (1935): 90-98 (Hebrew)
Scholem, *Jewish Gnosticism*	Scholem, Gershom. *Jewish Gnosticism, Merkabah Mysticism, and Talmudic Tradition*. New York: Jewish Theological Seminary, 1960.
Schwartzmann, "Image"	Schwartzmann, Julia. "Is She Too Created in the Image of God? Medieval Philosophical Exegesis of the Creation of the Woman According to Genesis 1-3." *Da'at* 39 (1997): 69-86.
Schwarz, "al-Fiqh"	Schwarz, Michael. "*Al-Fiqh*, a Term Borrowed from Islam Used by Maimonides..." In *Adaptations and Innovations: Studies ... Dedicated to Professor Joel L. Kraemer*, edited by Y. Tzvi Langermann and Josef Stern, 349-53. Paris: Peeters, 2007.
Schwarzfuchs, "Les lois royales"	Schwarzfuchs, Simon-Raymond. "Les Lois Royales De Maimonides." *Revue des etudes juives* 111 (1951-52): 63-86.
Schwarzschild, "Justice"	Schwarzschild, Steven S. "Justice." In *Encylopaedia Judaica*, 476. Jerusalem: Keter, 1971.
Schwarzschild, "Moral Radicalism"	Schwarzschild, Steven S. "Moral Radicalism and 'Middlingness' in the Ethics of Maimonides." *Studies in Medieval Culture* 2 (1978): 65-94.
Schwarzschild, *Pursuit*	Schwarzschild, Steven S. *The Pursuit of the Ideal: The Jewish Writings of Steven Schwarzschild*. Edited by Menachem Kellner. Albany: SUNY Press, 1990.
Schweid, *Crescas*	Schweid, Eliezer. *Ha-Philosophiah Ha-Datit Shel R. Hasdai Crescas*. Jerusalem: Makor, 1971.

Seeskin, "Faith"   Seeskin, Kenneth. "Judaism and the Linguistic Interpretation
                          of Faith." In *Studies in Jewish Philosophy: Collected Essays of the
                          Academy for Jewish Philosophy, 1980-1985*, edited by Norbert M.
                          Samuelson, 215-24. Lanham, MD: University Press of America, 1987.

Seeskin,   Seeskin, Kenneth. "Maimonides' Conception of Philosophy." In *Leo
"Maimonides'   Strauss and Judaism: Jerusalem and Athens Critically Revisited*, edited
Conception"   by David Novak, 87-110. Lanham, MD: Rowman and Littlefield,
                          1996.

Seeskin,   Seeskin, Kenneth. "Metaphysics and Its Transcendence." In
"Metaphysics"   *Cambridge Companion to Maimonides*, edited by Kenneth Seeskin,
                          83-104. Cambridge: Cambridge University Press, 2005.

Seeskin, *Origin*   Seeskin, Kenneth. *Maimonides on the Origin of the World*.
                          Cambridge: Cambridge University Press, 2005.

Seeskin, *Searching*   Seeskin, Kenneth. *Searching for a Distant God: The Legacy of
                          Maimonides*. New York: Oxford University Press, 2000.

Septimus, "*Madda*"   Septimus, Bernard. "What Did Maimonides Mean by *Madda*?" In
                          *Me'ah She'arim: Studies in Medieval Jewish Spiritual Life, edited by Alfred
                          in Memory of Isadore Twersky*, edited by G. Blidstein, E. Fleischer, C.
                          Horowitz, and B. Septimus, 83-110. Jerusalem: Magnes, 2001.

Septimus,   Septimus, Bernard. "'Kings, Angels, or Beggars': Tax Law and
"'Kings, Angels,   Spirituality in a Hispano-Jewish Responsum." In *Studies in Medieval
or Beggars'"   Jewish History and Literature*, edited by Isadore Twersky, 309-35.
                          Cambridge: Harvard University Press, 1984.

Septimus,   Septimus, Bernard. *Hispano-Jewish Culture in Transition: The Career
Hispano-Jewish   and Controversies of Ramah*. Cambridge: Harvard University Press,
                          1982.

Shapiro,   Shapiro, Marc. *Between the Yeshiva World and Modern Orthodoxy:
Between the Yeshiva   The Life and Words of Rabbi Jehiel Jacob Weinberg, 1884-1966*.
World   London: Littman Library of Jewish Civilization, 1999.

Shapiro, "Last Word"   Shapiro, Marc. "The Last Word in Jewish Theology? Maimonides'
                          Thirteen Principles." *The Torah U-Madda Journal* 4 (1993): 187-242.

Shapiro, *Limits*   Shapiro, Marc. *The Limits of Orthodox Theology: Maimonides'
                          Thirteen Principles Reappraised*. London: Littman Library of Jewish
                          Civilization, 2004.

Shapiro, *Studies*   Shapiro, Marc. *Studies in Maimonides and His Interpreters*. Scranton:
                          University of Scranton Press, 2008.

Shapiro, "Torah im Derekh Erez"	Shapiro, Marc. "*Torah Im Derekh Erez* in the Shadow of Hitler." *Torah U-Madda Journal* 14 (2006-07): 84-96.
Sheilat, "Uniqueness of Israel"	Sheilat, Yizhak. "The Uniqueness of Israel: Comparing the Kuzari and Maimonides." In *Me'aliyot 20: Essays and Studies on Maimonides*, edited by E. Samet and A. Fishler, pp 271-302. Ma'aleh Adumim: Ma'aliyot, 1999 (Hebrew).
Silman, "Halakhic Determinations,"	Silman, Yochanan. "Halakhic Determinations of a Nominalistic and Realistic Nature: Legal and Philosophical Considerations." *Dine Israel* 12 (1986): 249-66 (Hebrew).
Silman, "Introduction"	Silman, Yochanan. "Introduction to the Philosophical Analysis of the Normative-Ontological Tension in the Halakha." *Da'at* 31 (1993): v-xx.
Silman, *Kol Gadol*	Silman, Yochanan. *Kol Gadol Ve-Lo Yasaf: Torat Yisrael Bein Shelemut Ve-Hishtalmust.* Jerusalem: Magnes, 1999.
Sklare, "Are Gentiles"	Sklare, David. "Are the Gentiles Obligated to Observe the Torah? The Discussion Concerning the Universality of the Torah in the East in the Tenth and Eleventh Centuries." In *Be'erot Yitzhak: Studies in Memory of Isadore Twersky*, edited by Jay Harris, 311-46. Cambridge: Harvard University Press, 2005.
Solomon, "Intolerant Texts."	Solomon, Norman. "Reading Intolerant Texts in a Tolerant Society." *Tarbut Demokratit* 1 (1999): (Hebrew).
Solomon, *Analytic Movement*	Solomon, Norman. *The Analytic Movement: Hayyim Soloveitchik and His Circle.* Atlanta: Scholars Press, 1993.
Statman, "Authority and Autonomy"	Statman, Daniel. "Authority and Autonomy from the Oven of Akhnai." *Mehkarei Mishpat* 24 (2008): in press (Hebrew).
Stern, G., "Philosophical Allegory"	Stern, Gregg. "Philosophical Allegory in Medieval Jewish Culture: The Crisis in Languedoc (1304-1306)." In *Interpretation and Allegory: Antiquity to the Modern Period*, edited by Jon Whitman, 188- 209. Leiden: Brill, 2000.
Stern, "Covenant of Circumcision,"	Stern, Josef. "Maimondes on the Covenant of Circumcision." In *The Midrashic Imagination*, edited by Michael Fishbane, 131-54. Atlanta: Scholars Press, 1993.
Stern, "Enigma"	Stern, Josef. "The Enigma of *Guide* I: 68." In *Ha-Rambam: Shamranut, Mekoriut, Mahapkhanut*, edited by Aviezer Ravitzky, 437-51. Jerusalem: Merkaz Zalman Shazar, 2008.

Stern,
"Epistemology"

Stern, Josef. "Maimonides' Epistemology." In *The Cambridge Companion to Maimonides*, edited by Kenneth Seeskin, 105-233. New York: Cambridge University Press, 2005.

Stern,
"Maimonides on
the Growth of
Knowledge"

Stern, Josef. "Maimonides on the Growth of Knowledge and Limitations of the Intellect." In *Maimonide Philosphe Et Savant*, edited by Tony Levy and Roshdi Rashed, 143-91. Louvain: Peeters, 2004.

Stern,
"Parable of
Circumcision"

Stern, Josef. "Maimonides' Parable of Circumcision." *Sevara* 2 (1991): 35-48.

Stern,
Problems

Stern, Josef. *Problems and Parables of Law: Maimonides and Nahmanides on Reasons for the Commandments (Ta'amei Ha-Mitzvot)*. Albany: SUNY Press, 1998.

Strauss,
"How to Begin"

Strauss, Leo. "How to Begin to Study the *Guide of the Perplexed*." In *Guide of the Perplexed*. Translated by Shlomo Pines. xi-lvi. Chicago: University of Chicago Press, 1963.

Strauss,
"Literary Character"

Strauss, Leo. "The Literary Character of the *Guide of the Perplexed*." In *Essays on Maimonides*, edited by S W Baron, 37-91. New York: Columbia University Press, 1941.

Strauss,
"Maimonides'
Statement"

Strauss, Leo. "Maimonides' Statement on Political Science." *Proceedings of the American Academy for Jewish Research* 22 (1953): 115-30.

Strauss,
Philosophy and Law

Strauss, Leo. *Philosophy and Law: Contributions to the Understanding of Maimonides and His Predecessors*. Translated by Eve Adler. Albany: State University of New York Press, 1995.

Stroumsa,
"Sabians"

Stroumsa, Sarah. "The Sabians of Haran and the Sabians According to Maimonides: On the Development of Religion According to Maimonides." *Sefunot* 7 (1999): 277-95 (Hebrew).

Stroumsa,
Reshito

Stroumsa, Sarah. *Reshito shel Pulmus ha-Rambam ba-Mizrah: Iggeret ha-Hashtakah al Odot Tehiyyat ha-Metim le-Yosef ibn Sham'un*. Jerusalem: Makhon Ben-Zvi, 1999.

Ta-Shema,
"Hilkheta"

Ta-Shma, Israel. "*Hilkheta Ke-Batra'ei* – Historical Aspects of a Legal Maxim." *Hebrew Law Annual* 6-7 (1979-80): 405-23 (Hebrew).

Twersky,
"Epistemology"

Twersky, Isadore. "Aspects of Maimonides' Epistemology: Halakhah and Science." In *Maimonides and the Sciences*, edited by Robert S. Cohen and Hillel Levine, 227-43. Dordrecht: Kluwer, 2000.

Twersky,
"Non-Halakic
Aspects"

Twersky, Isadore. "Some Non-Halakic Aspects of the *Mishneh Torah*."
In *Jewish Medieval and Renaissance Studies*, edited by Alexander
Altmann, 95-118. Cambridge: Harvard University Press, 1967.

Twersky,
"Mishneh Torah"

Twersky, Isadore. "The Mishneh Torah of Maimonides." *Proceedings
of the Israel Academy of Sciences and Humanities* 5 (1976): 265-96.

Twersky,
Introduction

Twersky, Isadore. *Introduction to the Code of Maimonides (Mishneh
Torah)*. New Haven: Yale University Press, 1980.

Twersky,
Rabad

Twersky, Isadore. *Rabad of Posquieres: A Twelfth-Century Talmudist*.
Philadelphia: Jewish Publication Society, 1980.

Twersky,
Reader

Twersky, Isadore. *A Maimonides Reader*. New York: Behrman House,
1972.

Walker-Ramosch,
"Between the Lines"

Walker-Ramisch, Sandra. "Between the Lines: Maimonides on
Providence." *Studies in Religion* 21 (1992): 28-42.

Werblowski,
"Faith"

Werblowski, R. J. Zwi. "Faith, Hope and Trust: A Study in the
Concept of *Bittahon*." *Papers of the Institute of Jewish Studies* 1
(1964): 95-139.

Wolff,
*Musa Maimuni's
Acht Capitel*

Wolff, M. *Musa Maimuni's Acht Capitel*. Leiden: Brill, 1903.

Wolfson, E.,
Venturing Beyond

Wolfson, Elliot. *Venturing Beyond: Law and Morality in Kabbalistic
Mysticism*. Oxford: Oxford University Press, 2006.

Wolfson,
"Aristotelian
Predicables"

Wolfson, Harry A. "The Aristotelian Predicables and Maimonides'
Division of Attributes." In *Studies in the History and Philosophy of
Religion 2*, 161-94. Cambridge: Harvard University Press, 1977.

Wolfson,
"Double Faith"

Wolfson, Harry A. "The Double Faith Theory in Saadia, Averroes,
and St. Thomas." In *Studies in the History of Philosophy and Religion*
1, 583-618. Cambridge: Harvard University Press, 1973.

Wolfson,
"Classification"

Wolfson, Harry A. "The Classification of Sciences in Mediaeval
Jewish Philosophy." In *Studies in the History and Philosophy of
Religion* 1, 293-545. Cambridge: Harvard University Press, 1973.

Wolfson,   Wolfson, Harry A. "Note on Maimonides' Classification of the
"Note"   Sciences." In *Studies in the History of Philosophy and Religion* 2, 551-
                  60. Cambridge: Harvard University Press, 1977.

Wolfson,   Wolfson, Harry A. *Philo: Foundations of Religious Philosophy
Philo   in Judaism, Christianity, and Islam.* 2 vols. Cambridge: Harvard
                  University Press, 1962.

Wolfson,   Wolfson, Harry A. *The Philosophy of Spinoza: Unfolding the Latent
Spinoza   Processes of His Reasoning.* 2 vols. Cambridge: Harvard University
                  Press, 1969.

Wolfson,   Wolfson, Harry A. *Studies in the History of Philosophy and Religion.*
Studies   Vol. 1. Cambridge: Harvard University Press, 1973. Vol. 2, 1977.

Wurzburger,   Wurzburger, Walter S. *Ethics of Responsibility: Pluralistic Approaches
Ethics of Responsibility   to Covenantal Ethic.* Philadelphia: Jewish Publication Society, 1994.

INDEX

H

Habad 9, 158, 197, 243, 251, 314,

Hagigah, Maimonides on 42, 60, 65, 67, 195, 219-22, 224

halakhah, *see* commandments

Halevi, Judah 68, 69, 253, 256-58, 262, 273-75, 284, 286, 292, 299, 314, 322, 353-55

Harvey, (Warren) Zev 10, 12, 27, 34, 63, 115, 137, 203, 298, 340

heresy 87-103, 105-122

Hirsch, Samson Raphael 314

Hoch, Liron 28, 274

holiness 43, 165, 281, 289, 321-46, 353-56

Horetzky, Oded 231, 296

human beings, definition of 34-36, 43, 63-64, 68, 75, 80, 83, 222, 238, 297, 306, 308-11, 315, 339

I

ibn Bajjah 188

ibn Sina (Avicenna) 255

idolatry 42, 101, 204, 208, 228, 263, 289, 290, 315, 340

ikkarim, see dogma

imagination 38, 40, 53, 56, 64, 73-76, 124, 221-22, 290,
    see also perfection, of the imagination

immortality 15, 32, 36, 41, 66, 150, 152, 162, 189, 199, 254-57, 271, 275, 306, 311, 346

intellects, separate 34, 36, 53, 157, 63, 71, 127, 190, 195, 269,
    see also Active Intellect

intellectual perfection,
    see perfection, intellectual

instrumentalism,
    see science, formalist view

Islam 118, 209, 264, 281, 292, 303

Israel,
    see chosen people *and* election of Israel

J

Jesus 208, 303

K

Kabbalah 119, 275, 295, 350, 353

Kafih, Joseph 59, 124, 135, 169, 172, 177, 220, 223, 227, 267, 289, 296, 341

Kalam 118, 126

Karaites 152-54

Kellner, Jolene 11, 12, 292

Klein-Braslavy, Sara 11, 56, 291, 301, 376

L

Lasker, Daniel J. 11, 12, 20, 60, 77, 111, 152, 208, 273, 274, 297, 339, 343

Leibowitz, Yeshayahu 20, 164, 233, 235-41, 309, 332

M

ma'aseh bereshit and *ma'aseh merkavah* 16, 177, 195, 217, 219-24, 234, 241, 257

Maharal of Prague 299, 314

Melamed, Abraham 12, 70, 77, 293, 309

messiah, messianic era 8, 25, 64, 70, 94, 124, 129, 153, 158, 161, 166, 198-99, 208-09, 213, 244, 256, 257, 266, 271, 275, 291-319

metaphysics,
    see ma'aseh bereshit and
    ma'aseh merkavah

miracles 54, 93, 286, 357

Montag, Avram 11, 12, 237, 312

moral perfection, *see* perfection, moral

Moses 15, 29, 32, 42, 73, 76, 93, 99, 125-28, 134, 136, 139, 141, 161, 201-03, 218, 241, 26-62, 265, 269, 277, 284-286, 293-96, 299, 302, 306, 319, 326, 340-42, 351

N

Nahmanides 41, 138, 141-42, 160, 275, 293, 295, 309, 354

Noachides 295, 296, 299, 304, 315

Nissim Gerondi, *see* RaN

Nuriel, Abraham 101, 168-69, 173, 332-33

O

Obadiah the Proselyte 259, 268, 270, 302, 319,
    see also conversion

Orthodox Judasim 10, 15, 30, 33-44, 48, 109, 120, 122, 152, 157-64, 233-45, 291-92, 308-09, 340, 349, 351-52, 355-56